D1351340

'The great distinction of this book is that it is unremittingly and wonderfully offensive to liberal piety, that whispering ghost that sighs its sad way through the instituted wreckage of the education system. Ansgar Allen's genealogy of examination sets out education's passage from optimistic or sinister (as you will) Enlightenment dreaming to the structured chaos and brutality that today makes knowledge and its transmission safe for capitalism. If you can face up to what education has become, read this book.'
—*Dr Roy Goddard, University of Sheffield*

'Allen shows us that the classroom is a dangerous place, forensically and painfully he very convincingly spoils our love affair with education... Beautifully written and exquisitely understated – this should be required reading for every would-be educator.'
—*Professor Stephen Ball, Institute of Education, University of London*

'Brilliantly original and beautifully written... If you think that education should be guided by such high-minded liberal principles as freedom, equality and rational autonomy then this book will certainly make you think again.'
—*Professor Wilfred Carr, University of Sheffield*

'This book is subtly written and conceived, meticulously scholarly but above all it invites us, coolly, persuasively, to abandon what's left of our present faith and to commit to the serious, difficult business of forging new bearings.'
—*Dr Nick Peim, University of Birmingham*

'Full marks for this critique of examination. An antidote to contemporary educational platitudes and banalities of aspiration and meritocracy that sanitise and soothe away their technological continuities with eugenics. A rare Foucauldian critique combining outstanding scholarship with the incitement to action. Every teacher, parent and student needs to read this.'
—*Professor Erica Burman, Manchester Institute of Education*

'I thoroughly enjoyed reading the book. I loved the unique style... it was quite different from the usual academic literature I read.It is always refreshing and quite satisfying to read a book that is clear from the beginning and makes sense. There is a clear sense of rebellion.It is great to see an academic who does not sit on the fence and is not in fear of offending other academics. It's great to be different!'
—*Sumera Usman, undergraduate student, University of Sheffield*

'We should invert the old cliché: this book talks Power to Truth, and does so brilliantly... He tells us, in effect, to stick our liberalism up our holism.'
—*Professor Ian Stronach, Liverpool John Moores University*

Benign Violence

Education in and beyond the Age of Reason

Ansgar Allen
School of Education, University of Sheffield, UK

First published 2014 by
PALGRAVE MACMILLAN

Palgrave Macmillan in the UK is an imprint of Macmillan Publishers Limited, registered in England, company number 785998, of Houndmills, Basingstoke, Hampshire RG21 6XS.

Palgrave Macmillan in the US is a division of St Martin's Press LLC, 175 Fifth Avenue, New York, NY 10010.

Palgrave Macmillan is the global academic imprint of the above companies and has companies and representatives throughout the world.

Palgrave® and Macmillan® are registered trademarks in the United States, the United Kingdom, Europe and other countries

ISBN: 978–1–137–27285–0

This book is printed on paper suitable for recycling and made from fully managed and sustained forest sources. Logging, pulping and manufacturing processes are expected to conform to the environmental regulations of the country of origin.

A catalogue record for this book is available from the British Library.

A catalog record for this book is available from the Library of Congress.

Contents

List of Figures

Acknowledgements

This book would not have been written without Roy Goddard and Wilfred Carr, to whom, amongst others, I am indebted.

Preface

This book is not designed for academic consumption, in the sense that academia is complicit in the object of its critique. For that audience alone it must remain an *indigestible meal*.

* * *

Despite itself, this text is confined by its context. Written from within the physical and conceptual architectures of the university, it is placed alongside other academic projects that provide the frame of reference against which it is judged. In the past, these projects were regulated by a solitary fear, the fear of over-reaching themselves, of going beyond their scope. If ideas were stretched too far, they might snap.

* * *

A fear of becoming stretched, or drawn, is a fear of rupture, excision and division. In this context, the quality of an academic's output is deemed proportionate to the strength with which it adheres to the work of others. By sticking together, academics hoped to achieve the density that would prevent their work from appearing insubstantial. These academics were in pursuit of thickness.

* * *

Traditionally, academic life was a cloistered existence. Academics achieved density by enclosing their work, measuring the thickness and security of their intellect against the strength of the quarantine that contained it. Academic debate was very elite and very confined, carefully protected from outside interference. Those statements that were permitted within would be those that could say something 'original'. In order to judge originality, to decide whether a statement was sufficiently academic in its form, there was an expectation that those participating in the debate would be familiar with previous statements concerning the object of enquiry. Without this knowledge they would be unable to judge the 'newness' of a new statement. The quality of a statement, the feature that marked it as distinctive, and thereby permissible in this context, was its relation to other near equivalents. This relational positioning is what gave each statement its academic substance.

* * *

Through these arrangements, academic discourse excluded all those not inducted into the debate, those who were unable to place a statement within a series of statements to which it belonged and thereby make sense of it. Academic discourse denied access to those unable to understand a statement in terms of its positioning. It debarred those who failed, or those who *refused*, to make a contribution in the permitted terms of scholarly dialogue. This book does not belong to that tradition, and would prefer not to be judged by its standards. If judges appear, it would be better if their reviews were bad.

* * *

Academic conventions are not easily escaped. This text cannot entirely evade the form of an academic monograph, nor can it avoid the influence of its institutional setting. It can serve to irritate convention, but irritants are often welcomed. Without norms there are no perversions, and academics enjoy, perhaps even delight in, putting down those who make them itch. Alternatively, an academic balm is applied. This serves to domesticate the wayward intellectual by translating his or her perversions into acceptable discourse.

* * *

The environment in which I work is, nevertheless, undergoing transformation. My colleagues tell me that the age of individual scholarship is over. Instead, we researchers must collaborate with one another, and with others too. This kindly injunction is hard to refuse if one wishes to avoid the riposte that, by refusing to embrace those with whom one has little in common, one is thereby defending the old academic order of specialisms and seclusions. Refusal also has its material consequences. Those who wander between disciplines, creating glib networks and partnerships, are more likely to receive their recompense. The large funding agencies prefer collaborative enquiry, and what they prefer the academy delivers. Various devices ensure that those who cannot, or will not, accommodate themselves to this new environment are marginalised, perhaps even silenced.

* * *

As with all great extinctions, it is a change in the environment, rather than the weakness of a species, that renders individuals vulnerable. The academic species facing extinction today is not inferior to its successor; it just performed different functions. It was constructed and schooled for a different context, in which it found itself subservient to a different logic of examination, one that promoted thickness and exploited a fear of becoming thin. Whatever the pitfalls of this old way of life – a way of life that has not yet expired, and may still adapt – a new species of academic is in the ascendant. It retains some of the characteristics of its predecessor, but manages to approach the problem of thickness in reverse. Academics now over-reach themselves as a matter of routine.

* * *

It is said that the old seclusions of academic life are no longer viable. Distance and detachment are no longer praiseworthy attributes of the academic gaze. All research must have 'impact' and be accompanied by a 'pitch' explaining how this likely effect will be achieved. There is a repeated call to become relevant, or at least appear so, where appearances have been elevated above substance.

* * *

Reflecting on his own late nineteenth-century context, Friedrich Nietzsche put it like this: the journalist, he claimed, had become the 'paper slave of the day', having 'emerged victorious over the academic in all cultural areas'. The academic's only resort in such a climate is to undergo metamorphosis, whereupon the academic adopts the 'weightless elegance' of that journalistic sphere as its 'cultured butterfly'.[1] This description seems more appropriate to our century than the one from which it was taken.

* * *

Academics are cultured folk. Their most sophisticated representatives breeze through life exuding the fine tastes for which they are esteemed. And yet, that weightless elegance to which Nietzsche refers is never entirely achieved. As they look to the heavens, throwing aloft great sensibilities, academics also double over in anguish, seeking to connect with the world below. They are increasingly forced by the demands of their immediate environment to respond to the wider instrumental needs of society. Indeed, they experience a form of discomfort here that a spectator familiar with the haughty tones of the old academic may find pleasurable to watch.

* * *

The new injunction: academics will engage with reality, relating to the needs of the present as they are presently defined, speaking even if they have nothing to say.

* * *

Stalking one other and their stakeholders for opportunities to exploit, for angles that will give them the edge, those applying for funding must explain how they will be of service. Many self-styled progressives see this exposure to a new set of demands as a revolution in how they work. It is viewed as a momentous switch in academic discourse, one that gives voice to others and diminishes the influence of their own, too privileged, position. Progressives like to think they no longer speak from above.

* * *

As academics fall over one another in a display of respectful, cultured and salaried diffidence, they are pushed into the service of, and become subservient to, the existing social order. The university must now promote, support or pursue innovation, and thereby serve the interests of the wider economy. In writing their bids, researchers are encouraged to consider how their work might facilitate 'robust government' or 'private sector strategies to ensure sustainable growth'. In pursuit of wealth and opportunity, researchers adopt the demeanour of mineral prospectors in search of untapped opportunities, wading in the filth of those whose contents they have already exploited.

* * *

A good research project may promote resilience, or increase understanding between disconnected communities. It might act as a minor palliative, improving community well-being through its support of voluntary action or social enterprise. Good research always asks itself in advance how it can meet the needs of its users and beneficiaries. It identifies who those beneficiaries are likely to be and explains how they are likely to benefit. It justifies itself as a public good, using whatever language of social need may be current at the time. In effect, good research explains how it will build for the future *without offending the present*. Indeed, the futures imagined are nothing but more robust versions of the present. What this disallows, of course, is the possibility of objecting to the entire discourse within which contemporary needs are set. As academics chase each other about in ever-widening arcs across departments, faculties and institutions in search of the next big research project grant, they lose the protection of an earlier, more monastic form of existence. This way of life, one that unashamedly embraced its practices of seclusion, was able to stand aside and disregard the instrumentalities of the day. The old academic was deluded, of course, in claiming that his processes and utterances escaped the effects of power. And yet, the minor protections he did experience allowed the possibility of dissent.[2]

* * *

To say that this book was written whilst wearing a cassock, or some other vestment that distinguishes me as separate from society, and superior to you, would be misleading. And yet, in a marginal sense, this is a monastic exercise; it is an exercise in personal detachment. This book is the product of my desire for a different relation to the present.

* * *

The various forces of examination can be observed operating behind the normative orders I describe above. They define the relations we adopt with one another and codify how we relate to ourselves. Broadly conceived, examination forms the subject matter of this book, for which I offer a critique. This is a critique of examination, I might add. But that would be padding it out.

* * *

I hope you will be patient, and understand that it would be premature of me, at this point, in this preface, to give you my argument. 'Here it is,' I would say. I would, perhaps, denounce the global spread of this machinery, and declare us largely captive to a constraint without clear definition, to a force that we feel abstractly and cannot precisely locate.

To denounce examination in this way, from the outset, would be a mistake. Examination is not so easily grasped, and so our analysis would lack sufficient bite. We would cast about looking for conceptual resources, hoping to inflict some form of incision – to offer a critique even – and in doing so we would resort to the most tired metaphors. Critics of examination are, typically, all too eager to denounce its machine-like qualities and thereby contrast it with more holistic conceptions of what it means to be 'human'. Examination is portrayed as instrumental and reductive. We are portrayed as its prisoners, hoping for freedom. If only its mechanisms could be lifted, if only we could free ourselves from it…But to lift examination away, as if it were a great boulder, is impossible. We cannot separate ourselves from it, however Herculean the effort; examination will not come away without part of us attached. Examination has come to shape an entire set of perceptions. It conditions how we relate to ourselves, how we relate to one another and how we relate to our present. It declares what it means to be human; it defines how we understand human worth. It clarifies those human features that merit protection; it defines what should be celebrated or promoted, and what can be ignored, reformed or removed. For reasons such as these, examination cannot be simply lifted away. Social existence is in its thrall, and this book is no exception, having itself been written under a shadow. But examination is no simple monolith either. At any one time it is distributed across a whole series of arrangements, as a shifting set of functions. To grasp the significance of examination, we must pursue it in all its diffusion. Its features are layered across various sediments, which are the residues of former arrangements. A critique of examination must, therefore, adopt an historical line of enquiry. The examination of human worth and mapping of its social distribution has a past worth visiting. Examination has taken different forms and performed different roles in society. Human worth has been appraised differently throughout time, to a variety of purposes and variously nefarious ends. Examination and human merit: these two ideas are not timeless, nor are they universal. And yet, despite the profound contingency of examination, despite its distributed nature, examination has come to feel universal, inescapable. It has come to resemble a monolith.

* * *

At his trial more than two millennia ago, Socrates preferred to die than to live without examination. 'The unexamined life is not worth living,' he said.[3] Hence, according to legend, Socrates decided against flight and embraced his execution. We give Socrates too much credit, of course.[4] Still, this ancient story allows us to picture how today the scenario has reversed: in late modernity we struggle to *avoid* the unexamined life that Socrates seemingly refused to do without. That life, free from intrusion, free from examination, is no longer available to us. We are all examined now.

It seems odd that the site from which the examined life was *defended* from attack (a site once occupied by the solitary figure of Socrates) has since been crowded out by its champions. This is despite the global spread of examination, despite the fact that examination is now an inescapable fact of our lives. A crowded rampart has replaced the position once occupied by the solitary philosopher. This rampart is crammed with well-meaning individuals, all seeking to defend the examined life they now applaud. Philosophers were long ago cast aside by what became a rising horde of professors, eager to take up their chairs. Today, academics situate themselves at the vanguard (a somewhat oddly dressed vanguard, it has to be said), as they collectively shuffle forward under the banner of the examined life for which they presume to fight. It is assumed that the examined life is synonymous with the academy, so much so that, when the university is attacked, the fate of examined life is automatically associated with its future.[5] Its beleaguered employees are called upon to defend its reputation, the reputation of an establishment that is devoted (or so one is told) to the examined life, to a labour of learning and reflection.

* * *

My argument – in which I suggest that it has become increasingly difficult to avoid the examined life many in academia seek to defend – is easily attacked. I appear to be confusing two versions of what it means 'to examine'. I should, therefore, be explicit in saying that I *deliberately conflate* the examined life, in the high-minded Socratic sense, with examination in the mechanistic and lowly everyday sense of the word. My claim is that these two 'varieties' function together in the construction of docile subjects. As institutional sites of examination, universities are culpable in this venture, in a project that renders subjectivity open to the inquisitor. It is structurally absurd that members of these institutions should be encouraged to endorse the examined life and defend it from attack. Employees of educational institutions do not only serve as agents to examination; they also find themselves subject to its strictures. We are all at the receiving end one way or another; we are all impaled upon it. Admittedly, the nature of our discomfort varies according to our position, where we are each transfixed in a manner that depends on the resplendence of our dress. Upon graduation, those who don an academic cap and medieval cloak experience one of the more pleasurable thrusts that examination has to offer.

*   *   *

I am reminded of a childhood story once told to me at school. It concerns a boy seated in a large examination hall. In a fit of depression the boy inserted a sharpened pencil up each nostril and, so prepared, thrust his head downwards upon the desk. Presumably he died. I would think of him, whoever he was, when taking my examinations. Clearly, for that examinee, the examined life was *not* worth living.

*   *   *

During my twenties I experienced an infrequent but recurring nightmare. Whilst occupying this dream state, I would find myself back at school about to sit a Pure Mathematics examination completely unprepared. Upon waking I would remind myself, to some considerable relief, that the examination in question was long ago.

Now I have reached my thirties, the scenario has shifted. From within the recurring dream I am able to remind myself with pleasure that I hold a university degree, and that this degree renders all prior examinations superfluous. I have been elevated, educationally, and sleep a little higher.

*   *   *

The sensation returns in other contexts. When passing through airport security I experience a familiar discomfort, the discomfort of him who is being examined.

*   *   *

If I were to sit another formal examination in a hall of parallel desks, this would be the script I should like to return. It would be a numbered essay, divided into two, five, ten, 15 and 30-mark answers that disregard completely the questions my examiner poses.

* * *

The examination halls I once attended were invariably large, and yet they were intensely constricting in their effects. The aisles resembled those of the church, and the invigilator's steps would resonate just as well in a prison ward, or so I imagined. During the season, but long after my own graduation, I returned to the hall with which I am most familiar, seeking a picture for this book. The chief invigilator flatly denied access, though the scripts were not yet laid out and little, if anything, remained for him to conceal.

* * *

In the airport departure lounge I look at us standing in line, having emptied our nearby seats. We are lining up to board the plane even though the departure gates have not yet opened and will not open for some time. Where is it, I wonder, that we learn to behave as cattle, to submit ourselves to this social ritual as we collectively respond to its externally set, internally processed demands? We are all anxious, of course. There are no allocated seats on board.

* * *

Nietzsche argued that in other respects we are not bovine enough.[6] The world is not immediately apparent to our senses, and writing does not immediately reveal the world it describes. Understanding is a matter of interpretation. This takes time, and so we must learn to ruminate.

This text is an exercise in rumination. It is based on the suspicion that in responding to the urgent demands of everyday politics – with a heartfelt desire to reveal injustices, break down inequities, unearth corruption, prevent harm and so on – we already presume too much. Here the commitments of the politically engaged can function as a diversion. The urgency of conventional politics distracts us from the realisation – a product of rumination – that the very frameworks of the problems within which we live, within which we experience the dilemmas of the day, must also be approached, questioned and torn apart. For that reason, and to follow Nietzsche, I write 'neither usefully nor pleasantly'[7] for those who are overly wedded to the present.

I
Bodies

On Progress

I work in a building once occupied by architects. I am told they designed radio telescopes for receiving messages from outer space. It goes without saying that today our concerns are more immediate.

*   *   *

At its inception more than a century ago, the Department of Education that now employs me could boast the following equipment:

> The Department is equipped with the apparatus of a small pedagogical research laboratory, including a Hipp Chronoscope, Macdougall's Attention Machine, Rauschberg's Association and Memory Apparatus, Netschajef's Reaction Time Apparatus, Ebbinghaus Memory Apparatus, Jacquet's Sphymograph, Romer's Voice Key, Minnemann's Card Changing Apparatus, Wundt's Tachistoscope, Wundt's Control Hammer, Kymograph, &c., &c.[1]

In a school on the outskirts of the city similar devices reappear. A small girl stands about to be photographed, positioned on a weighing machine for the shot.[2] She peers at the camera whilst her teacher attends to the balances. Her head cocked to one side, and her face entirely blank, this photographic record tells us little of what was going on inside.

*   *   *

Measuring the child in 1911 was a physical activity by which features such as weight and height were collected and noted down. Examination of the mind in abstraction from the body was rare. As a technique, the mental test was still in its infancy and generally depended upon physical tricks, such as tests of reaction time, that were later found to correlate poorly with subjective impressions of intelligence. This would soon change. Within a mere

1

decade another type of test became common, one that would not depend on this circus of tricks. It became known as the intelligence or IQ test. A hundred years on this form of mental assessment is now so old that its use has become unremarkable. Today all young minds are routinely extracted, quantified and subjected to the language of statistical estimation. This form of extraction, a process by which the child is dissected and then reconstructed, has become entirely banal.

* * *

Children are today surrounded by the chatter of statistical work, a language informed by practices of assessment that are laced throughout schooling and its surrounding activities. Convention dictates that such extractions are part of a neutral process or, at least, that they should aspire to technical neutrality. This is the first denial of power.

Accordingly, knowledge of the child must be separated from the effects of bias; it must be objective, correct and reliable. If an assessment bias of some sort is discovered, it must be removed. This scientific procedure is governed by an explicit set of principles that have been rationally agreed. It is the product of a vast industry of professionals and their expert pronouncements. Examination must have an even and regular appearance; it should be without blemish. There is a sense of fairness and decency that comes with carefully designed, carefully administered assessment, or so we are encouraged to feel. This resides in its scientific, non-arbitrary, incorruptible technique.

Those critics who rightly claim that bias remains, who doggedly persist in searching it out, do not escape from the conceptual frame they appear to challenge. However shrill they become in their objections and denunciations, their objections still issue from within the terms of this debate: they speak in the language of bias and fairness. The framework of examination thereby remains intact, and is perhaps also a little reinforced.

* * *

Some educators seek to reject scientific measurement in its entirety. They hope to escape its assumptions concerning the nature of the learner or the nature and purpose of education more generally. As if their will to escape were enough!

Others try, more humbly, to diminish its effects. They promote our recognition of the whole child, of a human presence that must be respected, that must remain uncut, un-extracted. The individual learner ought to be accommodated in terms of his or her own unique completeness. We do violence to the child, they say, if we pare things down to the narrow language of a statistical judiciary. Believing that more humane forms of assessment are possible, that they are already on the horizon if only we were prepared to travel, those of this persuasion have developed other, rival techniques for appreciating the child. These practical innovations are, though, issued from a position of rivalry that is more apparent than real.

* * *

For those who reject the dominion of scientific measurement, grades and ranks are diligently avoided in favour of individual recommendations and constructive advice. The child is encouraged to avoid comparison with others and to focus on the process of learning. The key, it seems, is to avoid looking elsewhere for guidance or for reason to blame. One must focus on the self in order to celebrate the self and the unique developmental stage this self has reached. There are no generalisations, no universals against which the learner can be compared, and then ranked and judged. Each moment is its own. As such the ownership of each moment cannot be disputed; it is the learner's to possess. The learner must learn to take responsibility for that temporal slice, to diagnose it, and to deliver him or herself from it towards the next incomparable step of learning. This leads to a perverse situation in which 'there is no longer anything the self can hold on to, other than itself'.[3] Despite the surrounding warmth of feeling, the child is rendered alone. Examination becomes a process of extreme personalisation that functions *almost* 'like an amputation'.[4]

* * *

Extreme personalisation does not create selves that are perfectly atomised. These selves are not entirely cut off from one another. It remains true that 'no self is an island; each exists in a fabric of relations'.[5] What *has* changed, however, is that the self in question increasingly sits within a fabric of relations designed to *fold back* on the self, to refer back to each self in carefully individuated terms. This disguises the operations of a malevolent power, obscuring a set of relations that forms the wider structure of feeling.

* * *

The framework within which the individual is constructed remains hidden from view. In this way, social amputation operates as an insidious divider. From the perspective of its supporters this tradition of humanised assessment looks very different, of course. It has all but divorced itself from the deleterious effects of power, they feel. Their methods have been designed, quite deliberately to operate without bias and certainly without violence. Their pedagogy is presented as self-evident and neutral ('it is just the way we all learn'). And the experience of assessment and learning that it promotes is certainly intended to feel nothing like amputation! The child must be

kept whole, that is their basic tenet; the whole child is their aim and object. After all, these educators hold to higher principles; their activities are geared towards the flourishing of all. As with their rival (the statistical tradition), there is repeated here an insistence on neutrality, on the absence of power. This is the second denial.

*   *   *

There is a third denial of power that is associated with the examination of human worth. One stumbles across it frequently. I encountered it when overhearing an educator in conversation with a cynic. Actually I was part of the discussion, though I was experiencing one of those 'little touches of solitude' to which I am susceptible.[6]

The teacher was describing a scheme he had in mind to improve the prospects of state school pupils. The situation the teacher wished to confront is a familiar one: children of those parents who are able and willing to afford them a private education have a greater chance of making it to the country's elite universities. In these high-blown institutions, state school pupils are still, as a group, under-represented. The scheme he described was based on a simple hypothesis: children of the state are disadvantaged, he said, because they perform less well at interview. The proposed intervention follows naturally enough: to offer state school pupils mock interviews as a form of preparation.

The cynic poured scorn on the entire plan as you might expect: the system is already rigged, he said. It is hopeless to believe that a little interview technique could overturn an entire social edifice that is marred by injustices and systemic biases. If you are born poor you die poor; if you are born rich you die rich: the elites have ways and means of maintaining their advantage. The teacher agreed wholeheartedly, but then disavowed what he had just admitted. 'You are right', he said, *'but I just can't allow it.'* That, for me, was the crux of the matter: in all practical concerns the teacher was compelled to hold on to the illusion of duly awarded merit, otherwise where would that leave his scheme, and indeed his profession?

The details of the plan were also significant in their own way. The idea was to invite carefully selected 'strangers' to the school. This was based on the assumption that the true interview (the interview without bias) is an encounter with strangers. Leaving aside the elementary point that some strangers are stranger than others (the private school pupil may find the strangers on the interview panel more familiar than the state school pupil), there was something deeply ironic about this situation. Schools commence by telling their pupils: 'Never speak to strangers!' and finish with the concern that their pupils have lost the ability to do so.

*   *   *

Though there is plenty of cause for cynicism (it's all rigged, and so on), we do nevertheless reassure ourselves that privilege is no longer *publicly* supportable. In the liberal West, to bring attention to someone's privilege is to offer that person an insult. The implication, clearly enough, is that the person in question would have been unable to succeed on merit alone and does not deserve our recognition. Noble birth may continue to bring its hidden advantages, but these conveyances are said to be on the wane. Nepotism – the practice whereby those with power or influence favour relatives and friends – is no longer publicly defensible. It follows the fate of its precursor, the arrangement of judicious marriages, which has long been a topic of ridicule.[7] Though we admit that covert systems, systems that convey undue advantage, are still very much in existence – in which the middle classes are perhaps now the most adept game players in town – most people gaming the system today would be embarrassed to admit foul play. The cynicism that afflicts us is not quite that well set.[8] If we cynically 'buy' our way to a qualification or position, we still feel compelled to conceal what we have done. The felt need for concealment here can be taken as a mark of progress, progressives believe. This sense of shame rather proves the point from the perspective of the social optimist: meritocracy has become an unquestionable good.

*   *   *

It is commonly believed that we live in a meritocracy. The advocates of this faith remind themselves that power was once a brazen, openly patriarchal and unashamedly naked force. They flatter themselves with the idea that the blatant interventions of patronage have been largely replaced by scientific measurement and democratic correction, by tools providing better estimates of capability than birth, blood or noble origin ever could. Though some critics still complain of a continued class, gender or race bias in assessment, I would argue that their complaints are in a sense superficial. Their criticisms issue from, circulate through and are deposited back within the same system of meritocratic assumptions.

More baldly put, one might say that this entire debate finds itself located within a narrative of Western advance. According to this narrative, progress in the production of knowledge – including knowledge gained from examination – translates more or less directly into advances of justice, fairness and liberty. From this perspective, examination, and the knowledge it produces, needs only further refinement and better implementation as we work towards greater equality of opportunity through more perfected meritocratic techniques. Education systems are viewed as having become more transparent and more accountable through the production of knowledge about and within them. This transparency will, it is believed, overthrow those systems of power that are said to multiply when knowledge is thin and where the mechanisms of social life remain hidden from view. In such an educational context, with the effects of power largely 'removed', ability has, for the first time in history, a genuine chance to triumph over background and hence over power. Ability takes precedence over the influence of one's connections, of strings pulled in the shadows. Those who accept this progressive narrative flatter themselves that, even though imperfections remain, the aspiration to achieve perfected meritocratic order is firmly embedded.

* * *

As a regulating idea, meritocracy serves to structure and condition perception. In providing the framework upon which judgements are made, it functions as if it were timeless. Meritocracy is one of those moral touchstones many believe can be invoked without reasonable objection to judge social existence. The meritocratic ideal fulfils an essential role in those societies that have endured the combined onslaught of modernity and secularism, that are marked by the defeat of religious authority, and, as a result, no longer order their perception according to the metaphysical logic of a divine order. More earthly principles are now depended upon to regulate lived experience. It is here that the principle of meritocracy – a delicate but enduring concoction – has become the primary operator for a secular order.

* * *

In his commentary on Nietzsche,[9] Henry Staten contrasts the Christian order of discourse – which attempts 'to recuperate the suffering of history by projecting a divine plan that assigns it a reason now and a recompense later' – to the secularised narrative of a latter-day liberal humanism. Unable to cope with the possibility that there is no single explanation for the accumulated disorder of history – only the brute fact of that 'overwhelming spectacle of cruelty, stupidity and suffering' – left liberals and humanists find a secular replacement for the Christian precursor.[10] According to their revised understanding, 'all those lives ground up in the machine of history are assigned an intelligible role as victims of oppression and injustice'. This is the 'implicit teleology' of modern self-understanding, which 'gives form and meaning to the rest of history'. From their elevated perspective extends an 'invisible line of rectitude' used to judge human existence, a line of rectitude that would presumably continue to traverse history 'even though [its originating] community of belief my cease to exist'.[11] It is a position of self-professed pre-eminence that allows those who identify with it to stand outside history and act as supreme arbitrators, like gods, judging all societies alike according to their universal criteria. These defenders of our common humanity 'cannot accept', as John Gray argues, 'that a world in which their liberal ideals are constantly mocked does not secretly revere them'.[12] Like me, they sleep a little higher, and yet they refuse to wake up. Perhaps they should be permitted this temporal respite, as a prisoner might be allowed to rest on the way to the gallows. Eventually, though, liberals and humanists alike must leave this dream state and learn to admit the fragile foundations of their self-professed superiority.

The principle of meritocracy can be found within the ailing foundations of their humanistic tradition. It is remarkable, in fact, that such a fragile idea has been and still is used in this way, functioning as a key line of rectitude or 'sliver of light',[13] which somehow entitles those who possess it to illuminate and appraise the past, present and future alike. According to this singular line, a just society will be, amongst other things, a meritocratic one, in which meritocracy provides the scale against which social progress is judged. More advanced societies are deemed to be those that are more meritocratic. They make fewer decisions based on prejudice and extend opportunity further. Meritocracy is also used as a measure of corruption, whereby corrupt societies or corrupt institutions are thought to be those that violate the formula: merit = ability + effort. Meritocratic societies are open and fair; non-meritocratic ones are obscure and underhand. The conclusion is familiar; meritocracies are places where power is in retreat.

* * *

As a myth, meritocracy acts to support and legitimate unequal societies.[14] Whilst meritocracy is a comparatively recent social invention with no claim to universality, it performs an important and seemingly indestructible ideological function. It absorbs displeasure – a bitterness that is the product of inequality – by diffusing it and individuating it within a system that sanctions differential rewards, a system that assigns individuals to unequal economic positions according to their own 'effort' and 'merit'. It sets to work any remaining vexations issuing from those who retain a social conscience by diverting these desires for a different, more equal social order into the pursuit of system neutrality. This sublimation of desire is expressed through the fight against patronage or unfair influence, and through the development and distribution of accounting techniques and traditions of 'unbiased' measurement. It should be noted that, in the context of these earnest campaigns for more justly distributed inequalities, cases of residual nepotism are not as disruptive to the meritocratic ideal as they may at first appear. When individuals or groups are singled out for their unfair privilege, they serve an important function, reinforcing the principle of meritocracy amongst those who depend upon it to animate their contempt.

*   *   *

The ubiquity of meritocracy in liberal societies seems unassailable. If circumstances were different, perhaps we could let this spectre alone and allow it to continue as a ponderous, but harmless, preoccupation. But this continued faith in the eternal form of the meritocratic ideal has become embroiled in a scandal of perception, and this scandal has had its victims. Even though meritocracy clearly still exists as a collective ideal, as *a practical administrative project* it has long since been dismissed from the scene of government. It no longer persists in that corporeal form. We nevertheless remain *psychologically attached* to the idea of meritocracy, so much so that we are unable to fully perceive its departure, or take the measure of the system that replaced it. We cannot recognise our period as one in which *disorder* and the *impossibility of fairness* are principles that have been elevated above their opposites and incorporated within governmental technique. The period within which we live is one that exists *after fairness* and *beyond justice*, following a transition that took place largely unremarked. This transition occurred as the children of the late twentieth century learned how to live a life without fairness, as they were prepared for an existence where hope is more instrumental to their lives than the guarantee of justice, as they were schooled in a range of personal strategies and dispositions necessary for a docile and productive existence within a deliberately unsystematic social order.

Meritocracy, today, bears little resemblance to its former self, even though many resolutely hold on to its earlier definition; it has been transformed in spite of the fact that many are still preoccupied with its accompanying mission to eradicate power by removing the effects of unfair influence. A fissure has opened up between an abstract principle of justice and a social project within which reason has been suspended. This void now engulfs all well-meaning efforts oriented towards inclusion, fair opportunity and just desert. Within this space, which remains hidden from view (as does a quarry beyond the crest of a hill), machinations of government have been able to extend and multiply, adjusting and furthering their capacity to quell dissent.

*   *   *

False assumptions concerning the absence of power in scientific assessment, the benign intent of its rival anti-numerical approach and the universalism of the meritocratic ideal, were culpable in a wider transformation through which we entered this life beyond fairness. We cannot even complain that fairness is absent, for this complaint has been emptied of meaning. A belief in progress and an abstract faith in the institutions of liberalism and democracy also served to obscure the many 'dark sides' of power. Profoundly misguided in our commitments and in our estimates of the chief concerns of the day, many of us arrived at our current predicament staring intently in the wrong direction.

* * *

For those who maintain that it is time to inaugurate a resistance, perhaps even a collective refusal, the first step is to insist that power is *never* in retreat. Violence continues without interruption.

Modern Examination

To speak of the *history of examination* makes little sense. As a concept, examination is neither bland nor universal enough for such a history to be written. It cannot stretch across time gathering together all related events as their collecting term. Like the history it confronts, this is an unstable concept. It is, moreover, insufficiently distinct from close associates such as 'assessment'.

At times the words *assessment* and *examination* can be used almost synonymously. At others they drift apart. Whilst examination is often used to refer to the formal process by which candidates are judged for a particular qualification or post, assessment has a more general meaning and can refer to informal as well as formal activities.

There are other differences. In medieval alchemy, examination refers to the attempt to test or assay a precious metal in order to determine its purity. It is also associated with close scrutiny or investigation by inspection in order to establish the truth or qualities of an object, statement or calculation. Finally, examination refers to the interrogation of a person in order to determine his or her state of mind, knowledge or capacity. Assessment, by contrast, has been associated with the determination of a fine, charge or tax. It is also linked to the valuation of property. Whilst examination in its various uses is about inspection and truth, assessment adds to this the idea of distribution, remuneration and desert. Depending on my focus, I will switch terms. This chapter refers chiefly to examination, dealing as it does with the history of a device used to generate truth through inspection. Later chapters are concerned more directly with assessment: they investigate the valuation and distribution of human worth. This switch from examination to assessment is not without consequence, reflecting as it does a diminishing concern for truth.

*   *   *

In the West, two distinct traditions of examination can be identified, these being modern examination and its medieval precursor. Both were brought into being as institutional devices, assisting those institutions in games of subjugation.

Arriving during the twelfth and thirteenth centuries in Europe, medieval examination beat the Bubonic Plague by a century. This is not to boast on behalf of examination; it merely sets a scene. The pandemic was certainly a fearsome episode in human history, and yet there was a far more dangerous sickness already endemic in 1348 that is to be feared precisely because we do not experience it as such.

The plague arrived, so they say, on merchant ships upon which Oriental rats and their fleas hitched a ride. Examination has similar intercontinental connections, but we will remain in the West along with the fleas. Here we commonly perceive those who existed before medieval examination, and certainly those who existed before modern examination, as comparatively healthy. The ancients were particularly so; at least, this is how the story goes, where the hardy ancestor *par excellence* would be Socrates.

The medievalist Charles Haskins once quipped that a 'great teacher like Socrates gave no diplomas; if a modern student sat at his feet for three months, he would demand a certificate, something tangible and external to show for it'.[15] Unlike Socrates' companions, who were the victims of Socratic dialogue, modern students are the victims of institutional life, having been so formed that they cannot but share the expectations of organised education. 'Only in the twelfth and thirteenth centuries', Haskins continues, 'do there emerge in the world those features of organised education with which we are most familiar, all that machinery of instruction represented by faculties and colleges and courses of study, examinations and commencements and academic degrees.'[16]

* * *

Almost 900 years ago, the first medieval universities were established, their early development being closely associated with a certain pre-modern ritual of examination. Formal medieval education was a minority privilege. The favoured few entered a system that we may struggle to understand in retrospect because it failed to employ many of those features that we associate with formal education today. There were few graduated steps in the subjects taught. These subjects were not broken down into discrete units and then ordered into a hierarchy of difficulty from the most elementary components to the most difficult concepts. Also absent was the significance we now ascribe to age. A variety of ages were taught together.[17] So, whilst the life of a medieval student can be divided into three main phases, these divisions did not contain a graded hierarchy of steps and they are not best represented by age.

Roughly, then, the elite students of the first phase were called *scholars*. Four or more years were spent listening to lectures. These were delivered from a list of prescribed texts, with the number of times each text should be heard being defined in advance: 'Hard, close drill on a few well-thumbed books was the rule.'[18] But the required books were rare, and so the education was largely an oral one, divided between ordinary lectures that were delivered by masters and cursory lectures that were given by bachelors. The former expounded the text, whilst the latter offered little more than a running commentary on it. Lectures were augmented by disputations, in which the master would resolve any difficulties raised with respect to an authoritative text. A scholar would attend the disputations of his master for two years or so, during which period he would respond to questions posed by the master and receive training in textual reconciliation.

The second phase in the student's career was that of *bachelor*, a status that had been borrowed from the terminology of the Guilds, that is, a candidate for Mastership. The transition from scholar to bachelor was known as the determination, and eligibility for this step was ascertained through a series of preliminary examinations, called 'responsions'. The candidate and his master were then asked to swear an oath that the former had fulfilled the requirements, including attendance at the prescribed lectures. Determination itself involved the candidate holding a series of public disputations during Lent. Having successfully determined, the bachelor resumed attendance at his master's lectures. He was required to take part in further disputations over the next year and take on some teaching responsibilities by delivering a course of cursory lectures.

The next objective was to become a *master*. After several more years of study and teaching, the bachelor of promise reached the process of inception, through which admission could be gained to the masters' guild. The candidate would hold an inaugural lecture together with a disputation, following which there was a banquet held at the inceptor's expense.

* * *

All these examinations, commencements and academic degrees may sound rather tedious.[19] On those occasions when I find myself subjected to some ceremony or other, either participating in the ritual or standing by, I like to think that we would all rather be elsewhere. Those who find themselves fired up by such events exhibit, for me, the surface traits of a more troubling inclination.

It is with little pleasure that I spend effort recounting long-dead rituals, such as those detailed above. It would be far more entertaining, perhaps, to explore what medieval students got up to in their spare time. But the ceremonial particulars are important, and we should not allow our gaze to follow that of the wayward student. These events served a wider, moral purpose. At the very least, candidates could be rejected for inappropriate behaviour. Gambling and taking part in a knife-fight with local tailors were both recorded as reasons for rejection. Paying undue attention to the solemnity of the event itself was another reason for dismissal. In fifteenth-century Vienna one candidate made the unforgivable mistake of nipping out to see an execution during the examination – an irresistible spectacle, one assumes.[20] The threat of rejection for inappropriate behaviour was, nevertheless, only a blunt device for the regulation of personal conduct. The ceremonies themselves, these sites of medieval examination, were far more intricate in their effects as moral devices. To understand how they worked we must appreciate the regime of truth within which the medieval scholar was confined.

* * *

The medieval theologian and his student follower faced a basic difficulty: the various church canons contradicted one another. In this period a great deal of scholarly effort was expended to resolve these conflicts. Often since dismissed as 'mere scholasticism', this form of scriptural debate is so alien to our notions of rational discourse that we may indeed struggle to judge the scholastic agenda on its own merits. With an agenda that sets him at odds with our present, Alasdair MacIntyre provides a more sympathetic account. The key figure for MacIntyre was the influential theologian Thomas Aquinas (born 1225; levitated 1273; deceased 1274). Aquinas practiced a mode of scholasticism that coupled deep respect for authority with an effort to resolve contradiction and thereby reaffirm the pre-eminence of the church fathers. This was also the object of university disputations at which scriptural difficulties could be tidied up through dialectical argument. These carefully orchestrated disputes did provide a certain degree of creative space to develop counterarguments (for the sake of argument) before the final resolutions were applied in summing up. This opportunity was, nevertheless, short-lived, being cut short by the concluding remarks.

The medieval examination was an opportunity to demonstrate in discursive form the closeness and subtlety of one's understanding of and adherence to received tradition. 'Research' in the modern sense did not yet exist, with the 'research university' a thing of the distant future.[21] Knowledge of the truth did not emerge from an accumulation of facts; it was revealed following the correct reading of texts by someone who had developed those understandings that were valued by existing tradition. This is an affront to many ears today due to the enduring Enlightenment belief that rational thought must emancipate itself from the 'tutelage of authority'.[22] It is still often presumed that to be rational one must think for oneself. By contrast, scholastic rationalism was built on understandings that were largely tacit. These were absorbed gradually through, for example, attendance at and participation in the disputations that followed lectures. The bachelor would slowly learn through experience how to apply the acknowledged standards of his craft, and identify mistakes. The apprentice for mastership would also gradually learn to locate his efforts within the wider orbit of the scholastic universe, distinguishing between the 'kind of excellence which both others and he [for it would be a male] can expect of himself here and now, and that ultimate excellence which furnishes both apprentices and master-craftsmen with their *telos*', where the *telos* is their highest object or aim.[23]

Intellectual and moral virtues were deemed inseparable, where the effects of personal desires and inclinations were of particular concern when it came to textual interpretation. These tendencies were to be governed through an education in personal conduct. The apprentice would learn to self-regulate in working towards an ideal that was, in part, exemplified by the work of the craft masters in whom the apprentice placed trust. Personal 'defects and limitations in habits of judgement and habits of evaluation' that were 'rooted in corruptions and inadequacies of desire, taste, habit and judgement' would become evident through training. Though the individual concerned would develop a thorough appreciation of those personal attributes that were to be managed, the process was not individualising, and it would be a mistake to read it as such. Increased self-knowledge did not separate the individual from his or her environment as an increasingly distinct self-referential unit. The scholar was to become enmeshed, adopting the particular rationality or *Weltanschauung* of the craft. The apprentice would learn what it is about himself 'that has to be transformed, that is, what vices need to be eradicated, what intellectual and moral virtues need to be cultivated' if he was to become a master practitioner and so reside among like-minded peers.[24] The effects of medieval examination were deeply formative in this sense. This medieval ceremony was the culmination of a whole series of everyday personal reflections, inspections and petty ordeals. It was the medieval concentrate of a moral device that operated throughout the student experience.

* * *

The constraints of scholastic debate were not static; there was room for gradual transformation. Traditions adjusted over time, where the triumph of each successive stage came about under certain conditions. The superiority of a new interpretation was demonstrated if a later stage was 'able to transcend the limitations and failures of an earlier stage', according to 'the standards of rationality of that earlier stage itself'.[25] An earlier tradition could only be overthrown according to arguments that made sense to it, according to attacks that were advanced in its terms and according to its rituals of judgement. What this meant was that scholarship seeking the transformation of tradition demanded supreme efforts of self-cultivation in order to negotiate these complex transitions within a tradition. It would appear, then, that medieval change demanded an even deeper understanding of tradition than what was required when merely submitting to its existing mores. The rebel scholar would need to be the most ardent and skilful practitioner of his tradition. The rebel was marked by his alignment and acculturation, rather than his disaffiliation and militant disregard. Only the vanity of Enlightenment thinkers allowed them to believe that *radical* thought must be 'entirely deracinated' from formative authority in order to deserve that epithet.[26]

* * *

Histories are rhetorical deployments. For my purposes, medieval examination serves as a backcloth against which I hold up its successor. This history is not a progressive one. Indeed, my juxtapositions are designed to create a disturbance in the present.[27]

* * *

As MacIntyre would have it, the scholastic order of discourse was largely replaced by a post-Cartesian, encyclopaedic worldview.[28] Having awoken from our 'medieval slumber', we moderns no longer appeal to external authorities. Guided by reason, we are said to have developed independence from the tutelage of tradition.

* * *

That great mental sclerosis known as 'tradition' has been debunked, we say. A new freedom allows us to question without restraint and then verify our answers without prejudice. We love these answers dearly. We set them in typescript and file them away.

* * *

The cold and objective tools of modern examination would seem to epitomise the modern perspective. Examination, we believe, is no longer a device for cultivating a virtuous elite. It has become an impersonal, calculative tool. Examination, today, has little to do with the embodiment of moral virtues, in the medieval sense. It would seem that modern examination has displaced its pre-modern variant so completely that we can identify a total rupture in its history.

* * *

The logic of modern examination can be observed in a machine design once penned by the great utilitarian, Jeremy Bentham (who was born in 1748 and dissected at his behest for the purposes of science in 1832). As with the disputation, Bentham's modern examination was to be an oral and public ordeal. In all other respects, however, it was entirely at odds with its medieval precursor. Bentham's examination was not designed to secure entry to an order of masters; rather, as part of a constitutional code intended 'for the use of all nations and all governments professing liberal opinions', it would regulate admission to government posts. Here is an extract from his *Constitutional Code*:

> SECTION 16: LOCABLE WHO, *Enactive*, ART.1. This section has for its object the providing, as soon as may be, and in so far as is necessary, – but no further, at the public expense, in relation to the business of all the several Subdepartments comprised in the Administration Department, a system of arrangements, whereby in the several official situations, appropriate aptitude in all its branches shall be maximised, and at the same time expense minimized; say, a SYSTEM OF OFFICIAL LOCATION, or, for shortness, THE LOCATION SYSTEM.[29]

The abridged version is as follows. For each branch of art and science, a book would be provided in which 'the whole matter of it, or such portion as shall have been deemed necessary and sufficient, has been cast in the form of *questions, with correspondent answers'*.[30] The most advanced examinee would have the entire contents 'stowed in his memory' (for it would again be a male) and might be asked to respond to any question contained therein.[31] It would be 'impracticable' to examine the entire contents, and so only a selection of questions would be asked, these being selected by lot. This would ensure a 'maximization of the *inducement* afforded to *exertion* on the part of learners',[32] and would also prevent the examiner from having any 'power of favouring or disfavouring' individuals.[33]

All questions in the book would be numbered and accompanied by a corresponding set of square tickets. These would be arranged in numerical order, in the manner of squares on a chessboard, and enclosed in a square frame. This would 'suffice to render it manifest, to the requisite number of eyes, at one view, that for every question there is a ticket: and that for no questions there are tickets more than one'.[34]

The tickets would be placed in a cylindrical box and thoroughly shaken by a number of people in turn. For a cover, it would have a cloth, 'in which is a slit, long enough to admit a hand: – fittest hand, that of a child, not old enough to be exposed to the suspicion of having received instructions enabling it to act with discrimination'.[35] This would be a job for what Bentham describes as the non-discerning child. Finally, those who passed this test of aptitude would bid for the position advertised. In this way the overall machinery would maximise human resources at the minimum expense. He who passed, and was prepared to sell his services at the lowest price, would get the job.

*   *   *

It would appear from the overwrought novelty of these designs that the logic of examination they were attempting to describe was highly original. Whilst medieval examination cultivated the self – involving comparisons between the self being worked upon and surrounding tradition as exemplified by the craft masters – for Bentham, comparisons would take a different form; they would operate between individual learners. This would allow the efficient distribution and employment of individuals, maximising aptitude and minimising expense. Whilst the medieval disputation involved a competition of ideas, the aim of which was reconciliation and synthesis, the modern examination made a direct attempt to engender tensions between individuals, to stimulate their desires, instead of resolving tensions between their desires and the dictates of tradition. Modern examination appears to adopt a highly reductive logic, feeding from base inclinations to beat one's neighbour. With modernity, so the story goes, a sense of virtue is lost.

*   *   *

A corrupted form of disputation survived well into the seventeenth century,[36] further degenerating during the eighteenth century into prepared arguments, memorised beforehand.[37] The graduate disputation at Cambridge finally disappeared in 1838, with students submitted to uniform written questions instead. The decline was gradual. But, if we were after significant milestones, 1763 would be one to pick.[38] In this year the disputation became a mere preliminary method for matching examinees according to ability, following which differentiated *groups* of candidates would have questions dictated to them that they would answer together and in writing. Group dictation was eventually replaced in 1827 with printed questions, and, from 1792, questions were individually marked, generating increasingly fine divisions between examinees.

This has been identified as 'a most momentous step, perhaps the major single step towards a mathematised model of reality'.[39] Examinees were tested in batches, side by side with their competitors, alongside whom they would eventually be listed in order of attainment. A ranking procedure of 'unparalleled intensity and precision'[40] had been developed, and with it came the possibility of a new scientific reckoning that would take the individual as its prime target. At this point, only an elite minority were subjected to these dividing practices. It would take a century or more to extend examination to the general populace.

*   *   *

For England, the 1850s are sometimes viewed as the point of inflection after which modern examination really took off. In 1853, the India Act established a precedent. Examination was to be used in the public service, confined at first to the machinery of imperial rule. As the Whig politician Thomas Macaulay argued in parliament, with '800 men charged with the happiness of 120,000,000 people' there could be no room for incapacity; the aptitude of every imperial employee must be assured.[41] In this respect, the trialling of examinations mirrored other imperial experiments, in which the effects of newly invented techniques and devices, including genocidal ones, were first tested overseas.[42] With respect to government examinations, appointment through patronage or personal recommendation was now illegal: all 'Powers, Rights or Privileges' to 'nominate persons to be admitted...shall cease'.[43]

Within two years, the first examinations for posts in India were taking place.[44] Meanwhile, William Gladstone, Chancellor of the Exchequer and future Prime Minister, commissioned an enquiry that would recommend examinations for the Home Civil Service.[45] The prototype examinations at this point were of university origin. Indeed, the Indian Civil Service Commissioners hoped to call upon the expertise of recent 'moderators in the University of Cambridge' who knew 'by experience how to conduct the examination of large numbers

"Empire Day" Sheffield. Real Hindu Laddies.

of persons simultaneously'.[46] In the same decade, the Universities of Oxford and Cambridge began setting entrance examinations, marking one of the first incursions of qualifying examination into schooling. [47]

The rapid spread of modern examination generated a fear amongst some that selection by intellectual ability could not guarantee moral virtue (where such virtue was, of course, of a distinct breed in the context of imperialism). If modern examinations were to be the new gatekeepers, they might allow intellectually proficient, though morally deficient, inappropriate types into positions of influence. In correspondence with her Chancellor, the future Empress of India, Queen Victoria, gave vent to her fears:

> The Queen, although not without considerable misgivings, sanctions the proposed plan, trusting that Mr Gladstone will do what he can, in the arrangements of the details of it, to guard against the dangers...A check, for instance, would be necessary upon the admission of candidates [...] securing that they should be *otherwise eligible*, besides the display of knowledge which they may exhibit under examination.
>
> *Queen Victoria to Mr Gladstone:*
> *Buckingham Palace 17th February 1854*[48]

The Chancellor of the Exchequer presents his humble duty to your Majesty, and has the honour to acknowledge your Majesty's gracious letter.

He takes blame himself for having caused your Majesty trouble by omitting to include in his short memorandum an explanation of the phrase 'qualified persons'.

Experience at the universities and public schools of this country has shown that in a large majority of cases the test of open examination is also an effectual test of character; as, except in very remarkable cases, the previous industry and self-denial, which proficiency evinces, are rarely separated from the general habits of virtue.

But he humbly assures your Majesty that the utmost pains will be taken to provide not only for the majority but for all cases, by the strictest enquiries of which the case will admit; and he has the most confident belief that the securities of character under the system, although they cannot be unerring, will be stronger and more trustworthy than any of which the present method of appointment is susceptible.

Mr Gladstone to Queen Victoria:
Downing Street 17th February 1854[49]

This plea for modern examination is repeated elsewhere. Assurance is given that the moral character of persons selected by examination could indeed be guaranteed. Additional virtues said to be nurtured by examination include; 'a taste for pleasures not sensual' and a 'desire for honourable distinction'.[50] Testimonies confirmed that for the newly examined universities 'in more than nineteen cases out of twenty, men of attainments are also men of character'. The perseverance and self-discipline required for success in examination were 'a great security that a young man has not led a dissolute life'.[51] An intellectual test, so the argument went, was 'the best moral test that can be devised'.[52] Admittedly, these were mere defensive retorts. Nevertheless, they were also truer than their authors imagined.

* * *

Bentham's non-discerning child was just a convenient device, serving as a minor actor within the architectures of a larger machinery. It is with some irony, then, that, despite the small role it occupied, this child figure would eventually become the agent of a new moral order. With one hand extended into that cylindrical box – into an interior governed by number, lot and probabilities – childhood soon found itself subject to a new set of rules and regulated by a new order of discourse.

The instruments of moral formation were refashioned and massified for a new age. As a result, the soul of the child became the object of modern examination, instruction and enquiry. Subjected to a far more intense regime of petty ordeals than hitherto, this modern soul became so well regulated, and achieved such an elevated position, that it eventually developed into a 'prison of the body'.[53] Here Foucault draws from Nietzsche, who observed how the soul once 'looked contemptuously upon the body',[54] where all bodily diversions were suspected for their potential to corrupt the soul. With modernity this all changed; the problem today is its opposite. The soul has been so minutely prescribed, indeed, that the body should now regard the soul with great suspicion. Of course, we no longer speak of this soul as a 'soul', as we once did. It goes by other names. The modern soul is otherwise known as 'your true self' or 'your inner being'.

The popular phrase, *be true to yourself,* serves as a violent constraint. Those who attempt to obey this command search in vain for their inner self (which must, of course, remain elusive). They satisfy themselves with imported ideas that provide a sense of depth. Their inner self arrives as a constructed and constraining illusion.

Educated Bodies

Critics of modern examination are often its most deceptive representatives. They falsely depict examination as a mechanistic and lowly tool. As a blunt instrument, examination is said to trample over human life and prevent human flourishing. If we fail to resist its onslaught, examination will overcome every aspect of education with its reductive logic. Their retrospective accounts tell the story of examination as if it were a history of repressions. Even those histories that have a tendency to mimic the archives from which they draw – leaving us over-burdened with facts, and light on analysis – tend to reinforce the view that examination has spread almost everywhere. The facts are said to speak for themselves. We believe ourselves crushed, our life force running away through the drainage channels that examination has had the foresight to construct.

* * *

The good educator resists examination. Though few would remove examination entirely, many such educators seek to reduce its variously 'corrupting' effects. Here, resisting examination becomes a matter of allegiance to higher (rarely articulated) educational ideals. If only we could escape some of its influence, if only we could remove aspects of its imprint from the child. If only we could examine a little less and educate a little more. ... These sentiments are misconceived. The logic of examination constitutes modern schooling as its ontological condition.[55] Modern examination was not imposed on educational institutions as if from above: it is part of their very being. As such, it cannot be removed or meaningfully resisted without dismantling everything else.

* * *

The modern school arose through the accumulation of various dispersed techniques.[56] These techniques amassed between the late eighteenth century and the start of the twentieth, to form the distinctly functional architectures of modern schooling. This rise of mass schooling accompanied the formation of modern states that claimed to be serving the interests of their citizens. Newfound freedoms were established and old social ties (remnants of feudalism) broke down. It was important, under conditions such as these, that citizens were educated to use their freedom correctly. States came to depend on sophisticated techniques that would enable them to construct the subjects they required. This momentous formative endeavour, involving the material formation of an entire citizenry, no less, was taken up in part by the modern school. Early techniques focused on the training and regulation of bodies, and through the manipulation of

these bodies they constructed the modern soul. Whilst this soul has no vital or inextinguishable essence, it is no illusion either, being the product of its material reality. Unlike the soul of Christian theology, it was not born in sin, but was induced through various methods of punishment, supervision and constraint.

* * *

To those who defend the individual, here is a warning: the modern men, women and children you endeavour to free are already the product of something much greater than themselves. Their souls, your quarry, are 'the effect and instrument of a political anatomy' that is larger in extent than the reach of your compassion.[57] You seek to protect the sanctity of the individual? You are defending a phantom!

* * *

The technocrats who devised modern schooling employed techniques that would shape individuality in such a way that those concerned were isolated from one another but open to the influence of government. Here, modern examination in its various forms operated as a meticulous divider. Later contributions added a focus on interpersonal examining techniques. These would construct the modern soul as a self-regulating consciousness.

The overall strategy, as Michel Foucault once observed, was to combine dividing practices and practices of exclusion (where 'the subject is either divided inside himself or divided from others') with techniques that trained the child to 'turn him- or herself into a subject'.[58] These techniques enabled the individual to recognise externally defined traits within the self and then act upon them.

As a material reality, the modern soul depends on concepts and domains of analysis within which it can be determined. It relies on the carving out of categories ranging from more general ideas – 'psyche, subjectivity, personality, consciousness, etc.'[59] – to more child-specific notions – the troubled child, the child of promise, the borderline child, and so on. Examination performs a central role here in forming the frame of reference that informs the child, so that he or she may live within the scope it defines.

* * *

Together with schools, modern examinations evolved from practices that were developed at a number of sites and were influenced by a range of political, social, historical and psychological narratives. These practices were not variations on a single theme. They should be viewed as acts of differential creation.[60]

I have to say this, really. It forms part of my methodological mantra – one I inherit from the *genealogist*, a creature born of Nietzsche[61] and nurtured by Foucault.[62] The genealogist may be defined by the position he or she takes with respect to the following three terms. *Origin:* A genealogist should not pursue origins, as if the essence of things might somehow be discovered. *Descent:* The denial of absolute origins is linked to the idea of descent; every historical beginning is simply a fabrication derived from that which preceded it. Beginnings are nothing but events that have acquired a certain artificial status in retrospect. Thus, we should not search for beginnings. Instead, we should look for the 'myriad events' that coordinate to form the heterogeneity of descent.[63] *Emergence:* The emergence of historical events is to be understood as the product of confrontation. An historical event is the outcome of 'a particular state of forces'.[64] 'Consequently, no one is responsible for an emergence; no one can glory in it, since it always occurs in the interstice.'[65]

How the genealogist is able to function in this confrontational landscape will be explored in more detail later. For the moment it is sufficient to turn directly to Nietzsche for a description of the terrain:

> there is…no more important principle for all types of history than the following one…that there is a world of difference between the reason for something coming into existence in the first place and the ultimate use to which it is put, its actual application and integration into a system of

goals; that anything which exists, once it has somehow come into being, can be reinterpreted in the service of new intentions, repossessed, repeatedly modified to a new use by a power superior to it; that everything which happens in the organic world is part of a process of *overpowering, mastering,* and that, in turn, all overpowering and mastering is a reinterpretation, a manipulation, in the course of which the previous 'meaning' and 'aim' must necessarily be obscured or completely effaced … all aims, all uses are merely *signs* indicating that a will to power has mastered something less powerful than itself and impressed the meaning of a function upon it in accordance with its own interests. So the entire history of a 'thing', an organ, a custom may take the form of an extended chain of signs, of ever-new interpretations and manipulations, whose causes do not themselves necessarily stand in relation to one another, but merely follow and replace one another arbitrarily and according to circumstance. The 'development' of a thing, a custom, an organ does not in the least resemble a *progressus* towards a goal, and even less the logical and shortest *progressus,* the most economical in terms of expenditure of force and cost. Rather, this development assumes the form of the succession of the more or less far-reaching, more or less independent processes of overpowering which affect it – including also in each case the resistance marshalled against these processes, the changes of form attempted with a view to defence and reaction, and the results of these successful counteractions. The form is fluid, but the 'meaning' even more so.[66]

All this repels the fervent historian, who retreats to the archives in pursuit of historical truth. It implies a mode of historical enquiry that would be just as disordered as the history it perceives. The historian prefers calm, subscribing to the hope that insistent diligence, and the factual accumulations scholarly endeavour affords, will generate a fairly cohesive account of the object in question. I hope you will be reassured: I have no such ambitions. There is no desire to 'fill in the blanks' here. Ignoring the convention by which historical accounts are measured against the completeness of the picture they construct and all limitations are openly confessed by way of an apology to the reader, I focus on just two institutional sites without expressing regret for the inevitable limitations of my analysis. These two institutions will be contextualised, but only to a degree.[67] And I will generalise without undue restraint. My principal objective is confrontational. It is to engage with my chosen target: the 'relations of power'[68] Foucault once spoke of.

* * *

The purpose of this history is largely rhetorical. It has been devised to cast doubt on the present. Even a quick survey of the development of modern examination can, in my view, lead us to suspect the direction of contemporary reform efforts, however well-intended they may be. A history such as this should break down the current tendency in education to adjudicate between 'good' and 'bad' examining practices, between those examining practices that are seen as oppressive, impersonal and excessively mechanistic and those that are celebrated for their flexibility and attention to the needs of the child. Both traditions of assessment (mechanistic and humanistic) have as their object the construction of selves amenable to government. And so, the rejection of one tradition of examination in favour of another may do little to emancipate us from the effects of power. My claim is this: our entrapment on the horns of this false dilemma occurred at the emergence of modern examination. Indeed, the complex descent of the techniques that now afflict us should be traced back to their constitution in the nineteenth century

The institutions within which these practices were collected and developed have long since disappeared. The early nineteenth-century 'monitorial school' and the mid-nineteenth-century 'moral training school' were, nevertheless,

highly influential. These two short-lived institutions deserve far greater attention than they generally receive, having taken part in the transformation of practices from which modern schooling and examination were built.

The examining practices they employed were never simply oppressive, even in their darkest moments. They were, indeed, highly productive in constructing biddable subjects for the benefit of the modern state. In other words – and to repeat myself – the advance of modern examination did not trample the interior of the child. Even those examining techniques that seek to listen to the child – techniques that are celebrated for their benign attention to the unique needs of the individual learner – are not innocent of power interests and their effects. They are tied within a system of moral coercion that operates through carefully devised modes of examination, based on relationships that are often warm and kindly in manner.

* * *

My focus – a symptom of my place of birth – is the early development of the two schools in Britain. These two school types were global in their reach. Monitorial schools spread throughout Europe and across the Atlantic to the Americas,[69] followed by moral training schools, which can be traced to colonies such as Nova Scotia.[70] These institutions were devised for the wretched and dispossessed. Many feared that the urban poor, drawn to the cities in ever-larger numbers, were becoming ungovernable. When transplanted across the Atlantic to the Americas, these institutional techniques were applied to other 'difficult' groups, including the natives of that continent, who were bereft, or so it was assumed, living as they did without the benefits of modernity.[71]

These new institutional sites were contrasted with the disordered instruction already available in the slum. Run by social inferiors, scratching together a living on the margins of society, the private adventure or dame schools were judged too irregular and nomadic to function. Even worse, they were potential breeding grounds of vice and immorality.[72] Sir James Kay-Shuttleworth, secretary to the embryo Ministry of Education, complained that a great number of schoolmasters still 'plying their trade' in 1841 undertook this work either because they were 'incapacitated by age or infirmity' or because they had 'failed in all other attempts to procure a livelihood'.[73] Twenty years later a government commission lamented that these establishments were still springing up like 'mushroom growth'.[74] Indeed, it was felt that these places revealed a lot about 'what kind of education finds favour with that particular class of parents'.[75]

For a flavour of their decrepit construction, picture this particularly 'miserable' establishment, located 'at the top of a very steep and broken staircase' where the 'chief text-book seemed to be a kitten'. Again we are told that those working in this environment selected their profession 'because they have failed in other pursuits, or because, as in the case of widows, they have been unexpectedly left in a state of destitution'.[76] As one commissioner famously declared: 'none are too old, too poor, too ignorant, too feeble, too sickly, too unqualified in any way or every way, to regard themselves, and to be regarded by others, as unfit for school-keeping'.[77] The implications are clear enough: the poor could not be trusted with overseeing their own instruction. Those institutions they did manage to establish were 'of the most temporary kind'[78] and were not fit for purpose. The depraved masses required something rather more systematic and worthy than they were able to achieve without assistance from above.

Gradually, the responsibility for public education was adopted by large philanthropic organisations, and, following that, by the state. Having witnessed the birth of modern schooling, this period could be viewed as a triumph of educational inclusion. A chain of events unfolded here that would ultimately result in the guarantee that all children will have access to a formal education. 'Education for all!' – that is our great inheritance, this is our modern educational achievement. And yet, from the outset the newly invented institutions of schooling were based on practices of division; they generated fresh inequalities. They were, moreover, instruments of government. Children were institutionalised. They were made available for inspection, rendered legible and open to governmental calculation. These schools functioned as vast educational laboratories. They were founded for the production of knowledge and the proliferation of governmental techniques.

Each mode of schooling – monitorial and moral training – developed its own unique cluster of examining practices. In the monitorial school, examination was integrated within a disciplinary and functional architecture. As such, it cannot be understood apart from the entire ensemble of practices that made up this institution. Examination in the moral training school adopted a very different approach; it was based on the construction of intimate relations between teachers and pupils. And yet, it too relied on a larger functional organisation of space. The subsequent history of examination is a history of the relationship between these two basic approaches – one disciplinary, the other pastoral. They became entangled and generated derivatives, leading to the complex array of inscription devices and pastoral controls that constitute education today.

* * *

Schools and prisons often resemble one another. They share common histories and techniques. These techniques swiftly become so banal that we are no longer arrested by their grotesque presence. To take a contemporary example: children who use fingerprint scanners to pay for lunch no longer balk at the introduction of scanners elsewhere.

* * *

As the eighteenth century drew to a close there was a transformation in systems of punishment. Formerly public, and often brutal, the occasional display of retribution issued by the monarch and inflicted on the body of the condemned was withdrawn from open view. Punishment was dragged behind the prison gates so as to become an institutional and private concern. The new correctional order drew upon diffuse technologies distributed across prisons, hospitals, barracks and schools. Across these sites was developed a new mode of power that Foucault labelled *disciplinary*. Foucault describes its many components throughout *Discipline and Punish*[79] – in which he traces a transition from sporadic and vengeful punishments to regular and measured disciplinary techniques. These employed a far more advanced and better-calibrated economy of pain than the pillory was ever able to afford.

Certain formulations outlined in *Discipline and Punish* have since become commonplace. Scholars have claimed to find 'disciplinary power' everywhere. It has been depicted as a ubiquitous feature of modernity that has plagued us ever since it was developed in the early nineteenth century. Its fossilised structures are said to still influence schooling today. From this perspective, anything mechanical or reductive in appearance can find itself labelled as 'disciplinary'.[80] Disciplinary power is in danger of becoming a vague cipher for a form of subjection we are no longer able to identify precisely, because it has been applied to so many contexts in so many ways. It has become a promiscuous concept.

*   *   *

Jeremy Bentham's circular prison design, known as the 'panopticon', is the metaphor typically used to represent disciplinary power.[81] As a metaphor, it has some value, demonstrating how a disciplinary architecture could support the automatic functioning of power, where inmates become the bearers of the system that subjects them. Unable to discover precisely when they are being observed, inmates act as if observation were constant.

By referring to this metaphor, by emphasising the 'panoptic gaze', we avoid any reduction of disciplinary technique to notions of simple domination, for disciplinary power is said to operate through the dispositions and hence 'freedoms' of those it moulds. We should remember, however, that this prison design was no more than the 'diagram of a mechanism of power', one that has been 'reduced to its ideal form', and, by virtue of this reduction, details are lost.[82] Moreover, it exaggerates the principle of visibility.[83] Disciplinary power is about much more than optical surveillance.

*   *   *

The power of discipline is one of analysis, based upon its ability to locate and separate that which is to be studied. As Foucault put it: 'one of the primary objects of discipline is to fix; it is an anti-nomadic technique'. It is for analytic purposes that discipline 'arrests or regulates movements', clears up 'confusion', dissipates 'compact groupings of individuals wandering about the country in unpredictable ways' and establishes 'calculated distributions'.[84] The production of knowledge is an intrinsic part of its technique.

* * *

Partitioned individuals, a prerequisite for disciplinary analysis, are generated by various means. These include the basic spatial distribution of bodies, which is physical but can also be represented conceptually, such as through the distribution of inmates in cells or the register that records their arrival; a careful breakdown and coding of bodily movements, such as can be found in the sequential gestures of the military parade; the sequencing of activities through longer periods of time, which are made visible in documents such as a school curriculum; and efforts to coordinate the entire ensemble of bodies through a 'composition of forces'.[85] When combined, these techniques form the basic structure of a disciplinary examination. Whilst examination becomes through this ensemble the strategic hub of disciplinary power, it would be a mistake to treat disciplinary examination as if it were the hidden motor or essence of disciplinary technique.[86] Separated from its networks of associated techniques, examination has little specific gravity or strength of its own.

* * *

The monitorial school spread the simple, brute fact of confinement across its multiple, intersecting techniques. In Tennessee, when efforts to institutionalise children of the aboriginal population were reviewed, it was claimed that monitorial teaching 'relieves that bitterness which otherwise those would feel, who have not been accustomed to confinement'.[87] This was in 1818.

Viewed as both economical and effective, the monitorial school promised to transform ungovernable groups into useful and productive subjects at minimal cost. As a modern achievement it was raised above vaccination by its proponents, for it was said to offer 'a remedy for the disorders of filth, idleness, ignorance, and vice' that were 'more fatal', even, 'than the ravages of the Small-Pox'.[88] In the opinion of one colonial chaplain, this new system of education was nothing less than a form of *'mental vaccination'*.[89] It was the best means of 'arriving at *the cure* of those evils which at once disgrace society, and deprive it of many who might form its most active and useful members'.[90] It was able to 'correct those morbid humours which so corrupt the morals of society'.[91] Naturally, since both mental vaccination and social cure were now possible, the 'greatest

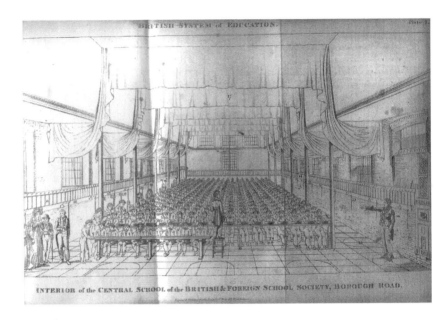

INTERIOR of the CENTRAL SCHOOL of the BRITISH & FOREIGN SCHOOL SOCIETY, BOROUGH ROAD.

discoveries, heretofore made for the improvement of human life, sink into comparative insignificance'.[92]

These were the views of the professed first architect Dr Andrew Bell and his expanding band of enthusiasts. Initially devised for orphans at a military asylum in Madras (founded in 1789), the system was imported with the return of Bell to Britain in 1797. Issuing from a rival denomination, Joseph Lancaster devised a remarkably similar system, and, with the support of their respective philanthropic societies and religious orders,[93] these school systems spread throughout kingdom and empire.

The Madras school run by Bell aimed to rescue mixed-race children, orphans of British officers, from the 'habits of wretched depravity' in which they had been 'educated by their mothers'.[94]

> It has long been said, that the half-cast children of this country show an evident inferiority in the talents of the head, the qualities of the mind, and the virtues of the heart. I will not enter into the question, How far government, or climate, and perhaps complexion as connected with climate, influence the character of the human race. Whatever may be the opinion on these heads, I believe that the effect of education will not be denied...I think I see, in the very first maxims which the mothers of these children instil into their infant minds, the source of every corrupt practice, and an infallible mode of forming a degenerate race.[95]

As a devout educationalist, Bell set out unperturbed to form his pupils in 'habits of diligence, industry, veracity, and honesty' as well as 'instructing them in useful knowledge'.[96] In 1839, following multiple experiments with the techniques he promoted, this educational optimism lives on in the teaching manuals of the monitorial school:

> However untoward a child may be found on first entering the school, no violence of temper, no perversity of disposition, no depravity of principle, no sluggishness of intellect, should discourage the hope of effecting a decided change, through the Divine blessing, on a patient and persevering application of the regulations prescribed.[97]

My contemporaries and peers maintain a similar commitment to education. They hold it to be a worthy, transformative and potentially life-changing endeavour. We agents of subjection take great pride in calling ourselves educationalists.

* * *

For want of proper assistants, who, when drawn from the local population, were felt to be poor in quality, Bell was forced to design a system that he could operate alone. One solitary master would conduct the school, transforming 'stubborn, perverse, and obstinate' boys into an 'annual crop of good and useful subjects'. This would be achieved by conducting the school 'through the medium of the scholars themselves'.[98] Dependable students, appropriately trained, would monitor and supervise their peers. Supervision was devolved within a tight scheme, across concerted systems of observation; it was spun through a network that was supported by its own interlocking web. This economy of power was designed to cope with the lower orders of society, which, it was presumed, required assistance in running their own affairs. These lower orders were to be an experimental population. Through the manipulation of their offspring they would become accustomed to a strategy of government that operated not from above but from below and within. The masses were to be instructed in procedures deemed appropriate for regulating and governing themselves.

Along with Lancaster, who believed that 'coercion' is 'the most disgusting word in the British vocabulary',[99] Bell asserted the mildness of his new technique. The moderation of force was adopted as a key principle: replacing a costly, sporadic, uncalculated use of violence with a far more carefully applied, constantly felt economy of power (using 'means as much more effectual as they are more lenient than usual'[100]). The problem with 'a system of terror' and the 'fear of punishment' is that neither is 'so constant nor so certain an operation'.[101] If 'newly-invented racks or screws, or whips, or cords' had been placed into his hands, Bell declares, the 'experiment should have perished in embryo'. Instead he devised a minute 'division of labour' which left the master with the 'simple and easy charge of directing, regulating, and controlling his intellectual and moral machine'.[102] Lancaster agreed: school keeping should no longer be a 'toilsome employ' if the school is 'conducted by a regular system'.[103]

*   *   *

In Nürnberg clocks have been striking the quarter hour since the sixteenth century.[104] With modernity, minutes became valuable. In the monitorial school time was to be maximised. The experience of time (its passing) was intensified by the maximal use of the slightest moment, 'as if time, in its very fragmentation, were inexhaustible'.[105]

A 'constant and perpetual attention' was desired of pupils. Usually this was limited by 'such a number of boys' as the master could 'at once have under his eye and within his reach'.[106] But the gaze of the teacher was only one of many devices. Constant activity was assured, or so we are told, by an 'uninterrupted succession of short and easy lessons', and through the 'perpetual presence and never-ceasing vigilance of its numerous overseers', the students themselves, who helped 'preclude idleness, ensure diligence, prevent ill behaviour of every sort, and almost supersede the necessity of punishment'.[107]

Discipline was the key to this 'simple, easy, pleasant, expeditious, and economical' system: '*as in an army*, discipline' was 'the first, second and third essential'.[108] We are told that a single master carrying out Bell's methods could 'without difficulty, conduct ten contiguous schools, each consisting of a thousand scholars' for the 'school teaches itself'.[109] Such machinery would not run in perpetuity without periodic maintenance: a 'scrutinising eye must pervade the whole machine'.[110] Its workings would be adjusted 'from time to time, so as to get the most out of it, with the least possible friction'. The 'smoothness, exactitude, and machine like regularity' of the school would then be assured.[111]

*   *   *

The school assembles in a single large room or hall, with windows at least six feet from the floor to prevent distraction. At one end is the master's desk; occupying the middle are forms (benches) and desks fixed firmly into the ground.[112] Upon entry, each pupil proceeds to his or her unique number printed on the school wall, where vacant spaces describe absences at a glance.[113] Once called to their seats, the hierarchy of classes and functionaries becomes manifest. Each allotted spot is a relative position within a route of progression that operates throughout the school, from the front, nearest the master's desk, to the rear. All monitors have their stations, a general monitor of order standing on a high stool at the lower end of the room, and the monitors of classes standing above the seated majority to the right of their respective subjects.[114] Through these arrangements in space, a disordered mass becomes a legible entity. The definition of each child, including his or her role within the school, is the direct result of his or her position within this conceptual and functional grid. A norm of progression is defined, constructing the terms in which pupils are to view themselves. Perched on the benches in front is their past; on the benches behind, their future.

* * *

At the end of each bench is a standard (a kind of notice board). Here class marks are displayed, forming a conceptual grid that defines the class and each individual within it. There are smaller boards called 'telegraphs' that turn freely on a rod, the lower end of which is fixed into the top of the standard just referred to. Inscribed on one side is the number of the class, on the other the letters E. X. By displaying these letters, class monitors inform the General Monitor when they have examined the slates. This procedure assures that testing is carried out on a regular basis.[115]

Even the precise movement of the child, seated with his or her companions along the regimented order of the bench, is defined according to a breakdown of bodily mechanics. Habits of 'prompt obedience' are to be

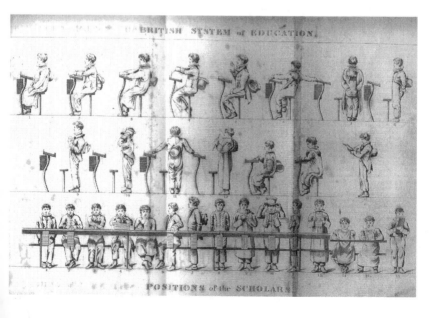

'universally established'. With children who are 'restless, volatile, and unused to restraint, mechanical motions of the body, as they are at once easily understood, and readily performed, afford the best means of inculcating these habits'. No teacher should rest until 'he has brought every child to sit, stand, speak, or be silent, on the instant of the command being given'.[116]

Positions of the Scholars, a popular illustration in monitorial school manuals, depicts a numbered frieze of bodily movements in which each figure corresponds to an associated command. Upon arrival at the writing desk, each pupil 'places his finger on the slate screw, and stops without turning' (figure eleven). When all have 'quitted the aisles', the monitor of order says 'front' at which 'they all turn and face him' (figure eight). At the command 'in' they 'spring in' (figure one). This continues, through figures two, four, five, two again, six and so on, and on, until they are eventually instructed to quit their desks, put on their hats (figure ten), and depart.[117]

* * *

These were idealised schemes. At times their claims to efficacy are almost mythological. Bell reports that the monitorial schoolmaster has at his disposal 'the hundred hands of Briareus, the hundred eyes of Argus, and the wings of Mercury'.[118] Surely this inflated statement renders all others suspect? The claims made on behalf of the monitorial school would appear to be wanton exaggerations. Even though failures are occasionally documented in the annual reports that were collated by the mother societies in Britain, their tone is generally pious. One school in Leith was an 'offence to the neighbourhood' when first established on account of 'the uncontrollable rudeness of the scholars out of doors, and the noise, insubordination, and misrule that reigned within'.[119] After five years it was transformed into a paragon of good order. How this was achieved remains unclear. In a Sheffield school, the account of moral rescue for one female pupil (who was 'violent to the extreme' and 'addicted to fighting, swearing, and almost every thing that was bad') takes the form of a sudden religious conversion, following exposure to scripture.[120] Clearly, monitorial techniques were far from uniform and employed devices other than disciplinary ones. These examples do not point, however, to a fundamental error in Foucault's disciplinary theory. For Foucault, disciplinary institutions are just like any other regime of power that has failed to achieve totality: these institutions are always-already failing, they are leaking at the edges. To reject disciplinary institutions as figments, as little more than the organisational fantasies of their architects, to say they never existed in this perfect form, and to call for research that finds out what 'really happened', misses the point. Indeed, as a non-total system of power, discipline draws strength from multiplication and dispersal, and not from isolated cases of perfection or conquest. The complex devices of the monitorial school were far more than the educational dreams of over-zealous pedagogues, eulogised in teaching manuals. These contrivances reflect a logic of design that extended well beyond the monitorial school, becoming too widely dispersed to be ignored.

*　*　*

Within the monitorial system and its arrangement of bodies, each scholar 'finds his own level, not only in his class, but in the ranks of the school, being promoted or degraded from place to place, or class to class, according to his proficiency'.[121] The steps were deliberately small. Even the differences between a class and its class monitor are modest. The monitors (who are pupils too) should know 'no more than what is level to the capacities of their pupils'. They will, as a result, 'lose no time in teaching what is beyond the comprehension of their scholars'.[122] Attention to the surface features of the pupil cohort, and not to its depths, was the epitome of good teaching.

*　*　*

Any boy 'lame, or deformed' or limited in his faculties can be rejected if he will become a 'burden' to the overall machinery of the school.[123] Those admitted must perform their function as a component part, where the basic drive is to 'obtain pre-eminence' in the class and then 'to rise above it and be promoted to a superior; and especially not to sink below it, and degraded to an inferior class'.[124] Promotion to a higher class only occurs when high rank has been held for some time, and is only permanent if the pupil can quickly rise to the middle of the new, higher class. Otherwise the pupil returns to the former group. Demotion occurs when a pupil fails to perform well. However, if high rank in the inferior class is maintained, the pupil is not 'doomed to permanent degradation'. A flavour of demotion is deemed sufficient to secure 'redoubled exertion'.[125]

Each class is itself divided into pairs of tutors and pupils (not to be confused with the monitors in overall charge[126]). The superior half of the class tutors the inferior half, and the seats taken along the bench reflect this: the lowest member of the class sits beside the highest, the next lowest beside the next highest, and so on all the way along. Achieving the status of tutor is an honour, but the tutor is responsible for a double fate. He must protect his pupil from demotion by teaching well, whilst retaining his higher rank by being proficient at what is taught, for 'what disgrace attaches to the boy who, by his negligence, is degraded into a pupil, and falls perhaps to be tutored by his late pupil, promoted to be a tutor'.[127] The overall effect of perpetual readjustment is that 'every boy in every class' finds himself fully occupied, his exertions maximised.[128]

*　*　*

Ranking depends upon an archive of past efforts. It begins with the individual scholar, who 'registers for himself all his daily operations in the last page of his copy, or ciphering book'. This is later compared with what he did the day before and what others of similar standing achieved. There are weekly, monthly, quarterly and annual reviews. The page in which 'these registers are kept, is ruled into thirty-one parallel lines, so as to last a month, and into as many columns as there are daily entries to be made'. The teacher also compiles a more general daily record containing the 'number of lessons read; pages or lines gone over in these lessons; and hours thus employed'.[129] In Lancaster's system, the monitor employed as 'inspector-general of reading' examines samples of each class on a periodic basis, getting round to 'some hundreds' in a few days.[130] This documentary trail ensures that each pupil has a 'permanent testimony' to 'merit and demerit'. Even if a pupil is 'overlooked in passing', the archive retains the relevant facts for later perusal.[131]

*　*　*

The 'black book' is seen as 'the most powerful operator'. All misdemeanours (including the failure to report misdemeanours) are recorded here. The schoolmaster then decides whether an 'immediate reprimand, or threat' is suitable, or whether the offence should become part of the weekly ritual of punishment. 'Abstract lectures are little attended to, and still less understood, by children. To reach their minds and touch their hearts, you must give a visible shape and tangible form to your doctrine.'[132] The reprimand passes through the body to the soul under construction.

Lancaster presents himself as a tireless innovator in this domain. Though he reputedly had 'a perfect horror' of the rod,[133] this came more from dislike of its tendency to arbitrary violence than its cruelty as such. He preferred a more regular economy of pain: modes of correction must be 'inflicted, so as to give as much uneasiness to the delinquents, without disturbing the mind or temper of the master'.[134]

Instruments of punishment include 'a wooden log' placed round the neck, which 'serves as a pillory'. The neck 'is *not pinched* or closely *confined* – it is chiefly burthensome by the manner in which it incumbers the neck, when the delinquent turns to the right or the left...Thus he is *confined* to *sit* in his *proper position*, and go on with his work.' 'When logs are unavailing, it is common to fasten the legs of offenders together with wooden shackles' and order them to walk round the hall until they are 'glad to sue for liberty'. If this fails, 'the left hand is tied behind the back, or wooden shackles fastened from elbow to elbow'. Sometimes 'the legs are tied together', preventing boys from wandering about. 'Occasionally boys are put in a sack, or in a basket, suspended to the roof of the school, in sight of all the pupils, who frequently smile at the birds in the cage.' This punishment 'is one of the most terrible' and is to be especially 'dreaded by the monitors'.

Frequent offenders are 'yoked together, sometimes by a piece of wood that fastens round all their necks' and forced to parade the school walking backwards', which makes them 'pay very great attention to their footsteps'. Others are 'dressed up with labels' describing the offence and are led round the school by two boys proclaiming the fault.[135] Dirty boys are cleaned before the whole school by a girl; truants are tied to a post; the most 'incorrigible' are 'tied up in a blanket, and left to sleep at night on the floor'.[136] In punishing by confinement after school, the master's attendance can be avoided 'by tying them to the desks'. Those who adopt 'a singing tone in reading' are ridiculed with a special costume; others are made to wear the 'fools coat'. A lazy boy will have a pillow fetched 'and placed on the desk for him to lay his head on, as if asleep, in the face of the school'; a 'boy wandering from his seat may be placed under a hen coop' – idle boys are rocked in a cradle.[137] All devices are to be applied with a cool, calculated temper. Despite their severity, these are carefully measured techniques. They are corrective in function, as the desired behaviour can be deduced from the punishment chosen.

* * *

A parallel 'system of encouragement' takes us away from these economies of bodily discomfort. Paper tickets are awarded for good work, and a monitor of tickets records these awards in a book. Accumulated tickets can be exchanged for prizes of varying value, from a separate monitor. There are several orders of merit, and those who reach a higher rank wear badges on a daily basis until they are forfeited by bad behaviour. We are told that pupils are 'more affected by their loss than coercion'.[138] Teachers and assistants also receive pecuniary and honorary awards, and 'silver medals' of varying size are 'distributed in the annual examination by the president'.[139] Many other duties have their respective officers and systems of encouragement. There is a 'sub-usher and usher' who 'watch over the whole', a monitor of slates, of cleanliness, of absences, and so on until every duty is discharged.[140]

* * *

Perhaps these paper tickets, prizes and medals will not distract you from the image of pupils yoked together, or boys confined in a sack. If it all sounds rather oppressive and alien to your finer sensibilities, do not be fooled. Taken as a whole, these techniques were profoundly constructive. We are their heirs, you and I. New ways of being, new understandings of the self were being formed here.

* * *

As an overall framework, disciplinary technique should not be misread as if it were the product of larger oppressions, such as the overbearing state, to name an obvious and frequently invoked example. Disciplinary technique evidently pre-dates state education in England. Of course, state institutions such as the elementary schools of the late nineteenth century later adopted some of these devices. But the state, of which we hear so much, is always limited by its dependence on techniques 'which it did not invent and whose consequences it cannot fully control'.[141]

In understanding the workings of power, we must avoid the phantom of an abstract oppressor. As Ian Hunter observes, the 'problem of total determination' only arrives under 'fantasmatic theoretical circumstances' that generate the abstract categories from which such a 'problem' first emerges.[142] The modern governmental state arose 'not as a new face for the timeless struggle between power and self-determination' but 'as a circumstantially-specific amalgam of political instruments'. These political instruments were of diverse provenance; each arrived with its own specific agenda. And so, rather than 'expressing the will of the absolutist state or its ruler', these instruments effectively 'colonized it in the name of a new range of political knowledges and imperatives'.[143]

*   *   *

In educational circles, examination is the exemplary case of an abstract oppressor. It has become a spectre in the eyes of its critics, one that stalks the corridors of the school, breathing its heavy stench into the classroom, obliterating all good intention, reducing teacher and student alike to shadows of their former selves.

The material presence of examination is far more diffuse, though, than its critics allow. In the monitorial school it was distributed widely, influencing bodily location and movement, rendering visible an otherwise obscured process of learning and effort. Examination was produced by the system of telegraphs that ensured it was taking place with coordinated regularity as part of every lesson; the keeping of records by pupils in the backs of their books at the end of each day and month, allowing comparisons between pupils and within pupils across time; the consequent distribution of scholars along the bench, pairing tutor and tutee in cooperative rivalry; the system that decided whether temporary demotion would become permanent; the records of overall class activity found both in a book and on public display; and, finally, the monthly, quarterly and annual reviews as well as systems of recognition and remuneration. Examination was a constant and diffuse presence in the overall economy of the school. All practices depended on this ability to locate, describe, record and compare, to raise up what was formerly 'below the threshold of description',[144] placing individuals within a 'network of writing' that would define them.[145]

Occasionally, Foucault encourages us to extend the reach of disciplinary power to the present when he remarks: 'It has always been *and still is* an intrinsic element of the disciplines.' Examination 'is *still* caught up in disciplinary technology'.[146] He does not, however, trace its development from the nineteenth century to the present as it appeared to him in 1975, leaving us with little more than these enigmatic claims. It is worth asking whether examination has indeed endured to the present day in the form described above. Does examination retain its disciplinary function in contemporary pedagogic practice? Or was examination in the monitorial school so specific to a particular organisation of space and hierarchy that, when the monitorial school dissolved, so did its disciplinary examination?

When we consider these questions, it must be remembered that disciplinary institutions, in this case monitorial schools, were 'mixed spaces' that were both real and ideal in their constitution.[147] Examination, in its disciplinary form, can still endure in the latter rarefied form even if many details of a material structure have long since departed. As an early nineteenth-century device, it also sits at the birth of the human sciences, at the dawn of partitioned, scientifically measurable, normalised humankind. In this sense disciplinary power is assured a continuing legacy. Its associated disciplinary knowledges, along with the examining experts they produced, are still in place in one form or another. At a very basic level, examination still renders the invisible visible, and situates the governed subject in a relative scheme. It was, though, only one technique amongst many. If disciplinary examination does indeed extend to the present, this must surely be in a highly revised form.

Modern examination has at least one other major nineteenth-century precursor. This antecedent technique produced a far more intimate regime of inspection, achieving a pastoral symbiosis that tied teacher to pupil in a pact of mutual salvation. It was at this point that school examination developed confessional attributes. The legacy of this pastoral symbiosis for the functioning of examination today is just as significant as, if not more so than, the legacy one might attribute to its more easily identifiable, disciplinary companion.

A Child's Interior

The spectacle of street life in nineteenth-century Glasgow inspired David Stow, son of a merchant, to confront the urban barbarities he witnessed whilst walking through the city. Stow decided that the fallen multitudes of the industrial age required his assistance. Charity he viewed as a 'mere expedient', believing that the proper solution lay in moral training. To surmount the effects of their poverty, the poor must develop the 'moral stamina' that would 'enable them to resist the viciousness of their surroundings'.[148] According to Stow, the problems faced by the urban poor were altogether new. Their predecessor, the Scottish peasant, had been far better cared for. This had little to do with the rural parish school and its claustrophobic interior: that institution 'was only one small portion of the machinery by which, under God, her peasantry were stamped with a high intellectual and moral character'.[149] In its wisdom the Scottish Church embedded itself in the rural community, providing 'a minister and a schoolmaster and a staff of elders for every small rural parish of perhaps 500 to 1000 souls'.[150] And it was the clergyman, we are told, who was the principal agent of moral rescue in this context. The close contact afforded by the realities of rural life enabled him to influence the family through its religious exercises, and thereby reach the child.

In the towns and cities, where intimate pastoral links were comparatively scarce, Stow claims that the 'natural tendency...is to evil'. Unable to rely on the support of the wider social environment, the pedagogue must now lay claim to *'the entire child'*, taking his or her very being into care.[151] Educational techniques suited to rural life had no place in the urban context. They could not countervail *'the sympathy of numbers'* – a social force Stow associates with the education of the streets.[152]

*   *   *

The spatial distribution of the moral training school, for which Stow was the acclaimed architect, would assist the schoolmaster in his efforts to lay hold of the entire child, to rescue it from a 'savage, brutalized existence'.[153] 'Pioneers of civilization' would be required when it came to work of this magnitude. These pioneers would run institutions that were able to effect a transformation in the child's interior. The obstacles faced by those engaged with this civilising mission were prodigious. Sir James Kay-Shuttleworth, perhaps the most eminent nineteenth-century proponent of moral schooling, recalls his experiences of the urban north, down upon which has 'floated a constant supply of an immigrant semi-savage population, bred on the moors of the Pennine Chain' and in other remote places. 'They probably have never lived but in a hovel; have never been in the street of a village town; are unacquainted with common usages of social life; perhaps never

saw a book; are bewildered by the rapid motion of crowds; confused in an assemblage of scholars. They have to be taught to stand upright, –to walk without a slouching gait, –to sit without crouching like a sheep-dog.' Their parents 'are almost equally brutish. They have lived solitary lives in some wild region' but the 'pressing wants of a growing family have induced them to accept the offer of some agent from a mill'. These are the children schools must 'civilise and Christianise'.

According to Kay-Shuttleworth, as they descend from the moors and wolds they arrive upon a 'different kind of brutishness' already entrenched in the 'most degraded parts of great cities'. Here the urban child, the '"Arab of the street"', learns a 'great deal of evil' from an already sinking and sunken population. 'Such children have of late years been netted in shoals, –got into schools, –have been won, tamed, and, in some degree taught.' But these efforts were never likely to entirely 'get rid of the wild, untamed barbarism of such children' and 'graft' onto them the 'civilisation' they so dearly needed.[154] Driven from the country; degraded in the city; disciplined in school. Moral training must now follow.

* * *

In its civilising mission the moral school introduced a unique configuration of architectural and interpersonal techniques to the educational landscape, systematising the work of pastoral care for the urban context. It devised strategies that accounted for life exterior to the school and developed for its operations a metaphor of depth. It intensified the relationship between teacher and pupil, working upon the child's constructed interior.

This was a major revision to the monitorial approach that depended upon comparatively shallow interpersonal relations. In the monitorial school, teachers recruited from the student body were selected not only for their reliability, but also for their intellectual equivalence (they were to know 'no more than what is level to the capacities of their pupils'[155]). The schoolmaster in overall charge also operated at the surface, maintaining the school's complex machinery of bodily manipulation. In these institutions, access to detailed records, accumulated by dispersed examining techniques, provided comparatively little in the way of depth; knowledge of each pupil remained shallow. By contrast, the soul of the moral training school teacher was selected for its apparent depth. This teacher was expected to convey some kind of indication or impression of the unfathomable depths of the soul. Teachers were now expected to be morally profound beings who exhibited in their bearing the rich qualities their students were expected to develop.

* * *

Monitorial schools were interior spaces. They opened to the pavement.[156] Whilst monitorial schools remained focused on their interiors, by gathering together large groups of children from the urban poor they nevertheless established the urban exterior as a problem space *in relation to* the school. The exterior now stood in direct contrast to the institutional order within, leading pedagogues to wonder how they might negotiate this relation between internal discipline and relative chaos without. This was a problem to which the moral training school provided its solution. It would counteract the effects of this exterior by relating it more explicitly to the work of the school. Strategies were devised with an explicit remit to counter the 'training of the streets'.[157] These strategies would mediate the relationship between exterior and interior through a simulacrum of the street, known as the playground. The objective was to *stimulate* the natural tendencies of children. This went against the monitorial philosophy, which, as Lancaster explains, 'prevents the natural vivacity of children'.[158] In the playground, by contrast, it was important to encourage the self-expression of children in order to derive moral lessons from their conduct. Through this use of space, children could be 'superintended in real life', where real life was a cipher for the life of the street. As a simulated urban exterior, the playground would supplement the '*unnatural* restraint of a covered school-room'. It would enable children to be 'freely at play', having 'free scope' and 'full vent' to display their true dispositions, revealing traits upon which the teacher would then operate.[159]

* * *

Do not be deceived by the liberal use of 'freedom' and 'truth' in these descriptions. The moral training school devised a unique economy of power in which these terms had specific and local meaning. The object of schooling was to cultivate the moral depth of teacher and child. In building a regime of instruction based on moral depth (or 'moral force' as it was later satirized[160]), this school relied on older, pastoral techniques redeveloped for its urban context. Here the moral training school formed part of a wider cultural shift whereby Christian governmental techniques were transformed for application in an increasingly secular context.

Relations were established between teacher and pupil that gave new life and fresh meaning to historic Christian devices – techniques seeking to relate the congregation, or flock, to its pastor or shepherd. Nineteenth-century schools drew heavily on religious discourses, in which themes of salvation, redemption and fear (relating to a potential fall from grace) were integrated within the discourses of modern schooling. In the American progressive tradition, to take just one example, Protestant themes were combined with the secular pursuit of reason, science and liberty.[161] An increasingly secular age was built on religious devices.

*   *   *

According to Foucault's tentative genealogy,[162] this 'pastoral power' originated as a governing technique in early Christian institutions. An arrangement was established within the church where certain individuals could, based on their religious eminence, serve others in order to achieve salvation in the next world. This governing regime would not issue commands from above with the expectation that obedience would be secured directly and through a unilateral relation. Rather, the exercise of power relied on the willingness of the pastor to develop a spirit of self-sacrifice that would guide his daily affairs. The pastor would deny himself not in the direct service of an all-powerful god, but through indirect means in the service of lower beings. These beings, in whose service he would place his soul, were his moral subordinates, the flock. To reinforce the connection between pastor and flock, the pastor's ultimate salvation was constructed so that it depended on the success of this relationship.

His attention to the flock was divided between supervising the flock as a whole and attending to the unique facets of each individual, however ignoble these particulars might be. This required intimate and confessional relationships to be established, through which the pastor's knowledge of the individual's conscience and his ability to direct it could be assured. Pastoral care was not removed and distant; it was coextensive and continuous with life. It was linked to a production of truth, the truth of the individual self.

Even though with the rise of modernity the pastorate lost a great deal of its former authority and reach, the techniques it devised spread and multiplied

outside the ecclesiastical dominion from which they originated. Its individualising devices were to become successively integrated alongside disciplinary mechanisms within the secular Western state. In this profane context
the idea of salvation took on different meanings, with a series of worldly
aims taking the place of the religious aims of the traditional pastorate. The
officials of this newly liberated pastoral power increased, including within
their orbit the nineteenth-century schoolteacher. Teaching became a form
of professional sacrifice for the present and future moral, social and educational well-being of the pupil.

Religious themes were not completely obliterated in this progressively secular
context. They were still invoked, though in a form that was increasingly subordinate to the concerns of a bureaucratic state. Kay-Shuttleworth declared that
the schoolteacher would require 'no small support from Christian faith' to
reverse 'the mental darkness, the stubborn tempers, the hopeless spirits, and
the vicious habits' of the pauper child. This demanded a 'spirit of self-sacrifice
and tender concern for well-being' based on a sober understanding of just
'how degenerate these children are'. The 'men who undertake this work should
not set about it in the spirit of hirelings'; a moral tether should be established
that would bind the subjectivity of the teacher to the pupil, establishing a relationship of mutual dependence.[163] This new relationship represented a 'significant shift from the view that the only interest a teacher might have in a school
is the fear of losing his situation. The teacher now had to be imbued with an
ethic of service.'[164] An ethic of this sort went far beyond the instrumental link
established by devices such as the Revised Code of 1862 that set in place a
system of personal and institutional incentives through what became known
as Payment by Results. The pedagogue's newfound ethic of service would,
indeed, survive the eventual repeal of this code, having created a teacher who
would associate his or her own subjective well-being with the fulfilment or
lack of fulfilment of his or her pupils. In other words, the teacher developed
an *educational conscience*. This was a portentous step; a secular educational
conscience had been constructed through institutional means.

A conscience of this kind is still in operation today. My colleagues and I
frequently experience its constructed effects. This conscience takes different
forms, admittedly, having been realigned for the problems of a different age.
In itself, this conscience is not objectionable. It should, though, always be
suspected for the governmental interests it serves.

*   *   *

Alongside his pupils, the pastoral teacher also required moral training. The
so-called 'normal schools' of nineteenth-century Britain were devised for
this purpose, preparing future teachers 'for a life of self denial'.[165] The newly
ordained teacher would then be placed in a school such as Stow's moral
training school, in which the carefully designed architecture of that school
would serve to amplify his moral presence. As Ian Hunter has argued, within

the more intimate spaces of such schools one finds 'the prototype of the modern classroom'. Organised as it was around the 'superintending eye and voice of the teacher', it replaced the 'molecular sub-divisions of the vast monitorial schoolroom' with the personal effects of moral force.[166] Pupils were arranged in the rising tiers of a gallery from which they would return the gaze of their moral exemplar, the schoolteacher. Direct supervision and an array of complex moral ties replaced, in part, the distributed supervision of the monitorial schoolroom.

* * *

Anticipating to some degree its progressive twentieth-century successors, Stow's school embodied an educational philosophy of collaborative enquiry. Moral formation was to occur in a mutually formed and contextually responsive environment, one that was open to the carefully educated whims of its co-participants.

The process would begin in the playground, where pupils were observed in their natural state. Upon their return to the gallery, any case of good or bad conduct was reviewed by the master, who would encourage the 'whole gallery to join in' as they did in all other exercises.[167] The entire school was thereby recruited to an investigation that would conclude by 'applauding the good deed, or condemning the misdemeanor'.[168] Here the effect of peers (the 'power of the Sympathy of Numbers') was elevated as a 'principle of the highest importance'. Stow viewed this socially mediated power as an 'influence, mighty either for good or evil'. At present it was 'all on the side of evil' due to the adverse training of the streets. 'To lay hold of this principle', Stow argued, 'and turn it to good, is the great desideratum.'[169] The gallery was designed precisely to harness this power.

Take the boy who steals his playfellow's toy: the master takes no action in the playground, but 'when the children are again seated in the school gallery, as usual, he commences the process of examination'. Today the pupils will investigate the case of the boy who stole a toy. At this point the story is abstracted from the culprit, whom it is unnecessary to name, as his head will hang down: '*he is visible to all* by his downcast and reddened countenance'. The master reminds his subjects that, although '*he* had not observed him, God assuredly had; or rather, he draws out this statement from the children themselves'.[170] Through yet more questions and answers the mode of punishment is discussed, negotiated and decided. Thus the whole group participates in moral correction.

As a school inspector explained in a manual describing various techniques for schooling the working classes, the teacher must 'be ready to seize every opportunity presented by passing events' for 'impressing on the child's heart some valuable lesson' from scripture.[171] Natural events occurring in and around the school, subjected to the collective judgement-making processes of the gallery, would transform 'wild beings' into moral subjects.[172] This mode of schooling would instil 'habits of investigation' enabling those instructed in these habits to interrogate the mundane events of daily life and expose them to religious appraisal. The child's soul would be 'formed and transformed into wholesome channels, which will benefit the child to his life's end and beyond it'.[173]

* * *

Even though the gallery school-hall, with its rising tiers of moral condemnation, may appear in retrospect to be the most striking feature of the moral training school, the mechanisms of examination were not exclusively concentrated here. They were distributed across the architectures and social relations of the school upon which the gallery depended. Throughout the school site, individuals learned how to construct the moral truth of each moment, where each moment became a potential case for whole-school examination. Through play, during conversation, and following instruction, the child developed a unique and devolved capacity to judge personal and interpersonal conduct, even though the gallery would in all likelihood never be assembled for the glory of that particular moment to which it would attach a collective verdict.

* * *

The pastoral teacher signified the moral template to which all would aspire. He would demonstrate those attributes his pupils were expected to develop.[174]

Whilst his moral bearing and composure would, from the perspective of his pupils, initially represent a distant ideal, his engagement with each individual child would be intimate from the outset. This relationship would demand that he place himself 'on such terms with his pupils so that they can, without fear, make him their confidant, unburden their minds, and tell him of any little mischief they may have done'.[175] This confessional practice would build upon, but also go beyond, the playground-gallery system of observation and correction. It would extend a truth procedure outside this architectural system, developing an obligation to confess on behalf of the child that would cover a whole range of activities far greater than mere playground misdemeanours.

* * *

The overall thrust of a confessional event, whether it occurs in a school, on a couch or in private, operates in a direction opposite to that which we might expect. The obligation to confess has become 'so deeply ingrained', Foucault argues, that we 'no longer perceive it as the effect of a power that constrains us; on the contrary, it seems to us that truth, lodged in our most secret nature, "demands" only to surface; that if it fails to do so, this is because a constraint holds it in place, the violence of a power weighs it down'. Every confession comes 'at the price of a kind of liberation'.[176] Confession frees, or so we are led to believe, and power reduces one to silence.

* * *

Be assured, confession will not liberate your inner truth. Your true self, your inner being is not awaiting its timely disclosure. We are materially constructed through confessional practices to produce truths about ourselves that reflect the discourses in which we have been schooled. If you were to resist these imperatives to expose your inner self, and become voluble about that which lies within you, perhaps silence would be your tactic. Can you not see how this injunction, this learned impulse to confess, renders your silence awkward? You would appear distinctly inhuman if you were to declare yourself empty, and affirm your superficial, socially distributed nature.

* * *

In the moral training school, pupils were expected to construct themselves according to an order of discourse they absorbed through the morally focused, morally saturated engagements of their environment. The idea was that every induced revelation concerning the child's inner being would generate intrinsic modifications in the child who uttered it. Inner truth was here a function of the larger framework of pastoral relations within which the child was positioned. The overall objective of confession in the moral training school was to develop the child's capacity for reflecting on and governing the self. Considered from a distance, pastoral power would allow mechanisms of state to develop a certain degree of purchase on the subjectivity of the child. Pastoral technique would facilitate the formation of a governable self-regulating citizenry once moral training was extended to the entire population. Here was developed a mode of examination that was more personal than the disciplinary technology described above, for it was no longer preoccupied with the operations of a complex disciplinary machinery. This is not to suggest that pastoral examination operated without external artifice. It, too, relied on distributed techniques and architectures in order to function. And yet, its focus in constructing the interiority of those subjected to its practices was more intensely developed, depending less on bodily manipulation, and more on interpersonal techniques of supervision and confession that were better able to endure outside any institutional confinements.

* * *

These two institutions – monitorial and moral training – employed relatively distinct methods of examination that were distributed within, rather than imposed upon, the relations that constituted the school. But these institutions also borrowed from one another, creating hybrid techniques. Those hybrids foreshadowed a more complete integration that occurred in the late nineteenth-century state-sponsored elementary schools of Britain and elsewhere.

* * *

The monitorial school slowly shifted in its approaches to an increased dependence on simultaneous moral instruction. Some very early examples of this can be found in the archive. In 1819, according to a report from France, one monitorial institution was making use of a pastoral technique similar to that which Stow would later 'pioneer':

> When a scholar has committed fraud, the teacher makes it known to the whole school, and asks the scholars, if they know any declaration of the Holy Spirit which is applicable to the case. [They] hasten to quote some passage of Holy Scripture [and offer other passages suggesting a route to correction]. Thus the teacher disappears before the Almighty...[the children now governed by the] Holy One who reveals himself to their tender minds, by means of their fellow scholars. Religious instruction becomes mutual.[177]

The critics of monitorial schooling did not, however, view it as an intimate space where tender instruction and moral discernment could be installed. They claimed that pupils were on the whole too numerous to benefit from the moral example of the master, and monitors were too ignorant. And so, those economies of instruction that were once a disciplinary selling point eventually came under sustained attack, and monitorial schools attempted to adjust their techniques in response. According to a monitorial school manual issued in 1856, the regimented hall should be overhauled and divided into three parts, with small groups sitting in semicircles at the front, standard fixed benches for classes in the middle, and larger groups assembled in a gallery at the back. With a heavy curtain partitioning off each section, the monitorial school would become a more intimate environment. Playgrounds were also annexed, now 'regarded by good teachers' in the monitorial school 'as places in which the dispositions of boys are frequently most strikingly manifested', and upon which subsequent instruction should rest.[178] Nevertheless, the school was still to be run according to a disciplinary framework: classes were to move from one section to the next according to a rigid timetable and on a regular basis; there would be a signal upon which the children leave their seats and march according to a beat, 'one, two, three, four, to indicate the time to which they are to move'.[179] Various other commands would regulate the raising of curtains, distribution of books, cleaning of slates and so on. In addition, the school was still taught and run by the scholars themselves, and if trustworthy assistants could not be found the curtains would be raised, returning the school to a less intimate disciplinary system.

* * *

Moral training appears allergic at first sight to a similar influx of disciplinary devices. Its proponents believed that the 'social body cannot be constructed like a machine, on abstract principles which merely include physical motions'. The social body also required 'the cultivation of religion and morality' and thereby necessitated the intimacies and methods of the moral training school.[180] Yet, disciplinary elements can still be identified in Stow's design: obedience must be 'instant' and children should move '*à la militaire*', with every motion of the class being 'as much as possible simultaneous' and according to precise verbal instructions.[181] The desired position and gait of the schoolmaster are minutely described,[182] and the school is referred to repeatedly as a 'machine'.[183] As with disciplinary power, any pastoral regime must be presumed to have its defects, and be seen as a system of only partial success. Alone, the pastoral teacher bore an impossible responsibility for the betterment of the lower classes and other socially marginalised groups. As it turned out, the success of pastoral technique depended on its integration with the activities of other actors and discourses. Fortunately for the pastoral schoolteacher, towards the end of the nineteenth century a rising concern for the health and hygiene of the population led to a proliferation of agencies concerned with the workings of the home. It was within this complex of agencies and 'tutelary agents' that the pastoral schoolteacher began to find support and adapt, supplementing a discourse of moral rescue with new discourses of hygiene and social health.[184] The confessional techniques of examination also expanded at an increasing rate, adapting in turn to new institutional sites, allowing the shaping of the private self to become a widespread activity.

* * *

It is, nonetheless, worth returning to the moral training school in order to focus on the precise functioning of a technique before its proliferation. This provides a conceptual grounding that can help clarify the significance of later developments. We can already see within the moral training school more modern ideas, such as those of a ' "child-centred" pedagogy, overseen by an unobtrusive yet vigilant teacher'.[185] It remains to be seen how more recent pedagogies maintained and modified a project once explicitly concerned with the formation of souls. For our current purposes it is sufficient to note that during the nineteenth century this parallel tradition in examination was already in existence. It followed a path that was distinct from the disciplinary route. This alternative approach makes a virtue of pedagogies that pay attention to the natural environment and dispositions of the child. In a display of openness, it recruits peers to the processes of assessment within a setting that has been carefully fabricated by the teacher and the school. The child is located very explicitly at the centre of examination for his or her own personal benefit. These clear affinities between Stow's nineteenth-century pedagogy and more recent trends in education should alert us to the potential for a moral scheme behind all traditions that are resolutely anti-mechanistic, traditions that 'prioritize' and listen to the child.

* * *

If we broaden our contemporary definition of examination to include the wide range of pedagogic techniques that extend beyond the examination hall throughout and outside the school, techniques that seek to reveal the truth of the child and use that truth to inform the educational encounter, that is, if we interpret examination broadly and acknowledge its widely distributed effects, it should be clear that a history of examination must pay attention to pastoral developments as much as it does to disciplinary ones. In other words, a history of examination should pay as much attention to techniques that respond to the child, in the child's own terms, taking into account his or her prior experience and wider nature, as it does to those more easily condemned techniques that seek to define the environment within which the child must exist and discipline the child according to its artificial terms. The line of distinction between these two techniques has, of course, been blurred. Extending our gaze back to a period when they can be more easily separated heightens sensitivity. It helps prevent our being blinded by a desire to challenge only the more conspicuous, heavy machinery of contemporary examination. It diverts our critical gaze either side of the manifest accountability techniques to which education appears increasingly subject. More humane-appearing traditions of examination may be just as dangerous as, if not more so than, their disciplinary analogues. Listening to the child –incorporating the child's experience into an examination procedure that has been lightened, and rendered formative – does not allow us to escape the grasp of power. It merely represents a switch in emphasis from one venerable tradition of power to another.

*　*　*

Today it is almost impossible to sense what it would be like to live an *unexamined* life. This is not simply due to the fact that examinations are everywhere, so much so that it would be difficult to pass through any modern system of schooling without being examined at one point or another. The problem is greater than objecting to the mere empirical spread of examinations, which have come to: regulate and record educational progress, or lack of progress; inform the relation between child and parent, guardian, relative or friend; suffuse practices of teaching and management; inform practices of social care, therapy[186] and incarceration; back up or undermine policy; control access to further education; inform employers; condition employees and so on. The empirical spread of examination is certainly alarming, and yet the problem is greater than objecting to the extent of its reach. Expressing our profound disapproval of examination, as a ubiquitous rationality that defines our epoch and limits how we think, cannot in itself solve the difficulty we face. We must confront the examined life more radically than this. Perhaps we do live in 'an age of examination'; perhaps it is indeed difficult to imagine how we could live differently without this incessant requirement to test and to score. But this is not a matter for the imagination to solve alone. This is not simply about picturing how we could educate differently, either without examination or with less of it. To say that it is about picturing how we could *relate* to each other differently would be closer to the point. Still, the difficulty we face in an age of examination cannot be combatted by dreaming what it would be like to go without examination and whether, by virtue of this vision, there is any scope for adjusting what we do, how we teach, how we learn, how we school. Examination cannot simply be removed and dreams cannot simply replace it.

First, examination constitutes the school as its ontological condition. To confront examination, one must confront the school. Second, insofar as dreams are wishes of the heart (as any Disney film will tell you), they will be limited by the sensibilities of the modern soul. As I have endeavoured to show, *this soul* may itself be the product of examination. Examination constitutes the soul of the child through a cluster of practices that make

up the school. Since the nineteenth century, examination has produced the concepts or conceptual frame through which we have come to know ourselves. The monitorial school was an early laboratory in this effort, integrating a process that rendered an amorphous mass legible, with a procedure that taught the partitioned mass how to behave. The moral training school further developed this construction of the soul by teaching its subjects how they should relate to themselves, initially through an external set of architectures and interpersonal relations, and later through the absorption of these procedures to an inner conversation that constructed the self to be confessed. These two early nineteenth-century sites established the frameworks of schooling from which later institutions were built. They developed examining strategies that would feed into the expansion of a far wider examining complex. Towards the end of the nineteenth century, the specific labour of producing souls was multiplying across an increasingly dense grid of social agencies tasked with revealing and directing the truth of personal and social life.

* * *

Any critique of examination and its deleterious effects should avoid the tendency we so often witness to high-minded indignation. It should avoid the temptation to denounce examination, that great institution, as a repressive influence against which the soul must fight in order to prevent its abridgement. The examining complex within which we were bred as infants now constitutes us as subjects; we owe our existence to it. A radical critique of examination must, therefore, begin by objecting to the subjects we have become. Here we must follow *The Immoralist*, who 'despised...the creature who was due to teaching, whom education had painted on the surface'.[187]

* * *

A radical critique of examination must, by definition, unsettle the soul. If you would prefer to avoid this experience, if you wish to remain secure from introspection and doubt, you must cultivate your attachment to historical constants. In particular, you should assert the uniform consistency of human experience throughout time. This consistency will enable you to connect in principle with all human life, as you share so much in common. Above all else, you must believe that there is an entity that endures through it all, 'something unchanging in all turmoil',[188] something that defines us as distinctively human. Then you must object to any theory claiming the contingency of the human form. Find reassurance by claiming to observe recurring human traits throughout time. Remain committed to these facts. With the facts pushed into view, you, yourself, can retreat from view because 'the facts speak for themselves'.

II
Populations

On Forgetting

Forgetfulness should not be confused with laziness. The ability to forget is an acquired skill, often held up as a marker of one's intellectual refinement. Indeed, nobody forgets better than the academic, who cultivates absent-mindedness as if it were a product of intellectual greatness. These benign appearances nevertheless belie the fact that forgetfulness is both a privilege (being the product of refinement) and a brutal imposition. It is an act of violence against those who contest the present.

* * *

In medieval Paris, theology degrees were once reported in rank order. Whilst the rationale for this ordering still eludes us, we can nevertheless distinguish it from the various kinds of disciplinary partitioning that arrived centuries later. Disciplinary division demanded precision and delivered functionality. Medieval ranking, by contrast, could not achieve such disciplinary effects because its inscriptions were not as embedded, penetrating, interconnected and 'scientific' as they would later become. Nevertheless, and in a way that is true to the mentality of our epoch, research has attempted to find the system behind this irregular medieval process for assigning rank, using a statistical method that correlates rank with other known features such as the examinee's eventual vocation.[1] In resorting to the statistical judiciary of our modern era, such research adopts a notably anachronistic under-standing of the purposes of medieval ranking: an order of discourse that is the product of modern examination is being used to assess the ranking system of a pre-statistical age. The modern disciplinary rationale is thus imposed, retroactively, on a medieval process, the unique disorder of which is consequently forgotten.

* * *

Our devotion to scientific ranking and the inscription of individual difference is a nineteenth-century bequeathment. Against those who commemorate this century for its progressive reforms and enfranchisements, one should recall what Foucault refers to as the 'dark side of these processes'. Developments that were 'egalitarian in principle' found support in those systems of division 'that we call the disciplines'. These disciplinary arrangements were non-egalitarian, inscribing difference on the bodies that were subjected to their operations.[2] Liberal advances in rights and freedoms were, in other words, accompanied by a 'considerable extension of procedures of control, constraint and coercion'.[3] With time, freedom itself became an object of government. Freedom no longer sat in opposition to coercion; it became its principal agent.[4]

* * *

The mechanisms of disciplinary power were widely distributed across a range of early nineteenth-century institutions. Within these walled compounds and throughout their complex interiors, individual bodies were carefully shaped. The effects of such activity nevertheless went beyond the construction of docile subjects; the disciplinary gaze also led to a transformation in perception that would eventually overhaul disciplinary practice itself. As individual bodies were subjected to the analytic gaze of disciplinary power, another, more complex, aggregate body began to emerge. The efforts of disciplinary supervision generated, in other words, a perception of the bodily mass from which the individual had been extracted. This population was found to have aggregate characteristics, distributions and averages.

A new realm opened up for the operations of power. Initially this new perception alighted on institutional populations that were already known and thereby available to power. But with time the previously indeterminate masses existing *outside* the institutional boundary became calculable, and available to government. A national population with defined characteristics emerged from the mix, and the old focus of disciplinary power on the institutionalised body broadened into a focus on the now knowable but dispersed body mass.

* * *

This rising perception – with each population now considered to be an entity in its own right – is associated with a novel form of power, a kind of 'biopower' that is directed at the body mass.[5] As a theoretical term, biopower describes a regime of calculation and force that seeks to nurture each mass of bodies that comes within its purview. It observes from a distance, giving space to the natural processes it perceives in the populations it endeavours to protect. The distinct movements of populations, their vital statistics, are

recorded so that the vitality of each population may be supported. Like an amoeba, gently distending and contracting beneath the lens of a microscope, populations are now watched and tended to. Where biopower seeks to promote already-existing internal movements, disciplinary power would put the amoeba in a small vessel and constrain its amorphous shape to corners and straight edges; only then would discipline attempt to impose novel movements upon its quarry. Biopower, by contrast, works with rather than against the characteristics of its object. It is an enabling dispensation of power.

*   *   *

One should not deduce that disciplinary power is, by contrast, an exclusively repressive technique. Biopower exhibits a basic ambiguity in its support of life processes, whereby totalitarian, even genocidal, violence has been configured from within its logic.

As a positive dispensation of power, disciplinary power must be understood in terms of its inherent productivity. Even though mechanical reduction and constraint, increased visibility, imposed hierarchy and minute division are all strategies that define its operations, disciplinary power aims to achieve high levels of 'docility-*utility*' in the bodies it subjects, and thereby requires the productive forces of those bodies to be unleashed rather than repressed.[6] By comparison to more direct and physically brutal means of subjection that are exerted from a position of concentrated power and strength, disciplinary power adopts a framework of dispersion and relative frugality in its operations, functioning through complex webs that render hidden the extended operations of its power. Through various forms of partitioning and observational technique, it prefers to condition bodies in comparatively mild economies of power, and thereby avoid subjecting them to overbearing compulsion, to a ferocity that would threaten to reduce bodies to an unproductive and broken state. The early nineteenth-century monitorial school was a case in point: due to the economies of power brought about through disciplinary technique, it was conceivable that an entire school could function under the supervision of a single master.

* * *

There are, nevertheless, important lines of difference between disciplinary power and its biopolitical scion: the overall concern of disciplinary power is bodily utility, whereas the issue for biopower is the maintenance of life. When populations are viewed as organic entities, a concern for the very fragility of their complex form supersedes all preoccupations with disciplinary calculation that are concerned with utility alone. Disciplinary power is only indirectly occupied with life, wishing to avoid broken bodies only insofar as that would impair their functioning.

* * *

A key link between biopower and discipline was established during the high watermark of early twentieth-century eugenic activity. This eugenic collaboration had enduring consequences for schooling, examination and meritocracy. The enduring relevance of eugenics may come as a surprise. It would serve a progressive narrative well to present eugenics as a long-abandoned project, one that can be located in, and resolutely confined to, a past era of despotic excess. The early twentieth century is our repository for many such excesses that we hold at a distance, thereby preventing a disturbance in the present. Eugenics becomes itself a disease, a short-lived malady that was overcome without enduring complications for the society of which it was once a part. Figured in this way, eugenics can be marginalised if not forgotten.

Here we must return to Nietzsche, for whom forgetfulness was an active capacity without which 'there would be no happiness, no serenity, no hope, no pride, no *present*'. For those 'in whom this inhibiting apparatus is damaged' a condition is suffered as a result of which they are never "through" with anything'.[7] Without this ability to forget we would never be 'through' with eugenics. Admittedly, eugenics is still mentioned from time to time. We are occasionally reminded, for example, of the eugenic motives that spurred on the development of intelligence testing in the early twentieth century. But this seems too weak a reason to recall and then dwell upon the horrors of a eugenic imagination. If we are to recall eugenics and risk a genuine disturbance in our capacity to forget, an influence more deeply formative than this must be discoverable. And so, in remembering eugenics, and promoting restlessness in those who wilfully deny themselves the pleasure of forgetting, I propose the following: it is my claim below that lesser-known aspects of the eugenic logic – combinations of eugenics with religious potential – provide us with a set of clues for unravelling later twentieth-century developments that extend, indeed, to the educational present.

The Violence of Power

The unity of the word does not guarantee the unity of the thing.[8]

Friedrich Nietzsche

When speaking of power, it is difficult to avoid a conceptual domestication of it. Power must remain in violent excess of all attempts to describe its presence. In this respect, to assert *the violence of power* is a plea against misapprehension.

        ★   ★   ★

The analytics of power here adopted draws from the work of Michel Foucault, which is full of traps for the self-styled devotee.[9] These serve as an implicit warning against infatuation. Nietzsche was more direct: he dismissed his followers in advance as an accumulation of noughts, or nobodies, as the German term 'nullen' implies: *Du suchst Anhänger? — Suche Nullen.*[10]

        ★   ★   ★

Those policing Foucault's legacy keep the traps well greased.[11] To suggest, for example, that Foucault was a producer of theories conveys an immediate signal to his followers: it betrays one's lack of sophistication. We are directed to Foucault's remark: 'I am an experimenter and not a theorist.' A theorist is here derided as 'someone who constructs a general system' that is mistakenly applied to divergent activities 'in a uniform way'.[12]

Viewed as a series of experiments, Foucault's corpus resists those who would perceive its various fragments as extracts from a systematic whole. In what was to become a hackneyed quote, Foucault invites us to regard his work as a 'tool box' from which we are to extract instruments to suit our purposes in local struggles against power. Foucault was not constructing a general theory of power. His only consideration was to pursue power to its multiple locations and render visible operations that have hitherto remained unremarked. This was an intellectual endeavour designed to remain in motion.

Do not ask who I am and do not ask me to remain the same: leave it to our bureaucrats and our police to see that our papers are in order.[13]

Foucault wrote in order to travel elsewhere, transporting his work beyond the constraints of existing thought, even if that thought had once been his own.

        ★   ★   ★

As one trap fails, another opens, for we are warned against presenting his genius in this way, as 'a perpetual surging of invention': this would only make 'him function in exactly the opposite fashion'.[14] When we seek the genius behind the invention, we are tempted to assume that a level of theoretical coherence must run through the ideas of the genius concerned. Commentaries tend to follow 'principles of evolution, maturation or influence' in their explications of the work of an author. Attempts are made to reach a point 'where contradictions are resolved' and the thinker stands before us, clarified and explicit.[15] With Foucault, this manoeuvre would be particularly damaging, as he embodied the principle of historical location, such that it becomes impossible to extract him whole from his temporal context.

* * *

In our use of Foucault we are faced with a set of difficulties. For a start, all efforts to uncover the 'essential Foucault' lead to a unified picture that is rather artificial. We could instead choose a particular theoretical point in his journey, yet that point is always embedded within its place of departure and its future destination. When attempts are made to interrelate two theoretical ideas that are located at different points in Foucault's corpus, we also run into difficulty.[16] These theories were never intended as component parts of some larger, precisely articulated theoretical framework. Hence, all usages of Foucault must remain partial: those who adopt Foucault can only deform him. This should be done without regret, for, as Nietzsche would say, 'one repays a teacher badly if one remains only a pupil'.[17] The challenge, nevertheless, is to deform Foucault's work in a way that is appropriate to it. This presupposes a sensitive understanding of Foucault, lest our deformation 'becomes a travesty rather than a tribute'.[18]

* * *

Foucault was interested in the actuality of power, not 'Power – with a capital P – dominating and imposing its rationality upon the totality of the social body'.[19] His aim was to explore *how* it operates rather than state once and for all *what* it is: ' "What is Power?" is obviously a theoretical question that would provide an answer to everything, which is just what I don't want to do.'[20] It could be argued that by avoiding a tight definition of its essential characteristics we leave ourselves open to criticism. We might be accused of turning power into 'a mysterious substance'. But that is exactly the point.[21]

To put it bluntly, I would say that to begin the analysis with a 'how' is to introduce the suspicion that power as such does not exist. It is, in any case, to ask oneself what contents one has in mind when using this grand, all-embracing, and reifying term; it is to suspect that an extremely complex configuration of realities is allowed to escape while one endlessly marks time before the double question: what is power, and where does power come from?[22]

To become preoccupied with the 'what' of power is to risk missing the complexity of its operations: 'It is a set of procedures, and it is as such, and only as such, that the analysis of mechanisms of power could be understood as the beginnings of something like a theory of power.'[23] Power is simply 'the name that one attributes' to a complex array of determining elements 'in a particular society'.[24]

Foucault was clearly set against all-encompassing notions of power; resisting global formulations concerning its nature and taking a flexible attitude to those formulations that he did propose. The point is to avoid a context-free theory of power. It is assumed that power is widely dispersed and locally contingent, so dispersed, in fact, that a single term almost fails to encompass its operations. Crucially, though, we can still comment on the nature of this dispersion (as a working hypothesis) without our thought becoming unduly fettered. A rough 'analytics of power' is still attainable and necessary.[25] It is important to reject, indeed, a strong tendency in neo-Foucauldian scholarship that fears pinning Foucault down as if any strong statement about Foucault or power, or any other aspect of his work, would automatically translate his ideas into a reductive and totalising discourse. Many scholars of a Foucauldian inclination do their level best to speak about Foucault 'without ever producing a definite object we call "Foucault"'.[26] Those explications of Foucault that do exist often begin with an apology, stating that overviews are impossible, that they risk exercising a constraint upon his work.

The difficulty with this fealty to Foucault is that it finds itself expressed through the work of his many acolytes as an ethic of self-restraint. This incurs a retreat on behalf of the neo-Foucauldian from those willing to resource political action. It fosters a growing detachment from any impulse for change. From a fear of bold pronouncements – as if any revealed polit- ical commitment would betray a lack of intellectual sophistication, doing violence to Foucault's thought, constraining the supple productiveness of his ideas, translating them at the very worst into epochal and totalising claims – theorists of this tradition learn to restrain their own impulses in what might be viewed, with some irony, as an exemplary case of self-government.[27] This fear, the idea that political engagement implies a betrayal of Foucault's care- fully developed critical ethos, has bred a fastidious and overly refined theo- retical appetite.

* * *

Foucault opposed all theories that would immobilise our understanding of power by giving it a specific theoretical form or structure. He sought to avoid those effects of analytic closure that were, in his view, a direct consequence of grand conjecture. The difficulty we now face is that the dispersion of power, to which Foucault's work subscribes, is also in danger of slavish deference to the point of absurdity. Power is perceived, by those steeped in this dogma, as too distributed and multi-faceted for us to launch condemnations. We are left unwilling to pinpoint and denounce the power we observe for fear of intellectual simplicity.

It is on account of these political effects that one must respond, in turn, by avoiding an overly reverent, doctrinally inflexible adoption of dispersed power. Indeed, a cautious approach to Foucauldian notions of power mirrors the approach once taken by Foucault to those all-embracing theories of power that were suspected for their damaging analytic effects.

* * *

The above-claimed dispersion of power is composed of a few basic propositions. Power (for Foucault) is a relational force. It is a system of associations that pervades the social body, becoming manifest in human interaction. It is not a 'general system of domination exerted by one group over another', although this may be one of the 'terminal forms power takes'. Blockages may exist at certain times and places, but, unless power has reached a terminal point, an excess remains that is 'mobile, reversible, and unstable'.[28]

* * *

In the liberal and democratic regimes of late modernity, *freedom* serves as an agent of government. In this context, the pursuit of freedom generally helps to reinforce power, 'as the frenzied movements of a newly captured fly only serve to entangle it hopelessly in the spider's web'.[29] The web is spiderless, of course.

* * *

Under liberalism, power is largely 'exercised over free subjects'. Indeed, without a certain degree of freedom, the mechanisms of liberal government would be largely inoperable. There must be 'some possible mobility' in those subjected; they must have a 'field of possibilities' from which to choose.[30] If subjects were perfectly enslaved, there would be no need for the exertions of power so defined. The liberal order would be extinguished, and instead of power we would have *domination*, a condition entailing an *absence of power*.

* * *

A degree of *resistance* is always to be found when power is present. Indeed, by definition resistance can only exist in the strategic context afforded by power. Resistance is 'inscribed' in power as its 'irreducible opposite'. It can be found 'spread over time and space at varying densities' within the frameworks that power provides.[31] Normally this resistance is fragmentary, local and transitional; it is spontaneous and solitary. More often than not, it takes the form of subtle provocations rather than singular direct confrontations. It occurs within the spaces that a certain degree of freedom allows, and it is largely unseen. Great 'radical ruptures, massive binary divisions' are far more occasional, reliant as they are upon 'the strategic codification' of those more dispersed 'points of resistance'. According to Foucault, what makes a revolution possible in such a context is the successive alignment of these various manoeuvres, enabling their dispersed points to connect in a larger scheme. There is 'no single locus of great Refusal, no soul of revolt, source of all rebellions, or pure law of the revolutionary'.[32] Mass action depends upon the alignment of dispersed offensives.

This synchronisation of power does not only occur at times of mass resistance; it is also achieved through successful efforts to govern. These efforts can only succeed by taking advantage of *existing force relations*, and it is in this sense that we must offer 'an ascending analysis of power', examining how such relations are 'invested, colonized, used, inflected, transformed, displaced, extended, and so on by increasingly general mechanisms and forces'. Power 'is not something that is pluralized and then has repercussions down below'.[33] Power is propagated below with the potential for hijack from above. *Government*, broadly conceived, is the term that refers to this process of hijack and steering.

* * *

To focus on this process of colonisation – in which dispersed power relations become mechanisms of government – is typical of the Foucauldian viewpoint. When power is taken as an entity that is widely distributed throughout the social body, concentrations of power are explained in terms of the successful manipulation of such dispersion. These concentrations of power are not thought to be the exclusive construct of a dominant force. Power relations are 'not the projection' of a 'great sovereign power on individuals; rather, they are the shifting and solid ground in which it has taken root'. Power relations, indeed, provide 'the conditions' that allow sovereign power to function.[34] Government, as conceived within this conceptual framing, relies upon the co-option of already-existing movements that are located below, whereby a government policy is simply a 'global strategy that tries to coordinate and finalize' more dispersed forces.[35]

* * *

We are to invert a commonly received view, which dominates perception outside Foucauldian circles, according to which power comes from above. The top-down view of power is nevertheless persistent. Even when we deal with power at a local level, we are tempted to suggest that it *represents* the wider interests of capital, patriarchy, state power and so on. And yet, these are just displacements by which we dodge the real question of power in all its complex detail, deciding instead that 'all of this derives from a market economy, or capitalist exploitation, or simply this rotten society'.[36] To suggest that power comes from below, and that it is only co-opted from above, is a bold reconfiguration. Foucault is, of course, candid enough to acknowledge its counterintuitive effects. He realises that this is 'essentially asking the elliptical god of battles to explain the long days of order'.[37] That, indeed, is our challenge. Here we adopt 'Nietzsche's hypothesis' locating the 'basis of the power-relationship' in a 'warlike clash between forces'.[38] The type of war metaphor Foucault has in mind here is the metaphor of civil war or insurgency, where direct confrontations between amassed forces are rare. Foucault viewed grandiose metaphors of struggle – accounts influenced by the metaphor of a clearly defined battlefield of opponents – as inappropriate.[39] Such conceptions encourage us to think in terms of victors and vanquished, oppressors and oppressed in a way that purges analysis of subtlety and insight. If *struggle* is to become a cipher for power, it must be explored in all its terrestrial and contradictory detail.

* * *

Order, Foucault argues, is 'something fragile and superficial' that is then 'built on top of this web of bodies, accidents, and passions, this seething mass which is sometimes murky and sometimes bloody'.[40] It is built through a growing 'rationality of technical procedures that are used to perpetuate the victory, to silence, or so it would seem, the war, and to preserve or invert the relationship of force'.[41] This is the scaffold within which the apparent calm rests. To invert the ascending axis and analyse from the top down would be to revert to traditional methods that are too 'easy' and capable of any explanation.[42] A top-down analysis also exaggerates the fixity and self-evidence of power, where disorder has been replaced, or so we are encouraged to believe, by peace, resolved conflict and legitimate force. We are tempted to assume that current structures are stable and timeless, and to forget the complex and bloody web upon which they sit.

* * *

As a conceptual tool, violence has its limitations. When 'we speak of violence, and this is what bothers me about the notion, we always have in mind a kind of connotation of physical power' which 'allows one to think

that good power' is power that is 'not permeated by violence, is not physical power'. [43] Foucault was at pains to demonstrate that the violence of power could at the same time be rational, calculated and controlled. And yet, following Nietzsche, we should also emphasise the reverse and companion view, that 'reasonable' power is also underwritten by violence. The challenge is to explain how one thing can 'arise from its opposite' (reason from violence, altruism from egoism, truth from error, etc.).[44] The 'typical prejudice' is to believe that entities such as truth and reason 'cannot be derived from this perishable, seductive, deceptive, lowly world'.[45] Indeed, this idea is 'probably bound up with the whole Western organisation of knowledge' which cannot allow that truth be found 'on the side of violence, disorder, and war'.[46] Only those with sufficient grit are able to contemplate the possibility that all 'higher' things may indeed find their origin in violence and cruelty. This is not to make an ontological claim about power or reason, to claim, for example, that power and reason are essentially vicious or warlike. The provocation – violence is the wellspring of reason – is simply a device to help us escape equating power with the absence of reason, or reason with the absence of power.

* * *

A confrontation with violence is what sustains the radicalism of philosophy. It can be observed in Nietzsche: 'how much blood and horror is at the bottom of all "good things" ',[47] Marx: 'capital comes dripping from head to toe, from every pore, with blood and dirt'[48] and those, such as Benjamin, who found influence in both and notoriously remarked: 'There is no document of civilization which is not at the same time a document of barbarism.'[49] To be found occasionally in Foucault,[50] this emphasis retains within view the continued violence of power even when it becomes codified in governmental devices. It is a perspective on the nature of power that perpetually incites radical critique, rousing the theorist who holds it from intellectualised detachment. Perhaps, then, it is significant that, when exploring the dispersion of power, many Foucauldian analysts diligently avoid such bold and incendiary proclamations, as if reference to 'this seething mass'[51] or something like it would destroy analysis. With violence suppressed, the importance of struggle beneath systems of power is given little attention, and the possibility of an equally violent response is silenced.

* * *

The architecture of violence can be observed in this relationship between codified power and its un-codified remainder. Here one can resort to military metaphors, and note a division between tactical and strategic relations:[52]

> the rationality of power is characterized by *tactics* that are often quite explicit at the restricted level where they are inscribed (the local cynicism of power), *tactics* which, becoming connected to one another, attracting and propagating one another, but finding their base of support and their condition elsewhere, end by forming comprehensive systems: the logic is perfectly clear, the aims decipherable, and yet it is often the case that no one is there to have invented them, and few who can be said to have formulated them: an implicit characteristic of the great anonymous, almost unspoken *strategies* which coordinate the loquacious tactics whose 'inventors' or decisionmakers are often without *hypocrisy*.[53]

Tactics operate throughout the spaces that exist within a system of power. When they become systematised, they transform to form codified strategies. These codified architectures are not the invention of any single architect; rather, they represent a complex configuration arising from diverse relations of (tactical) force. This, roughly, is how violence becomes systematised.

Convention tends to ascribe token architects or decision makers to these systems; those Nietzsche refers to as 'the apparent weather-makers of politics'.[54] And yet, one must insist (with some reluctance, it is true) that the hypocrisy of an organisation is not necessarily of its own deliberate making. Hypocrisy is often the product of those odd coagulations between disparate tactics of power, between a web of bodies, accidents and passions that coalesce to form a 'winning strategy'.

The un-codified play of tactical manoeuvre does not operate without constraint. 'Each [tactical] power relation can be referred to the [strategic] political sphere of which it is a part, both as its effect and as its condition of possibility.'[55] Here there is the 'double conditioning' of strategy 'by the specificity of possible tactics, and of tactics by the strategic envelope that makes them work'.[56] In other words, tactical power works within the strategic envelope that it once produced but which, in turn, now provides it with the environment of possibilities within which it subsequently moves. Tactics form strategies, and strategies form the envelope within which tactics occur.

Undeniably, these are mere abstractions, but they are important. They allow us to perceive power and resistance in a way that circumvents the claim that Foucault is ultimately pessimistic, that for Foucault 'resistance is co-opted in advance' and therefore 'cannot seriously undermine the system'.[57] The excesses of tactical relations and the perpetual failures of strategic power to codify these tactics (power is always a failing project) leave room for power to outgrow and explode its current configurations.

* * *

Contemporary and critic Michel de Certeau further clarifies the relationship.[58] For Certeau, *strategies* are localised in space or institutions, whilst *tactics* are the movements that occur in a given environment. Strategies define the field within which the subject tactically pursues a set of possibilities allowed by that field. In this way *the violence of power precedes the individual subject*. This is a crucial distinction. It undermines the discourse of 'individual responsibility', a legalistic rationale, which only serves to obscure the various kinds of systemic violence that accompany the individual actor.

* * *

Whilst strategic power can be identified by its spatial and conceptual architectures, the individual tactical manoeuvres made within this environment cannot be so easily perceived. We might say that the *tactics of power* are only fully evident within a 'fourth dimension', where there is a combination of three-dimensional space with temporal movement. Tactical power sometimes leaves artefacts, but never the full trace of its journey. To fully perceive tactics it would be necessary to chart their development through space *and time*, as the time traveller explains to his guests in *The Time Machine*:

> 'Clearly,' the Time Traveller proceeded, 'any real body must have extension in *four* directions: it must have Length, Breadth, Thickness, and – Duration. But through a natural infirmity of the flesh, which I will explain to you in a moment, we incline to overlook this fact. There are really four dimensions, three which we call the three planes of Space, and a fourth, Time. There is, however, a tendency to draw an unreal

distinction between the former three dimensions and the latter, because it happens that our consciousness moves intermittently in one direction along the latter from the beginning to the end of our lives...This line I trace with my finger shows the movement of the barometer. Yesterday it was so high, yesterday night it fell, then this morning it rose again, and so gently upward to here. Surely the mercury did not trace this line in any of the dimensions of Space generally recognized? But certainly it traced such a line, and that line, therefore, we must conclude was along the Time-Dimension.'[59]

According to such multi-dimensional thinking, tactical power becomes an operation that is performed in the fourth dimension. It is an action that occurs within, but also runs alongside, overarching and pre-existing frameworks of possibility.

*   *   *

If tactics are, according to Certeau, just movements, and if, returning to Foucault, these movements are the power relations that are performed in everyday life, the target for analysis cannot be the power relation itself. It would be impossible to trace something that is so radically pluralised throughout time and space. Indeed, it would be impossible to recognise a power relation in the singular, not only because it rarely leaves a trace but also due to the fact that, being a relational entity, it only makes sense within a wider scheme. It is also rather optimistic to believe that we can arrive at a precise understanding of the general frameworks within which tactical movement takes place. Even though these strategic frameworks are easier to see – being found in the relatively permanent architectures of knowledge and space – they are widely distributed. Moreover, these strategic frameworks are in motion, being the shifting products of tactical iteration.

*   *   *

The analysis of power is embedded within a framework that it cannot fully perceive or transcend. There is no escape from power and there is no privileged point from which its operations can be rendered transparent. Once one accepts this position – where power analysis cannot escape its conditions of production – there is a strong temptation to conclude that the analytics of power must be rather *partisan* in its pursuits; it will always speak (whether it likes it or not) from a particular political position. But this over-states the case. Whilst it may not be possible to *transcend* power and reach a viewpoint beyond its influence, this does not mean that critique is unable to *transform* power (*and itself*). We must not assume that *partial* critique invariably occupies a stable *partisan* position. As Foucault famously remarked, the problem of political analysis and critique is not about 'defining a political "position" (which brings us back to a choice on a chessboard that is already set up), but to imagine and bring about new schemas of politicization'. This quote is frequently cited but rarely embodied.[60]

* * *

To embody such a critical impulse, one must adopt the ways of the *'genealogist'*. This creature is described and personified in the work of Foucault, and his predecessor, Nietzsche. The genealogist sets out to challenge what is given to us as universal, necessary, obligatory, and present this given as it sits upon a complex history of contending forces. The objective is to develop a form of 'practical critique' that explores how we have been constituted so that we may then 'separate out, from the contingency of that has made us what we are, the possibility of no longer being, doing, or thinking what we are, do or think'. This critical ontology is an experimental one. It is a practical critique that engages with reality in a direct though tentative way.[61] The uncertainty of its approach is not matched by an associated taste for caution, however. As a writer, the genealogist actively seeks confrontation. As Foucault put it:

> Writing interests me only in the measure that it incorporates the reality of combat, as an instrument, a tactic, a spotlight. I would like my books to be like surgeon's knives, Molotov cocktails, or galleries in a mine, and, like fireworks, to be carbonized after use.[62]

Genealogy mirrors, indeed, the early stages of guerrilla war, of the sort waged in the Cuban Revolution and later described by 'Che' Guevara.[63] In the early phase of guerrilla war, the revolutionary band is still small and depends entirely upon its terrain. The great weakness of the guerrilla force is its diminutive size. Its great strength lies in its flexibility. Whilst large armies operate according to a relatively inflexible protocol of engagement, the guerrilla band is free to adjust its tactics to the specific situations it encounters. Unconventional methods combined with constant reinvention can subvert the conventional and predictable strategies of a larger army. Detailed knowledge of the terrain is also essential so that the guerrilla may use this landscape to best advantage. Finally, the revolutionaries must be attentive to the needs of the local population, for without their support and recruitment the movement cannot grow.[64]

In a similar way, the survival of genealogy depends on a detailed understanding of the environment in which it operates. If it is to be politically effective, it must combine this understanding with its appreciation of the local population, of those needs and hopes that are silenced by the dominant regime of power. And yet, unlike the guerrilla, who has aspirations to statecraft, genealogy must remain within the early stages of struggle in this guerrilla metaphor, even though the revolution it promotes may gather momentum and support. The latter stages of war involve more conventional military tactics, formalised procedures and the firming up of ideology. These tendencies are to be rejected. The true revolutionary will abandon this seizure and, finding dissatisfaction in it, will look for a new front.

This is, of course, easy enough to describe schematically. In the entangled practices of intellectual work it is rather more difficult to enact. For Régis Debray, combatants engaged on intellectual fronts experience this limitation as a kind of vice.

> That an intellectual, especially if he is a bourgeois, should speak of strategy before all else, is normal. Unfortunately, however, the right road, the only feasible one, sets out from tactical data, rising gradually towards the definition of strategy. The abuse of strategy and the lack of tactics is a delightful vice, characteristic of the contemplative man – a vice to which we, by writing these lines, must also plead guilty. All the more reason to remain aware of the *inversion* of which we are victims when we read theoretical works. They present to us in the form of principles and a rigid framework certain so-called strategic concepts which in reality are the result of a series of experiments of a tactical nature. Thus it is that we take a result for a point of departure. For a revolutionary group, military strategy springs first of all from a combination of political and social circumstances, from its own relationship with the population, from the limitations of the terrain, from the opposing forces and their weaponry, etc. ... This slow climb from tactics to surrounding and corresponding strategy ... is to some extent the history of the Cuban Revolution.[65]

This 'bourgeois vice' is difficult to avoid. The contemplative man or woman will struggle to mimic the tactical sensitivity of a revolutionary guerrilla. Obvious constraints here are the frameworks of understanding within which the genealogist must work, which must be closely read if they are to be subverted. To free up genealogical analysis, this recourse to facts and interminable academic debates must be accompanied by a dose of rhetoric, even fiction.

*　*　*

Foucault once said 'that there is no question' of his work 'being anything else but fiction',[66] which repeated an earlier remark: 'I have never written anything but fictions.' This did not mean that 'for all that' his work was 'outside truth'.[67] Fiction in this context does not refer to 'the dissemination of falsehoods' but to the 'transformative effects' of a 'rhetorical deployment'.[68] Fictive devices are used to generate a sense of the power relations that condition us, creating a disturbance in the subject, generating within the reader an impression of one's own external construction and lack of inner authenticity. This effect of fictive affectation would be impossible without the reality of power relations to which a fictionalised account refers. The disturbance in the reader is an effect of their recognition. An account of power that makes use of fictive devices *must ring true.*

*   *   *

In some respects the genealogical project could not be more ambitious. In order to gain an impression of the way in which power conditions us, we must set a very broad remit. Our analytic target must be, rather impossibly, the strategic envelope in all its shifting forms. We should seek to describe the overall framework in which power plays out – its key rationalities, stakes and weak points – even though this view can never be complete. This was Foucault's approach in those moments of gestural rhetoric when he appears to deliver the whole panorama.

Once bound and printed, these deployments do not take the form of a novel.[69] These genealogical accounts are still constrained to provide a certain degree of 'proof in historical matters'.[70] Indeed, one cannot escape discourses of truth if the terms of engagement are to create a disturbance in the production of truth. A relationship with more conventional methods of veridiction is therefore combined with the tone of speculative fiction. It is this combination that provides genealogy with its rhetorical strength. The ultimate truth of a Foucauldian engagement is to be found at the level of its catastrophic effects, in which it helps us to work towards a political reality that does not yet exist.

*   *   *

That genealogy asserts the necessity of fictive devices to the analysis of power is a mark of its optimism. It is perhaps only when we move towards the opposite of power, where we experience not freedom but domination, that objective worldviews will finally be within our grasp. This would be the point at which the circulation of power becomes blocked and freedom almost ceases to exist. It is here, approaching domination – where power relations are more fully codified, leaving little in excess – that a fictional account (were it possible to relay) would most closely approximate the factual reality. When speculative fiction finally graduates to become a factual account, our hopes for political contestation and change are likely to be over.

*   *   *

Foucault's work is predicated on a logic of engagement that links specula-tion to political action. It begins with a refusal to translate speculation into the terms of conventional political debate. As a critical intellectual with a growing reputation, Foucault was desperate to avoid becoming the 'alter ego, double, or alibi' of any existing party or social movement.[71] His success here can be measured by the distance he maintains not only from mainstream politics, but also from the conventions of a more radical politics, from the received wisdom of those seeking to overthrow political systems according to theories of society that, Foucault would argue, are located in the systems they seek to replace.

* * *

In discussion with Maoists on the topic of popular justice, Foucault provides an essential counter to militant presumption.[72] Whilst his interlocutor spec-ulates that the liquidation of bosses in a country the size of France might not be practical, and that popular justice requires the careful guidance of a revolutionary court, Foucault patiently explains that the Maoists are already assuming too much. Their problem is more fundamental. The structure of a court, the idea of a neutral third party, the processes of power and enforce-ment, and the reference to a 'universal' idea of justice, are all embedded in the old order. Revolutionary terror, if it can be supported at all, requires *better calibration*.

* * *

To succeed, a revolution must be fundamental in its reach. In a deliberate attempt to upset liberal-left sensibilities, the philosopher Slavoj Žižek claims that revolutions have failed not because they were 'too extreme' but because they did not question their own presuppositions adequately enough.[73] Foucault would presumably agree, having argued himself that one can 'perfectly well conceive of revolutions that leave essentially untouched the power relations that form the basis of the functioning of the state'.[74] To the extent 'that the problem of the mechanics of power' was 'not posed or analysed', communist regimes (to take one example) may have 'rein-vested the very power-mechanisms constituted by the capitalist State'.[75] Radical, emancipatory theory failed to anticipate these outcomes because of its tendency to reduce the complexities of power to simplistic relations of domination and exploitation. The age of revolution was hindered by the way in which the idea of 'revolution' was configured:

> For two hundred years this idea overshadowed history, organized our perception of time, and polarized people's hopes. It constituted a gigantic effort to domesticate revolts within a rational and controllable history: it gave them a legitimacy, separated their good forms from their bad,

and defined the laws of their unfolding; it set up their prior conditions, objectives, and ways of being carried to completion. Even a status of the professional revolutionary was defined.[76]

In opposition to these conceptual restraints of radical theory, which, Foucault would argue, serve to foreclose revolutionary possibility, gene-alogists hope to remain alert to insurrectional possibilities as yet un-codified by theory. Their work becomes a profusion of 'grey, meticulous, and patiently documentary' investigations.[77] These investigations will not consider society as a whole and then recommend universal solutions, for '"the whole of society" is precisely that which should not be considered except as something to be destroyed'.[78] In other words, speaking at this level of abstraction generates a form of blindness that allows old forms of power to be smuggled through, including the tyrannical notion that society can be ordered according to a single unifying law. Since power is radically dispersed and locally contingent, its overthrow 'does not, then, obey the law of all or nothing'. Power is 'not acquired once and for all by a new control of the apparatuses nor by a new functioning or a destruction of the institutions'.[79] The revolutionary challenge is to unveil power and overthrow it in all its dispersion and specificity. This changes the perceived role of intellectual or critic. Without reference to a dominant principle or underlying rationale, critique can no longer adopt the 'premise of a deduction that concludes, "this, then, is what needs to be done" '.[80] To make such recommendations would demand precisely the sort of global and unitary view that is no longer deemed possible.

Rejected here are the standard conventions of critique. Limited to a practice 'characterized by deficit, dependency and distance', conventional critique perceives 'epistemological problems' as cognitive errors requiring correction – it corrects deficits in understanding and is dependent on something other than itself; it relies on a 'normative infrastructure that specifies its lawful foundation and its legitimate objective'. Finally, it establishes a system of distance, creating an opposition between 'those who know and those who do not'.[81] Our challenge, it seems, is to transform the critical enterprise by exploring the limits imposed on the production of knowledge and the operations of power; relating each normative infrastructure to its historical genesis; and then working within these normative frameworks in order to render them unstable, liable to collapse, and open to reconstruction on different terms by those who were once subjected to them.

* * *

If we are to follow Foucault's occasional and more obviously militant remarks, this determination to localise and particularise problems, to eschew legislative statements and political allegiances, to avoid, in other words, the usual tendencies of critique, does not reduce the critical enter-prise, as if by default, to a weakened state. Foucault speaks of his desire to 'break through that rigid yet fragmented crust' formed by the dogmas and 'endless discussions' of intellectual debate, and his wish for a 'personal, physical, and real involvement' in political events.[82] Foucault was indeed no stranger to political protest, direct action, police brutality, arrest and deportation.[83] He confessed admiration for practical revolutionaries, most famously commenting on the Iranian Revolution of 1978. This revolu-tionary moment was, in his view, praiseworthy for being relatively unen-cumbered by revolutionary expertise, by that 'gigantic effort to domesticate revolts within a rational and controllable history'.[84] The Tunisian revolts of 1968 had a similar quality: The 'Marxist education of the Tunisian students was not very deep', Foucault claims, but their level of understanding 'wasn't essential'.[85] Theoretical 'exactness' or subtlety was not necessary for a revolt animated by desire, myth and spirituality, in which practical decisions were located in the 'logic of events'.[86] The crucial factor in the relation-ship between Marxist theory and the accompanying logic of events was its productivity. Here Foucault contrasts the 'vehemence and intensity' of appeals to Marxism in Tunisia with the Marxism he experienced in France, in which the revolutionary impulse was reduced to the format of 'cold academic discussion'. After May 1968 these discussions fragmented into a 'proliferation of theories', into an 'irrepressible discursivity' that was far removed, in his view, from the practical impulses of revolt.[87] The practical–intellectual task, one might interpret, was to help shape an 'enthusiasm for the Revolution'[88] by bringing into question all that appears 'universal, necessary, obligatory'[89] without then crushing such enthusiasm under the weight of excessively scrupulous intellectual enquiry.

* * *

In taking a bellicose view of power – an approach that is rejected by the Foucauldian mainstream, which prefers less violent metaphors – one must adopt an approach to theoretical work that is fittingly political. Some hints towards a critical ontology of power can be found in those historical figures who have adopted a similar approach. In his 1976 lecture series, Foucault provides a tentative and experimental historical survey, recalling a time when notions of war and struggle were used to conceptualise the past and contest the present. This occurred during what Foucault identifies as the second stage in a three-phase shift that took place in the activity of writing up history.

Historical discourse during the first phase identified by Foucault performed a ceremonial function. It was used to justify and reinforce existing power. History would show how existing sovereigns were preordained with an indisputable right to rule by 'extracting from' all the 'vicious and violent accidents' of the past, 'which are linked to error, a basic and permanent rationality which is, by its very essence, bound up with fairness and the good'.[90]

At various points in and around the seventeenth century another mode of retelling the past began to emerge in the margins, where it remained until finally disappearing in the nineteenth century, when it would be 'denounced as the discourse of a biased and naive historian, a bitter politician, a dispossessed aristocracy, or as an uncouth discourse that puts forward inarticulate demands'.[91] It is precisely this uncouth discourse, or something in the spirit of it, that I seek to emulate.

The crucial advance for counter-historical discourse was to drop the implicit assumption that people and sovereign were a unified cause. This opened up historical discourse, enabling divergent histories of races to be told (where 'race' must be understood in its original French sense, meaning: 'membership of the royal (and noble) families of the Middle Ages'[92]).

Within these rival factions, the role of sovereign history was inverted and fragmented. It was inverted because the vicious and violent accidents of the past were no longer linked to error; they were no longer explained away so as to reassert sovereign right. Fragmentation occurred because history now provided the source material for rival and contending accounts. These accounts were 'deployed within a history that has no boundaries, no end, and no limits'. The 'drabness' of histories that were organised around 'a few basic, stable principles' was replaced by something more fiery and ephemeral.[93] Multiple histories were now told in support of rival factions that were laying historical claims to their respective legitimacy and importance. These rival nobilities might argue on behalf of their hitherto neglected but noble lineage, or they might tell a more discontinuous history that accounted for their current subjection. There was no longer one history for all; rather, history became an oppositional tool by which the status quo could be challenged. As forgotten struggles were unearthed, and as the 'blood that has dried in the codes' was rediscovered, these multiplying histories of races broke apart from the old homogenising history of the sovereign:[94]

> the subject who speaks in this discourse, who says 'I' or 'we,' cannot, and is in fact not trying to, occupy the position ... of a universal, totalizing, or neutral subject. ... that person is inevitably on one side or the other: he is involved in the battle, has adversaries, and is working toward a particular victory. Of course, he speaks the discourse of right, asserts a right and demands a right ... [but] in all cases, it is a right that is both grounded in history and decentered from a juridical universality. And if this subject who speaks of right (or rather, rights) is speaking the truth, that truth is no longer the universal truth of the philosopher ... It is interested in the

totality only to the extent that it can see it in one-sided terms, distort it and see it from its own point of view. The truth is, in other words, a truth that can be deployed only from its combat position, from the perspective of the sought-for victory and ultimately, so to speak, of the survival of the speaking subject himself.[95]

This 'established a basic link between relations of force and relations of truth' and 'dissolved' the 'identification of truth with peace or neutrality'.[96] Once historians became more than the mouthpieces of sovereign right and transformed themselves into the spokespeople of rival noble groups, they were able to interpret the world in a deliberately agonistic way. They began to make 'history function within the political struggle' by recovering a knowledge of their past.[97] For these historians, truth did not begin once violence ceases. Rather, truth was one of the effects of struggle.

> History encounters nothing but war, but history can never really look down on this war from on high; history cannot get away from war or discover its basic laws or impose limits on it, quite simply because war itself supports this knowledge, runs through this knowledge, and determines this knowledge. Knowledge is never anything more than a weapon in a war, or a tactical deployment within that war.[98]

Through a detailed study of historians such as Henri de Boulainvilliers, Foucault was able to show that these histories were not always simple tales of 'victors and vanquished'. At times they were far more finely drawn, analysing fluctuations of power, showing how sources of strength could become principles of weakness. They were able to explain how 'a certain relationship of force' was slowly 'and for obscure reasons, inverted'. This led to 'the emergence of a diversity of struggles' and 'shifting front lines' as the analysis proceeded towards finer historical distinctions. Larger struggles were 'divided and transformed by multiple channels'. The relationship of war became 'part of every social relationship', fragmenting into 'thousands of different channels', revealing war to be 'a sort of permanent state that exists between groups'. History now appeared as a 'calculation of forces',[99] and historical discourse became a political device, having established in effect a form of 'historico-political continuum' where the recounting of history was 'not simply a matter of describing a relationship of force' – it was an attempt to adjust 'current relations of force' by interrupting present politics with revised historical understandings. History thus became 'a knowledge of struggles' that was then deployed 'within a field of struggles'. There was now 'a link between the political fight and historical knowledge'.[100] It is precisely this connection, whereby the discourse of historical struggle became tied to a political fight, that Foucault was, in his own words, 'praising'.[101]

The work of a counter-historian was not arbitrary, using any means to elevate one particular nobility above its rivals. There were heavy constraints placed upon such work. The various historians Foucault examines, with their diverse political dreams, used methods of analysis that were 'closely interrelated'.[102] These were not the methods of 'biased and naive' historians who were busy generating falsehoods.[103] They may have been radical opponents of conventional understanding, but they did not reply with imaginary or contrived accounts. These historians challenged conventional knowledge 'by reimplanting it' within their 'own discourse'.[104] This required subtle inversions and careful attention to detail. The counter-historian had to reconstitute the past from a common resource of historical events. As the contested terrain became better known, the work of the historian multiplied into ever more detailed analyses of relations of power. Through these constraints, the counter-historian was forced to become increasingly adept.

> We have all these historical discourses, and they form a very closely woven web, no matter what their historical theses or political objectives may be. Now the fact that this epistemic web is so tightly woven certainly does not mean that everyone is thinking along the same lines. It is in fact a precondition for not thinking along the same lines or for thinking along different lines...If different subjects are to be able to speak, to occupy different tactical positions, and if they are to be able to find themselves in mutually adversarial positions, there has to be a tight field, there has to be a very tightly woven network to regularize historical knowledge. As the field of knowledge becomes more regular, it becomes increasingly possible for the subjects who speak within it to be divided along strict lines of confrontation, and it becomes increasingly possible to make the contending discourses function as different tactical units within overall strategies (which are not simply a matter of discourse and truth, but also of power, status and economic interests). The tactical reversibility of the discourse is, in other words, directly proportional to the homogeneity of the field in which it is formed.[105]

In certain attenuated respects, counter-history can be taken as the model for, or at least the ancestor of, genealogical work. The task is similar, in that a tightly woven network of historical understanding has to be carefully rewoven if the genealogist is to reconfigure or invert conventions. Though the genealogist will not ally with any political position, or be the spokesperson for any one faction, noble or otherwise, genealogical discourse is still designed for dissemination and use in a bellicose world. Genealogy is distinguished by the value it places on 'voluntary inservitude' and 'reflective indocility'.[106] It seeks to invert the common politics of historical truth, famously summed up by George Orwell: '*Who controls the past, controls the future: who controls the present controls the past'.*[107] Accordingly, resistance in the totalitarian society Orwell describes would take the form of a campaign for the return of Truth, an effort to rescue the facts of the past, a refusal to become subject to a falsified and instrumentalised history. The genealogist, by contrast, seeks to *intensify* the contested nature of history. Genealogy is opposed to any single historical account becoming the dominant narrative (which applies also to the history that a genealogist writes), suggesting an alternative solution, one that fragments history in such a way that subjugated discourses are able to speak.

Foucault's interest in counter-history betrays a methodological commitment. It is the *function* of history as an oppositional tool that he admires, even though such discourse was used as a tool of rival nobilities, even though, as Foucault observes, it was often 'basic, clumsy, and overloaded', and contained 'the most insane hopes'.[108] We are, as readers, perhaps somewhat disappointed to discover that, during the nineteenth century, the counter-history Foucault celebrates was transformed into something rather different, and this is where any praise of his comes to an abrupt halt.

*   *   *

Counter-historical discourse was co-opted and transformed in two important respects. According to Foucault's tentative genealogy, in the nineteenth century the multiplex discourse of struggle was reduced to the revolutionary idea that one final battle could end all struggles and result in utopia. At the same time, the rhetorical deployment of counter-historical discourse became concentrated in a revolutionary elite.[109]

During a similar period, attempts were made to 'recode the old counter-history not in terms of class, but in terms of races – races in the biological and medical sense of the term'. This 'biologico-medical perspective' crushed 'the historical dimension that was present' in the old discourse.[110] It was internalised within the logic of statecraft. Coupled to the idea of biological purity, this co-opted discourse led to the rise of state racism (including Soviet state racism[111]). Struggle was recast in the terms of modern racist discourse, and, with it, war became conceptually reconfigured as an 'internal war that defends society against threats born of and in its own body'.[112] In this switch from an 'emancipatory project to a concern with purity', struggle transformed into a fight for the overall well-being of a state, into a biopolitical fight to preserve the state from impurity or contamination. Counter-history – a political tool of rival and contending groups – was thereby turned back on the mutineering dispositions of those who had once forged it. It was reduced to a tool of state, a rationale for removing 'heterogeneous elements' by 'medico-normalizing techniques'.[113]

*   *   *

It has been argued that Foucault's 'celebration of militant thought' in the form of counter-historical discourse 'exposed the limitations and immense dangers of that style of thought' by hinting at a line of descent which connects it with both the rise of revolutionary terror and the rise of state racism.[114] This objection is too absolute. Whilst Foucault's conclusion to his historical survey of the counter-historian serves as a warning, it does not entail a rejection of counter-historical modes of enquiry. Instead, we should consider whether a form of power analysis that models itself on disparate struggles could again become internalised within the operations of government, or find itself becoming reduced to a potentially tyrannical singularity. The challenge for counter-historical work is to devise a resistive strategy that maintains its distance from both government and tyranny.

*   *   *

One resistive strategy in vogue amongst neo-Foucauldian writers is to promote 'the art of not being governed so much'. This, Foucault once suggested, is the 'preliminary definition of critique'.[115] We should note the irony of this position when it is translated from Foucault (and from the specific context in which it was uttered) to become the avowed methodological commitment of subsequent work. The difficulty with this definition of critique is that it is notably close to the liberal order of discourse, which, as a particularly dominant discourse today, such critical activity would presumably set out to challenge. The problem that critique of this type must confront is that its opponent (a liberal or neoliberal order) is just as preoccupied with the problem of *too much government*, of inserting economy into political practice, as it finds itself to be.[116] The basic impulses of such critique and of its object are closely linked in this case. As Foucault himself conceded, the art of not being governed so much 'is at once partner and adversary of the arts of [liberal] government'. A critical attitude that takes this form operates, therefore, both as a means for challenging the liberal arts of government, and as a way of refining them by 'finding their right measure'.[117]

There is a basic ambiguity in this conception of critique, one that continues to be expressed in the work of Foucault's followers. To the extent that Foucault had a political orientation, it was based, so we are told, 'not on our status as human beings but on our status as governed beings'.[118] Whilst 'we may not share an essence, a soul, an identity or any other fixed attributes with others', there is 'one status that we do share, and that is our status as subjects of government'.[119] We even 'have the right as governed subjects', these commentators tell us, to contest the practices that govern us in the name of so-called freedom.[120] The idea of a 'right' in this context has a specific meaning and does not necessarily imply an essential humanism, according to which we are somehow born with inalienable rights – it is only the contingent fact that we are currently 'subject to government' that gives us the right to collectively 'resist government'.[121]

These are mere prevarications, however. They are elaborations laid over a more basic fault, and should not distract us from our realisation that the critical perspective adopted in the work of those who take this neo-Foucauldian line is severely limited. Those who would like 'not to be governed so much' are constrained to a normative horizon that is *defined by government*.

* * *

The determination to avoid a more explicit normative commitment than this minimal 'art of not being governed so much' holds the line against a critique once made of Foucault by Jürgen Habermas. Habermas' claim was that, without a normative foundation, Foucauldian critique is unable to answer the question *'Why Fight?'* Without a positive vision to work towards, it is unable to suggest why we should 'muster any resistance at all'.[122] Why not simply adapt to power instead?

As any Foucauldian will tell you, this critique misfires to the extent that it is concerned with separating legitimate from illegitimate power so that one might pursue the former and resist the latter. Foucault rejected this entire conceptual framework as wedded to a contractual conception of power. This conception – 'articulated around power [viewed] as a primal right that is surrendered, and which constitutes sovereignty' – elevates the social contract as the 'matrix of political power'.[123] The contractual conception of power serves a regulating idea, constraining discussions concerning power into normative questions of right, responsibility and obligation. From a Foucauldian point of view, this conception is severely lacking in that it is unable to account for the multiple, entangled forms in which power manifests itself.

Now, these arguments have been repeated often enough. The key and neglected point to add is that, in escaping the implicit normativities of contractual power, Foucault was able to gesture to more radical forms of political engagement. Take, for example, these remarks from an interview in 1971:

> we can't defeat the system through isolated actions; we must engage it on all fronts – the university, the prisons, and the domain of psychiatry – one after another since our forces are not strong enough for a simultaneous attack. We strike and knock against the most solid obstacles; the system cracks at another point; we persist. It seems that we're winning, but then the institution is rebuilt; we must start again. It is a long struggle; it is repetitive and seemingly incoherent. But the system it opposes, as well as the power exercised through the system, supplies its unity.[124]

Evident here is an acknowledgement of the need for collective action against a set of forces *to be opposed*. These opposed forces still supply resistive activities with their unity (and to that extent they remain limited to the horizon defined by power), but this recognition of strategic constraint is combined with a militant demand, one that acknowledges the necessarily extended and interminable reality of the political fight, in which one must take account of the multiple and duplicitous natures of power. It is precisely this militant aspect that remains neglected in neo-Foucauldian work, where the accompanying critique of utopianism, which arrives several lines later in the same interview ('to imagine another system is to extend our participation in the present system'), is given exclusivity.[125]

*   *   *

We should return to Habermas and yet reframe his question, switching from *why* to *how?* To begin with the strategic question 'How Fight?' is to investigate the conditions of conflict most suited to critique. This would evade what Foucault referred to as Enlightenment blackmail, a form of conceptual imprisonment that imposes the constraints of 'a simplistic and authoritarian alternative'.[126] According to this system of coercion, one is told to either justify critique in terms of a strong normative framework of judgement, or admit that it subscribes to no such framework, and that one consequently has no right to insist that others take it seriously. Clearly, we should not be drawn into this dispute if it means that we subsequently become held captive by it. To begin by asking whether a historically contingent, embattled and anti-foundational form of critique can ever answer Habermas's query 'Why Fight?' is to set out in the wrong direction. We should become 'less concerned with *why* this or that than with *how* to proceed'.[127]

Described as 'the first key move' of a Foucauldian analysis of power, this switch 'from why to how' has been applied to effect a breach of self-evidence, 'making visible a singularity at places where there is a temptation to invoke a historical constant'.[128] To ask *why* things occur entails questions such as: Who invented this technique? What wider social process does it represent (capitalism, social disintegration, modernisation, class conflict, etc.)? Whose interests does it favour? And so on. By contrast, Foucault adopts a resolutely descriptive tone in explicating the 'how' of power, seeking a 'multiplication or pluralisation of causes'.[129]

Applying this logic to its own enterprise, we might argue that genealogy should not begin by telling us why it generates a particular form of critique (i.e. whether it is for emancipation, human rights, equality, autonomy, freedom, etc.). Instead, it could investigate how we could better practise critique, what conditions are conducive to the critical enterprise. The issue of normativity does not vanish, but it is deferred somewhat. It is no longer assumed that 'why' comes first, or that to answer 'why' provides the necessary foundation upon which all else must rest.

* * *

So how does a Foucauldian critic fight? If we take our lead from respected Foucauldian scholars, it would appear that the critic barely fights at all. Members of this prolific, yet small and politically detached, cadre of academic writers ordinarily distance themselves from struggle, urging caution, intellectual modesty and analytic reserve.

It is remarkable that even the foremost proponents of this tamed critical ethos, the 'governmentality' theorists in Britain and elsewhere, have been subjected to their own methodological critique. The claim is that they, too, have failed to exercise sufficient Foucauldian caution in their research. It would seem that even the most devoutly cautious intellectual practitioners of Foucauldian scholarship are not immune to attack. The suggestion is that governmental theorists are, despite their methodological intentions, still prone to global pronouncements. A yet more 'supple analysis' is possible and necessary, one that shrinks still further from a 'diagnostic style' of thought given to 'epochal announcements and totalizing claims'.[130] Foucault himself, it is claimed, was prone to these attacks in his earlier work, and yet managed to restrain this impulse in his last years through a diligent investigation of 'patterns of correlation in which heterogeneous elements – techniques, material forms, institutional structures and technologies of power – are configured'. This was the work of a more restrained Foucault, so the argument goes, who explored assemblages of power and 'broad configurational principles'.[131] Suitably matured, Foucault became analytically cool and resolutely descriptive, no longer relying on implicit mythologies of oppression, or appealing to a broader politics of refusal.

A typical response to this critique would be to assert that Foucault was never given to epochal claims, or, if he was, that these were minor slips in an abiding project of more carefully measured statements. But this response concedes too much, too willingly. Present throughout Foucault's output is a dissonance that was never resolved. One can sense an enduring desire in his work that was never entirely disavowed, to combine meticulous investigation with the urgency born of a militant impulse. This productive dissonance is what makes his work so engaging and provocative.

* * *

The most eminent scholars of the 'governmentality' school should be given their due as having in many cases successfully achieved the critical distance they so diligently seek. It is only regrettable that the critical enterprise they promote is the remainder of a more vigorous, once bolder form of engagement. In the hands of its originating thinker and for a brief period during the twentieth century, this critical work formed a provocative and stimulating countervailing force against tendencies towards revolutionary singularity, reductive theoretical unity, and transcendence found in the doctrines and politics of Marxism, Maoism and other radical Left groupings of the time.

In a different political climate any critical endeavour that relies heavily on Foucault's analytics of power should carefully examine its political strategy, or risk becoming 'at its last gasp' mere scholarship of a variety once castigated by Nietzsche.[132] If organised militancy oriented towards a singular and despotic truth were to emerge once more, perhaps genealogy, taken as a research project to be practised by an elite and fastidious few, might be appropriate again. An academic cadre could again produce monographs that work to destroy, or at least cast doubt on, the simplistic tales of oppression and domination foisted on us by revolutionary teleologies. In our current climate, however, this model of critical intervention is unable to function to any perceivable effect. It has lost the foe against which it defines itself, the unifying militant project, which has disintegrated into 'discontinuous, particular and local critiques'.[133]

* * *

Foucault was perfectly explicit that 'political analysis and critique, for the most part, have to be invented',[134] and that this would be a 'permanent political task'.[135] His analytical and conceptual innovations produced a line of supple, sensitive enquiry, which afforded a more detailed and rigorous examination and account of governmental power than anything hitherto achieved by radical critique. Neglected, however, is the accompanying statement, in which Foucault is explicit in his recommendation that the creation of new forms of political analysis and critique must be accompanied by the invention of 'strategies that will allow both modifying these relations of force and coordinating them in such a way that this modification will be possible and register in reality'.[136] This call for 'new forms of politicization' remains open and demands equal attention alongside the accompanying demand for better-tuned critique.[137]

* * *

There is a temptation evident amongst those who use Foucault to adopt a division of labour between political analysis and critique, on the one hand, and political action, on the other. This neo-Foucauldian tendency arises from an excessive fidelity to Foucault's well-known rejection of the 'imperative discourse' of universal intellectuals, which 'consists in saying "strike against this and do so in this way" '. Foucault's point here was that 'the dimension of what is to be done' can only appear within a field of forces that 'cannot be created by a speaking subject alone and on the basis of his words'[138] – all of which may be admitted – but this does not mean that critical scholarship should confine itself to descriptive analysis and oblique political observation.

It is here, perhaps, in the work of those determined to remain connected to political praxis, that even utopia may have a role to play. It would take the form of shifting visions of possible lives, a visionary process that is nevertheless brought to earth and muddied, as it is tied to bitter struggles against the governing effects and the domesticating influences of power. Utopian thought would dirty itself in order to become connected to Foucauldian critique, and Foucauldian critique would entertain the possibility of risk and embarrassment by its association with dreams.

* * *

Through its opposition to the teleological schemes of organised militancy, genealogy once attempted to provide revolutionary discourse with distant assistance of a calibrating sort. Today, by contrast, it must establish a different and closer relation to militancy. The *disorganisation* of militant work, which has become both a fact of struggle and at times a normative ideal, demands an adjusted form of political enquiry from the Left. The academic monographs of the fastidiously aloof neo-Foucauldian academic still deserve careful reading, but the critical ethos they have come to represent should be cast aside.

To reinvigorate analysis and achieve greater purchase on political actualities, the violence of power must be repeatedly insisted upon. As a conceptual frame for those seeking to position their work politically, it suggests that we attend to the *quality* of struggle. In our current climate, this entails working towards the construction of new forms of militancy after a long period of Left militant decline and strategic realignment. This would involve an investigation of the material conditions that are required to support, maintain and assist militant work, an investigation that may involve, indeed, genealogies of previous struggles, looking in particular at those battles that were relatively unfettered by theoretical globalisms, and were locally situated and responsive to the immediate logic of events. This is not to suggest that struggle should be elevated as an ontological principle or goal. Rather, the task for critique today is to investigate the conditions that are required to enhance the potential for a more incisive and practically influential critique of a genealogical kind: that is, a model of political intervention that is careful to avoid simplistic condemnations of power, a type of oppositional practice that is open to counterintuitive and anti-foundational critique, a militancy that attends to the multiple, diffuse and unexpected ways in which power conditions our daily lives and forms us as myopic, docile subjects, wedded in the very formation of our character to the systems which oppress us.

* * *

The analytic perspective afforded by an insistence on the warlike, violent nature of power entails a practice of critique that has far greater potential for challenging existing dispensations of power in general, and interrupting liberal complacencies in particular, than the generally acquiescent neo-Foucauldian formula I have described. The real advantage of an insistent focus on violence is that it emphasises the basic Foucauldian point, which is that, when peace arrives, so does domination. This implies two objectives for genealogical critique. *First*, genealogy and any political practice with which it may become associated must hold with resolution to its founding suspicion of peace: where benign peace is just a cover for 'blood that has dried on the codes',[139] and despotic peace is the same wound but without the bandages. *Second*, genealogy works towards insurrection, rejecting those forms of militancy that embody in their revolutionary efforts either a tendency to peace or a tendency to domination.

This militant positioning need not contradict the governmental wish to be governed less. However, it does imply an important switch in emphasis, from individual subjective resistance to collective material refusal, from a personal desire to take control over the practices that form the self, to a communal project that seeks to promote disorder and assist the insurrectional activities of those denied access to the construction of truth. The genealogical task is to promote a productive engagement with power on behalf of those who have been subjected to its dictates. It is to work around the all-too-common consequences of resistive activity: the intensification of power, on the one hand, and the self-destruction of those who once rebelled, on the other.

Make Live and Let Die

Militancy relies upon the terrain in which militant action takes place. Government is similarly dependent, and yet its formative resources are far greater in scope. With the spread of modern examination, new forms of knowledge, new fields of perception and new possibilities for governmental action were produced. Examination was tied into the construction of a logic of power that was uniquely concerned with life processes and their supervision. This was a form of 'biopower' that exercised its gaze upon the living populations it brought into view.[140] To bring life into the realm of political calculation was a momentous step. It hugely expanded the responsibilities of government. Phenomena 'peculiar to the life of the human species' were now located in 'the sphere of political techniques'.[141] Life was to be administered. The administration of life would not crush or restrain its impulses, but assist in its production.

* * *

Once it was the sovereign's right to decide who should die and, by implication, who might continue to live. This right was gradually diminished until it was exercised only in 'cases where the sovereign's very existence was in jeopardy'.[142] When threatened, the sovereign could still expose the life of his or her subjects in war. If the monarch was directly challenged, the death penalty could still be applied. And, in cases of regicide, death was drawn out and multiplied in a vicious spectacle of retributions.[143] But the sovereign only exercised an asymmetric right over life and death, where the balance was always tipped in favour of the latter. The sovereign could either exercise the right to kill or expose to death, or choose to refrain from killing. The options were, in a vital sense, pretty limited. There was little in it for life.

* * *

The logic of political right was reconditioned during the nineteenth century for a new regime of power. The old right 'to take life or let live' was complemented and permeated – that is to say, it was not entirely replaced – by a new right which was its opposite; this was the right 'to make live and let die'.[144] The balance was tipped in favour of life, whereupon its maintenance and optimisation became the major political concern.

* * *

The introduction of biopower was dependent on its disciplinary precursors.[145] Centred on the body, these disciplinary techniques were required to first separate out, align, serialise and render visible individual bodies. They manipulated each body 'as a source of forces that have to be rendered both

useful and docile'.[146] These precursors employed 'techniques for rational-
izing and strictly economizing on a power that had to be used in the least
costly way possible'.[147] They extended disciplinary power across a network
of relations and throughout a 'spiderless web'.[148]

*   *   *

Despite its diffusion, disciplinary technique could still function to some
extent in a state of relative isolation, confined at times to a single institution. Biopower, in contrast, required 'complex systems of coordination
and centralization' from the outset.[149] It could not function without a
wider network. Operating in a realm of population-level characteristics, that is, in a realm defined by the abstractions it created, biopower
depended upon systems of knowledge production that went beyond
the constraints of institutional boundaries. Unlike discipline – which is
concerned with 'man-as-body' as he is put to work in a particular locale –
biopower exerts itself upon 'man-as-species' as he is seen to develop
across space and time.[150] Individuals are now perceived in a diminished
form, in those terms afforded by the grand abstractions of a species-view.
Whilst discipline 'tries to rule a multiplicity of men to the extent that
their multiplicity can and must be dissolved into individual bodies that
can be kept under surveillance, trained, used, and, if need be, punished',
biopower is 'addressed to a multiplicity of men' to the extent that they
form 'a global mass that is affected by overall processes characteristic of
birth, death, production, illness, and so on'.[151] Unlike disciplinary power,
which acts by individualising, this new power operates by 'massifying', by
addressing itself to the species. The 'anatomo-politics of the human body'
is now accompanied, and to some extent replaced, by a ' "biopolitics" of
the human race'.[152]

*   *   *

A biopolitical view can be found latent within discipline: the segmenta-
tion of time and activity, both hallmarks of disciplinary power, was initially
conceived in mechanical terms. These forced divisions, geared towards
the more systematic deployment of bodily functions, were later refined.
Disciplinary activity brought about a 'whole series of researches' into 'the
natural machinery of bodies', and with time 'the simple physics of movement' it assumed was replaced by an effort to accommodate the more
complex, 'organic' features of the bodies it sought to employ.[153]

Disciplinary power would also come to depend on the collected features
it constructed: for example, the effects of 'normalizing judgement' are
secured in part through the process of ranking.[154] So, whilst discipline as 'a
mode of individualization' depends upon a division and ordering of disordered multiplicities, it also comes to rely on the aggregate features of the

institutional population it reconstructs.[155] The disciplined individual comes to exist in relation to *a reconstituted institutional population*.

* * *

Biopower is distinctive, nevertheless, in that it entails a different mode of construction, a different conception of the norm, and a new and vital concern, the concern for population.

Beginning with construction, whilst biopower builds upon pre-existing processes, aiming to *construct with* already-existing forces in mind, discipline operates according to the principle of *complete reconstruction*. It structures a space as if nothing had existed before it. Generating an architecture that will decide the distribution of bodies, discipline manufactures the environment that is to become a site of supervision, constraint and modification: 'A good discipline tells you what you must do at every moment.'[156] It seeks to 'circumscribe a space in which its power and the mechanisms of its power will function fully and without limit'.[157]

Biopower sets out very differently: it invests the space of its operations with a certain pre-existing right. It acknowledges the already-existing life processes and relations of force within which it will locate its activities. 'Like disciplinary mechanisms', biopower aims 'to maximise and extract forces'.[158] Unlike discipline, it relies upon 'a number of material givens' – biopower constructs its regime with existing relations in mind. It is 'a matter of maximizing the positive elements' and of 'minimizing what is risky and inconvenient'.[159] Operating in a realm of abstraction where the common conditions of life become manifest, it 'intervenes at the level of their generality'.[160]

Taking the example of risk, which is ascertained through a calculation of probabilities, attempts are made to manage the indefinite play of variables, where 'security mechanisms' are 'installed around the random element inherent in a population of living beings so as to optimize a state of life'.[161] Biopower does not believe in the possibility of absolute suppression (or, conversely, in the point of utopian dreaming). Rather, it defines 'a bandwidth of the acceptable that must not be exceeded'.[162] It dreams of an environment in which uncontrollable forces can unfold without posing any major threat. This technology of power decides to let things happen; it brandishes the principle of *laissez-faire* as its foremost commandment. The 'free' movement, interaction and life of individuals are to be nurtured, not extinguished. Biopower is pragmatic and sensitive. Its abiding concern is to function within the pre-existing nature of things. It configures action in the political domain as if it were action within the domain of nature. The natural environment of the human species becomes the target of knowledge production, the point of intervention, and the rationale for limited action.

* * *

Looking back over his earlier treatment of discipline, Foucault decides that a switch in terminology is required. Discipline is preoccupied with 'normation' and not 'normalization', as it was earlier labelled.[163] Discipline *begins* with a norm: it 'breaks down individuals, places, time, movements, actions, and operations' and attempts to recombine them according to its prior conception of the object. Successful conformity to the norm is defined as normal behaviour.[164]

Biopower, by contrast, begins with the measurement of existing phenomena and derives norms from the results obtained. Here it observes a logic that is 'exactly the opposite of the one we have seen with the disciplines'. Instead of starting with the norm, data are plotted in order to discover what is normal. Only after normality is defined can *normative action* begin. The 'normal comes first and the norm is deduced from it'. And so we have 'no longer normation, but normalization in the strict sense'.[165] Biopower works backwards from the discovered traits of a population and the *normal distributions* they reveal.

*   *   *

Normal distributions are obtained by plotting. The score of a particular phenomenon is plotted against the frequency of each score in a population. The result for many 'natural' phenomena is a frequency distribution in the shape of a bell. By virtue of its shape, this curve exhibits a central tendency: the average, mean or norm. This bell-shaped curve also exhibits the extent of deviation from that central score on either side, which declines rapidly at first and then tails off into a relatively low number of extreme outliers. Variance about the central tendency is defined in standard deviations, with 68 per cent of all scores being found within one standard deviation from the middle. Anything beyond two or three standard deviations is a distant outlier, and, in terms of normalisation, a great abnormality. Normal distributions, so it goes, are frequently observed in nature, or for phenomena that result from the combined influence of many factors acting independently of one another, each making a small contribution to the outcome. In its abstractions the bell curve is well suited to a logic of power that grapples with the ultimately obscure relations of cause and effect that occur within a human population. The bell curve is a reassuringly graphic representation of that which must remain, by definition, invisible.

*   *   *

Normative action seeks 'to reduce the most unfavourable, deviant' scores so as to bring them into better alignment with the central tendency.[166] This corresponds to the modern usage of the word 'normal' as it entered the English language in around 1840. The verbal form, 'normalize', was in common use from 1865 onwards.[167]

'Normal' described an entity that constituted, conformed to, and did not deviate or differ from the common type or standard. This early usage can also be observed in nineteenth-century teacher training institutions, called 'normal schools', which were set up as 'model' or 'exemplary' schools. In this context, the statistical centre point represented the ideal against which deviations either side were to be compared.

This would all change. Once held up as the aspirational ideal, average man would later become mediocre. The average became a mere symptom of the overall population, which was something to be improved upon. The average or central point of the normal distribution was reduced in status as the higher, diminishing tail of the normal distribution came to represent the distant ideal.

*   *   *

When deviations from the norm achieve their modern status as points of interest, the entire length of the normal distribution acquires significance from the perspective of government. The full distribution of a population becomes the reference point and rationale for intervention.

Biopower intervenes at multiple points, reflecting in this way the statistical narrative of the normal distribution, which is the product of small interlocking forces, each making only a minor contribution to the overall outcome. Normalisation, as a set of procedures, must learn to act within existing relations if it is to deal with nature and its material givens in all their great dispersion.

*   *   *

Despite the extent of its operations, the dominion of biopower should not be exaggerated. The 'normalizing society' is not a 'generalized disciplinary society' whose institutions 'have swarmed and finally taken over everything'.[168] The vast majority of a population exists, by definition, within a bandwidth of the acceptable where power can be lightly felt.

*   *   *

Intervention at its most severe removes the deviant arm of the distribution. This does not shift the rest of the distribution towards higher figures. The curve simply becomes lopsided or skewed.

To move the distribution as a whole, concerted action is required. Taking eugenics as an example of biopolitical intervention, and taking the normal curve to represent the distribution of a trait within a *breeding* population, concerted action operates as follows. To the left of the central tendency, breeding is at first only mildly discouraged through strategies of power that seek to influence the multiple social factors impacting on breeding rate. Further from the central point, these discouragements increase in terms of their severity. A similar process of graduated encouragements must occur at the opposite end. Only joint action across the distribution and the populations and processes it represents will effectively adjust the overall characteristics of the curve.

*   *   *

PLATE II
SIPHONING WATER OVER A WALL

Another partial approach that is similar to the removal of deviant scores in its lack of effect upon the overall distribution is to merely siphon off and encourage those with the highest scores. The idea here is to remove and segregate by upper-end selection, creaming off and creating a social elite. Criticisms of meritocratic systems often focus on this principle.[169] In doing so they ignore the biopolitical scope of meritocracy, which seeks to manipulate the conditions of life *across* the normal distribution. A critique of upper-end siphoning misses its mark.

*   *   *

As both a descriptive and an operational term, 'population' acquired new meaning in a shift that coincided with adjustments to how that entity could be approached. Population was once understood as a factor that, together with territorial size, defined sovereign strength, where a strong sovereign would be one who rules a large territory that is rich in resources, including a large and useful population. This was on the condition, of course, that it was an obedient population. And so the population was seen as something that had to be subjected to Sovereign Will. To the extent, therefore, that disciplinary power also hoped to shape conduct in 'the most homogenous, continuous, and exhaustive way possible', it was 'the oldest dream of the oldest sovereign'.[170] This is not to forget that sovereign power was arbitrary and sporadic, whilst disciplinary power was measured and economical. However, this comparison renders biopower distinct, insofar as a new factor came into play, one that supersedes questions of utility. The existing characteristics of the population were now to be given greater respect, as the overall well-being of the population had become the supreme concern. This new dimension to the logic of power arrived once a disorganised mass of bodies to be disciplined came to be seen differently, as a social organism. The population became an entity that contained its own systems of organisation, its own 'processes to be managed at the level and on the basis of what is natural in these processes'.[171] Once disciplinary examination carved out 'in reality, as a field of reality' a 'population and its specific phenomena',[172] this population came to form the 'pertinent space within which and regarding which one must act'.[173]

* * *

The so-called constraints of nature came to define how one interacted with a population. The population no longer exists as 'the simple sum of individuals inhabiting a territory'.[174] It is governed by collective phenomena that 'become pertinent only at the mass level'. These phenomena are 'unpredictable when taken in themselves or individually', and yet are able to display at the collective level a set of 'constants that are easy, or at least possible to establish'.[175]

When the population becomes 'a datum that depends upon a series of variables', the relation between a population and its sovereign shifts, from attempts to over-determine individual conduct, to efforts that are made to tame forces governed by probability and chance.[176] The relation between a population and its sovereign is no longer 'one of obedience or the refusal of obedience, of obedience or revolt'.[177] It is governed by a more permissive ethic. The overall care of and respect for these distributed processes comes to form part of the repertoire (and self-identity) of government.

* * *

The population now appears 'as a kind of thick natural phenomenon' that through its very complexity becomes something that 'cannot be changed by decree'. It requires new techniques, applied to entities that seem far removed from actuality.[178] Here the government of populations increasingly depends upon 'the birth of the sciences of man', on human sciences that are able to make sense of these aggregate effects.[179] These sciences begin to observe collective events, such as suicide rates, that have a peculiar constancy from year to year. Frequency distributions are plotted that demonstrate central tendency. This central or average point has no individual reality, belonging to no one in particular. It is an abstract feature of the population as a whole.

* * *

The population, so perceived, is much more than a discovery of the sciences of man. The population, so constructed, defines the purpose of government, the new 'final end of government', and as such inaugurates a new system of value.[180] The role of government is no longer to maintain sovereign strength, but to nurture the vital statistics of the population; to organise it around its central tendencies, to remove undesirable outliers, to enhance desired strengths and ensure its overall security. The interests of the population become the new and ambiguous targets of government in a self-perpetuating, self-reinforcing interplay between techniques of power and forms of knowledge that repeatedly carve out new objects for supervision, new processes to investigate, new populations to oversee.

*   *   *

In claiming that 'the natural course of development has to be carefully monitored, supported and even corrected in order to emerge appropriately',[181] biopower develops a pernicious ambivalence with respect to the phenomena it seeks to support. Whilst biopower makes social phenomena appear natural, and thus inevitable and limiting, it also expends great effort to ensure that what will naturally occur actually occurs. This biopolitical injunction to obey what is natural does not necessarily imply reversion to a simpler form of life, one that is closer to nature. Biopower can involve a thoroughgoing use of artifice. At times its functionaries will even claim to replace these natural processes by simulations of nature that are construed as if they were its evolutionary successors.

The ambiguity of biopower is located between the discovery *and imposition* of what is natural. This facile combination conceals a moral and political gap that might otherwise mediate between the scientific directive of a naturalistic perspective and the social governance it inspires. This link between scientific knowledge and governmental command is also a short circuit. This is where the project of biopower, a form of power that is concerned with the promotion of life, obtains its ambivalence. Within the paradox of this odd connection, between scientific inevitability and necessary governmental intervention, a site of dangerous possibility emerges. This pact, involving the discovery and imposition of what is natural, opens up a vast space of governmental opportunity, enabling a potentially dangerous biopolitics to emerge *from within* the established conventions of politics. Excluded here are those forms of dissent that reject the biopolitical terms of debate, those voices that refuse to engage in a discussion that can only raise a toast to our collective health.

*   *   *

Biopower grafts itself onto older techniques. With respect to discipline, it was able to 'integrate it, modify it' and, above all, use it by 'infiltrating it, embedding itself in existing disciplinary techniques'. Biopolitical technologies do not substitute themselves for discipline. They exist at a different level and on a different scale.[182] Discipline was, indeed, 'never more important or more valued than when the attempt was made to manage the population'. Management did not mean 'just managing the collective mass of phenomena or managing them simply at the level of their overall results'. It meant managing 'it in depth, in all its fine points and details'.[183] In fact, biopower led to the *intensification* of disciplinary work. Disciplinary power was now redeployed within a different overall logic. This combination peaked in the mid-twentieth century, after which there was a long period of decline in favour of other forms of individuation. It is here that the history of eugenics is instructive.

From the eugenic perspective, population becomes the end of government, with the improvement of the species as its target. Eugenics aimed to enhance natural processes, and suppress those processes that it perceived to be unnatural, such as charity for those who find themselves in difficulty. It was to operate through the removal of 'undesirable' outliers (by cutting off the inferior tail in the distribution of a particular trait), as part of a process that would shift the normal distribution in a more 'desirable' direction. Eugenics supposed that degenerate outliers could be virtually eliminated not just from this generation, but also from future generations by inheritance. Such negative actions at the deviant end were to be complemented by positive actions at the other end of the distribution. These would incrementally promote the reproduction of bodies with more favourable traits. Ultimately, it was hoped that within a few generations degeneracy would be bred out of the population, and superior characteristics would be enhanced. The central tendency would move towards favourable characteristics.

The late nineteenth-century rise in eugenic thought provided a strong impetus for the development of biometric assessment. In order to promote that which was deemed biologically favourable, eugenics required the tools to identify these traits. Whilst bodily function was relatively easy to assess, innate qualities of mind were far more difficult to pinpoint. If mentally superior individuals were to be encouraged to breed, they had to be identified first by 'objective' testing. In a similar way, those who demonstrated an inferiority of the mind would have to be identified so that their degenerate traits could be bred out of the population. Here it became the function of psychometric measurement to discover the 'natural' distribution of traits within a population, and to subsequently classify levels of degeneracy, normality and superiority. At the same time, evolutionary theories were called upon to explain the reasons for such a distribution, and to recommend appropriate action. Rising degeneracy was explained away as the consequence of inappropriate social action, as the result of an interruption of the natural course of things by which social interventions had prevented natural selection from taking place. In other words, what was natural to the population had been undermined by artificial intervention. It was felt that the natural processes by which the human species is improved (through a survival of the fittest) had been hindered by human activity. For these reasons, eugenic action was proposed to be in line with evolutionary theory, and therefore in line with the natural course of things.

* * *

A brief survey of eugenics, one that exhibits key features of a biopolitical worldview, highlights a problem at the very heart of biopower. How can negative action, or any action against the unfavourable end of a normal distribution, be justified by an order of discourse that takes life as its supreme ethic? How can a form of power that is oriented towards life and not death become involved in killing or, at the very least, in the denial of life? Foucault was nothing if not direct in making these associations:

> In all history it would be hard to find such butchery as in World War II, and it is precisely this period, this moment, when the great welfare, public health, and medical assistance programs were instigated. The Beveridge program[184] has been, if not conceived, at least published at this very moment. One could symbolize such a coincidence by a slogan. Go get slaughtered and we promise you a long and pleasant life. Life insurance is connected with a death command.[185]

To suggest a connection between welfare reform and totalitarian violence is provocative, if not reckless, and to make a slogan out of this coincidence appears, at the very least, lacking in taste. Nevertheless, there is an apparent paradox here. It seems more than coincidental that during a time of mass destruction major plans for the reorganisation of welfare were, indeed, afoot. Foucault's claim is that this 'coexistence in political structures of large destructive mechanisms and institutions oriented toward the care of individual life' should be seen as 'one of the central antinomies of our political reason'.[186] Its formation is accounted for in Foucault's lecture series of 1976, in which the rise and fall of counter-historical work is told. The series title, *Society Must Be Defended*, encapsulates well the biopolitical injunction that replaced the older counter-historical discourse.

To recapitulate: biopower can trace its genealogy back to a counter-historical precursor, to a series of investigations carried out by rival groups that accounted for and challenged their present state of affairs by investigating the complex descent of past struggles upon which reality was thought to rest. These histories told a story of race struggle, where 'race' is used in its pre-modern sense. As interventions they sought to challenge the status quo, where that which was self-evident, right and proper was undermined through rival accounts of history, allowing alternative visions of the future to be advanced. In this respect, these counter-histories can be taken as proto-genealogies, even though they were often clumsy and brutal, and were employed in support of the cynical interests of elite social groups. Foucault's loosely veiled eulogy comes to an abrupt halt at this point, when he observes that this discourse was later co-opted, eventually leading through various mutations to mass destruction.

According to Foucault's tentative[187] genealogy, rival groups were now identified in biological terms, and reorganised according to new systems of classification across vast ethnic, criminal and mental taxonomies. Counter-history was transformed almost beyond recognition, as race was connected to biological purity, and the function of history was lost. Retained, however, was a discourse of struggle, which became internalised within the state. This was a struggle to protect the state from internal dangers. It was here that a new form of power oriented towards life ('make live and let die') became state racism, and in so doing gave fresh impetus to the older sovereign approach to death ('take life or let live'). This, so it goes, was how 'the power of death, the function of death' came to be 'exercised in a political system centered upon biopower' and life.[188] Biopolitics was mirrored by a 'thanatopolitics', or politics of death, which would become its strategic counterpart.[189] Indeed, wars were 'never as bloody as they have been since the nineteenth century' – 'never before did regimes visit such holocausts on their populations'. The great ruse of the twentieth century is that this 'formidable power of death' was often able to present 'itself as the counterpart of a power that exerts a positive influence on life', endeavouring to 'administer, optimize, and multiply it'. This, precisely, was the cynical trick through which 'the power of death so greatly expanded its limits'.[190]

Operating at the level of populations, the survival of the species now became paramount. In other words, *society must be defended* at all costs. It was in the name of the vitality of the whole that death was justified, as we justify the eradication of disease in order to promote the life of the body. This operation depended on strategies of power that introduced breaks 'into the domain of life that is under power's control'.[191] State racism fragmented a population into those who must live, and those who were deemed a threat to this vital order. Their death became 'something that will make life in general healthier'.[192] Thus, biopower was connected to a death command, to the extent that it constructed the notion of a biological threat. And this did not entail 'simply murder as such, but also every form of indirect murder: the fact of exposing someone to death, increasing the risk of death for some people, or, quite simply, political death, expulsion, rejection, and so on'.[193] A type of power that acted in the interest of life brought about a whole raft of sinister consequences and interventions following the construal of entities, groups and individuals as biologically dangerous. Historical struggle was recast as a struggle for the species in a discursive switch with genocidal consequences. Hence, biopower was not good or bad, but it *is* dangerous.

Here we have an obvious switch in tense. Biopower has not extinguished itself, nor has it released us from its constraint. We should, of course, and with great resolve, *become tense*. Yet we find the experience uncomfortable and yearn for security. We will not fully acknowledge the wellspring, nor will we recognise the consequences, of this *biopolitical* desire.

Improving the Breed

> Individuals appear to me as partial detachments from the infinite ocean of Being, and this world as a stage on which Evolution takes place, principally hitherto by means of Natural Selection, which achieves the good of the whole with scant regard to that of the individual.
>
> Man is gifted with pity and other kindly feelings; he has also the power of preventing many kinds of suffering. I conceive it to fall well within his province to replace Natural Selection by other processes that are more merciful and not less effective.
>
> This is precisely the aim of Eugenics. Its first object is to check the birthrate of the Unfit, instead of allowing them to come into being, though doomed in large numbers to perish prematurely. The second object is the improvement of the race by furthering the productivity of the Fit by early marriages and healthful rearing of their children. Natural Selection rests upon excessive production and wholesale destruction; Eugenics on bringing no more individuals into the world than can be properly cared for, and those only of the best stock.[194]
>
> *Francis Galton*

Eugenics is a distinctly positive science. Even though all members of a population are rendered subordinate to the good of the whole and can be extinguished if the greater good requires it, most individuals will find themselves above the line that demarcates degeneracy. These individuals are to be supported and nurtured in a way that natural selection could never allow.

*   *   *

The most positive dimensions of the eugenic rationality are those that survive to the present day. Their continuity can be understood by situating eugenics within a longer timeframe, against a political programme that preceded it and then existed alongside it during the early twentieth century, adopting its procedures and tools, and which continued after eugenics fell out of fashion. This parallel programme can be found within the history of meritocracy, which received fresh impetus with the 1948 universal declaration of human rights and with the overall 'retreat of scientific racism'[195] that did such apparent damage to the eugenic cause.

*   *   *

The eugenic cause was directly connected to the development of intelligence testing, its techniques, rationalities and procedures. The impetus to develop such tests often came from those with eugenic aspirations. We learn little from this association with eugenics, however, if we decide that the danger of testing lies in its potential misuse. Equally, we learn little from eugenics if we judge it according to a similar language of deviancy, as illegitimate, immoral or unscientific. These are the conceptual tricks by which we miss its continuing effects. We must *rehabilitate* eugenics if we are to explore its continuing influence.

* * *

Eugenics is commonly seen as the wayward project of a more deeply ingrained social Darwinian worldview. Its canonical text, *On the Origin of Species*, was set in print in 1859.[196] Charles Darwin has since become a great scientific and secular hero, even though some would argue that his *magnum opus* recycled conceptions of the natural world that were already in circulation. The success of his book owed more to the context in which it was received than its genius. Speaking to that context, Herbert Spencer coined what became its catchphrase. A sober spectator, equipped with the knowledge of science, could now confront the brutality of existence devoid of any romantic illusions. Life is little more than a 'survival of the fittest', he said.[197]

* * *

The *Origin* focused upon the natural world to the exclusion of 'man', even though in private Darwin confessed this to be the 'highest and most interesting problem for the naturalist'.[198] This omission was corrected in *The Descent of Man*, published in 1871, though by that time natural selection had been applied to the problem of human evolution by several other biologists.[199] Francis Galton was prominent amongst them, connecting human evolution to the problem of regression and the possibility of a eugenic response.

* * *

The human race now faced the prospect of its own degeneration. The biological ramifications of civilised living were laid out in books such as *Descent*, in which it was argued that charity and other sentimental activities had interrupted the logic of natural selection, allowing the weak to multiply:

> With savages, the weak in body or mind are soon eliminated; and those that survive commonly exhibit a vigorous state of health. We civilised men, on the other hand, do our utmost to check the process of elimination; we build asylums for the imbecile, the maimed, and the sick; we institute poor-laws; and our medical men exert their utmost skill to save the life of every one to the last moment. There is reason to believe

that vaccination has preserved thousands, who from a weak constitution would formerly have succumbed to small-pox. Thus the weak members of civilised societies propagate their kind. No one who has attended to the breeding of domestic animals will doubt that this must be highly injurious to the race of man. It is surprising how soon a want of care, or care wrongly directed, leads to the degeneration of a domestic race; but excepting in the case of man himself, hardly any one is so ignorant as to allow his worst animals to breed.[200]

Unable to sustain the radicalism of his position, Darwin concedes that it would be impossible to restrain our sympathy for the weak 'without deterioration in the noblest part of our nature'.[201] Darwin decides that sympathy, and hence charity, should be retained against the recommendations of science. Galton had fewer scruples, recommending a more robust response. In his view, charitable attention should be diverted away from those judged to be biologically inferior, and distributed instead according to the biological calibre of the recipient:

It is known that a considerable part of the huge stream of British charity furthers by indirect and unsuspected ways the production of the Unfit; it is most desirable that money and other attention bestowed on harmful forms of charity should be diverted to the production and well-being of the Fit. For clearness of explanation we may divide newly married couples into three classes, with respect to the probable civic worth of their offspring. There would be a small class of 'desirables,' a large class of 'passables,' of whom nothing more will be said here, and a small class of 'undesirables.' It would clearly be advantageous to the country if social and moral support as well as timely material help were extended to the desirables, and not monopolised as it is now apt to be by the undesirables.[202]

It had long been supposed that care of the poor, and those otherwise in need, only stimulated the tendencies they exhibited. Here we have a proposal to put this hypothesis to the test, to work towards a calculation of benefits, and thereby estimate the likely returns of welfare.

*   *   *

Herbert Spencer once defined 'the universal law of Nature' as 'the law that a creature not energetic enough to maintain itself must die'.[203] Here, in its basest form, is a rationale for reduced assistance to those deemed unfit. Barbaric statements such as these are distracting, though. They over-stimulate our senses. We will not absorb the saccharine fact that eugenics was a positive science.

*   *   *

Do not be fooled into confusing positivity with goodness – a science such as eugenics is only positive in that it seeks to promote features that are already in existence – equally, do not be overawed by that which appears good.

Positivity is dangerous, of course. Supportive activities are often savagely felt by those on the receiving end, as many who avoid the brutal experience of today's benefits office (leading to a statistic in unclaimed benefits that far exceeds the total value of benefit fraud) know only too well. Each calculation of benefits hurts the recipient to the extent that the subject in question is taken to pieces in search of 'productive' traits.

* * *

As Galton explains, eugenics – the science of improving stock – was 'by no means confined to questions of judicious mating'. Knowing there to be multiple reasons for the distribution of a certain trait, this would be a science that 'takes cognisance of all influences that tend in however remote a degree to give to the more suitable races or strains of blood a better chance of prevailing speedily over the less suitable than they otherwise would have had'.[204] Eugenics would be concerned with much more than mere excision. True to the logic of biopower, it aimed to look deeply into the complex relations of social life and assist them in their proliferation.

* * *

Galton 'felt little difficulty', he tells us, in understanding the *Origin*, having 'devoured its contents and assimilated them as fast as they were devoured, a fact which perhaps may be ascribed to an hereditary bent of mind that both its illustrious author and myself have inherited from our common grandfather, Dr. Erasmus Darwin'.[205] So inspired, Galton turned a calculating eye on the human species, seeking to demonstrate in particular the 'hereditable transmission of talent'. To prove that 'mental qualities' are transmitted from one generation to the next, Galton selected a number of notable men from between the years 1453 and 1853, and discovered a relatively high proportion of kinship links in his group of 'original minds'.[206] This was followed by a more substantial work, *Hereditary Genius*, in which Galton provided yet more biographical evidence for the descent of intellectual ability.[207]

* * *

To the eugenic mind, high traits, such as talent or natural giftedness, are not the only characteristics that we inherit. From a eugenic–evolutionary perspective, 'man was barbarous but yesterday, and therefore it is not to be expected that the natural aptitudes of his race should already have become moulded into accordance with his very recent advance'.[208] High civilisation has not been accompanied by the eradication of the savage in man, for within our populations the baser traits are still evident, and the danger of atavism looms.

In constructing this apparition, eugenics also laid claim to the resources to fight these dangers. In this way, eugenics presented itself with a very practical problem, for the tools had not yet been developed to separate those who transmit superior qualities from those who transmit degenerate ones. Without proper tools, Galton had to assume in *Hereditary Genius* that ' "eminence" may be accepted as a criterion of natural gifts'.[209] This assumption can be justified, he argues, if we 'look upon social and professional life as a continuous examination'.[210] As 'ordinary scholastic examinations' assign marks to individuals, 'the world, in the same way, but almost unconsciously, allots marks to men. It gives them for originality of conception, for enterprise, for activity and energy, for administrative skill, for various acquirements, for power of literary expression, for oratory, and much besides of general value, as well as for more specifically professional merits.' And 'those who have gained the most of these tacit marks are ranked…as the foremost men of their day'.[211]

This mention of the modern examination is significant. In 1869 its techniques were still relatively new, and yet we find it swiftly adopted as a metaphor to explain the *natural* workings of the social world. The examination evolved with cynical speed beyond its initial conception as imposed artifice, to become a reflection of naturally occurring, competitive forces. It fell within the ambit of a sociological naturalism, according to which in its artificial forms examination merely formalises what is already going on. Examination becomes unavoidable, inescapable. It is reconfigured as a commonplace occurrence, as just another banal fact of social life.

* * *

Eminent men and women generally distinguish themselves in later life, that is, long after peak fertility, which limits their utility as breeding subjects. Specialist tools were required for judging innate potential, and yet, when Galton's research was first presented in 1865, neither he nor anyone else could be sure how to go about measuring so elusive a thing as natural giftedness.

Anticipating his twenty-first-century successors, the great research funding agencies of late modernity, Galton issued his own research call. He proposed a vast network of 'anthropometric laboratories, where a man may, when he pleases, get himself and his children weighed, measured, and rightly photographed, and have their bodily faculties tested'. This would allow 'anthropometric registers' to be amassed for statistical analysis, and mark the beginnings of a science that might, after much refinement, develop a test for natural ability in the fertile young.[212] It was at this point that the ancient remark – 'the unexamined life is not worth living'[213] – acquired a new and potent significance.

* * *

Galton set up a prototype laboratory at the International Health Exhibition of 1884. For a three-penny fee visitors would enter a small enclosure and submit themselves for measurement. The interior of this enclosure was partially visible to spectators through a trellis as an enticement. The measured visitor would eventually depart with a 'card containing the results furnished him', with a duplicate kept for the register.[214] Over 9000 visitors were logged and tested for 'keenness of sight; colour-sense; judgement of eye; hearing; highest audible note; breathing power; strength of pull and squeeze; swiftness of blow; span of arms; height, standing and sitting; and weight'.[215] As it turned out, these tests of reaction time, energy and sensory acuity 'failed to correlate with any independent signs of accomplishment or intelligence'. And yet, the idea of 'mental testing' was now established as 'a major research problem for the future'.[216]

* * *

In 1869, Galton advanced a bold hypothesis concerning the distribution of intellectual power, ranging from the most 'conspicuously eminent' scholar at Cambridge to the lowest 'idiots and imbeciles among the twenty million inhabitants of England and Wales', with the various grades of able, mediocre and 'silly' persons in between.[217] He claimed that the range of mental power is 'enormous', and yet, when you place men 'according to their natural abilities' in 'classes separated by equal degrees of merit', the number of men in each class is far from equal. Indeed, the distribution of ability will follow 'the very curious theoretical law of "deviation from an average" '.[218]

The Belgian statistician Adolphe Quetelet had already reported a bell-shaped distribution of chest sizes in a sample of Scottish soldiers.[219] Similar results were reported for the distributed heights of 100,000 French conscripts.[220] Galton's conceptual leap was to assume that 'if this be the case with stature, then it will be true as regards every other physical feature – as circumference of head, size of brain, weight of grey matter, number of brain fibres' and so on. By analogy, Galton continues, there 'must be a fairly constant average mental capacity in the inhabitants of the British Isles' with deviations from this average 'upwards towards genius, and downwards towards stupidity' following the shape of a bell.[221] To support the argument, Galton contrives an experiment in which the actual distribution of examinees is placed alongside a predicted distribution using the law cited above.[222] The correlation is fairly close, leading to the 'undeniable' conclusion 'that eminently gifted men are raised as much above mediocrity as idiots are depressed below it'. The 'differences of intellectual gifts between man and man' are found to be 'enormous'.[223]

Despite first appearances, this was a significant departure from the work of Quetelet. Not only did it travel beyond observable characteristics (such as height or girth) to speculate a normal distribution in unmeasurable capacities, it also revised the idea of average man. When Quetelet applied the normal distribution to human variables in 1844, the normal or average represented man in his ideal form (the man of ideal height and ideal girth). This average was not yet seen as mediocre or middling. Indeed, all variations from this average were aberrations from the norm. Transmitted here were assumptions deriving from the early history of the normal distribution. As a mathematical function it had first been used decades earlier to remove measurement error from astronomical observations. The average derived from this function was the *true value* of a measurement. The distribution of readings either side of this average, observed in the raw data, represented error and the imperfection of measurement techniques. When this logic was first applied to human phenomena, observed social regularities were also associated with the idea of a true reading. Average social phenomena were no longer seen as mysterious regularities. They represented the key properties of a population, and stood for 'real quantities' with 'underlying truths and causes'.[224] This raised statistical traces to the realm of social realities that could be targeted for control.

When the normal distribution was first extended to the measurement of human variation, its exclusive association with error was not immediately abandoned.[225] There was only a gradual transition from the term 'law of error' to 'normal distribution'.[226] For earlier theorists (including Quetelet), error was something to be eliminated; for Galton, 'these errors or deviations were the very things I wanted to preserve and know about'.[227] Deviations from the norm were no longer associated with error, but were linked to human potential.

*   *   *

The Possible Improvement of the Human Breed under the Existing Conditions of Law and Sentiment sets Galton's ideas against those of his more timid contemporaries. Delivered in 1901, this lecture offers a carefully succinct outline of the practical implications of eugenic improvement.[228] Improvement is narrowly defined according to a diagram that depicts a 'standard scheme of descent'. The distribution of 'talents' associated with 'the formation of civic worth' in 1000 breeding couples is shown at the top, in a rough frequency distribution that displays the rough contours of a pyramid.[229] These breeding couples follow the 'Normal Law of Frequency'[230] and are graded from left to right, from those far below average, to the bulk of breeding couples contained in the central pillars, down to those few who exhibit exceptional and very rare eminence to the far right of the diagram.

Galton does not explain how such talents are to be assessed. However, he does assume that 'civic worth' and its associated hereditary talents roughly match the class divisions in society, where those who display high levels of civic worth are most frequently found in the highest social classes. Following the classifications of the English philanthropist Charles Booth, these

STANDARD SCHEME OF DESCENT

PARENTAL GRADES NUMBER IN EACH	u 22	t 67	s 161	r 250	R 250	S 161	T 67	U 22
1000 COUPLES BOTH PARENTS OF SAME GRADE AND ONE ADULT MALE CHILD TO EACH								
REGRESSION OF PARENTAL TO FILIAL CENTRES								
22 CHILDREN OF u	6	8	6	2				
67 CHILDREN OF t	7	17	23	15	4	1		
161 CHILDREN OF s	5	22	50	52	25	6	1	
250 CHILDREN OF r	2	14	51	86	68	25	4	
250 CHILDREN OF R		4	25	68	86	51	14	2
161 CHILDREN OF S		1	6	25	52	50	22	5
67 CHILDREN OF T			1	4	15	23	17	7
22 CHILDREN OF U					2	6	8	6
SUMS	20	66	162	252	252	162	66	20

divisions extend from 'criminals, semi-criminals, loafers and some others, who are in number at the rate of 1 percent', through 'very poor persons who subsist on casual earnings, many of whom are inevitably poor from shiftlessness, idleness or drink', to the class of 'hard-working people' who, nevertheless, have 'a very bad character for improvidence and shiftlessness'. We then continue upwards to regular earners of 'twenty-one shillings or less a week, so none of them rise above poverty, though none are very poor', to earners of 'twenty-two to thirty shillings a week' who are known for 'all forms of co-operation and combination; in short for trades unions'. This last group is very numerous and thereby constitutes 'the mediocre class'. Above this 'large mass of mediocrity comes the honourable class…which consists of better paid artisans and foremen. These are able to provide adequately for old age, and their sons become clerks and so forth'. Then we have the 'lower middle class of shop-keepers, small employers, clerks and sub-ordi-nate professional men, who as a rule are hard-working, energetic and sober'. The traits of those above lower middle class, Galton declines to specify. Presumably they are very refined indeed.[231] Despite these claims that there is a close correspondence between class position and 'civic worth', we are assured that exceptions do occur. Here, Galton cites Booth, who corrects those who would misread him: when referring to the savagery of the lowest classes, he did 'not mean to say that there are not individuals of every sort to be found in the mass. Those who are able to wash the mud may find some gems in it.'[232] In other words, some individuals with a human worth that is higher than their fellows can be found in the lower echelons.

The scheme of descent also depicts the 'worth of children' in the smaller distributions that appear further down in the diagram.[233] As an aside, Galton speculates that children of the highest and rarest class would be 'a cheap bargain for the nation to buy' at the 'rate of many hundred or some thousands of pounds per head'. By contrast, the worth of an average baby, taking into account his or her earning potential measured against the cost of childhood and old age, would be around five pounds. Naturally, these are gross simplifications. For example, adults from the most eminent class will not always produce similarly eminent offspring. The offspring of a group of these parents will be normally distributed about its own average, and that average will regress (or shift) towards the population average from which the parents were extracted. In other words, the average child of a superior parent will be slightly less eminent. We are told that the extent of regression will be about a third of the way towards the original popula-tion mean. This reversion to mediocrity is depicted on Galton's diagram by the dashed diagonal lines. The implication is that those who wish to encourage talent must work within an 'economy of effort'. Though Galton first suggests that individual children, the *outputs* of breeding, could be given a value according to their relative position, what Galton now adds is the idea that *effort* itself can be placed on a relative scheme. Here, by far the 'most profitable parents to work upon' are those from the highest class.[234] In this economy of effort, class mixing is to be avoided. Indeed, with parents of dissimilar classification 'regression of the genetic centre goes twice as far back towards mediocrity'. Thus, mixed couplings are very bad economy indeed.[235]

This discovery of a law of regression had clear practical consequences for eugenic intervention. Before this law was devised, there was a tendency in Galton's work 'to overrate the speed with which a great improvement of the race of mankind might theoretically, be effected'.[236] But natural phenomena were far more intransigent than was initially presumed. It became ever clearer that these phenomena must be carefully respected and understood if one is to work effectively within them. Here, the limitations imposed by nature must not inspire despondency; rather, they only make it more urgent to pursue an economy of effort. The eugenic mind is now concentrated on this question. The law of accelerated regression will sting those who do not give natural process its due respect.

$$\star \quad \star \quad \star$$

The last chapter of Galton's autobiography provides a general review of his work and its reception. He notes that 'confusion is often made between statistical and individual results'. It is commonly objected that the effect of 'a particular union cannot be accurately foretold' and thus 'the application of the rules of Eugenics is vain'.

As any good statistician will tell you, this is a mistaken view. It is based on a misunderstanding of statistical perception. Statistics only 'give us assurance concerning the fate of such or such *percentage* of a large number of people which, when translated into [individual] terms, is the probability of each of them being affected by it'.[237]

With statistics a new reality appears, one that arrives with its own rules and procedures. This reality is the actuality of the *case*, where each individual case is the effect of a twofold process: first, a statistical move that individualises a collective phenomenon, and, second, a governmental injunction that seeks to align each individuated case with a collective endeavour.[238] In eugenic terms, each breeding union is a singular case within a larger population: it will have its own probabilities of reproductive success, estimations of desirability, and calculations of cost. It is at this abstracted level and in these terms that government will operate:

> From the statesman's point of view, where lives are pawns in the game and personal favour is excluded, this information is sufficient. It tells how large a number of undesirables or of desirables can be introduced or not into a population by such and such measures. Whether their names be A, B, or C, or else X, Y, or Z, is of no importance to the 'Statistician,' – a term that is more or less equivalent to that of 'Statesman'.[239]

The challenge for the everyday 'statesman', otherwise known as the case-worker, is to transmit this heartless logic into personalised guidance, preferably with a humanistic twist. The practical task is to place the heart within a scheme of probabilities.

* * *

Sometimes it feels as if one's early publications were designed to embarrass a later self. Galton certainly felt queasy about some of his early work, in which he mistakenly argued that

> The power of man over animal life … is enormously great. It would seem as though the physical structure of future generations was almost as plastic as clay, under the control of the breeders will. [240]

Upon reflection, Galton decides that the power of a breeder is far more limited than this statement suggests. The breeder is restricted to only 'perpetuating and intensifying qualities which have *already appeared* in the race'.[241] One must work within the constraints of life, and nurture or deny only that which is already taking place. Eugenics is a humble pursuit, always restraining itself to the facts of the case.

* * *

The success of eugenics would rely heavily on its popular appeal. And so, mindful of their public, its 'advocates should move discreetly and claim no more efficacy on its behalf than the future will confirm; otherwise a re-action will be invited'.[242] These advocates, Galton declares, should also demonstrate that eugenics is a gentle, enabling science. Its methods are not in the main those of 'stern compulsion'. In fact, compulsion should be relied upon only to prevent the 'free propagation of the stock of those who are seriously afflicted' by degenerate traits (including 'lunacy, feeble-mindedness, habitual criminality, and pauperism'). It is merely in the 'self-defence' of society that we must 'withstand the free introduction of degenerate stock' and engage in punitive measures (such as sterilisation or prohibited breeding). The organisation of marriage, meanwhile, is to be left open. As the intrinsic sense of the eugenic creed becomes manifest in the general population, it 'should form one of the many considerations by which marriages are promoted or hindered, as they are by social position, adequate fortune, and similarity of creed'. If someone of 'exceptionally good stock' should marry 'an inferior', this 'will be felt as derogatory' and therefore such unions will become unlikely.[243] Finding a good eugenic match would become a matter of moral and civic obligation, a matter of enthusiasm for the race that might eventually develop into a sort of 'religious obligation'.[244] In effect, punitive measures are only necessary for the worst stock. Self-restraint is to be the watchword for the middling masses; and only the best are to be practically encouraged. Life is to be supported in its current arrangements, where existing traditions of marriage and mate selection are those aspects of social life that must be fortified and conditioned.

* * *

The association between eugenics and national survival was a pragmatic one. Ronald Fisher, Professor of Eugenics and father of statistical science, makes this point in his 1914 preface to *Eugenics Review*, an organ of the eugenic cause:

> Eugenics is not inherently associated with nationalism; but in the world of nations, as we see it, nationalism may perform a valuable eugenic function. The modern nation is a genetic, a territorial, and an economic organism, and the modern tendency is to emphasise its essential unity.[245]

By projecting eugenics as a national-level concern (rather than a concern for humanity in general), biological logic is able to invest state logic. The good of the nation becomes equivalent to the good of the biological species. According to Fisher's predecessor Karl Pearson, who worked at the Francis Galton Laboratory for National Eugenics, the title of this laboratory was not accidental:

> It will be noted that Galton added the word National to Eugenics. This addition has been often overlooked, or when not overlooked misinterpreted. Critics have glibly talked of the 'international character of science,' and said that no branch of real science can be national. The word is, however, essential to the idea Galton had in mind... Galton had in mind the statecraft which would elevate a whole nation and make it fittest for its work in the world... No more than there is equality between man and man of the same nation is there equality between race and race... there is a relative fitness of nations, their racial history, their environment, and their traditions fit them best for definite forms of work. Each nation has its own eugenic problems. The best type of man for Germany may not be wholly the same as the best type of man for Great Britain... [Many] races have hardly yet found their true place and function in the community of nations. Science will not flinch from the conclusion, if such be inevitable, that some of these races scarce serve in the modern world any purpose than to provide material for the history of man.[246]

Brutal writers such as Pearson make few attempts to soften the blow. In this case, we see how an effective eugenic programme will target national institutions, constructing each country as an entity with its own unique eugenic problems. These efforts will not be governed by a restrictive paro- chialism, however. A global view is adopted here, formed as it is by a scien- tific community that communicates across borders. If some nations are judged inferior, they will be allowed to diminish. Otherwise they will be forcibly removed. ... Perhaps this sounds excessive? Pearson would agree. These achievements will be impossible without a shift in values.

* * *

Under biopower, systems of value were indeed disturbed. One explanation would be to claim that there was a shift in social and intellectual authority and hence a transformation in the engines of value. During the nineteenth century a scientific worldview came to challenge its theological rivals. In the early part of that century, scientific research stood subordinate to established moral values; its materialism was trumped by the imperium of theology. Towards the end of the century, this situation reversed as the professional status and authority of the scientist gained ground.[247] The scientist became concerned with popular perceptions, and, as Galton explains, sought to reform the 'popular notion of life':

> Most persons seem to have a vague idea that a new element, specially fashioned in heaven, and not transmitted by simple descent, is introduced into the body of every newly-born infant. Such a notion is unfitted to stand upon any scientific basis with which we are acquainted ... [for] the terms *talent* and *character* are exhaustive: they include the whole of man's spiritual nature so far as we are able to understand it.[248]

Galton exaggerates the case, of course. The ascent of a non-theological, scien- tific morality was not entirely divorced from its theological antecedents. In the study of demographic constants (such as the ratio of male to female births, or the differential mortality of boys to girls, which led to a balance of the sexes by the time the age for marriage was reached) theological explanations were often given. Until the nineteenth century, in fact, statistical regularities such as these were taken to indicate divine wisdom and planning. This logic was disturbed only when other regularities suggesting a somewhat less impec- cable god became prominent. From 1827 the French government published records of criminal activity in which similar year-on-year regularities were observed. Here, the predictable frequency of murder, theft and suicide was more difficult to explain in theological terms. It was better to interpret these anomalies as entities in their own right.[249] Still, even though divine inten- tions were gradually replaced by probabilistic renditions of reality, residues of the old worldview remained. The injunction to respect the will of our (now absent) creator was modified to become a demand that we respect the will of nature. As Pearson put it, 'our god is the welfare of the race'.[250]

* * *

In a collection of lectures and essays, entitled *The Ethic of Freethought*, Galton's protégé, Karl Pearson, sets out his scheme for an explicit moral naturalism. A statistician by vocation, and socialist by political inclination (preferring the bureaucratic socialism of professional elites), Pearson developed an accompanying moral philosophy, promoting what he called a 'rational basis of morals'. A rational approach, he decided, is surely 'the only safe guide to right action'. By contrast to the moral clarity afforded by this rational position, all prior attempts 'to create self-consistent gods' were 'a mere waste of intellectual energy'.[251]

Pearson's new rational morality would accompany the discovery of objective social facts. A natural order is now found in things, or, at least, things are naturalised, and this naturalness becomes the operating principle for a novel form of political calculation. Even though a degree of moral continuity can be observed here (for one must revere the natural processes that have been discovered), there is an important difference. From a materialist perspective one respects these processes not from obedience to god, but for their own sake, and in order to nurture them. If one fails to abide by what is natural, there will be negative consequences of a material kind. As Foucault puts it, 'there will be either success or failure; success or failure, rather than legitimacy or illegitimacy, now become the criteria of governmental action'.[252] What is legitimate is replaced by what is successful, what is right by what is valid. These laws of nature are only violated when errors are made. These violations are not the effects of wickedness; they are the mistakes of ignorance.

* * *

According to this ethic of freethought, it was time to separate morality from rite and dispense with conceptions of 'good and evil, as if they had an absolute or abstract value'. 'Immoral' is 'simply another term for what is antisocial'. And that which is antisocial can be decided a rational basis. This connection of (a) immoral behaviour, to (b) behaviour that is antisocial, to (c) rational decision-making is the basic schematic for Pearson's moral order. The 'welfare of society' against which (b) is defined forms the connecting idea, serving at the centre of this moral scheme.[253] Morality becomes a 'question not of feeling but of knowledge and study'.[254] This exacting task requires sufficient expertise to ensure a 'gratification of the social passion in one's actions'. Computations of what is social and what is antisocial in terms of the welfare of society are demanding; so demanding, indeed, that very few people are 'capable of being really moral'. A truly moral person 'must be in

possession of the highest knowledge of his time'. This would entail 'possession of all that is known of the laws of human development. He, and he only,
is capable of fulfilling his social instinct in accordance with those laws.'

Clearly, 'the ignorant and the uneducated cannot be moral', for morality 'is
not the blind following of a social impulse, but a habit of action ... moulded
by that knowledge of truth which must become an integral part of our
being'.[255] The ignorant are not *immoral* either; they are just ignorant and in
need of education. A large part of the labouring classes fall into this category, and, 'incapable of moral action', they represent a significant threat to
social stability.[256] Faced by problems such as these, education performs an
important function in lifting people out of their ignorance and endowing
them with the sense to act in ways that accord with the overall welfare of
society (as defined by those 'capable of being really moral'). The calculation of conditions favourable to overall welfare 'is a problem requiring the
careful and scientific investigation of the state itself – only by such investigation will we be able to determine what is social or antisocial, what is
healthy or unhealthy' for the population as a whole.[257]

* * *

The existence of a normal distribution of intelligence was soon confirmed
by those committed to its discovery. Its existence was used to justify interventions that were now underwritten more or less explicitly by the new
moral order.

> *I.M. Girl, age 14–2; mental age 9; IQ approximately 65.* Father a laborer. Does
> unsatisfactory work in fourth grade. Plays with little girls. A menace to
> the morals of the school because of her sex interests and lack of self-
> restraint. Rather good-looking if one does not hunt for appearances of
> intelligence. Mental reactions intolerably slow. Will develop but little
> further and will always pass as feeble-minded in any but the very lowest
> social environment.[258]

The above description combines biographical and observational data to
predict a life of vice and dependence, where the most important details
seem to be those that are provided in italics. By 1919 it was possible to
quantify this daughter of a labourer in a way that would allow her case to be
assessed in relation to the vast population of which she was a part. This was
an important development: in order to make administrative decisions both
strict and correct, eugenics, and other social projects, required an objective
test of human qualities. It was felt that the quantification (and definition) of
intelligence could perform this role, as a proxy for the measurement of civic
worth. Galton's anthropometric laboratory had clearly failed in this respect.
Tests of sensory acuity and reaction time exhibited poor correlations with

external measures of intelligence, such as academic success, as both Galton and those who followed his example were to discover. It was fortunate, therefore, that more effective laboratories were already in existence. These were the elementary schools that were in hot pursuit of their utopian target: *education for all*. These schools, and others like them, provided much more than instruction. They afforded the motivations and conceptual architectures that were to be crucial in the development of mental tests.[259]

* * *

The success of mental tests followed a switch from physical attributes to abstract qualities of mind. The French psychologist Alfred Binet is the hero of this story, even though his particular involvement was born of mundane institutional requirements. Recently enacted French law required that all children be given a public education, including those deemed 'subnormal'. For the latter category of child, specialist schools were to be provided. This raised an administrative difficulty: the problem of allocating those children who were considered to be on the borderlines of abnormality. As the member of a commission appointed in 1904 to investigate the problem, Binet found diagnostic procedures to be woefully unreliable. Assignment of children between the three major categories of deficiency – 'idiots' (the most severely mentally deficient), 'imbeciles' (moderately deficient) and 'débiles' (those at the lower limits of normality) – was fraught with confusion. Mistaken assignment would obviously have negative consequences. Hence, improved diagnostic tools were urgently required to resolve borderline cases. Along with Theodore Simon, Binet devised a test (the Binet–Simon test) that would perform these classifications more precisely. This test was published in 1905, revised in 1908, and again in 1911 just before Binet's death.

* * *

The conceptual architectures of mental testing were found within the institutions of mass schooling. These institutions had already generated norms of conduct and performance. They had organised behavioural space, establishing the standards against which variations between children could be charted. Within these institutional confines a new category of child emerged, who, though appearing fully functional at first sight, did not seem able to benefit from instruction. These children, who had done little except fail to fit, came to be known as educational imbeciles or the feeble-minded. In such a context, when a separation of the population became necessary (following the arrival of universal schooling and the problem of borderline children), the response was to use criteria of separation that were directly educational and behavioural [260]: that is, criteria that can be derived from the artificial context of schooling, with its arbitrary codes of conduct and favoured activities.

The tasks in the Binet–Simon test were arranged according to the assumed (and institutionally specific) development of a 'normal' child. According to this framework, a 'normal' child of, say, five years of age would have an equivalent mental level of five years, whereas a child with arrested development would have a mental level lower than its chronological age. The tasks used in the Binet–Simon test were standardised on a population of 50 'normal' and 45 'subnormal' children. The examiner proceeded through a hierarchy of activities, with so-called idiots engineered to drop out at a mental level of two years, imbeciles managing questions between two and five years, and débiles passing tasks that a normal child of five to 11 years would be able to complete. This introduction of age-related tasks (tasks corresponding to the development of a 'normal' child) was a key advance. It was now possible to assign an 'intellectual level' to the individual, which later became known as his or her 'mental age'.

*   *   *

There were two hypotheses: either the measured intelligence of an individual was a single attribute, or it was the accumulated effect of diverse factors. Charles Spearman (a member of the Eugenics Society) advanced the former hypothesis, arguing that intelligence is a sort of mental energy. He labelled it 'g'. The Binet–Simon tests had come very close to measuring this underlying brainpower, Spearman argued. However, all tests are complicated by more specific factors, which he labelled 's'. These are special abilities that help in some tasks but not in others (unlike 'g', which helps in all tasks). The strategic advantage for Spearman of his two-factor theory of intelligence was that it neatly explained the profound difficulties involved in designing a perfect intelligence test, that is, a test that measured pure 'g'.

The two-factor theory of intelligence also had something important to say about more conventional tests of scholarly attainment. It seemed that even school examinations tested for 'g' to varying degrees. Indeed, Spearman reported that school disciplines could be arranged according to the hierarchy of their saturation by 'g'. In Spearman's study, Classics came top of the list as being the best indicator of intelligence. Mathematics was ranked below English and French, indicating the disciplinary prejudices of the day.[261]

Spearman was triumphant: 'here would seem to lie the long wanted general rational basis for public examinations', he wrote. It was now possible to defend 'high marks in Greek syntax' as a good indicator of 'g' and therefore as a reasonable test of the 'capacity of men to command troops or to administer provinces'.[262] It was now feasible, Spearman contended, to objectively measure the extent to which public examinations reflect underlying ability. 'One can even conceive the establishment of a minimum index to qualify for parliamentary vote, and, above all, for the right to have offspring.'[263]

The great liberal philosopher John Stuart Mill made a similar point decades earlier, suggesting that only the better educated should be allowed to vote. Any man should be allowed to qualify for this privilege, Mill argued, 'if he can prove that *in spite of all difficulties and obstacles*, he is in point of intelligence' entitled to it.[264]

* * *

A unitary scale for the measurement of intelligence was still lacking. Subtracting the recorded mental age from the actual age on a Binet–Simon test provided a measure of delay, but it was limited in that children of different ages could not be placed on the same scale. They were not comparable. A *division* of the two terms, by contrast, would provide a relative rather than an absolute measure of disparity. This relative measure could then be compared between individuals of different ages. William Stern made this recommendation in 1912. He called his ratio (mental age divided by chronological age) the intelligence quotient. In 1916 Lewis Terman removed the fractional appearance of the ratio, multiplying it by 100. This brought into existence the modern IQ scale with which we are now so familiar. Properly quantified, human intelligence was arranged as a universal reference point against which individuals could be compared, and through which interventions could be justified.

* * *

The Binet-Simon tests were translated and popularised in the United States by Henry Goddard, a psychologist seeking to better identify the débile class, to which he applied the new term 'moron'. Residing just outside the outer fringes of normality, this group was the most difficult to identify. Consequently, its members would pass on their defective traits relatively unimpeded (assuming the more obvious idiots and imbeciles were taken care of). With the mental age of a child, so defined, they were liable to become paupers, criminals, drunkards and prostitutes, or at least form an irresponsible group of 'ne'er-do-wells'. At least, these were the prospective futures for the so-called moron type that so exercised his imagination. Goddard justified 'exercising as much control over them as we do over normal childhood'.[265] They should be identified, segregated and prevented from breeding, a process for which the new mental tests would be a useful tool. As Goddard speculates, these tests might also be used to prevent the admission of immigrants of degenerate traits, for low intelligence was deemed a serious threat to national well-being.

* * *

A revision by the psychologist Lewis Terman, known as the Stanford–Binet, was introduced in 1916 and soon became the benchmark against which subsequent intelligence tests were measured. It was standardised on 2300 individuals and, unlike the Binet–Simon test, could be used for adults and in the measurement of high intelligence. This allowed testing to be extended to the entire population, from degenerate, through normal, to exceptional persons. Terman was optimistic that intelligence tests would soon become indispensable to the 'educational engineer'.[266] He also believed that they could play a supplementary *eugenic* role with respect to the moron.

> It is safe to predict that in the near future intelligence tests will bring tens of thousands of these high-grade defectives under the surveillance and protection of society. This will ultimately result in curtailing the reproduction of feeble-mindedness and in the elimination of an enormous amount of crime, pauperism, and industrial inefficiency. It is hardly necessary to emphasize that the high-grade cases, of the type now so frequently overlooked, are precisely the ones whose guardianship it is most important for the State to assume.[267]

We find delinquency associated once again with mental deficiency. As Terman put it: 'Morality depends upon two things: *(a)* the ability to foresee and to weigh the possible consequences for self and others of different kinds of behaviour; and *(b)* upon the willingness and capacity to exercise self-restraint.' Thus, 'all feeble-minded are at least potential criminals' and 'every feeble-minded woman is a potential prostitute'. Repeating the position taken by Pearson, we find that moral judgement 'is a function of intelligence'. 'Morality cannot flower and fruit if intelligence remains infantile.'[268] It is not 'the blind following of a social impulse'.[269] Morality is the product of rational calculation.

According to the normal distribution, those of superior intellect are in a similar proportion to the feeble-minded. It was clear enough to those of a eugenic mindset that the 'future welfare of the country hinges, in no small degree, upon the right education of these superior children'.[270] These superior children also, must be identified.

> Through the handicapping influences of poverty, social neglect, physical defects, or educational maladjustments, many potential leaders in science, art, government, and industry are denied the opportunity of a normal development. The use we have made of exceptional ability reminds one of the primitive methods of surface mining. It is necessary to explore the nation's hidden resources of intelligence. The common saying that 'genius will out' is one of those dangerous half-truths with which too many people rest content.[271]

The educational engineer now faced a range of possibilities. Intelligence tests could be used to reveal exceptional ability and allow early promotion up the school. The risk of not taking such action was that exceptional children might fall into 'lifelong habits of submaximum efficiency'. Terman felt they must be pushed as hard as 'their mental development would warrant', 'under proper medical supervision, of course'. The main 'danger in the case of such children is not over-pressure but under-pressure'. Intelligence tests could also be used more broadly, for placing all children within the school. This is said to be of particular use for the pupil of completely unknown abilities 'who enters the school system from another'.[272] Finally, Terman argues, intelligence tests could be applied to ascertain vocational fitness, a point to which I return.

*   *   *

> **Case 13. Mary N.** 26 years old. Mentally 10. Has been here 19 years... Mary is a splendid illustration of that type of girl that is most dangerous in society. Pretty and attractive and with just enough training to enable her to make a fair appearance she deceives the very elect as to her capacity. Responsibilities would be placed on her which she could never carry. She is absolutely incapable of controlling her own instincts and impulses, and incapable of exercising any judgement in matters that are at all complex. In Institution life she is happy and useful. Unprotected she would be degraded, degenerate and the mother of defectives.[273]

On the question of intelligence and its relation to social life (paupers, criminals, drunkards, prostitutes, etc.), one crucial point of clarification was provided. As Galton and his successors argued, intelligence is distributed continuously from very low to very high. In that sense it is a relative matter: the intelligence of a specific individual can be described in its relation to the normal distribution of all other intelligences. But it was also argued that the relativity of intelligence operates on a socio-temporal axis too. As Goddard would have it, the *social significance* of each particular level of intelligence is 'fixed not arbitrarily but by the social necessity', which itself is a function of historical progress.[274] The boundary between lower normality and upper abnormality is defined as *the point at which a person cannot deal adequately with his or her environment*. Social environments, we are told, are graded in complexity just as much as intelligence. Here, Goddard cites Binet, who points out that 'normal intelligence is a relative matter and that which is sufficient for a French peasant out in the country is not sufficient for a Frenchman in Paris'. Some types will 'have intelligence enough to live in certain environments and care for themselves but in a more complex social group it is impossible for them to function properly'. As civilisation advanced, the bar was raised. The 'persons who constitute our social problems are of a type that in the past and under simpler environments have seemed responsible and able to function normally'. The difficulty for them today is that 'the present environment has become too complex'.[275]

We can see in this rationale how arguments for national self-defence against the pernicious effects of the defective are justified in terms that are defined by the nature of the society to be defended. The contextually specific demands of a complex society designate the point at which a citizen who fails to cope thereby becomes a threat to that society. The nature of society is appealed to and used to justify a line of distinction between those that society will 'make live' and those that it will 'let die'. As already noted, this does not only entail murder as such, but also every form of indirect murder: the fact of exposing someone to death, increasing the risk of death, or, quite simply, political death, expulsion, rejection, and so on; to which we must add institutionalisation, prohibited breeding and sterilisation. This is an exemplary case of the kind of self-referential thinking and justification that is definitive of biopower, *where the population is both the object of government and the source of guidance as to how that government should operate.* Intelligence is defined in terms of social necessity. It is defined in terms of population-level requirements, and yet, at the same time, it is the device used for managing a population.

* * *

During the First World War, a group of psychologists contributed to the war effort by ranking army recruits according to their mental abilities. Goddard and Terman joined a group of scientists led by Robert Yerkes. Their leader was a eugenicist and primate expert. Several years later, he was teaching table manners to chimpanzees.

* * *

In 1917, Yerkes published recommendations for converting the Stanford–Binet, age-based scale to a point scale. This would make test data more amenable to statistical analysis. The Binet tests had always been limited in this respect.[276] In their construction, specific activities were matched to the age at which a 'normal' child was expected to achieve mastery. For example, a normal five-year-old child was expected to name certain colours, and a normal eight-year-old was expected to count backwards from 20 to zero. These assumptions were then verified by testing them on a sample of children. Roughly speaking, the problem with this approach is that the test was limited to a specific group of children for whom the tasks were devised. These tests were useless in other contexts, being inflexible by design.

With a point scale approach, however, the tasks were less specific to context. They were no longer selected to match a certain age, and each task was divided into stages of difficulty. Though age as a criterion for task selection was no longer important, norms could still be established *in retrospect* for each different age. Indeed, norms could now be established for any variable in a population. In addition, once these tests were administered to increasing numbers of people they would become increasingly reliable. Any new group could be tested so long as a sufficient number of initial examinations were conducted in order to establish preliminary norms. As Yerkes explained, the test was now 'universally applicable'.[277]

*   *   *

An exploratory norm-generating device had replaced its precursor, which had been limited to a specific population, relying as it did on certain preconceived ideas about what members of that population should be able to do at a particular age. Here we now have a tool designed to discover the norms and traits of particular groups, a tool that would claim to have developed a non-biased, culturally and socially non-specific platform of discernment. This was a key development in biopolitical strategy, representing a shift from normation towards normalisation, from the prescription of norms to the discovery of normative traits latent within a population. Biopower requires methods that are able to reveal essential truths about our social world. A proper, technically respectable diagnosis is necessary so as to make the biopolitical remedy appear legitimate. The shadow of power must be removed if a diagnosis is to be believed and obeyed.

*   *   *

In a disciplinary context, the concealment of power was just another component technique in the creation of productive bodies. Disciplinary truth was judged not according to its neutrality as such, but according to its productive facility. Biopower brings with it an added dimension; it must conceal power because the apparent absence of power and the apparent presence of unadulterated truth form the basis of its claims to be able to compute the social good. Here a more deliberate and self-conscious attempt is made to obscure the operations of power. In order to make recommendations for the good of society, expert groups must portray themselves as neutral, scientific and uncorrupted.

To the extent that the emerging human sciences owed their existence to disciplinary technique, they appeared neutral as if by accident. This was because disciplinary technique practised a mechanical concealment of power. Once the human sciences were connected to a biopolitical logic, however, the concealment of power and the appearance of neutrality became a necessary part of their existence. Biopower supplemented the mechanical concealment of power with the concealment of a rhetorical deployment. This concealment for the sake of appearances is a whitewash imposed by those committed to the overall coherence of biopower and its ability to make truth claims about our social world.

The frameworks of dispute also shifted, from a debate that was primarily concerned with pointing out inefficiencies or brutalities, to a debate that was far more concerned with tearing away the veil of appearances. Indeed, we are today surrounded by those claiming to tear down this veil. They issue their claims to truth whilst also denouncing the biases, errors and hidden commitments of their opponents. There is a scramble for neutral ground, for a position once occupied by those of righteous indignation. It is as if social relations can be stripped away to reveal a neutral substratum upon which we can then build.

These preoccupations suit biopower well: the fight for neutrality and the fight against bias pose no threat to the biopolitical order. We have been set up, in other words. Our assigned task is to be enraged by that which is unfair, to fight again and again over the same ground-up terrain.

*   *   *

Biopower evacuates politics by claiming that it is only concerned with apolitical calculations of welfare. Of course, this evacuation is in itself an ideological operation of power. Normalisation, involving the discovery of population-specific traits, was a core strategy in this deployment. It claims that these traits are independent phenomena, that they represent discovered truths that are inherent to the population under study. The self-evidence of biopolitical truth becomes almost incontestable.

In the early years of normalisation, mass testing of World War I recruits was a major spur, returning data on 1.75 million men and providing norms on a national scale. This United States programme developed tests that were no longer administered individually by a trained psychologist, but could be administered to large groups. These tests were designed for positive as well as negative selection, broadening an earlier focus upon the subnormal. Recruits were graded for army purposes from high officer types, through good private types, to those unfit for service. Although there was some resistance to the psychological expert within the army,[278] the scientific status of testing was now established, and after the war there was a steady and lucrative stream of requests for the technology.

The point scale approach was refined through the introduction of the Wechsler Bellevue Scale in 1939, and its revision, the Wechsler Adult Intelligence Scale (or WAIS), in 1955. These provide IQs that are no longer based upon the relative difference between mental age and chronological age, and are known instead as 'deviation IQs'. Individual raw scores are converted to deviation IQs according to their deviation from the central tendency in a particular individual's group. Thus, IQ is now directly expressed as a *relative* performance in a specific age group. The average score is arbitrarily set at 100 to allow comparability with earlier IQ tests that were also set at 100.[279] Standard deviations for all groups are set at 15 so that more than two-thirds of all IQs will fall between 85 and 115 by default (that is, between one standard deviation above and one below the mean). This is now the typical approach for IQ tests that refer *directly* to the normal distribution. Overall, from Binet, through Spearman, Stern, Terman and Yerkes, to Wechsler, these were some of the steps that made normalisation, the elevation of population-level traits, a scientific possibility.

This 'full appreciation' of the population was a statistical perception. Population norms were derived from a pilot study of the test in which a representative portion of the population was examined. One could now rank geographically dispersed individuals according to a 'unitary' trait, where each individual could be identified and dealt with according to his or her relative position in the normal distribution, becoming a case in an overall population. It was no longer necessary to assemble all those to be ranked in one place and compare them directly. One no longer had to amass individuals in a single institution and observe them for a period of time. The test had become a 'mini-laboratory for the inscription of difference'.[280] It performed this geographic feat by assembling the population in its statistical constructs.

*   *   *

When promoting life and paying respect to existing relations, biopower was not always light in its touch – this much we can freely admit. Still, in its early eugenic incarnation a more *laissez-faire* approach was imaginable from the outset, as illustrated by this extract from the work of Georges Vacher de Lapouge, writing in 1896:

It would be very ingenious to achieve the destruction of the degenerate in such an amicable way, by making alcoholism, debauchery and an idle life so easy for them...the disappearance of the Red Indians and various peoples of Oceania has been largely facilitated by low-priced alcohol. The African Negroes at the present time are being very largely weakened by the grain spirit that they are so greedy for. It is likely that this process will run its full course, using this dangerous passion against them. In Greenland, the Eskimos persist only thanks to measures taken by the Danish government; access to the country is prohibited without special authorization, and the introduction of alcohol proscribed under severe penalties. I can well believe that if there were one town in France in which alcohol was free, alcoholics would congregate there like garden slugs under a buttered cabbage leaf, a succulent and fatal trap...If the reform of humanity could be achieved in this way by the simple play of human passions, without having to sacrifice people or be in any way violent, it would be likely to proceed at a more rapid pace.[281]

Against this imagined scheme in which debauchery (viewed as a product of degeneration) was to be left to its own devices, perhaps even encouraged, we should observe that in its early history biopower functioned in the opposite direction. It was at first associated with highly interventionist strategies of power, ignoring Galton's call for public self-regulation. In this period biopower tended to work as a disciplinary *intensifier*. It was only much later that a more liberal strand developed, and discipline played a relatively minor role.

* * *

In the late nineteenth and early twentieth centuries there was an effective partnership between a biopolitical interest in species health and a disciplinary concern with the productive coordination of bodies. Whilst biopower operates at the species level, it still depends upon bodily techniques. Early on in its development, biopower relied upon those disciplinary institutions that were already in existence. As Foucault would argue: 'discipline was never more important or more valued than when the attempt was made to manage the population'. This did not mean 'just managing the collective mass of phenomena or managing them simply at the level of their overall results; managing the population means managing it in depth, in all its fine points and details'.[282] A century or more ago, the problem of population health only made 'the need to develop the disciplines even more acute'. Discipline was not replaced by biopower, but population health now became the major concern, with discipline working in a subordinate fashion within this broader scheme.[283] This strategic combination can be observed in four exemplary cases: (1) the identification and training of feeble-minded

children, (2) plans for the custodial care of subnormal adults and children, (3) the internationally widespread practice of voluntary and forced sterilisation, and (4) the deployment of a biopolitical logic by fascism.

* * *

Reporting in 1898, a committee tasked by parliament with considering the plight of 'defective and epileptic children' framed the biopolitical challenge as one of suitable training:

> children exist who, on the one hand, are too feeble-minded to be properly taught in ordinary elementary schools by ordinary methods, and, on the other hand, are not so feeble-minded as to be imbecile or idiotic... From the normal child down to the lowest idiot, there are all degrees of deficiency of mental power; and it is only a difference of degree which distinguishes the feeble-minded children, referred to in our inquiry, on the one side from the backward children who are found in every ordinary school, and, on the other side, from the children who are too deficient to receive proper benefit from any teaching which the School Authorities can give... [But] these children show themselves capable of receiving considerable benefit from the individual attention and the special instruction given in the special classes. By the age of 13 or 14 they may sometimes arrive at a stage of elementary instruction equal, perhaps, to that attained by ordinary children of eight or nine years of age, and they *often show themselves capable of being trained in some manual occupation*. Thus there is a fair prospect, that, with favourable surroundings, they may take their place in the world, and may not become inmates of workhouses, asylums, or prisons.[284]

Compulsory schooling had enlarged the scale of the educational problem. Though distinct groups of children, such as those working in mines and factories, cleaning chimneys, and so on, had already invited concern as victims of the industrial age, social commentators now began to take an interest in the state of the child population as a whole.[285] Attention turned to moderate cases of 'defective' children and the problems they posed for compulsory schooling. In the interests of *national efficiency* (which was a fashionable phrase at the time), all educable children were to be given a basic course of instruction. Those who resisted the efforts of ordinary education would receive special training. It was hoped that these children could still become *productive economic subjects*, and not be a burden on the population as a whole. This combination of (a) institutional training to enhance individual productivity, and (b) the idea that a specific group of the child population is in need of training to prevent it from becoming a *social burden*, is an example of how a biopolitical logic was deployed in a disciplinary setting.

In true disciplinary spirit, those who resisted ordinary education were to be reclassified, segregated and educated in separate institutions and according to a carefully designed normative order that would ensure a basic level of economic productivity for each individual subject.

* * *

Plans for the custodial care of subnormal adults and children were similar in tone, as this 1908 parliamentary report on their 'care and control' makes clear:

> Of the gravity of the present state of things, there is no doubt. The mass of facts that we have collected, the statements of our witnesses, and our own personal visits and investigations compel the conclusion that there are numbers of mentally defective persons whose training is neglected, over whom no sufficient control is exercised, and whose wayward and irresponsible lives are productive or crime and misery, of much injury and mischief to themselves and to others, and of much continuous expenditure wasteful to the community and to individual families.
>
> We find a local and 'permissive' system of public education which is available, here and there, for a limited section of mentally defective children, and which, even if it be useful during the years of training, is supplemented by no subsequent supervision and control, and is in consequence often misdirected and unserviceable. We find large numbers of persons who are committed to prisons for repeated offences, which, being the manifestations of a permanent defect of mind, there is no hope of repressing, much less of stopping, by short punitive sentences. We find lunatic asylums crowded with patients who do not require the careful hospital treatment that well-equipped asylums now afford, and who might be treated in many other ways more economically and as efficiently. We find, also, at large in the population many mentally defective persons, adults, young persons, and children, who are, some in one way, some in another, incapable of self-control, and who are therefore exposed to constant moral danger themselves, and become the source of lasting injury to the community.[286]

The British Mental Deficiency Act of 1913 took on those adults and children who were harder to instruct.[287] It recommended custodial care under the auspices of a new central authority, the Board of Control. Those who demonstrated social incapacity would be removed from the community.[288] There was an expressed need for a 'public organisation to train them according to their ability, and to control and supervise them'.[289] As a 'first principle', those *'who cannot take part in the struggle of life* owing to mental defect...should be afforded by the state such special protection as may be suited to their needs'.[290] Without protection, moral defectives suffered at the bottom of a Darwinian struggle. They were, rightly, disadvantaged; this was to be expected. And yet, for their sake and for the sake of society, it was better to remove them. Moreover, it was feared that, despite the harsh conditions of their lives, a lack of self-restraint was resulting in high rates of propagation. For this reason alone, 'during the years of procreation and childbearing' there should be 'control or supervision in the case of mentally defective men and women'.[291]

In retrospect, the historian will observe that in 'the bleak economic climate prevailing after 1918' these recommendations would 'look more and more like extravagant fantasies'.[292] They are, nevertheless, worth attending to in their utopian form. These dreams of government are built from the social and political possibilities of the day. They demonstrate the distinctly disciplinary form in which the biopolitical logic was to be enacted.

*   *   *

In some pre-war states of America the bodies of so-called degenerates became a direct surgical target in the name of population health. Fears for the degeneration of the human race were shared by professionals, who would occasionally sterilise the unfit without legal sanction. This occurred in a disciplinary setting where individuals were already subject to institutional control, taking the existing manipulation of bodies to a new level.

In the mid-1890s a physician at the Kansas Home for the Feeble-minded chose to sterilise 58 children. Local citizens condemned his actions, even though to the board of trustees he was a pioneer. In 1899, a physician at the Indiana Reformatory began performing vasectomies on inmates in order to prevent the propagation of a criminal class. These were isolated acts, and yet they followed a logic that was soon to be enacted in the legislature. In 1905 an *Act for the Prevention of Idiocy* failed to reach law in Pennsylvania, but in 1907 a bill was ratified in Indiana to legislate for the forced sterilisation of its mentally impaired patients, poorhouse residents and prisoners.[293] Whilst failed attempts followed in Oregon, Illinois and Wisconsin in 1909, in that same year the state of Washington targeted the procreation of habitual criminals and rapists, Connecticut allowed sterilisation in its asylums, and California permitted castration or sterilisation of state convicts or residents at a home for 'feeble-minded' children. Over the next three years a legislative attempt in Virginia failed, but there were successes in Nevada, Iowa, New Jersey and New York State. Eventually, 29 states enacted legislation, though many were initially slow to implement their laws. Of the 6244 state-sanctioned operations between 1907 and 1925, 4636 were in California, where mental patients were sterilised before discharge as a matter of routine. Gradually, this activity intensified in other states, and by 1940 35,878 sterilisations had occurred, 14,568 of these in California.[294] Sterilisation before discharge assured the sustained influence of institutional life. This was a 'disciplinary career' of permanent effect.[295]

In England, compulsory sterilisation never reached the statute books, despite pressure from the Eugenics Society and other groups. In 1930, a physician was caught castrating young men at an institution in London. He was made to promise not to do it again until it was legalised.[296] Lobbying of civil servants at the Ministry of Health and its Board of Control secured the appointment of a *Departmental Committee on Sterilisation* in 1932.[297] They confirmed the seriousness of the problem, observing 'the dead weight of social inefficiency and individual misery which is entailed by the existence in our midst of over a quarter of a million mental defectives'. Many more were thought to be 'mentally subnormal', and, considered as a whole, this group was 'probably growing'. It was unfortunate that the 'ascertainment of defectives' was severely neglected by some local authorities, for without this detailed knowledge of their populations sterilisation could not proceed.[298] With compulsory sterilisation ruled out, the committee advised in favour of voluntary sterilisation (by consent of the patient, parent or guardian).

For those with a eugenic conscience, the situation was becoming desperate. According to the psychologist Raymond Cattell, 'a real deterioration of our race is going on here and now, day by day, hour by hour'.[299] In *The Fight for our National Intelligence*, Cattell described what he saw as the immediate social predicament: birth rate is inversely related to intelligence, and overall national intelligence is declining as a result of this dysgenic imbalance. In

300 years, at the present rate of uneven reproduction, half of the population will be mentally defective.

For context, we are told that the decline of ancient Greece and Rome 'was primarily due to a biological withering of those strains of the population bearing high mental capacity'. 'England and most civilized nations' now face a similar threat, Cattell implores. 'Not one civilization has yet escaped this sequence', in which men of 'great natural mental capacity' create a civilisation that subsequently decays as the 'sub-men' begin to outbreed the superior. And yet from these ashes 'the ancient law of the survival of the fittest constantly accumulated through blood and agony, a preponderance of survivors'. These survivors broke out of 'the decrepit civilization' within which they found themselves to create a social order with a level of vigour and commitment that had been 'dropped from the nerveless fingers of its former keepers'.

The history of civilisations is one of great wastes and wastelands. Fortunate are we who have 'the temper of the scientist', which inclines us to regard all this as 'a natural disease', which, 'if the scientist is given a chance, may yet be understood and mastered'.[300] Cattell's suggestion is that we devise a coordinated array of mechanisms that would address themselves in a comprehensive fashion to the entire range of citizens in our normally distributed population. He set this vision against the reality of contemporary policy, which he viewed as impossibly disjointed in this area. Its 'boasted progress

and reforms' were 'often only the digging away of what is continuously silting up'.[301] Successful intervention required concerted action at all points of the bell curve.

* * *

A mobilisation of forces, of the scale required to have a lasting impact on the demographic, was carried out under the Nazi regime. This was the most prominent example of a rising 'state racism' where governments took upon themselves a responsibility for 'the biological protection of the race'.[302] The Nazi state was, unlike others, in a position to act with sufficient might.

The Nazi regime relied, in part, on a biological rationale. As Adolf Hitler explained in *Mein Kampf*, 'any crossing of two beings not at exactly the same level produces a medium between the level of the two parents: the offspring will probably stand higher than the racially lower parent, but not as high as the higher one'. For Hitler, such mating was not only 'contrary to the will of Nature'[303] but also contrary to the will of the state, which must adopt a 'philosophy of life' that corresponds to the 'innermost will of Nature'.[304] Such a state is tasked with: 'the preservation of the racial existence of man. Thus, it by no means believes in an equality of the races. It recognises their higher or lesser value and feels itself obligated, through this knowledge, to promote the victory of the better and stronger, and demand the subordination of the inferior and weaker in accordance with the eternal will that dominates this universe.'[305]

For Hitler, absolute priority is given to this conception of Nature. Indeed, according to Hitler, 'man has never yet conquered Nature in anything'. At most he has 'caught hold of and tried to lift one or another corner of her immense gigantic veil of eternal riddles and secrets'. In reality, 'he invents nothing but only discovers everything'. Man does not 'dominate Nature, but has only risen on the basis of his knowledge of various laws and secrets of Nature to be lord over those other living creatures who lack this knowledge'.[306] This, we should observe, is a good example of the biopolitical perspective, where biopower builds upon pre-existing processes, aiming to construct with already-existing forces in mind. It does not entertain pure invention or attempt complete reconstruction.

By operating in terms of population health and of biological threats to that health, the Nazi regime could justify waging war on its subjects, for their own collective good. Of course, the Nazi rationale went far beyond the naturalistic lore of biopower, and so it would be a mistake to say that it represented biopower in all its solitary glory. As George Orwell noted in his review of *Mein Kampf*, though 'nearly all Western thought since the last war, certainly all "progressive" thought, has assumed tacitly that human beings desire nothing beyond ease, security and avoidance of pain', Hitler felt that something more was desired. He decided that 'human beings don't only want comfort, safety, short working-hours, hygiene, birth control and, in general, common sense; they also, at least intermittently, want struggle and self-sacrifice, not to mention drums, flags and loyalty-parades'.[307] The Nazi regime appealed to folklore, mythology and sentiment just as much as it made use of biological discourse. In Foucault's terms, however, these appeals to mythology are to be expected. Successive historic periods rarely achieve absolute separation or total rupture. In its early development, biopower did not effect a complete break with the 'symbolics of blood' that preceded it. As Foucault would admit, there were indeed 'overlappings, interactions, and echoes'.[308] Nazism revived 'in a regressive mode' the mythological discourses of counter-history that biopower had once co-opted, inverted and de-mythologised. We find here 'a Nazi reinscription or reinsertion of State racism in the legend of warring races'.[309]

The place of the biological discourse of race in the elimination of Jews is well known. Still, we should observe that, before exterminations began, mainstream science was relatively uncertain about the extent to which Aryan and Jewish peoples could be divided along clear racial lines. In this respect, the genocide of European Roma was more closely connected to scientific ideas current at that time, which confirmed their racial separateness. Similar scientific support backed the forced sterilisation of racially mixed children of French African troops in 1937.[310] The sterilisation and elimination of those already institutionalised (the diseased and handicapped), which preceded and anticipated the later purges, also followed a clearer biological rationale. Between 1934, when the sterilisation law was brought into force, and 1945, there may have been as many as 350,000 to 400,000 sterilisations for those judged to be suffering from a heritable disease. This was mirrored by the *Lebensborn* programme, established in 1935, that organised the breeding and care of Aryan infants at six specially designed institutions. Meanwhile, the 1935 marriage law prohibited the communion of fertile partners if one or both suffered from a mental or physical disorder that might damage the health of any descendants. The SS marriage code of 1933 required proof that a fiancée's parents had 'no physical or mental disease, that she was not sterile, and that there were neither Jews nor Slavs in her genealogy as far back as 1750'.[311] Together these measures amounted to a systematic attempt to rationalise human resources and increase species health, and hence productivity, through institutional, essentially disciplinary, means.

From 1939, doctors were required to register the birth of 'malformed' children, who would then be killed. This was followed by an order to remove 'mentally impaired' patients in a similar fashion. *Aktion T4*, which pioneered the use of gas chambers, was eventually suspended in 1941 following public unrest (though extermination continued by other more sporadic institutional means). This is often referred to as Nazi euthanasia, a term that André Pichot, in his history of *The Pure Society from Darwin to Hitler*, objects to as euphemistic.[312]

It is, indeed, true that euthanasia derives from a Greek root meaning quite literally 'easy or happy death'. And so we can, of course, sympathise with Pichot's objection. But this terminology is, in one sense, appropriate. The terms 'eugenics' (good birth) and 'euthanasia' (good death) aptly represent the biopolitical logic with its promotion of species well-being.

The refinement of biopolitical–disciplinary intervention was further advanced by the use of data management facilities supplied by IBM.[313] A system of punch-card tabulators provided the computing power that would help orchestrate the categorisation and movement of millions of people. This would allow disciplinary power to extend the management and coordination of individual bodies well beyond its institutional boundary. Once bodies had been extracted from the population and assembled in the camps, their utility was secured (during the 'extermination by labour' programme) by manipulating a system of dials on a machine that contained a card for every prisoner, each card divided into columns with punched holes designating their vital characteristics. These dials 'were adjusted to isolate certain professions, labour skills, age groups, or language abilities needed for work battalions'. The names of selected prisoners would be listed on a printout for 'transport to nearby sub-camps, factories, and even local farms'.[314]

* * *

Today, by contrast, candidates for work face the personality test. The punch-card tabulator developed for the concentration camp, and the personality test devised for the contemporary job seeker, may appear, at first sight, to be similar technologies, divided only by decades of technical refinement. The differences between them are crucial, however. To the extent that it examines more affective competencies, the personality test is distinct:

> Are you sensitive, conscientious, autonomous, gregarious or extroverted? Are you a lively and bubbly individual? Are you emotionally intelligent? Are you a team player? Are you a leader? What is your leadership style?

These are not specific labour skills, and could not be operationalised in the functional regime of the Nazi labour camp. In operational terms, a bubbly personality would be a ridiculous assignment. Personality tests are designed for a radically altered workplace where job requirements are just as diffuse as the competencies that are listed for them. The personality test only *simulates* the work of its predecessor, the labour camp tabulator. In today's radically altered environment, during a period that deals increasingly in simulations (thereby disguising the brute fact of labour exploitation), these competencies and personality traits multiply without restraint. Future employees 'log in' online of their own volition, to test themselves in advance, discovering personalities and traits that condition their workplace aspirations. These tests also occupy many idle moments. We learn to live with them lightly. They are titillating diversions that bear resemblance to the buttercup test: if you like butter, so it goes, the flower will reflect yellow light under your chin. It comes as no great shock, therefore, to hear that these tests and the competencies to which they refer are, in practical instrumental terms, meaningless.

*　*　*

An older colleague and I stand at a cash machine. He enters his pin code and waits for the money. A box containing a row of randomly changing digits appears at the centre of the screen. This throws him into a short-lived yet fiendish temper. 'What is the point! These numbers are meaningless!' he spits out. Being a member of the younger generation, I struggle to empathise. Perhaps they are designed to pass the time, I offer, as if a rationale would help. Perhaps they indicate that the machine is thinking or counting your money, I continue. They are indeed meaningless, I think in silence. And what is so enervating about that? My generation is accustomed to this experience.

*　*　*

At the opening ceremony of a Berlin factory in 1934, and in an exemplary combination of biopolitical and disciplinary themes, the manager of IBM's German subsidiary explained what was on offer to the Nazi regime:

> The physician examines the human body and determines whether...all organs are working to the benefit of the entire organism...We [IBM] are very much like the physician, in that we dissect, cell by cell, the German cultural body. We report every individual characteristic...on a little card. These are not dead cards, quite to the contrary, they prove later on that they come to life when the cards are sorted at a rate of 25,000 per hour according to certain characteristics. These characteristics are grouped like the organs of our cultural body, and they will be calculated and determined with the help of our tabulating machine. We are proud that we may assist in such a task, a task that provides our nation's Physician [Adolf Hitler] with the material he needs for his examinations. Our Physician can then determine whether the calculated values are in harmony with the health of our people. It also means that if such is not the case, our Physician can take corrective procedures to correct the sick circumstances...Our characteristics are deeply rooted in our race. Therefore, we must cherish them like a holy shrine, which we will – and must – keep pure. We have the deepest trust in our Physician and will follow his instructions in blind faith, because we know that he will lead our people to a great future. Hail to our German people and *der Führer!*[315]

Foucault refers at one point to the two great 'pathological forms' or 'diseases of power', these being Stalinism and fascism. One of the 'numerous reasons why they are so puzzling for us is that, in spite of their historical uniqueness, they are not quite original. They used and extended mechanisms already present in most other societies.' In spite of their own 'internal madness', they relied 'to a large extent' on 'the ideas and the devices of our political rationality'.[316] Reflecting on the Nazi State, Foucault concludes:

> No State could have more disciplinary power than the Nazi regime. Nor was there any other State in which the biological was so tightly, so insistently, regulated. Disciplinary power and biopower: all this permeated, underpinned, Nazi society.[317]

Whilst biopower alone cannot explain Nazi mobilisation, an account of this regime and its atrocities can illustrate how biopolitical and disciplinary logics were able to function together. Crucially, this regime made use of techniques of power and forms of knowledge that were already in existence. Foucault's provocation is to suggest that post-war welfare programmes designed to improve society also developed at their inception from similar assumptions and techniques. The point of this provocation is not to condemn post-war welfare by association. Rather, it is to demonstrate how a disposition of power persists through the shifting configurations it is able to adopt. These techniques extend across contexts and throughout great social upheavals. These strategies of power cannot be defeated as wars are won. They remain because they form us.

III
Meritocracies

Our Eugenic Religion

These are uncertain times, so we say. We have 'grown accustomed to our *angst'* – having become attached to the spirit of post-modernity which makes a virtue of our lack of commitment[1] – yet we still repeat, in a whole series of low, feeble tones expressive of our fear, that lives have become irregular, institutions unfathomable, and sociality impossibly diffuse. In this climate of lamentations, formed of statements that are themselves equally blurred, greater precision is required when speaking of present disorder. We require a genealogy of its prior construction.

*   *   *

Meritocracy has undergone its own dissolution; it has broken down into a less determinate, more fluid form. It has dissolved in the technical sense, where dissolution refers to the process by which a rigid structure becomes incorporated in a liquid. This development is far from benign. A fluid meritocracy is just as regulating as, perhaps more so than, its comparatively solid predecessor. This last collection of aphorisms explores how, with eugenic assistance, meritocracy developed as an insidious form of social regulation.

*   *   *

Dissolution also means to end, close down or dismiss. My contention is this: if meritocracy can no longer be held up as a timeless ideal against which we compare and judge our institutions, if it has a history, it is capable of further change, including its dismissal.

*   *   *

This final collection, which bears the title *Meritocracies*, would make little sense without the preceding histories contained in *Populations* and

Bodies. Initially confined to disciplinary institutions, a few decades into the nineteenth century modern examination was at the forefront of a rising awareness of populations. Bodies in their collective form appeared before the gaze of power, exhibiting their own unique characteristics and requirements. This new perception depended upon earlier procedures of disciplinary assessment that provided the data required to form this new level in operations of power. The collection of disciplinary apparatuses in that strategic hub, the modern examination, marked the high point of disciplinary power whilst generating the possibility for a transition towards a new biopolitical mode of power. Older forms endured, of course. Disciplinary precursors continued to operate in combination with biopower well into the twentieth century, even though biopower was in some respects their successor. It was here, in the relations between disciplinary power and biopower, that the histories of *Bodies* and *Populations* – one of institutional disciplinary artifice, the other of population-level government – could be seen to overlap and interlink. *Meritocracies*, adopts a similar approach, overlapping with these previous histories at key points, whilst charting a divergent field of development. In pursuing connections with eugenic discourse, the history of meritocracy borrows from *Populations* whilst extending beyond its endpoint in 1945 and the associated decline of openly eugenic projects. In the post-war years there was a shift from disciplinary artifice to the management of freedom. Though examination once distinguished itself as the archetypal technique of institutional control, over the twentieth century its reach extended far beyond its initial confinement. It came to invest the wider social body in a transformation that caused it to adopt a more fluid, less disciplinary form. The logic of assessment that examination established has come to occupy our minds, defining the frame through which we view one another and ourselves. Personal advancement and institutional reform are allowed greater freedom to operate, now that we interpret our actions within its pervading rationality.

* * *

The fragmentation of these histories is deliberate. It follows what Foucault once described as a 'methodology of discontinuity'.[2] The historian who emphasises historical continuities is treated here with suspicion. Traditional history is to be derided as a 'discipline by means of which the bourgeoisie showed that its reign was only the result, the product, the fruit of a slow maturation, and that this reign was thus perfectly justified, since it came from the mists of time'. To lay claim to historical truth, to emphasise continuity and ward off those who would seek to challenge this methodological imperium, is to ward off, by implication, threats of revolution.[3] By contrast, and in its revolutionary role (where genealogy serves as analytic companion to those activities and hopes that are, properly speaking, insurrectional), genealogy is preoccupied with exploring hidden breaks and concealed shifts. And yet, though Foucault had no difficulty in defining the beginning or end of a particular period of history as such, and was pleased to record such historical discontinuities where they were to be identified, these historical breaks were not treated as if they were complete (or incommensurable) ruptures. Instead, each break presents a problem: to investigate how the end of one period was to become the beginning of the next. Here Foucault sought to identify and describe the various transformations that enabled precisely this 'passage from one state to another'.[4] These periodisations overlap, of course, where each layer of historical events demands its own specific timeframe. Events occur in their own distinct time periods, and as we refine our analyses, multiplying the events with which we are concerned, these discontinuities also multiply.[5] 'History appears then not as a great continuity underneath an apparent discontinuity, but as a tangle of superimposed discontinuities.' In other words, history is shown to contain a multiplicity of timespans. This perspective avoids sweeping 'up all human phenomena in a single movement' and is entirely opposed to the biological view, which posits at 'the root of historical time … something like a biological evolution'. From this perspective, human societies 'have no other lawfulness, no other determination or regularity than life itself', which is to say that human societies are 'incapable of revolution'. Against this view, we must insist on the presence of many different timespans, each obeying its own laws and principles of development, each being the bearer of its associated events. One might say, in other words, that to grasp the discontinuity of events is to promote the transformation of societies.[6]

* * *

When histories of meritocracy and eugenics are divided into their respective phases, certain shared transitions become evident. The transformation of meritocracy into a more permissive, yet equally divisive, system of rewards was matched by a similar transformation in eugenic discourse. In 1938 both Wells and Cattell anticipated this switch, noting the liberal and religious potential of eugenic discourse. Indeed, from its very inception, eugenics was about far more than exclusions and exterminations; it was formed within a much wider and more constructive scheme. Recent commentators, who mistakenly ape Foucault by adopting a neo-Foucauldian display of intellectual restraint, would nevertheless seek to distance us from eugenics and consign it to the past. As Nikolas Rose has argued, if 'we are to be clear about the specificity of the present, beyond rhetoric', then we need to realise that eugenics was part of a biopolitical strategy that was specific to the first half of the twentieth century only. Eugenics is finished, he claims, and it makes little sense to invoke it in denouncing contemporary phenomena.[7] In its day, eugenics was confined to a 'rigid policing of the boundary between those in society and those who threatened it'.[8] The basic eugenic preoccupation was to segregate the subnormal. As such, it had little to contribute when it came to governing those who remained in society following such acts of subtraction. Admittedly, Rose concedes, eugenic strategies were sometimes connected with other approaches, such as medical 'neo-hygienist' strategies aimed at enhancing the home environment and the quality of mothering for those deemed normal. But, according to Rose, these neo-hygienist approaches were, nevertheless, of a different order:

Eugenics entails a direct coercive intervention into the sphere of personal existence, an intervention which operates by, first of all, ascertaining who is pathological, and how many such individuals there are, and secondly by removing and isolating these dangerous elements to prevent their number increasing further. This strategy works by an attempt to subtract, as it were, the pathological from the normal: it is negative and deductive. It leaves the 'normal' untouched, and where it does intervene into families to remove individuals its objective is to prevent such families from functioning, or rather malfunctioning, spawning more defective progeny ... But we have already seen that the neo-hygienist strategy is both wider in scope and more flexible in application than this. It certainly has disablement and segregation as one of the weapons in its armoury. But it does not limit itself to the neutralisation of this pathological minority; it aims rather to utilise its clinical expertise in a preventative way, through moralising, training, reforming those who fall within the range of the normal. To inject new norms of health and household management into the home through the instrument of the child. To make the family take on to itself the responsibility of its own hygiene.[9]

It is important to Rose that we limit eugenics both temporally and strategically. This is due to the evocative nature of the topic. Mainstream Foucauldians are conspicuously silent when it comes to more obvious and brutal manifestations of power. The lesson is this: in the analysis of power we must not overlook the mundane by focusing on the extreme, for it is in the mundane and everyday that we find the more treacherous operations of power. Eugenics is too obviously brutal; hence, Rose limits it to a negative project of biological subtraction. It is precisely because the neo-hygienist strategy retrospectively appears relatively benign (for, indeed, who

would argue against improving the home environment and the quality of mothering?) that Rose must demonstrate how hygiene has a 'potency and flexibility far beyond anything which psycho-eugenics could provide'.[10] To reveal the potency of neo-hygiene, Rose must prevent it from becoming overshadowed by eugenics. He must show that eugenics occupied a limited and dwindling realm.

*   *   *

Eugenics has long been condemned for its negative and deleterious tendencies. By the late 1930s the eugenic movement was increasingly threatened by association with Nazi practices[11] – an accusation that solidified once the enemy was confirmed as an enemy of the West. Suffering from the 'taint of fascism', its advocates were forced to adopt 'a policy of crypto-eugenics',[12] and the term once coined by Galton fell from active use. I have no intention of following this retreat of eugenics from acceptable discourse and transforming this investigation into one of underground, clandestine operations, where support for old schemes continues under new names. My interest, rather, is in the collapse of that alliance between biopolitical and disciplinary techniques, an alliance that defined the high watermark of eugenic practice. This process of collapse occupied much of the latter half of the twentieth century. The disciplinary excesses of this union would invite the most obvious revulsion, leaving the systematic abstractions of biopower relatively untouched. It was the physical manipulation of bodies that was objected to most clearly. This objection did not lead to a post-disciplinary era, though it did entail the development of a regime of power that relied less and less upon its disciplinary ancestry. This was not about the withdrawal of discipline, but about an expanding realm in which discipline became less important. The challenge I set is to investigate how technologies and perspectives born in the eugenic union – tests of individual difference and modes of statistical treatment – continued to operate once eugenics itself became taboo. Moving beyond discipline changes our focus to a concern with new modes of connection between biopolitical discourse and an evolving cluster of techniques that would manipulate bodies differently. Once discipline fell from favour, biopower attached itself to other individualising techniques that would serve as its replacement.

*   *   *

Galton would be the first to argue that eugenics should gain purchase on individuals through non-disciplinary means. Though punitive measures can be relied upon to prevent the 'free propagation' of poor stock, Galton felt that marriage should be left for individuals to organise. This would be productive so long as eugenic sense became common sense, forming 'one of the many considerations by which marriages are promoted or hindered, as they are by social position, adequate fortune, and similarity of creed'. If someone of 'exceptionally good stock' wishes to marry 'an inferior', this 'will be felt as derogatory' and hence such unions will become uncommon.[13] Finding a good eugenic match would become a matter of moral and civic obligation. Propelled by an enthusiasm for race improvement, this sense of duty could eventually develop into a sort of 'religious obligation'.[14] Major Leonard Darwin, son of Charles, put it like this:

> Eugenics demands self-sacrifice, and religion is indeed the only power which it can call to its aid in this respect.[15]

*   *   *

Religious tendencies themselves have eugenic effects, so we are told. Galton speculates that religion provided barbarian societies with 'sufficient cohesive force' to triumph over those groups with a lesser inclination towards superstition.[16] In today's societies, 'the social system of every nation including its religion' has 'adjusted itself into a position of stability that is dangerous to disturb. Deep sentiments and prejudices, habits and customs, all more or less entwined with the established religion of each nation, are elements of primary importance in the social fabric.'[17] And so, if we are to adjust the social order, Galton argues, we must acknowledge a role for religious senti-ments in human societies. Indeed, a 'national religion' could be established on eugenic lines.[18]

Here biopolitical logic receives an important addition. Religion itself is added to the list of natural human phenomena. It becomes just another natural social process to be accommodated as part of the overall biopolitical manipulation and government of populations. As a biopolitical strategy that aims to build upon natural processes and work with existing tendencies, eugenics must make use of these inherent religious inclinations. The best way of doing this, Galton claims, would be to absorb these religious tendencies within eugenics. Hence, Galton reconceives eugenics as if it were a national religion.

* * *

Galton was responding to a late nineteenth-century study by Benjamin Kidd. His book, titled *Social Evolution*, claimed that there is a non-rational dimension to social behaviour, a religious aspect that has been crucial to the progressive evolution of humankind.[19] These religious attributes promote doctrines that are beyond reason, that command unthinking support, and have the capacity to evoke socially useful behaviour. As a supplement to egotistical behaviour, these doctrines have been essential to human evolution, helping societies orient their members towards the good of the whole. Naturally, there is a hier-archy of religions. Of all the religions, Kidd finds that Christianity is by far the most progressive in promoting self-abnegation for the corporate good:

> The Christian religion possessed from the outset two characteristics destined to render it an evolutionary force of the first magnitude. The first was the extra-ordinary strength of the ultra-rational sanction it provided, which was developed throughout the long period we have been considering [the Middle Ages]. The second was the nature of the ethical system associated with it, which, as we shall see, was at a later stage in suitable conditions calculated to raise the peoples coming under its influence to the highest state of social efficiency ever attained, and to equip them with the most exceptional advantages in the struggle for existence with other peoples.[20]

Following Kidd, biopolitical governance would have to rely on more than rational administration and technical prudence. There are, he argued, deeply traditional yet eminently progressive social processes at work within human societies. These processes can, moreover, be linked to evolutionary developments. In regulating and enhancing human vitality, biopower has as much reason to be concerned with rites as with disciplinary technique.

* * *

Christianity was not the only religion with eugenic potential. A representative of *The Jewish Chronicle* was despatched to interview Galton shortly before his death. His report of the discussion is prefaced with the following hypothesis: 'It may be said that from the days of Moses Jews have been "eugenicists"...'

When asked by his interviewer whether 'the hygienic regulations of the Mosaic code have contributed to the fitness of the Jewish race', Galton was prepared to admit an indirect influence. He was less obliging when asked to comment on the likely eugenic effects of their historic persecution. Galton's preference is clear: positive techniques embedded within existing traditions are to be favoured against those instruments that are imposed against traditions and from without.[21]

*   *   *

This preference for positive methods is echoed, with greater urgency perhaps, in the work of Raymond Cattell. His claim is that whilst 'we can only cut off the tail of stragglers by direct eugenic methods; we must leave to culture the breeding of vanguard qualities'.[22] The best hope for eugenics is to embed a eugenic sensibility in the free action of individuals, and to rely on compulsory action only in the most extreme cases. This would achieve a far closer match between birth rate and fitness, where fitness depends upon the present requirements of civilisation. Eugenic activity must become an intrinsic part of the day-to-day self-regulation of individuals.

A 'social revolution' is within our grasp, Cattell implores, if only we can develop a widespread commitment to the happiness of those yet to be born; a commitment that is driven by the condition that they 'shall be fit for the world' in which they will live; for happiness and fitness, Cattell claims, are intimately linked.[23] This cultivated love for the unborn may result in 'the greatest turning-point in the history of the human race' at least since the advent of Christianity. A eugenic religion, promoting love for unborn children, could even be considered as 'a continuation of Christianity, an extension of its values to the field of the unborn'.[24] Indeed, Cattell went so far as to claim that 'Christianity is impossible without eugenics, or, rather, eugenics is a growth of Christianity.'[25] This eugenic development of Christian sentiment 'as love of the best in man' (rather than love and propagation to all, feeble and strong alike) would substitute for the 'reckless, cruel and wasteful methods of Nature the humane control of kindness and reason'. At last, a 'thoroughly Christian treatment of the defective' would be possible, for 'the defective' could be given the best available care and support once one is assured that further propagation is impossible.[26] When the 'admitted ideal of civilization' is to 'shift regulation entirely to the individual',[27] the eugenic visionary must realise that the 'maintenance of morality by conscience' is the key.[28] Guided by religion, we would live

ethical eugenic lives, concerning ourselves with the quality of our children, and regulating ourselves accordingly.

*   *   *

Even though the eugenic cause was soon to be discredited, this appeal to religion provides a clue to the endurance of its more fundamental eugenic rationality. Envisaged by Cattell as an extension of Christianity and Christian values into the realm of the unborn, the developing eugenic rationality recalls a more ancient, pastoral regime from which it draws inspiration.

According to Foucault's tentative genealogy, whilst Ancient Greece sought to establish the unity of the city-state, the Hebraic tradition developed a more dispersed, pastoral approach to government. For the Greeks, state power and pastoral responsibility lay in separate domains, and so pastoral care remained outside the activities of statecraft. More than two millennia would pass before there was a fusion between state power and pastoral control. This demonic combination offered modern states huge potential to extend their activities.[29]

The recent fusion of state power and pastoral control relied upon its Christian precursors. Christianity appropriated and developed Hebraic pastoral techniques. These became highly individualised, designed to govern in a continuous and permanent way. In the shepherd–flock game of the Christian pastorate, the shepherd wields power over the flock in a way that guarantees the flock's existence. This form of power aims to ensure, sustain and improve the lives of each and every member through individualised concern. It is oriented towards the good of the flock, keeping watch and basing its supervision on the intimate knowledge constant observation allows. Within the flock, 'total obedience, knowledge of oneself, and confession to someone else' were to be combined.[30]

* * *

Pastoral power, with its attention to the 'good of the flock', sounds vaguely biopolitical. It was, though, the technique of a pre-scientific age when the 'good of the flock' was not defined in scientistic terms. Following the modern development of biopower with its statistical perceptions of population health, pastoral power was, nevertheless, redefined and reinvested for a secular age. It was placed within a biopolitical scheme, where the good of the flock, defined formerly in theological terms, becomes equivalent to the biological and statistically measurable health of the population. Kidd made an important step forward in this respect when he naturalised religion and gave it a key evolutionary role in the development of human societies.

* * *

Techniques of pastoral supervision were put to use by modern educators such as David Stow, long before the appeals to religion of Galton, Kidd or Cattell. The moral training school was already organised in response to its rough simulation of the street, the playground, where children would reveal their natural dispositions for subsequent modification in the gallery. In this respect, it differed from the monitorial school, which paid scant attention to the pre-existing, natural states of its subjects. Here the moral training school anticipated later biopolitical developments. Importantly, though, whilst it is true that the moral training school governed its subjects by responding to their natural dispositions, its moral code was not derived from the population that it sought to guide. It paid attention to the natural dispositions displayed by pupils at play, but then inflicted its own independent morality upon them. The ambiguous circularity of biopower, whereby moral principles are derived from the population under study, was not evident here. The moral training school only attended to natural dispositions so as to better replace them with its theological principles. When Galton, Kidd and Cattell speak of religious potential they invoke a very different logic of correction. Whilst they recognised the beneficial effects of existing traditions and moral codes, these traditions would ultimately face judgement before their evolutionary jury. Only those traditions judged to convey an evolutionary edge were to be supported. And so, when pastoral power was inserted within the biopolitical logic, its theological principles of moral guidance were revised so that they would refer to scientific principles and statistical truths. These truths now provided the substance for its basic tenets. Pastoral guidance was only supportable within a biopolitical scheme if its principles of self-regulation were shown to advance the collective good, where the collective good is defined in scientistic terms.

In suggesting that Christianity bore the potential to go beyond disciplinary artifice in the eugenic scheme, both Galton and Cattell lead us to reconsider the operation of pastoral power in this context. It is necessary to examine how a form of pastoral power that promotes self-regulation is able to adjust when it is situated within the biopolitical scheme. In its earlier form, pastoral power operated by combining confession, or the ability to construct and divulge certain truths about oneself, with standards of conduct set by a moral exemplar. It was a matter of revealing the truth of one's spiritual self and comparing this truth with the ideal self. By contrast, in its emergent twentieth-century mode, confession would increasingly come to refer to a scientific rather than spiritual truth about the self.

*   *   *

In the eyes of its most perceptive supporters, the survival of eugenics would depend on these new relations of power, where a population-level awareness becomes attached to the self-regulating practices of individuals. As Cattell explained, religious techniques would be crucial to the cause: eugenics 'should not throw away the great, slow-built, emotional attitudes, with all their poetry and wealth of human associations, which have grown up through the centuries around the concept of God'.[31] Eugenics must adopt from religion an adjusted, pastoral mode of power whereby individuals willingly submit themselves and the details of their lives to a higher authority. Cattell argued that these individual acts of submission must orientate themselves towards an adjusted religious creed. As the 'greatest turning-point in the history of the human race' since the advent of Christianity,[32] this new religion was to be accompanied by a new conception of God, whereupon God ceases to be a transcendental being. His symbolic form is located in the material realities of our universe. In Cattell's view, this new entity, which we will soon come to identify as 'God', is to be linked to an age-old accumulation of human effort. It is a being to be found in the 'collective mind' to which we are all unwittingly linked, an entity he calls our 'Theopsyche'. This psychic entity is the legacy and continuing project of all good human action, where 'Goodness is the human tendency towards progress.'[33]

> This God which is all that is altruistic, intelligent, wise, powerful, courageous, and unselfish in the group mind of man is a reality in the fullest

sense. We meet it in every kind action, every effort to discover further secrets of the universe, every creation of beauty, and every sacrifice for a super-personal object. It lives in the idealistic organisation of all minds, and each one of us is part of it in proportion to his idealism.[34]

This 'Theopsyche' is a God that has grown out of our collective labours. The accumulated result of individual efforts towards progress, it has developed into a reality that anticipates and outlives all of us. Whilst it may have been formed of human interaction, it is ultimately based in nature: 'It perishes in part if mankind perishes, but it is inherent in matter and will emerge again.'[35] It 'has its roots in the material cosmos from which it is an emergent', and so we must conclude that the 'worship of nature is one with the worship of God'.[36] It is to this deification of the human project that individual conscience is to be wedded. Religious overtures will now prepare individual lives for acts of devotion that are to be coordinated with the overall progress of humanity. With an updated conception of religion, eugenics can draw upon forces far more pervasive than mere techniques of disciplinary compulsion. Individuals will adopt procedures of self-examination and a willingness to confess, all of which is ruled by absolute submission to the eugenic creed.

This is a bold extension into the religious realm of that strain of moral naturalism earlier identified in Pearson,[37] where that which is good is that which promotes overall social welfare. We find again with Cattell that evil deeds are those that are 'opposed to group welfare',[38] and sin is a 'failure to make the best out of the whole race'.[39] All calculations of welfare are to be framed in evolutionary terms.

Whilst Pearson believed that only very few are 'capable of being really moral', for only they would be 'in possession of all that is known of the laws of human development', Cattell appears to be more optimistic. By adopting religion and reformulating God, we may all come to worship and obey 'a super-individual consciousness with which the individual can maintain a communion'.[40] In theory, any individual may contribute in a positive fashion to the group project, just as any individual may enter the more conventional religious fold. Of course, from the eugenic perspective, relative contribution is dictated by the normal distribution, where 'the lower variant' can 'achieve happiness and avoid criminal self-assertion by [direct] submission', whilst 'the upper variant' is 'rescued from cynicism and despair' by commitment to the communal project towards which all genius will turn with religious fervour.[41] Across the spectrum of human variability, we will be governed by our emotional commitment to a religion of human progress. Everyone will seek to contribute according to what is deemed biopolitically good and beneficial. And all troubles and hardships will be justified as necessary steps through the reassuringly circular logic of biblical discourse:

And we know that in all things God works for the good of those who love him, who have been called according to his purpose.[42]

*   *   *

In a secular context, the indifference of the statesman to the plight of the individual transforms pastoral power. There is an eventual separation of the shepherd from his flock, allowing the flock to roam without direct supervision. The abiding hope is that the flock maintains a conscience and commitment to self-rule that is in line with the dominant rationality. In many places the shepherd disappears, but the function of shepherd as moral exemplar continues in the guise of its ideological successor, which holds aloft any activity that promotes population well-being and collective security.

*   *   *

Cattell hoped that the scientific expert would replace an erstwhile pastorate in guiding us towards the social good. As he put it, 'society must have an adequate supply of watchers in the field of sociological and psychological research in order that the consequences of modified moral laws may be accurately worked out'.[43] This mode of mandarin rule, one that takes overall well-being as its driving aim, would rely upon a substructure of motivated (rather than disciplined) individuals. It would depend upon a common drive that would be expressed in the day-to-day commitments of its members, through a mixture of obedience and a desire to do good, as defined by the latest scientific morality.

*   *   *

The strategic polyvalence of biopolitical discourse allows shifts in priority, where the place occupied by population health is occasionally given over to a concern for economic vitality. Here, action on the population in the name of overall economic well-being adopts a logic of action established by those projects that were in pursuit of collective biological health.

The separation between eugenic pursuits and economic ones was never absolute. Galton, as we have seen, speculated about the economic value of children to the state.[44] The eugenic movement was itself closely associated with early twentieth-century efforts to secure 'national efficiency', where executive control, coupled with the wisdom of science, was to fulfil this aim.[45] In the United States, the enhancement of population health was advanced as a partial solution to the problems of economic stagnation.[46] In Britain, it was argued that birth control for poorer stocks offered a solution to unemployment.[47] In Germany, the unfit were already in 1911 referred to as the *Minderwertigen* – a term meaning 'those of inferior value' – whereupon efforts were made to estimate the cost of the unfit to state and society.[48] Nazi propaganda would later revile disabled people in terms of their cost:

> *60000 Reichsmarks kostet dieser Erbkranke die Volksgemeinschaft auf Lebenseit! Volksgenoffe das ist auch Dein Geld!*
>
> Sixty thousand Reichsmarks is what this person suffering from inherited defects costs the Community of Germans during his lifetime. Fellow Citizen, that is your money, too! [49]

Such horrific statements are far from unique. In our century, the undeserving poor, the scroungers, skivers and shirkers – those who lack the virtuous drives of bourgeois aspiration – are said to live lives of abject, self-imposed torpor that can and must be measured against the heavy costs they impose on the taxpayer.

*   *   *

These are only the more obvious manifestations of a connection between eugenic rationality and the pursuit of economic health. Behind lies a history in which eugenic rationalities and meritocratic schemes developed complex and evolving relationships. At one point they were tied to that mutual reinforcement between biopolitical and disciplinary techniques, an alignment between modes of power that defined interwar eugenic history. Early meritocratic schemes sought to increase overall economic productivity by dividing, classifying, training and reassembling the population in a more efficient form. This would all change. Following the decline of conventional eugenics, and the reduced dependence of biopower on discipline, it was necessary to devise a replacement scheme for the formation of individual subjectivities.

During the last two decades of the twentieth century, with disciplinary techniques occupying a diminishing position in the meritocratic order, subjects were encouraged to adopt a new kind of economic morality. This morality would seek to guide subjects on an individual basis through the diffuse economic activities of everyday life. The social order for which they are prepared increasingly operates in the realm of appearances. To be favoured are those individual and collective actions that merely *look as though* they promote economic vitality. This cultivates an individual mindset from which it has become much harder to perceive the insistent demand to pursue economic returns as an ethic subservient to its capitalist master. In late modernity, the pursuit of economic returns has become profoundly disordered, having abandoned its older utopian aspiration to high functionality and efficiency in production, in favour of a chaotic economy of frantic individual pursuits. This, in brief, is our eugenic religion.

The Occasional Hero

Jeremy Bentham's *Constitutional Code* of 1830 outlines a system, both rigid and mechanical, for the allocation of government posts. By integrating a question book, tickets, ticket board, cylindrical box and non-discerning child within the overall mechanics of employment, it was hoped that rigor in assigning posts could be assured. The manner of delivery from examination to job would be direct. Examination was to convey candidates straight to their posts, in a way that maximised human resources and minimised cost.[50] In the decades that followed, the guiding idea was to generate an efficient distribution of human talent through direct and prescriptive means. The radical proposition of the era was to reorganise society in a way that assured the prevailing social hierarchy accurately reflected the hierarchy of talent found within a population. During the second half of the twentieth century this mechanistic system was radically overhauled through a whole series of refinements that would in the end break it open and force it to embrace complexity. A fluid meritocracy operating according to a completely different governmental logic came to rule. The efficient distribution of human resources no longer mattered as it once had. Achieving a perfect match between the social hierarchy and the hierarchy of talent ceased to be the driving aim. Instead, individuals were expected to relocate themselves; social redistribution became *their responsibility*.

*   *   *

Today's Left-leaning liberal has been the victim of a facile parody.[51] This individual is said to believe that 'all can have prizes'. Nobody is to be written off by the system. All individuals will be able to achieve if they are given the opportunity to do so. ...

Whilst these reactionary quips may contain a grain of truth, describing to some extent the ethic of our times, the inclusive-sounding rhetoric that is attacked here has no chance of translating itself into an egalitarian reality, as its opponents seem to fear. Against this rhetoric, we must insist that a fluid meritocracy remains highly organised and highly regulating. It is a system of government that uses liberal Left sentiment as a cloak. Far from being the consequence of muddled egalitarian ideals, our contemporary predicament is shaped by an extended and divisive regime of power. Its ancillary function is to conceal widening inequalities.

*   *   *

A fluid meritocracy is achieved when the free movement of individuals conforms to its aspirational rhetoric, a switch that is accompanied by the disappearance of those more obvious machinations of power that once held them in check. It is a system where a particular conception of 'freedom' has come to rule. By contrast, location systems such as Bentham's were essentially rigid, adopting a disciplinary logic of design. In 1830, Bentham stood at the dawn of a traditional conception of meritocracy. At this point the utopian aspiration of disciplinary power was shared by a traditional meritocracy, where bodies 'trained to function part by part for particular operations' would be combined to 'form an element in a mechanism at another level'. Disciplined through the coding and sequencing of their activities, located in analytic pedagogies of rank and progression, these bodies could now become 'part of a multi-segmentary machine'. The dream of disciplinary power, which was also the dream of traditional meritocracy, was to 'construct a machine whose effect will be maximised by the concerted articulation of the elementary parts of which it is composed'.[52] The mechanical allocation of jobs, if fully realised, would be the perfect realisation of disciplinary schooling.

* * *

Eugenic thinkers were quick to adopt vocational location as a biopolitical tool. In *Feeble-mindedness: Its Causes and Consequences*, Henry Goddard admits that a campaign of mass institutionalisation or sterilisation would be politically and practically impossible, for two very practical reasons. First, feeble-mindedness was seen as far too widespread for such measures. Second, many apparently normal human beings were thought to transmit feeble-mindedness as a recessive trait. Goddard concludes that the problem must be managed from within society by adjusting the demands of the social environment to the mental age of the individuals concerned. A vocational machine was required, one that would work alongside and complement more severe eugenic incisions. This machine could be justified in the name of 'self-defense if for no other reason'.[53] Admittedly, Goddard adds, it would also prevent the 'unjust and cruel' situation whereby society allows low-grade individuals with childlike intelligence to fall into lives of poverty and vice.[54]

Based upon his experiences at an institution for the feeble-minded, Goddard decides that so-called 'idiots' would always require custodial care, and 'imbeciles', with an intelligence of three to seven years, really ought to be institutionalised in one form or another. The range of useful tasks they can perform are narrow, he argued, and even these tasks are limited to the more able imbecile who could, perhaps, do little errands in the house, wash the dishes, and dust. Only simple tasks of short duration should be assigned. The so-called 'moron', of between eight to twelve years in mental age, will be of greater use. Under supervision a range of simple industrial tasks become possible, from scrubbing, mending and caring for the bathroom to simple jobs involving machinery. Whilst the high-grade moron 'cannot plan', supervision may become occasional, or be removed entirely

INDUSTRIAL CLASSIFICATION

MENTAL AGE	INDUSTRIAL CAPACITY	GRADE	
Under 1 year	(*a*) Helpless. (*b*) Can walk. (*c*) With voluntary regard	Low	Idiot
1 yr.	Feeds self. Eats everything	Middle	
2 yrs.	Eats discriminatingly (food from non-food)	High	
3 "	No work. Plays a little	Low	Imbecile
4 "	Tries to help		
5 "	Only simplest tasks	Middle	
6 "	Tasks of short duration. Washes dishes	High	
7 "	Little errands in the house. Dusts		
8 "	Errands. Light work. Makes beds	Low	Moron
9 "	Heavier work. Scrubs. Mends. Lays bricks. Cares for bath-room		
10 "	Good institution helpers. Routine work	Middle	
11 "	Fairly complicated work with only occasional oversight	High	
12 "	Uses machinery. Can care for animals. No supervision for routine work. Cannot plan		

for routine tasks. For our convenience, these levels of 'industrial capacity' are summarised in a table defining how those at the outer fringe of normality will be put to work.[55]

*   *   *

The eugenic argument for meritocracy runs like this: if we cannot remove all defectives from society, we must identify their kind and care for them within society, demanding of them no more than their capabilities allow. A 'registration bureau' will be required, where the grades of all persons of suspect mind will be recorded. In the meantime, schools will have to serve in this capacity.[56] Appropriate training will be provided, taking care not to teach more than any particular child is judged able to learn. Whilst they have so far been a burden to society, with proper care this would all change and we might eventually come to value such large numbers of high-grade morons. When properly managed, they will be 'able and willing to do much of the drudgery of the world, which other people will not do'.[57] Employers will allocate jobs according to the mental capacities of applicants, placing workers in positions that suit their ability. Thus, examination will decide job allocation in the direct Benthamite sense. Graded individuals will be matched to graded jobs.

*   *   *

Goddard's industrial classifications were limited by the scope of his book, which was exclusively concerned with the lower fringe of normality. Cyril Burt, by contrast, widely viewed as the first *educational* psychologist, would later extend the logic Goddard applied to the feeble-minded, so that it would encompass the entire range of human capacity, from so-called idiot to genius.

Burt claimed that expert vocational guidance should be offered at an early age, whereupon every child 'should be made the subject of special study', following which the child is then 'recommended to enter, or to train for, that particular type of occupation for which (so far as can be judged) he seems by mental constitution best adapted'.[58] These specific recommendations would be buttressed by large-scale studies that could define the 'optimal range of intelligence' for various occupations 'with an upper limit as well as a lower'.[59] These occupations would then be organised in a manner that corresponds with the normal distribution of intelligence. As a preliminary hypothesis, designed to inform these future research efforts, Burt arranged vocations into eight categories, where *Category VIII* contains those here defined as unemployable:

> I. Higher professional (0.1%)
> II. Lower professional (3%)
> III. Clerks and highly skilled workers (12%)
> IV. Skilled workers (27%)
> V. Semi-skilled labour (36%)
> VI. Unskilled labour, etc. (19%)
> VII. Casual labour, etc. (3%)
> VIII. Imbeciles and idiots (0.2%)

According to this carefully engineered 'discovery', the proportions of a population engaged in these various positions follow the normal distribution. The majority were to be found in *Category V*, with only a fraction of a per cent to be found in the highest and lowest categories. These minorities were the distant outliers of the employment curve.[60] With jobs classified in this way, it would be a matter of fitting applicants to jobs in a manner that would involve perfect fit between the distribution of intelligence and the distribution of jobs. Around the mean or average, difficulties increase, though not in a way that contravenes the overall principle of allocation. For the large bulk of the population which is clustered in this central area, Burt envisaged that tests of special abilities would supplement tests of general ability. This would facilitate the finer distinction of such a large and closely matched group.

Overall, these technologies would rationalise an irrational system of vocational guidance where 'the predominating element in the choice of occupation' had hitherto been 'the wish or the whim of the parent and of the child'. Irrational motivations are said to include 'selfish' desires for a 'quick financial return', potentially misplaced though 'fond ambitions', 'gossip' and 'fantasies'. The average parent also suffers from a 'lack of psychological insight' and 'cannot possibly have the range of information necessary for a satisfactory choice'. [61] Teachers often fill this gap in expertise, but 'the teacher is an educational not an industrial expert, and of all the professions his is perhaps the least in contact with the world of business'.[62] According to Burt, a centralised administrative machinery making use of precise and rational techniques was urgently required.

*   *   *

The disciplinary element of these schemes consists in their effort to achieve the most utopian objective faced by disciplinary power, which is to bring partitioned lives into a state of mutual synergy, to 'construct a machine whose effect will be maximised by the concerted articulation of the elementary parts of which it is composed'.[63] In this context the machine is no longer the individual disciplinary institution. It is to be much larger, containing a variety of institutions distributed throughout the socio-economic order, all working in sync with one another. The production of docile subjects is now matched to a national endeavour that seeks the perfection of its meritocratic distributions.

*   *   *

Burt describes a factory involving 'trade-processes of two different levels of difficulty, the one dull and mechanical, consisting mainly in the minding of machines, the other demanding alertness and resource, and consisting mainly in the arranging and packing of delicate articles in fancy boxes'. All employees were required to take an intelligence test in an experiment seeking to enhance the allocation of employees to posts. The prevention of intellectual wastage was on the agenda, but it was not the only concern:

Whilst it is 'sufficiently obvious' that 'the unintelligent girl would not only be slow and incompetent, but possibly spoil half the material that she handled' in the more demanding post, it is less obvious but just as important to note 'that the bright and active girl put on to dull mechanical work would become irregular and discontented', possibly disturbing 'her fellow-workers by the overflow of her superfluous energy'. In effect, a poor match between a person's ability and the assigned industrial task may lead to distraction. Burt claims that such low-level disruption could be prevented by rationalising the distribution of workers according to an assessment of their intelligence. In the factory experiment, we are told that this was achieved 'without dismissing a single employee'. The 'output and quality of work' were 'enormously increased'.[64] Regrettably for Burt and those like him, industrial experiments such as these were comparatively rare.

*   *   *

Goddard was also of the opinion that incorrect vocational allocation was endemic to the system. Again we find that efficiency is not the only issue at stake. Misallocation could lead to, or at least exacerbate, worker unrest.

> When one contemplates the enormous proportion of misfits that must exist in the industrial world and that such misfits mean discontent and unhappiness for the employee, one can but wonder how much of the present unrest in such circles is due to this fact. A man who is doing work that is well within the capacity of his intelligence and yet that calls forth all his ability is apt to be happy and contented and it is very difficult to disturb any such person by any kind of agitation.[65]

The rationale here was that careful, scientific and benevolent management of human societies is required in order to provide the appropriate environment for each type of person, and thereby prevent disquiet. Each must be assigned his or her place in society according to his or her ability. The normal distribution of intelligence renders any effort to seek equality of condition senseless, even dangerous for those raised above their station. Equality would torment lower types who are unable to cope in an environment that demands more intelligence than they have to offer. Some types require custodial care, others supervision, and the mediocre majority need to realise that in societies as complex as ours expert guidance and intelligent rule is required if we are to achieve well-being. Vast differences in intelligence force advanced societies to become unequal. These societies are, nevertheless, fair if these inequalities reflect innate intelligence. In other words, advanced societies are those that are both unequal and meritocratic. Each person must take his or her place in a social hierarchy of merit, responsibility and influence, where this positioning reflects relative ability:

> Socialism[66] is a beautiful theory but the facts must be faced. One of the facts is that people differ in mentality and that *each mentality requires its own kind of life for its success and happiness.*[67]

Democracy, for Goddard, is a far better formula than socialism in that it recognises the inequality of man. The democratic challenge is to maximise liberty whilst engaged in the pursuit of collective well-being. The 'greatest liberty and the highest happiness is only attained when each individual is properly adjusted to the rest'. A 'perfect democracy is only to be realized when it is based upon absolute knowledge of mental levels and the organization of the social body on that basis'.[68]

Observable once again is the 'dark side' of democratic political reform, where the creation of 'an explicit, coded and formally egalitarian juridical framework, made possible by the organization of a parliamentary, representative régime', is mirrored by insidious disciplinary powers.[69] These are the meritocratic and disciplinary arrangements that Henry Goddard brings to the fore in his deliciously candid text. Democracy, for Goddard, is dependent on achieving a good match between each individual and a social environment that is appropriate to his or her abilities. Only under controlled conditions such as these can liberty and happiness be achieved.

* * *

The democratic relation established between citizens in a system that is necessarily unequal but, in principle, open to all along principles of merit conceals operations of power that have, as Foucault argues, 'the precise role of introducing insuperable asymmetries'. The formal assurance of equality of opportunity is mirrored by the disciplines, which 'characterize, classify, specialize' and 'distribute along a scale'. Operating behind our celebrated ideals is a machinery of more specific normative discretions, a machinery 'that is both immense and minute, which supports, reinforces, multiplies the asymmetry of power'. Hence the importance given to the sciences that provide this process with its 'respectable face; hence the fear of abandoning them if one cannot find any substitute; hence the affirmation that they are at the very foundation of society, and an element in its equilibrium'.[70]

* * *

We ask with bewilderment: How could we ever live without science? How could advanced democratic societies *not* be meritocratic? How could they *not* assess, classify and allocate according to a regrettable, though necessary, vocational hierarchy? How could a perfected democracy avoid this necessity that people of ability are assigned to positions of responsibility and influence, positions that are appropriate to their talents?

* * *

Despite the great optimism that is displayed in their schematic outlines, each method of job allocation, from Bentham through Goddard to Burt, would eventually fail to find its way into practice. Nevertheless, each method demonstrates a particular logic for advance by merit, a logic that lay behind early efforts to replace patronage. Early meritocratic logic and subsequent arrangements were rigid and hierarchical, and essentially disciplinary.

* * *

It has been said that the earliest meritocratic developments were 'peculiarly aristocratic'.[71] An exemplary case would be the civil service arrangements employed during British colonial rule of India. As the Earl of Cromer recollected in 1911, the aim of reform was to 'acquire for the public service' an 'aristocracy, in the proper and original sense of the term; that is to say, not the aristocracy of birth, but that of intellect and of character'.[72] 'Aristocracy', we are reminded, comes from the Greek *aristokratia*, combining *aristos* 'best' with *-kratia* meaning 'power' or 'rule'. It was imperative to ensure that representatives of 'an imperial race' were of the highest calibre,[73] a mission which could not be assured in the bad old days of patronage:

> I am one of the band, not now very numerous, who can speak with some personal experience of the pre-competition days...Some fifty-six years ago, being then a boy of fourteen, I was admitted into the Royal Military Academy at Woolwich...At that time there was a sort of sham entrance-examination, but I never heard of any boy who had been nominated by the Master-General of the Ordinance being rejected. Lord Hardinge, the grandfather of the present Viceroy of India, who was a friend of my family, gave me my nomination. On presenting myself at Woolwich for medical examination, I was very rightly rejected for short sight. I returned to London and told my mother, who was my only surviving parent. She acted with promptitude. She instantly rang the bell, ordered her carriage, and went to the Horse Guards to see Lord Raglan...another friend of the family. The result was that next day I returned to Woolwich with a letter addressed by Lord Raglan to the medical officer, asking him to 'reconsider the matter.' I was, of course admitted...The practical working of the system may, however, best be illustrated by an anecdote which is related to Lord Melbourne. A friend of his who occupied a high position and who disposed of a good deal of patronage, said to him: 'I do not in the least mind confessing that if I had to deal with two candidates, one of whom was the son of a friend or relation of mine, and the other was a stranger, I should, *ceteris paribus*, give the appointment to the son of my friend or relation.' To which Lord Melbourne dryly replied, 'So should I, but *ceteris paribus* be d – – d'.[74]

* * *

The civil service examinations of the mid-nineteenth century were intended to establish open competition 'in such a manner that no part of the kingdom, and no class of schools, shall exclusively furnish' those who would rule India.[75] To this end a range of subjects were offered for examination in order to prevent bias against the curricula of any particular class of school. Nevertheless, up to 1500 marks were available for knowledge of Latin and Greek, and up to 1000 for Mathematics, whereas only a maximum of 500 were available to natural science. In this respect the examinations faithfully reflected the dominance of Classics and Mathematics at Oxford and Cambridge.[76] Only those who attended institutions of this sort would be able to compete in these more lucrative subject areas. It was claimed, nevertheless, that knowledge of the Classics and Mathematics was not essential. By 1876, 11 candidates from a total of 894 succeeded in gaining entrance 'without showing any knowledge of Latin, or Greek, or mathematics'.[77] The figures are hardly encouraging.

Later in the same report it is admitted that 'a large proportion of the appointments [still] fall into the hands of youths connected with India by birth or parentage', though it is assumed that 'such youths, having more reasons than others for wishing to go to India, make greater exertions to attain their wish'.[78] Of the '668 civilians sent out to India between 1860 and 1874, as large proportion as 78 per cent were the sons of parents belonging to the aristocracy, gentry, army, navy, Indian Civil Service, or one of the learned professions'.[79] This affirmation of social hierarchy seems entirely in accord with that other desire of its architects: to admit only those who 'have received the best, the most liberal, the most finished education that his native country affords'. The requisite knowledge would be that which typical 'English gentlemen' choose to cultivate.[80]

* * *

As Terry Eagleton once quipped: 'In the bad old days, it was assumed that culture was something that you needed to have in the blood.' 'Countless generations of breeding' went into the formation of 'gentlemen'. The cultured disposition of these natural rulers 'was not really something you could acquire, any more than you could acquire a second pair of eyebrows or learn how to have an erection'.[81] The cultured elites just were, simply, elite. We should not downplay, therefore, the significance of this shift to a test of acquired competence. A battle was fought on this terrain, where reform efforts were constantly restrained and conditioned by preconceived ideals of gentility.

* * *

In late nineteenth-century England access to education was stratified verti-
cally by class and by wealth. The labouring poor attended elementary schools
until their early teens, whilst the middle and upper classes had the benefit
of secondary schooling until a later age. Secondary education was divided
into elite schools for those aiming at the professions, and less expensive
schooling for those who could not make 'gentlemen' of their boys or 'ladies'
of their girls and yet were not willing for their children to associate in school
with children of the labouring poor. Their children would aspire to commercial and clerical occupations.[82] The curricula on offer varied greatly, with
a proper teaching of the Classics reserved for the higher echelons. Unless
parents could afford to send their offspring to the right sort of school, or
could pay for an intensive period of 'cramming', civil service examinations
were well beyond reach. Initially, only university graduates were encouraged to take the Indian Civil Service examination. The architects of this
scheme thought it 'desirable that a considerable number of the civil servants' should be 'men who have taken the first degree in arts at Oxford and
Cambridge'.[83] It was felt that in 'the two great ancient languages there ought
to be an examination not less severe than those examinations by which the
highest classical distinctions are awarded'.[84] Clearly, with entrance defined
by such lofty criteria, great challenges faced those who would never enter
an Oxbridge quadrangle.

* * *

British candidates would only apply for the most senior appointments in the
Indian Civil Service. All other workers were recruited from the indigenous
population. For the Home Civil Service the situation was more complex,
as all grades of work were open to the British candidate. As a result, reform
proceeded at a much slower pace and sporadic, limited competition between
select nominees was initially favoured above comprehensive, 'open' competition, which was eventually introduced in 1870. In theory, there would
be two schemes of assessment and two levels of post. The first-class posts
would be limited in number, and their examinations would focus upon the
curricula of that highest class of school, the English public school.[85] The
great bulk of recruitment would be for subordinate clerks who were to be
examined in handwriting, spelling, arithmetic, bookkeeping, geography
and history, areas for which the sort of training offered by 'a commercial
education' would be most suited.[86]

* * *

The distinction between higher and lower-division clerks maintained a
basic hierarchy in the civil service. Lower-division clerks complained that
'members of the lower class are almost ineligible for promotion into the

higher'. They argued that a system in which there is little hope for advancement causes those of the lower division to 'degenerate' into 'mere routine'.
In order 'to stimulate the zeal of the junior members it is necessary that
each should feel himself more than a mere machine'. 'Great class feeling
and jealousy are engendered by the present distinction, and harmony and
efficiency seriously impaired.'[87] In situations such as these, 'no machinery
or supervision, however elaborate, can so well promote economy and efficiency in large establishments as contented officials, animated by hope'.[88] If
only the civil service could be reconfigured in a way that would allow it to
operationalise desire, making use of this impulse for advancement. If only
it could adopt aspirational hope as its operational logic, efficiency would be
assured – or so their argument implied.

The riposte of the higher clerk is to insist that 'it would generally be
acknowledged that a man with a public school and university training is,
prima facie, more capable' of undertaking duties involving 'responsibility,
discretion and power to direct'. Men of this calibre are better able to 'uphold
the credit and efficiency of their Departments' than those with little more
than 'a board school education'.[89] Here lines were clearly drawn along
explicit class boundaries. It seemed that only efficiency arguments invoking
the animating effects of hope could threaten to reform a rigid hierarchy.

The homogeneity of recruits was, nonetheless, hard to maintain. The
diversity of applicants was on the increase, with second-class clerkships
attracting a growing number of competitors. In the mid-1870s, the proportion of competitors to vacancies was about three to one. By 1884 this reached
eleven to one. Responding to the pressures of high demand, special agencies
had been established to provide coaching to those who could just about
afford it, gradually breaking down the deliberate hierarchy of the examination syllabi. These special agencies offered a new mode of education that
came to be feared as instrumental and dangerously effective. Cramming, as
it came to be called, was now 'rampant'.[90]

*   *   *

In the higher class of India appointments there were similar fears: it was
felt that 'methods of special preparation' failed to 'impart sound and well-
digested knowledge', being 'directed solely to obtaining the largest possible
number of marks from the examiners'. And so it was suggested that a certain
proportion of appointments should be reserved for university graduates, to
maintain a direct connection with these institutions, and thereby maintain the calibre of recruits. Those responsible for the examination system
disagreed. Special preparation was indeed common, but the Commissioners
could find no evidence to suggest that it led to inferior competence. The
data accumulated by such examinations (which were, after all, conducted
by 'eminent University scholars' who were presumably not easily tricked)

proved that, if anything, specially prepared candidates were obtaining on average 'higher marks than the University candidates in the very subjects which are most studied at the Universities, viz., classics and mathematics'.[91] In marshalling these facts the Commissioners did not wish to question the good work of these higher seats of learning. Theirs was merely a pragmatic calculation. The climate had changed in the two decades since the inception of competitive examinations in 1854. The 'attractions of an Indian career' had since 'lost something of their brightness', and thus 'the most distinguished students from our greatest Universities' were no longer coming forward as competitors.[92] Despite this switch in recruits, the aptitude of men who now entered the service was, on the whole, felt to be higher than it had been under the former system of nomination. The accumulated evidence of successive examinations was now able to exert its own authority over traditional prejudice. Special preparation, or cramming as some chose to label it, was providing men of adequate competence and was, therefore, not to be rejected out of hand. Special preparation had, indeed, provided an alternative route that circumvented the old guarantee of good breeding. Evidently, the very success of a competitive system in attracting competitors was acting to weaken the 'direct connection' between government service, on the one hand, and the old schools and universities, on the other, a connection 'which the administrative reformers had been so keen to achieve'.[93] The early system of rigid, hierarchical meritocratic advance – envisaged by Bentham, Goddard and Burt, and attempted in the civil service – was to an extent breaking down in favour of an aspirational, or hope-driven, system of merit. A rigidly stratified system was developing a certain degree of porosity. In this respect, the civil service can be taken as the rough prototype, acted out in miniature, of a more general social experiment that would unfold at a much slower pace in systems of public education.

* * *

Across schools in England, early systems of scholarship offered a degree of mobility through a stratified system. In principle, talent would rise to its rightful place, which is a position within the system where the level of education is matched to the level of ability. In this sense, advance by scholarship differed from advance through cramming or special preparation. Whilst the latter were sporadic and unplanned activities (and to some extent ahead of their time), scholarship was mechanical and relatively precise. It was a principle and technique of disinterested rational reallocation. In theory, the occasional genius from a lower class would be allowed to step up, and intellectual wastage would thereby be avoided. Overall, the system of merit would maintain its rigidity, for educational provision was still arranged according to a deliberate hierarchy of schools. Rigidity was assured, even though a limited internal dynamic would enter its hierarchies and quality stratifications. Scholarship would guarantee that these hierarchies would be protected from critique as they became increasingly accurate through an internal process of corrections. Hierarchies would become ever more justifiable as the homogeneity of their contents increased, as they came to better reflect the distribution of talent. ...

With the benefit of hindsight, we can observe that the envisaged technology of corrected hierarchies would never achieve perfection according to its own parameters of success; the stratified system it sought to correct was eventually overwritten by a fluid ethos of self-propelled movements. Efforts to fill 'gaps in the upward ladder', as it was described in 1895,[94] would later become redundant as new logics of advance were implemented. As rigid hierarchies broke down into something less determinate, scholarship came to resemble a transitional technology. Once the principle of meritocratic perfectibility, it transformed into a generalised principle of movement. Formerly a technology of small corrections within hierarchies, meritocratic advance came to invest entire populations as their logic of admixture, as their eugenic religion.

*   *   *

A Royal Commission reporting in 1868 divided existing schools into three broad groups, which were felt to correspond 'roughly, but by no means exactly, to the gradations of society'.[95] A perfected system would have this typology formalised into three precise grades of school, whereby each school type would cater for a specific sector of the population and a specific category of vocational futures.

First-grade schools 'would make it their chief aim to prepare for the Universities' and their curricula would be guided by 'what the Universities require', that is, they would be dominated by the Classics.[96] These schools would retain pupils until 18 or 19 years, and would be split into a lower and an upper division, with an examination regulating entry to the latter. They would also charge the highest fees.

Slightly cheaper would be the second-grade schools that would 'cease at about 16. After that the boys are not supposed to go to the Universities, but either to the employments or to special preparation for employments'.[97] These schools would be suited to 'the richer shopkeepers', 'many professional men' and 'all but the wealthier gentry'. Latin would receive less emphasis and Mathematics would be 'at once strictly scientific and yet of a practical cast; not aiming at subtle refinements, but at practical applications'. As a general rule, the concrete would replace the abstract.[98]

Schools of the third grade would 'carry education up to the age of 14 or 15'. These would serve the class of artisans, small shopkeepers and smaller farmers, for whom suitable education was most wanting. Essential to the prosperity of industry, these 'industrial classes have not even that basis of sound general education on which alone technical instruction can rest'. They are left in want of the 'disciplined faculties and sound elementary knowledge' upon which such technical education depends.[99] According to the Commissioners, this 'lowest portion of what is commonly called the middle class' required far more basic instruction. Their third-grade schooling would be further split into two divisions, with entry into the upper division regulated by a qualifying examination. The upper division would have 'a regular examination of its higher classes' to 'ensure the efficiency of the work'.[100]

All that remained were the elementary schools established under limited funds since 1833 for the labouring poor. In principle, these schools could be attached to schools of the third grade. The elementary school ending at 12 years would be almost equivalent to a lower-division third-grade school. The Commissioners foresaw, however, that many lower middle-class parents would be unhappy if the two were merged. In many elementary schools the schoolmasters 'are of a lower social rank, and are not felt by the parents to be equals to the children whom they have to teach'.[101] Nevertheless, whilst parents may be 'unwilling to be confounded with the labourers whom they employ', one might still bring these schools 'into relations with each other' so that 'arrangements might be made for promoting the most promising boys of the elementary school'. 'Both kinds of schools would gain by this. The prospect of such a promotion would stimulate the boys in the lower [elementary] school, and the third grade school would be perpetually supplied with picked scholars'.[102] It was a win-win scenario, they felt.

* * *

The general idea that schools could assist those of exceptional ability to climb the social ladder was, in 1868, already established in practice. It can be observed in those occasional schools that combined the rigid stratifications of the nineteenth century within a single institutional complex. At a school in Liverpool there were three divisions. The pupils were 'absolutely separate'; the 'line of buildings is so arranged that they cannot mix in school hours. There are separate playgrounds, separate dining rooms, and separate entrances'.[103] At a school in Buckinghamshire, boys of the lower division even 'left half an hour before those of the upper, to avoid mixture in the streets'.[104] Back in Liverpool, uniforms varied according to division, and each division had its allotted staff. There was only one point of connection: 'every half year one boy can be "nominated" from the lower school to the middle school' based upon merit, and 'one boy from the middle school to the upper in the same way'. It was a 'stream of promotion' that might, in principle, 'reach the Universities'.[105] The flow of exceptional talent was, nonetheless, strictly limited, with no more than six promoted boys allowed in any one division at any one time. In a complex of upper and lower schools in Oxfordshire, promotion was even less frequent, with only two pupils passing to the upper

school in seven years.[106] It seems that existing divisions were to be protected against excessive dilution. Heroic climbers were to be limited in number.

*   *   *

In 1868, the figure of the occasional hero also prevailed in a mythological sense. As the Commissioners report: 'Our history is full of names of men who have risen by their learning' and there are 'few schools which cannot point to at least one such hero in their past history'.[107] 'Three centuries ago' many founders of the old endowed schools 'appear to have desired to give those children of poor parents who are fitted for it by nature, opportunities of obtaining a higher cultivation than would otherwise be within their reach'. For these gifted, poor individuals, education was provided free of charge. At the time 'when most of the [endowed] grammar schools were founded, there was', we are told, 'by no means a universal desire for education, still less the education which these schools were intended to give, the education of a scholar'. As a result, the system was self-selecting; only those children of 'peculiar natural aptitude' stayed on, having attracted the notice of an intelligent master, the rest being 'speedily removed to commence their various occupations'. The 'process of selection' was 'perpetually' taking place, as masters uncovered one by one those pupils thought able enough to be instructed further. In 1868, however, these old traditions were no longer deemed viable.

No such system of selection 'can be expected now', we are told – some other system must be 'substituted for that which' once 'acted spontaneously'.[108] When the provision of schooling expands to encompass the entire population, the old tradition of selection by sporadic adoption must be rendered systematic. As T. H. Huxley proclaimed in 1871, 'no educational system in the country would be worthy the name of a national system, or fulfil the great objects of education, unless it was one which established a great educational ladder, the bottom of which should be in the gutter and the top in the University and by which every child who had the strength to climb might, by using that strength, reach the place intended for him'.[109] The administrative task, in effect, was to ensure that enough ladders were provided, and that those already in place were without gaps. The Commissioners, indeed, made recommendations for such a ladder, permitting ascent for those able to climb. Their advice was as follows: even though the 'schools of the third grade are not, and are not intended to be, preparatory to schools of the second; nor schools of the second to schools of the first', this differentiated system must, nevertheless, allow that 'real ability shall find its proper opening'.[110] Scholarships should be 'open to merit and merit only, and, if possible, under such regulations as to make it tolerably certain, that talent, wherever it was, would be discovered'.[111] The division of education into distinct grades would not 'be complete unless it were possible for boys of exceptional talent to rise to the highest education which the country could supply. And this of course implies that there should be some connecting thread pervading education at every grade'.[112] This 'connecting thread', or 'leading study', would serve as a link between the three grades of school.

When selecting this leading study, the Commissioners felt that Latin was the obvious subject to choose. Even though Latin would only be taught to a limited extent in schools of the third grade, boys of exceptional talent would presumably be able to pass to a higher-grade school, and, 'fired by the natural ambition consequent of their own success, would be found quite capable of making up, perhaps of more than making up, for the disadvantage of changing from one system to another'. Despite the disadvantages of their prior and distinctly inferior third-grade education, being 'clever boys', once promoted, they would quickly surmount such drawbacks.[113] The hero rises by virtue of his strength.

* * *

The extent to which such recommendations were carried out is unclear. Historians note that 'no central or regional authority was set up to mastermind this reconstruction' of schooling, and, whatever the changes that were made, 'this scheme was not brought in in the pure form here proposed'.[114] Still, even without the impositions of a central authority, later Commissioners noted that the tripartite classification had been 'followed by subsequent writers, and indeed, has largely passed into common speech'.[115] The Elementary Education

Act of 1870 is often celebrated as the beginning of state education, and yet, in the face of continued hostility to state control, this Act only sought to fill in gaps at the lower end of school provision. State influence in schooling would only grow over the decades through a process of gradual attrition.

Without central control, no central thread or clear route of progression could be established. And so, without properly mechanised systems of advance, local tactics and sporadic educational adjustments were allowed to spread. For example, lower schools developed additional and superior classes so that they could retain their more gifted scholars. The Commissioners had anticipated and feared this outcome, noting that the 'tendency of successful schools is always to make their success a stepping stone in the social scale'.[116] This would break down hierarchies and lead to encroachments. It was as a preventative measure that they recommended each 'kind of school should have its own proper aim set before it, and should be put under such rules as will compel it to keep that aim'.[117] 'A boy of 14 [at a third-grade school] ought to be required to quit a school of this grade at the end of the current half year. A rule of this sort is necessary to prevent successful schools of this grade from encroaching on the work of the schools of the grade above, and slipping into their places.'[118]

The problem of 'overlapping' was duly reported in 1895. Between schools of the same grade it was comparatively rare. More frequent were those incursions

that arise 'when a lower school retains pupils who are ripe for a higher'. For the time being, it was felt that this overlap was not serious enough to result in severe competition with superior schools. The 'higher grade elementary schools' were to be tolerated as 'agencies which supply a widely-felt need' so long as they did not overstep 'the fair limits of a province which they have legitimately and usefully made their own'.[119] Still, the Commissioners felt that these schools should be brought into a more 'definite and organic relation' with secondary schools, so that they shall 'rather co-operate than compete with the latter'. This would be achieved by imposing 'stricter limits of age, and by establishing graduated scholarships'.[120] Incursions continued, however. By the turn of the century, money intended for elementary education was still being used to fund scholars retained beyond the prescribed 14 years. In London, auditors eventually stepped in, closing the system down as an illegal use of funds.[121] According to the Commissioners, a better scholarship system would have prevented this. With the able few properly extracted, hierarchies would have been easier to maintain.

* * *

In principle, the number of ladders could multiply *ad infinitum*. In 1895 it was suggested that systems could be made more 'elastic', providing opportunities for those of uncommon ability to step up into higher-grade schooling throughout their school career.[122] Scholarships should be 'carefully graduated', varying in terms of value, age and 'class of school' for which they were tenable.[123] The idea was to introduce multiple points of advance by which talent could ascend. In London a system of 'double promotion' was later trialled in elementary schools, whereby children were reclassified twice a year in order 'to secure a more rapid passage' through school for a special few. Annual promotion of the bulk of children from class to class was to cease, implying as it did that progress between scholars was uniform. Double promotion, carefully targeted at the most able, would allow their swift advance and early transfer to secondary education. In principle, ladders could be lowered into the depths of schooling, extending pathways of ascent throughout the institutional architecture.[124]

* * *

More than a mere offering or token gesture to the lower classes, scholarship was viewed as a form of relief, reducing class pressure and maintaining internal hierarchies against the trespasses of lower-grade schooling. The hero was a by-product, a high-powered discharge to be tolerated by the system, and occasionally revered. During the twentieth century all this changed. The academic hero became so commonplace that the heroic function he had once served was depleted of its original force. The occasional hero receded behind an inclusive, more democratic logic of social redistribution.

*   *   *

The Commissioners of 1868 claimed that 'the wealth and prosperity of the country' depends to a great degree 'on the industry, and that industry on the intelligence' of the poorly educated lower middle classes. There is a 'deficiency' in 'general intelligence', they said, 'and unless we remedy this want we shall gradually but surely find that our undeniable superiority in wealth and perhaps in energy will not save us from decline'. It was felt that the labouring classes most of all required 'disciplined faculties and sound elementary knowledge'.[125] Their members should only be educated in a manner suited to their eventual job prospects. The lower sections of society must be improved only so that they can better contribute to the goals of industrial development and enhanced national competitiveness.

The imperatives were not only economic, however. Arguments for a minimal level of instruction also responded to the recent enfranchisement of working men. Both points are made in William Forster's address to Parliament in 1870:

> Upon the speedy provision of elementary education depends our industrial prosperity. It is of no use trying to give technical teaching to our artizans without elementary education; uneducated labourers – and many of our labourers are utterly uneducated – are, for the most part, unskilled labourers, and if we leave our work-folk any longer unskilled, notwithstanding their strong sinews and determined energy, they will become over-matched in the competition of the world. Upon this speedy provision depends also, I fully believe, the good, the safe working of our constitutional system. To its honour, Parliament has lately decided that England shall in future be governed by a popular government. I am one of those who would not wait until the people were educated before I would trust them with political power. If we had thus waited we might have waited long for education; but now that we have given them political power we must not wait any longer to give them education. There are questions demanding answers, problems which must be solved, which ignorant constituencies are ill-fitted to solve. Upon this speedy provision of education depends also our national power. Civilised communities throughout the world are massing themselves together, each mass being measured by its force; and if we are to hold our position among men of our own race or among the nations of the world we must make up the smallness of our numbers by increasing the intellectual force of the individual.[126]

According to Forster, the expansions of democracy and industry demanded an educational parallel. This call to enhance the intellectual force of each individual said nothing, however, about the redistribution of intelligence. Each individual must be enhanced only as a representative of his class. In 1887, an elementary school headteacher put it in these terms:

> The general condition of the human intellect is like the surface of the earth, there are mountains and valleys; and all that education will do will be to lift up the whole crust of it, still leaving the mountains and the valleys. We shall always have the hewers of wood and the drawers of water.[127]

By 1895, and with the publication of a new government report, migration between valleys and mountains was now permissible if it favoured the national interest. Even though scholarship was still envisaged as a pressure-release valve and pathway for the able, even though first-grade schools still occupied themselves with cultivating the most genteel and cultured of men, the governmental rationale was changing. As the Commissioners boldly stated, the 'more highly organised our civilisation becomes, the more imperative grows the need' for promoting men of talent by recruiting to their ranks 'the best blood and brain from all classes of society'.[128] In effect, advanced democratic societies are now said to depend upon more than the docility and operational functionality of their various class members. These classes must also exhibit between their divisions an efficient distribution of talent.

*   *   *

Scholarship was viewed in 1868 as an extension of opportunity to the hidden genius. It was a system that would assist the meteoric rise of the academic hero. Against this scheme, reference to 'best blood and brain' in 1895 contains in a more explicit form the idea of overall intellectual redistribution. Basing scholarship upon the principle of blood – where blue blood is rejected as an illusion, for all blood is red – leads to a set of justifications that rely less upon a mythology of the occasional academic hero (to whom ladders descend from the ramparts of class privilege), and borrow more from a population-level, biopolitical perspective.

*   *   *

The genius-hero was the object of Galton's first enquiries in the 1860s.[129] And yet, this preoccupation with the descent of eminent men was also the point of departure from which a population-level rationality later developed. In this respect, Galton's work passed through a broader transition, from a mythology of the genius-hero to a more mundane, statistical awareness of the distribution of intellectual traits. In tracking men of eminence between 1453 and 1853, Galton's initial foray into hereditary genius performed a dual function. It inaugurated a new population-level science and governing rationality, whilst also marking the end of an era. The hero, with whom Galton's first publications were so obsessed, was soon to be retired.

Lives Redistributed

> For institutions to exist there must exist the kind of will, instinct, imperative which is anti-liberal to the point of malice.[130]
>
> *Friedrich Nietzsche*

Architectures of devious intent are the ones we enjoy hearing about. These are the ghosts of our past whose hauntings we take pleasure in recounting. Architectures of benign intent are always less interesting, and are only used for ceremonial purposes in progressive histories of the present. Here I offer something different. This history of good intentions is not without its share of malice. Offered here is a history of benign violence, one that seeks to invert perception and locate devious forces in kindly reforms. It is designed to arouse suspicion. It is designed to disturb *you*, dear reader.

* * *

The ubiquity of Latin as the language of advance disappeared with the development of intelligence tests. Latin no longer served as the connecting thread regulating advance between different types of school. With tests of mental capacity, a new science of schooling became possible. Subject-based achievements, otherwise known as 'attainments', were separated from measures of underlying ability. School attainments, so the argument went, were riven with confounding variables that masked the effects of underlying intelligence. Whilst high attainment could be achieved artificially through extra training, underlying intelligence was not so malleable. The educational ideal was to divorce attainment from ability, for ability was raw and pure, and, by consequence, easier to administer.

* * *

Writing in 1919, Lewis Terman embraced this new dawn as the age of the 'educational engineer'.[131] The 'nation's hidden resources of intelligence' could now be located in a systematic way, he claimed, so as to rationalise the distribution of talent. 'The common saying that "genius will out" is one of those dangerous half-truths with which too many people rest content.'[132] To match the distribution of talent to the hierarchy of jobs requires deliberate and thoroughgoing intervention.

* * *

The engineer was not always welcome. Mental tests covered a terrain once occupied by professional judgement. Faced by the inertia of recalcitrant pedagogues and the institutions they served, Terman's psychometric utopia was never fully realised. It would only ever adopt more partial forms.

* * *

The technocratic cause did prosper. State schooling, for example, became increasingly systematic. In England and Wales, quotas were levied in 1907 to ensure that grant-aided secondary schools admitted a minimum percentage of ex-elementary school pupils.[133] Throughout the nation's schools the point of transition slowly clustered about the age of 11. Elementary schools became 'primary' schools that fed directly into a secondary system.[134] The old system of scholarship by which candidates jumped to a parallel system of education became a common moment of transfer at 11 plus. Individual ladders became a collective incline.

* * *

At first the system was patchy and slow to develop. Many pupils lingered on in elementary schools until 14, never progressing to secondary education, and for much of the interwar period the provision of education beyond 11 years of age was in very poor supply. In this climate, where structures

THE MAP IN THE GARDEN (CHAPTER XVIII)
" That's the way to London "

failed to match an envisaged distribution of abilities, the scholarship ladder became a point of contention. Pugnacious conservatives, such as one Lord Birkenhead, would claim that it was both complete and effective:

> There is now a complete ladder from the elementary school to the University, and the number of scholarships from the elementary to the secondary school is not limited, awards being made to all children who show capacity to profit.[135]

Other commentators, such as an ex-President of the National Union of Teachers, felt that the distribution of opportunity was tight-fisted at best:

> The restrictive, ineffective scholarship system in vogue for the vast majority of children coincides with a commonly held view that secondary education is something to be doled out with a sparing hand to the bright child of impecunious origin.[136]

In his 1926 study, *Social Progress and Educational Waste*, Kenneth Lindsay estimated that 'of the 550,000 children who leave elementary schools each year, 9.5 per cent of an age-group proceed to secondary schools...while 1 per 1,000 reach the University'. For the elementary school child, vertical mobility was very poor indeed.[137] Poverty, combined with a limited supply of secondary schools, distorted the system of advance. For Lindsay, this turned what should be 'a qualifying examination into a competitive one'.[138] He argued that a better system would arrange secondary schools according to the 'rich variety of capacity among children'; it would substitute 'selection by differentiation' for 'selection by elimination'.[139] The irrational element introduced by competitive forces would be replaced by a 'scientific organization of education and industry, and a reorientation of the idea of secondary education' so that secondary schools would prepare more than just 'black-coated workers' for employment. Secondary schooling would cater for '*all* children, based on their tendencies and desires and the evident needs of production'. Here was 'a plea', in other words, 'for an alternative theory to that of the "ladder" idea'.[140]

* * *

In Lindsay's critique, the limitations of selection itself were not under attack. Despite an obscure reference to 'untilled ground',[141] the material disadvantage faced by the elementary school child, and the effects of this deprivation on his or her educational attainments, abilities, and prospects for advance, are not raised with any particular force. In 1926, the reform objectives were comparatively simple: expand secondary provision and make it free.

* * *

The development of school transfer technologies was a task willingly adopted by the educational engineer. In 1920, a *Departmental Committee on Scholarships and Free Places* rejected 'nomination' as a method of scholarship allocation. A 'well-conducted examination' was far more preferable. It would test for 'capacity and promise rather than attainments', where examinations should be confined to English and arithmetic. As Cyril Burt, their expert witness, now confirmed, these subjects 'correlate most closely with general capacity'.[142]

Once 'general capacity' was invoked, Spearman's '*g*' entered the language of the report. The assumption behind '*g*', the idea that core intelligence exists as a single measurable capacity, was an assumption that arrived with its close associate: the envisaged normal distribution of '*g*' throughout the population. From a psychometric perspective, the task was clear: the 'country cannot afford to miss intelligent children'. As the committee reports, 'the impression left on us by the evidence is that at present a great many excellent fish slip past the net'.[143] A scholarship system that made use of psychometric tests, with all their precision and exactness, would perfect the net. To 'discover capacity apart from attainment', these 'psychological tests would constitute the best method'. It was regrettable, therefore, that the technology was still under-developed. Hesitant when it came to such *avant-garde* techniques, the committee hedged their bets: 'At present applied psychology is in an experimental stage, and the validity of its methods is not yet sufficiently firmly established to justify their employment in the place of ordinary tests.'[144]

* * *

Undeniably, with individual nominations replaced by testing, the 'burden of examination' on schools would be increased. Nevertheless, with the rise of statistical perception, the demand that all school children must be tested was unavoidable. Teachers might complain that such examinations could lead to 'invidious' comparisons between teachers and between schools, but in saying this they missed the point. The aim of scholarship testing was not to measure attainment; it was to uncover general intelligence, a capacity over which schools were thought to have no influence. This would avoid the 'evils of a general external examination' because the closer a test comes to revealing innate capacities, the less it reveals about the efforts of a particular teacher or school.

Aside from the evident need to introduce psychological advances as they arrived, the remaining problem said to be holding up dispassionate allocation was the 'ignorance, apathy, or selfishness of some parents'. Here the authorities, including elementary school teaching staff, would need to take responsibility, ensuring that 'the advantages of further education' were 'made known' to all custodians of a child's future. The 'co-operation of the parents' was viewed as 'one of the most important factors in the success of a scholarship scheme', where the challenge was to foster 'a tradition or habit of scholarship winning' in those who lacked ambition.[145]

* * *

A century later, I find myself bombarded on a regular basis with inducements of a similar kind. If I resist, I too appear lacking in ambition. Increasingly we are expected as university employees to spend our time generating a research income for the institution. Our habits must change as we learn to engage in the frenetic activity of bid writing that now defines the profession. As an employee, I am encouraged to feel personally responsible for the economic future of my department, the university it serves and the wider economic order that it is expected to support through innovative and timely research. In this environment, little space remains for *untimely* meditations.

At a glance, the inducements planned for the early twentieth-century parent appear similar. The parent becomes a guardian of success, positioned as a key actor, encouraged to comply with the economic dictates of traditional meritocracy. The activity of parenting is to be channelled in support of the national economic interest. It is configured as a personal responsibility: parents are to prevent offspring from indulging in wasteful activities; those capable of winning scholarships must always be forced into the ring. To be capable of success and yet remain untested is to fail prematurely.

Despite these apparent similarities, the aspirational logic described here was entirely at odds with the hope-driven ethos that rules our present. Though some university employees remain obsequiously subservient to the university they serve – even believing the self-congratulatory platitudes that are farmed out in press releases and degree celebrations – many know that success in academia comes at a definite cost. Personal relationships are sacrificed in pursuit of eminence and recognition amongst peers, whilst intellectual commitments are given up and quickly forgotten wherever the pursuit of eminence finds itself unable to cash them in. Those seeking to enhance their personal esteem indicators, and hence their careers, must learn to exist in a realm populated by other similarly pumped up phantoms. Those seeking research grants must reconcile themselves to the fact that available funds are diminishing. The various organisations to which one can apply for cash have less and less to give out these days, and few academics expect this situation to reverse. Bid writing is a decidedly manic affair, to which they commit with grim resignation. In a traditional meritocracy, by contrast, situations like these were viewed, quite rightly, as systematic failures. These wasted energies would have to be rationalised, or so the argument went. If scholarships still failed to identify talent, they would be reformed. If school provision did not match the distribution of ability, it would be adjusted so that it did, indeed, fit. Whilst the systems that made up a traditional meritocracy were often, in practice, still highly dysfunctional, its bureaucrats viewed any chaos in the system as an operational defect. Disorder did not yet serve a governmental function. Chaos was yet to be operationalised as an agent of power.

* * *

In today's academic environment I come across as pretty eccentric if I remind my colleagues that we are surrounded by phantom activities and operational stupidities, that we absorb these systems, indeed, into our everyday activities and perceptions. This complaint appears odd, not because it is original or globally denied. After a few beers, many of my colleagues would freely admit that much of an academic's time is wasted in senseless activities. What is odd about my complaint, simply, is that it appeals to an out-dated system of government. By complaining, I appear a little too quaint to be taken seriously.

* * *

In a more systematic era, those with a commitment to order could still express their regret at systematic failures and find themselves in sync with the governing rationality. It made perfect sense to criticise the continued failures of scholarship systems. These systems were still remarkably uneven, including as they did various forms of oral examination; the testing of only those pre-selected by the head; and the use of a variety of *ad hoc* procedures that were passed off as intelligence tests but failed to live up to the rigors of contemporary science.[146]

Where state agencies failed, industry took over. Though today's businesses thrive on disorder, in the early twentieth century the opportunity to inject a little order was a steady business investment. In the newly established market of mental testing, an agency based at Moray House in Edinburgh secured the greatest market share. The first Moray House Tests began to appear in 1925, with its client base expanding throughout England, providing academy-approved tests of English, Arithmetic and Intelligence. By 1954, most authorities were using such tests in selections at 11 plus.[147] This industry would slowly permeate the entire education sector. Adaptable and unscrupulous, it would serve whichever regime of power came to rule.

* * *

During the initial phase of expansion, the perfectibility of testing faced some basic structural challenges. In the 1924 *Report of the Consultative Committee on Psychological Tests* the problem was stated clearly: no 'mere improvement in the methods by which selection takes place – eminently desirable though such improvement is – can act as substitute for the large increase in the Secondary School accommodation and in the supply of free places which is so urgently needed'. There would always be a 'waste in capacity', whatever the state of examination, if provision failed to match the distribution of talent.[148] The

1926 report on *The Education of the Adolescent* argued that 'diversities of gifts' require a 'diversity of educational provision'.[149] Schooling should be reconfigured so that all are educated together for the primary phase, after which they would move *en masse* to secondary education. Secondary education should be reorganised so that it is divided into three broad types to which pupils would be allotted at 11 plus. With all pupils moving to another school at the end of primary education, an educational ladder for the heroic and fortunate few was no longer appropriate. Lindsay's earlier mantra is repeated: 'selection by differentiation takes the place of selection by elimination'.[150] Once the competitive element disappeared, selection by differentiation would be mandatory, purely administrative and utterly scientific.

* * *

The meritocratic rationale had by now passed through a number of stages. An aristocratic system was initially transformed by the metaphor of ladders, whereby a degree of mobility was to be allowed, allowing the occasional migrant of 'exceptional ability' to climb through the social strata.[151] As the distribution of intelligence became a matter of national concern, this modified system itself began to appear inadequate. A decade after intelligence tests were first developed, those at the forefront of this science would look with a derisory gaze at contemporary efforts to celebrate those of exceptional ability. They found themselves reminded of 'primitive methods of surface mining'.[152] The technical challenge, as they saw it, which had been almost entirely neglected, was to search more deeply, and with greater determination, looking beyond those who were most obviously exceptional and easy to spot. It was necessary to replace a system that allowed those of exceptional strength to rise up by a system that employed a universally applied technique to test and position all without exception. The collective instrument that was developed, an instrument that was to serve as a tool in pursuit of national efficiency, came to be known as the 11 plus examination.

These population-level objectives were served by disciplinary techniques, which were ideal for inverting traditional visibilities. Visibility had once been a mark of eminence that was reserved for a noble elite. The bulk of the population was only rendered visible in occasional outbursts, such as those moments when a member of their group was punished in a public display of sovereign retribution. With the development of disciplinary institutions, this visibility was inverted. Previously ignored, unknown and marginalised people rose to prominence as strategies of power sought to regulate the detail of their lives.[153] In this respect, the occasional academic hero was a throwback from the past. The sporadic discovery and celebration of talent was replaced by an inverted system of visibility, by an inescapable system of measurements seeking the redistribution of all for purposes of national efficiency.

* * *

Within the logic of a traditional meritocracy – where the allocation of jobs is to be mechanical and direct – perfection is achieved when the normal distribution of abilities traces the same trajectory as a normally distributed hierarchy of jobs. The same applies to the distribution of schooling, as encapsulated in this quote from the Board of Education: 'In a wise economy of secondary education pupils of a particular type of mind would receive the training best suited for them and that training would lead them to an occupation where their capacities would be suitably used.'[154] In 1920, with six million children registered to public elementary schools and only 300,000 children attending grant-maintained secondary schools, this was hardly the case.[155] In such a climate, competition was tolerated as a necessary evil. It was used to encourage wider participation in testing at a time when 'examination for all' was still a utopian dream.

* * *

In his 1911 lecture, *Examinations in their bearing on national efficiency*, the educational reformer Philip Hartog sought to refine the logic of examination. He claimed that its precise function should be more carefully defined:

> One must be clear about the purpose of examinations used 'to distinguish between candidates of different merit', he wrote. The 'competitive idea' that lingers behind merit can lead us into confusion; it can tempt us 'to forget the distinction between the efficiency of an examination and its difficulty'. Very difficult examinations are likely to be highly competitive, but are they efficient? An efficient examination is one that says something useful about those who pass it. This means that superior examinations are not simply those which are harder to pass: 'The main question is, surely, not which candidate can do the most difficult things, solve the most Chinese of puzzles, remember the most unrememberable of formulae.'[156] Rather, superior examinations are those devices that match people to tasks and are able to divide candidates who can perform certain pre-defined social functions from those who cannot.

* * *

It was hoped that the eventual reorganisation of schooling would make competition a thing of the past. When educational structures were finally matched to population characteristics, competition would necessarily cease. This would allow examinations to become truly efficient. They would no longer resemble a narrow gateway that guards limited opportunities against a throng of able bodies. Instead, the natural distribution of ability would be reflected in a complementary distribution of educational provision. The fight for a relatively small number of secondary school places would be replaced by efficient and useful distributions. People would be allotted their position in the system of production, and they would recognise this position to be a just reflection of their intellectual desert.

*   *   *

It is interesting to note that some feared competition *for* schooling would be replaced by competition *between* schools. It was suggested that inter-school rivalry might be the unintended consequence of an increased number of schools in the secondary sector. Government officials agreed that this should be prevented: competition that leads to one school 'attracting to itself pupils better qualified to profit by the other' school 'is to be avoided', they wrote. It would complicate and potentially obstruct the proper allocation of places according to ability.[157]

*   *   *

The marginal position given to competition in these early meritocratic developments seems entirely in accord with Foucault's treatment of disciplinary power. Foucault rarely mentions competition in *Discipline and Punish*,[158] and this omission would appear to be more deliberate than accidental. Disciplinary power is concerned with achieving a precise composition of forces. It might use techniques of rivalry and mutual comparison, but these devices are carefully located within a wider technocratic scheme. Competition performs a minor role in discipline; it occupies a subordinate position. As a strategic organising principle, competition is a post-disciplinary, late twentieth-century device.

*   *   *

The 1924 report on psychological tests addressed the issue of vocational allocation with a prudent hope: 'When psychological tests had been made more satisfactory, they could be used to discover persons having a relatively high degree of the capacities required for a given occupation.'[159] Moreover, they could be used to 'dissuade children from entering occupations for which they are shown to be naturally unsuited'.[160] This would be a positive move, for a lack of general intelligence 'might be an advantage for some kinds of mechanical work'.[161]

The committee cited research on 'The Selection of Mill Workers by Mental Tests'. Here no correlation was found between higher intelligence and greater efficiency at work. Automated machinery had generated work 'so specialized and monotonous that an intelligent person is very likely to revolt'. Only those with very low intelligence can 'do nothing but put full spools of silk in place of empty ones, week after week, year after year, with seeming contentment'.[162]

Once again, social stability is said to depend on the correct allocation of jobs to intelligence. This was a period when it made sense to look to the regulating potential of disciplinary technique, rather than to the productive effects of manufactured hope, mutual rivalry and competitive effort. Assisted by a rising awareness of population-level characteristics, the existing disciplinary logics of schooling – residues of the monitorial school – were to be extended beyond their institutional walls to embrace movements between schools as well as within them. Individuals were to be rationally distributed amongst schools and eventual employments in order to achieve productive efficiency and social harmony. In this climate, competition was a potentially dangerous force, erosive towards rational planning and social contentment.

*   *   *

Group intelligence tests were only 'tentatively' added to 'the customary written examinations'. It was hoped that by 'calculating the correlation between the separate results and the subsequent development of the pupils' the 'relative merits' of these systems of examination could be compared. Intelligence tests might well assist in the 'classification and promotion of pupils' and in 'making recommendations for the transfer of individual children to other types of school', but the implementation of such techniques should be based on the future study of carefully maintained records, a process of research that would gradually lead to the 'elimination of untrustworthy tests of whatever kind'.[163]

The language is cautious: only the 'experimental use' of intelligence tests is recommended by government.[164] And yet, these recommendations already relied heavily on psychological and statistical discourses. Detailed school record keeping and a search for correlations were both suggested. Oral examinations should be 'standardized'[165] and 'pains' should be taken 'to frame the written [subject-based] papers on sound psychological lines'.[166] Indeed, 'if effective steps were taken to apply a knowledge of psychology and of the new technique of testing to written examinations of the ordinary type', the case for using group tests of intelligence would be *pro tanto* weakened'.[167]

Even reports issued by those with an aversion to testing could not avoid the assumptions of psychometric science. The 1941 report on *Curriculum and Examinations in Secondary Schools*[168] is well known for its hostility to testing. Its committee was chaired by Sir Cyril Norwood, who had already published his views on the 'cramping and deadening influences which may proceed from the too rigid working of the necessary [educational] machinery'.[169] In this earlier work Norwood argued that the 'soul' of the educational system, which had 'grown out of the life of the nation',[170] faced a very real 'danger from mechanization'.[171] On the topic of examination, he feared that overly mechanistic approaches would result in the pupil treating the examiner 'as if he were a foe instead of a friend'.[172] Norwood was the proponent of a gentler pedagogic model, one that practised care and moral guidance.

In the 1941 report, the 'judgement of the teacher' is viewed 'as the most important factor to be taken into consideration' when deciding where a child was to be placed. School records compiled by teachers would provide 'the best single means at present available of discovering special interest and aptitude and general level of intelligence'. Intelligence tests were still of an 'experimental nature' and should not be used in isolation. It is the expert judgement of the teacher, expressed in school records, which must be trusted; intelligence tests can only ever be a 'supplementary method of arriving at a true judgement'.[173] And so it goes on.

Here was a clear attempt to resist the incursions of the educational engineer. The idea was to resurrect expert judgement and pedagogic wisdom. It is notable, therefore, that the report does not succeed in escaping the underlying problem. The presence of a 'general intelligence' that is distributed to varying degrees throughout the population is still presumed. It is still a matter of matching 'secondary education of the various types' to this distribution of ability.[174] Psychometric assumptions can thus be found in a report that is known for its hostility to psychometric technology.

* * *

Her Majesty's Inspectorate had long since been peddling psychometric techniques. When monitoring the conduct of local education authorities, it promoted key principles of intelligence testing: accordingly, entire age groups should be tested rather than a selected few; oral tests were condemned as unstandardised and inconsistent in operation; group intelligence tests should be supported as one element in an armoury of techniques designed to discover hidden ability; marking procedures for attainment tests should be checked alongside the results of standardised intelligence tests; either an age allowance should be calculated, or pupils ought to be tested twice a year to ensure the youngest and oldest candidates are separated by no more than six months' development; examinations must deliver a broad spread of marks rather than the bunching of candidates; English and arithmetic scores should correlate well, and poor correlation should be viewed with suspicion; examination questions are best piloted in other areas of the country first; short questions are more desirable than longer essay-style questions, facilitating more objective marking; and, finally, questions should be graded in difficulty around the abilities of the average pupil. The overall message was that opportunities for subjective discretion in marking were to be reduced; tests would be trialled, standardised and adjusted for age.[175] Through mechanisms such as these, the new principles of testing were firmly embedded in educational practice.

* * *

The idea of meritocracy had broad appeal. Beyond its attraction for various technocrats, imperialists and defenders of the national interest, it appealed to those with more progressive, egalitarian dreams, including representatives of the moderate and radical Left. To affirm and promote 'The Inequality of Man' did not imply that one was a social conservative wedded to existing distributions of wealth and opportunity. In the crass terms of socialist J. B. S. Haldane, a recognition of innate inequalities served only to further justify his politics:

> In the remote future mankind may be divided into castes like Hindus or termites. But to-day the recognition of innate inequality should lead not to less, but to greater, equality of opportunity.[176]

It was a Labour government that eventually reformed schooling, extending opportunity to all by matching educational provision to the distribution of talent. The great range of ability was to become the principle 'to which the bias or objective of each school' would be 'naturally related'.[177] Secondary schools were to be classified as grammar, technical and modern, where secondary modern schools would cater for the bulk of the population. It was assumed that there 'are far more pupils for whom a Modern School is appropriate than there are pupils for whom a Grammar School is appropriate'. The modern school would, therefore, provide a 'general education for the majority of the boys and girls in the country'.[178] Although this tripartite system was patched onto existing institutions and thereby reflected some of the historic divisions of schooling, it nonetheless followed the normal distribution of ability in its design.

> ...we can think of an area, typical of much of the country, in which up to about a quarter of all the pupils who leave the primary schools go on to secondary grammar or secondary technical schools. The remaining three-quarters apart from a small number who may be provided for in 'special' schools for the severely physically or mentally handicapped, will go to secondary modern schools. In the latter, there will be an 'above average' group, including some pupils who show themselves capable of doing work similar to that done by many pupils in a grammar school. There will be a second group, generally much larger, who represent the 'average' boys and girls of their age; and a third, usually smaller, group, of those who have considerably more difficulty in remembering and applying what they learn, and who certainly work more slowly. Finally, we can pick out a fourth group of really backward pupils who have a struggle to attain an elementary mastery of reading, writing and calculation.[179]

It seemed fortuitous that the 'evolution of education' had 'in fact thrown up' three 'rough groups' of children.[180] Each group could be sent to its respective school. Their traits were as follows:

Those associated with the grammar school are, typically, 'interested in learning for its own sake', 'can grasp an argument or follow a piece of connected reasoning', are 'interested in causes', and are 'sensitive to language as expression of thought'. They can 'take a long view' and 'have some capacity to enjoy, from an aesthetic point of view, the aptness of a phrase or the neatness of a proof'. Those who demonstrate this 'particular type of mind' tend to enter the professions.

Technical education provides for those 'whose interests lie markedly in the field of applied science or applied art'. 'The boy in this group' often 'has an uncanny insight into the intricacies of mechanism whereas the subtleties of language construction are too delicate for him. To justify itself to his mind, knowledge must be capable of immediate application' and must be 'concerned with the control of material things'. 'He may have an unusual or moderate intelligence'.

The final group deals with those who cope 'more easily with concrete things than with ideas'. Interested 'in things as they are; he finds little attraction in the past or in the slow disentanglement of causes or movements'. 'His horizon is near' and his intellectual 'movement is generally slow'.[181]

We see here the outlines of a hierarchy, with grammar schools taking the most intelligent, technical schools following with those of 'moderate' intelligence and, finally, modern schools largely taking the remainder.[182]

* * *

For the system to function, it was deemed 'essential' that 'parity of schools in the secondary stage of education' could be assured.[183] Variations in esteem would undermine the smooth working of the system. They would impede the proper allocation of individuals by generating aspirations and desires for social advance that were in excess of individual abilities. Variations in prestige would nurture unrealistic hopes whereby individuals of lower intelligence would mistakenly seek entry to school types that were higher than their abilities allowed. As the 1938 committee on secondary education advised, equal status would 'make it easier to transfer pupils to schools better suited to their needs' without 'creating any sense of slur or failure'.[184] The 'legacies of an age which had a different educational and social outlook from our own', that gave 'certain schools a prestige' based on 'other than educational grounds', must be swept away. Once established, equality of status would ensure that all schools are 'equally acceptable to parents' and would enable allocations to schools that could 'best develop' the 'particular abilities' of their children.[185] This ideal of parity was repeated in further government reports,[186] extending to the following statement in *Half Our Future*, which considered the plight of the 'average' and 'less-than-average' child:

> Most boys and girls are able to accept realistically differences of ability among themselves; it is not the fact that they all cannot attempt the same work, but the realization by some pupils that what they are doing is not valued by the community, which is most likely to produce a sense of rejection, apathy or hostility.[187]

The post-war Labour MP and Minister of Education, Ellen Wilkinson, was a staunch supporter of this view. She claimed that a differentiated array of schooling is necessary in order to accommodate the great range of human aptitude. Indeed, whatever we do to our education system, 'coal' would still have 'to be mined and fields ploughed'. What had to be removed, simply, was the 'fantastic idea' that 'you are in a higher social class if you add up figures in a book' rather than tend the land.[188] The population at large must be educated to ignore vast inequalities in status; indeed, these must be collapsed, so that individuals are able accept the redistributions that are imposed.

*   *   *

Parity of esteem was never achieved, of course. The suggestion that it could be realised in a divided system looks ridiculously optimistic, if not completely disingenuous, from a twenty-first-century perspective. The challenge for us, however, is to view the problem through its contemporaneous lens. In schematic terms, for a traditional meritocracy, hierarchies themselves are relatively unproblematic. Problems arise at an auxiliary level, where school esteem varies according to school type. Unrealistic hopes and desires are seen to be the chief limitations to technocratic perfection. These interfere with administrative efforts to distribute children between schools according to their ability, and tailor schooling to their aptitudes. When schooling is provided for all, the distortions of competition, with all the emotive forces that competitive desire unleashes, are no longer admissible. Competition between individuals and schools is to be 'deplored'.[189]

The parity ideal only looks odd to us now because we are so familiar with its replacement. In the second half of the twentieth century, esteem was transformed from a limiting factor, to be levelled at all costs, to a principle of organisational enhancement as one school is pitted against the next in pursuit of 'innovation' and 'improvement'. Competition has long since emerged from its formerly subordinate position.

*   *   *

As psychometric perspectives and assumptions came to infuse interwar educational practice and policy, a parallel debate rumbled on concerning the factual claims upon which intelligence testing was said to rest. Initially, at least, the practical consequences of this dispute were limited. Mental measurement had been securely adopted by educational policy.[190] Its assumptions were reproduced in successive government reports and in the activities of the inspectorate. By the 1920s, 'general intelligence' was a term in widespread popular use. Its progenitor concept, Spearman's '*g*', was, nevertheless, under sustained attack in the academic literature, and a rival theory embracing multiple factors was gaining ground. Though the widespread utility of intelligence testing would in the end ensure its survival, uncertainties concerning its validity would soon force it to operate within an altered regime of power. What was disrupted here was that clear-cut and deterministic notion of measurable, innate and uniform '*g*', which proposed that mental energy of a uniform and quantifiable kind is distributed to various degrees throughout the population. Intelligence, it appeared, might actually be far more multiple and dispersed. This realisation acted as a slow puncture, gradually deflating the technocratic dreams of early meritocracy. In the years that followed, this entire scheme, with its anti-competitive, anti-aspirational and pro-administrative biases, slowly fell apart until a point was reached at which statisticians would have the temerity to suggest that *random preferment* is the best form of promotion in bureaucratic organisations.[191] Though random job promotion may appear completely irrational and would strike many as undesirable, it is not in itself an innovative concept in the context of present-day strategies of power. As we will discover, the idea of an irrational system of job allocation is entirely in accord with current systems of merit.

*   *   *

In the late twentieth century, the irrational forces of competition were gradually admitted into the scope of government. Competition became something to be encouraged, though not in the form of its mythological raw state, summed up most famously by Hobbes as 'every man, against every man'.[192] Competition was to be constructed artificially from a range of favoured dispositions, norms, frameworks and practices. Meritocracy gradually forgot its technocratic dream, no longer holding to grand plans of scientific repositioning. The engineered movements of a population were replaced by disorderly conduct of a kind favourable to government. Meritocracy became an ethic of admixture, one that took a highly individuated form, conditioning the various activities of day-to-day existence. It sought to guide solitary movements rather than control their eventual configuration. It passed from the administration of outcomes to the regulation of processes.

* * *

In order for meritocracy to become the guiding aspirational logic that conditions human interaction, making direct bureaucratic intervention less and less necessary, older, mechanical systems had to be superseded. A toilsome form of mechanical distribution that sows variations in so-called 'intelligence' alongside carefully matched educational provision had to be replaced by a system that allowed greater freedom to the social form. Formerly rigid and relatively overt, allocation would have to become far more fluid. Once doggedly mechanical, the technocratic distribution of bodies would recede into the mind, where it could regulate self-positioning activities. Meritocracy came to occupy the individual's interiority, impacting on his or her self-understanding, self-appreciation and practices of self-development. It would eventually oversee the redistribution of talent through its internalisation within the individuated practices of the population.

* * *

The transformation of meritocracy precipitated about an axis that was defined by the nature–nurture debate and related discussion concerning the role of social, cultural, race and gender bias in assessment. Here there was a growing awareness of the role environmental factors had to play in the distribution of 'intelligence'. These debates brought to prominence the general and increasingly intractable problem of complexity.

* * *

The changes were gradual, and this was part of their success. This allowed individuals to believe that the old tenets of a traditional meritocracy were still reflected in the new social order.

* * *

Whilst histories of meritocracy are very rare indeed, the phase from 1900 to 1940 was once dubbed a 'genetic meritocracy'.[193] This description is problematic insofar as it suggests a self-contained period ruled by the imperium of genetic determinism. It forecloses the possibility of a more gradual adjustment. Indeed, the replacement of deterministic ideas was never complete, and, after a brief absence, advocates of a link between genetic makeup, race, class and intelligence did return. These self-styled realists took on what they saw as a post-war consensus that was, for them, inflating the role of environmental factors.[194] The damage carried out by their opponents was irreversible, however. A longstanding commitment to counter the effects of environmental conditioning had already led to a series of adjustments that pushed traditional meritocracies into an advanced and chronic state of decline.

*   *   *

In the post-war years there was a growing sense that environment or nurture had a large and hitherto undervalued influence on mental development, ability and attainment. Hereditary, genetic and deterministic world-views were on the wane, and the pre-war designation of three types of child requiring three types of school became increasingly untenable. There were rising calls for an alternative system of education that would replace the old hierarchy of schools. So-called comprehensive schools, where all children were to be educated together, gradually won support.

It is tempting to view this point in educational history, with hereditary determinism on the back foot and comprehensives a real possibility, as the dawn of a golden era lasting until the late 1970s, when the hopes of this period were eventually dashed by a resurgence of the Right led by Margaret Thatcher. It is certainly undeniable that radical changes to the educational landscape were made during this post-war period of reform. Egalitarian demands were bolstered by changes in the perception of ability, the social conditioning of which received ever-greater attention. It was argued that the ideal of equal opportunity was not served simply by examinations for all at 11 years. Social conditions would have to be equalised too; the old demand for parity of esteem would need to be changed into a concerted effort to achieve parity of experience. These were the new egalitarian demands. This golden age, though, was digging its way along a dangerous seam, for this period was a transitional one, during which the egalitarian cause prepared the groundwork for its replacement.

*   *   *

The Holocaust raised the question of race to a new pitch. In the years that followed, some hoped to confront this question and finish the debate once and for all. UNESCO issued *The Race Concept: Results of an Inquiry* to settle the matter. There is 'no proof', it was reported, 'that the human groups of mankind differ in their innate mental characteristics'.[195] The negative effects of miscegenation were also denied. Indeed, it was claimed that race 'is not so much a biological phenomenon as a social myth'. On the question of human 'educability', the 'plasticity' of man was emphasised, and on mental characteristics the report claimed 'that intelligence tests do not in themselves enable us to differentiate safely between what is due to innate capacity and what is the result of environmental influences, training and education'.[196]

The report generated the controversy it sought to end, with critics arguing it over-reached the evidence. Under pressure, UNESCO issued a more reserved statement in 1951. Science, it seemed, could not make conclusive pronouncements in either direction, and so, in the spirit of dispassionate enquiry, German scientists such as Eugen Fischer, Fritz Lenz and Hans Nachtsheim, all of dubious pre-war and wartime repute, were invited to comment on the statement and suggest revisions.[197] The report did, nevertheless, signify a broader transition. According to one analysis, scientific racism was now in retreat. From this point onwards, any 'hereditarian explanation of social or cultural characteristics or ability was prone to be classified as racist. Naturalism and biological reductionism were generally viewed with suspicion, an attitude that continues to the present.'[198]

* * *

A central organising rhetoric informs *The Race Concept*. It pits the rationalism of genuine science against obsolete or pseudo-scientific notions, which, we presume, should never have been admitted in the first place. The findings of a reputable scientific community, disseminated widely throughout the UNESCO member states, would, we are encouraged to believe, provide a solution to the dangers of the recent past: 'Racial doctrine is the outcome of a fundamentally anti-rational system of thought', we are told, 'and is in glaring conflict with the whole humanist tradition of our civilization.'[199] The implication in the report is this: a return to rationality and science is a return to civilised life.

* * *

We can, of course, put this rhetoric to one side. The argument that science, instrumental rationality, bureaucratic machinery, statistical purview, disciplinary technology and the like were put to violent use by the Nazi regime has already been made by Foucault and others.[200] Though the Nazi regime did appeal to pre-modern mythologies of supremacy, this did not entail a departure from modern principles of rationality. The real problem posed by this event is that the Nazi regime was able to use and magnify existing rationalities and techniques. It mobilised the most banal practices of modernity, and that is what makes it so disturbing.

* * *

Beneath the distracting rhetoric of a dichotomy between rational and anti-rational tendencies, *The Race Concept* as formulated by UNESCO represents an attempt to destroy the race question through sublimation, diverting it into an intractable realm of complexity. Indeed, the ensuing debate made any 'simple explanation' of differences even more remote.[201] *The Race Concept* represented a return to science only insofar as it expressed the self-professed limitations of science and embraced uncertainty. Scientific thinking now acknowledged that the origins of mental characteristics could not so easily be deduced, for environmental and hereditary influences were heavily entangled with one another. According to this perspective, if we lay the foundations of policy on a vulgar and simplistic hereditary determinism, such policy will always be iniquitous and morally suspect simply because it fails to recognise the intractable nature of its object.

* * *

In meritocratic terms, the problem of complexity was initially absorbed by a social project that sought to achieve some sort of levelling effect when it came to environmental influences. In terms of formal education, a thorough-going redistribution of ability throughout the existing hierarchy would be insufficient. Ladders were now deemed unable to counteract environmental influences because these influences would self-perpetuate throughout the educational system they sought to correct. Eleven plus allocation within a tripartite system was a marginally better option. Its success would, however, depend upon highly accurate tools for human sorting and on all examinees having had similar educational experiences in their early years. Either schools and home environments would have to be homogenised, or their negative effects would have to be opposed by countervailing techniques. As a new breed of sociologist would soon confirm, however, the effects of the home environment are not easily reversed. Selection at 11 would always retain a social bias.

Selection procedures were also failing in terms of their predictive validity. By 1959, government advisors claimed that 'the extent of overlap' in ability between secondary modern and grammar schools had been 'underestimated'. For these advisors the policy consequences were clear: as it was 'much easier to change forms than to change schools', a comprehensive system of education, whereby all ranges of ability are catered for in one school, would be preferable.[202]

* * *

Unpopular Education, a critique of schooling and social democracy from 1944 to 1980, makes the point that during the immediate post-war era 'educational politics focused, very narrowly indeed, on *access*', entailing questions such as: Who has access to grammar schools? Are access examinations fair or do they discriminate?

At a similar time, social class was redefined in a 'fundamentally distributional' manner. Social classes were not permitted to have contradictory interests. Irresolvable conflicts demanding revolutionary, or radical, solutions were unthinkable once class difference was reduced to a matter of unequal distributions. With the distinction between classes reduced to a matter of distance, a gradualist approach seeking successive reductions in the separations between classes became reasonable.

According to the gradualist vanguard, a reduced gap between social groups could not be brought about through equality of opportunity alone; this kind of approach would only further deepen class divisions under existing conditions. The pursuit of equal opportunity had to be combined with the pursuit of greater equality of condition. There would need to be some degree of structural equalisation, or at least some sort of compensation for the disadvantaged. This was, of course, a profoundly revisionist strategy, one that did not tackle the deeper processes that led to class difference in the first place. When class became a matter of distribution, it could also be represented 'as a *matter of degree'*. The degree of equality could now be thought of as a ratio to be perfected, where too much equality leads to reduced incentives to take up burdensome work. In effect, social arrangements 'should be equal enough but not *too* equal'.[203]

The consequence of this for education was that comprehensive schooling could still function without contradiction alongside retained grammar schools and the ever-enduring private sector. The comprehensive schools themselves would not aspire to the abolition of selection; instead, they would allow internal divisions according to 'ability' that were softened and increasingly negotiable. Comprehensives would retain the meritocratic logic, still acting as institutions of human sorting, even though this meritocratic logic was now open to the vagaries of environmental influence. The issue of human sorting was more problematic now, but it was not in any way rejected.

* * *

Comprehensive schooling was to become the favoured project of the egalitarian reformer. It responded to the demise of determinism and a rising appreciation of the effects of environmental conditioning. These schools could be safely established, as the 'tripartite' system was not obligatory. It was merely an influential recommendation to be found within government reports preceding and post-dating the 1944 Education Act, which mandated nothing in this regard. Though secondary modern and grammar schools dominated early post-war development in England, a handful of comprehensive schools were opened in the first decade. During the late 1950s, amid mounting critique of the rigid hierarchies of school provision, the pace of reform increased. By 1962, 152 comprehensives had opened, providing for 10 per cent of all secondary school pupils. Many of these schools existed within authorities that still practised selection and retained grammar schools. More extensive reform followed an initiative in 1965 made by the incoming Labour government. It asked all authorities to submit plans for reorganisation on comprehensive lines.[204] Between 1966 and 1970, the percentage educated in comprehensive schools rose from 12 per cent to 40 per cent. It reached 50 per cent by 1973, 80 per cent by 1977 and 83 per cent by 1981.[205] This progressive advance seemed unstoppable. It was viewed by its supporters as a great triumph for social democracy.

* * *

A new breed of social scientist now occupied the position of social critic,[206] indicating with expansive gestures how multiplex were the environmental factors to be considered. These factors reinforced systems of exclusion. In 1953, it was reported that sons of the lower working class were still under-represented in grammar schools, whilst the middle classes were correspond-ingly under-represented in secondary modern schools, suggesting a class bias in the selection procedure.[207] Assuming that intelligence was distributed randomly amongst the social classes, this bias should not have occurred. One year later, this problem of selection was compounded by the findings of a government report in which it was announced that a disproportionate number of able, working-class grammar school pupils were leaving school early. There was also a clear gender bias, with girls tending to leave earlier than boys.[208]

Supporters of an older meritocratic order were not immediately converted. The incumbent Minister of Education, Sir David Eccles, speculated that: 'In the long run our ... schools will not be judged by how fairly a child enters at 11 but by how successfully he leaves at 15+, i.e. how he makes his way into the big world.' According to Eccles, the *outcomes* of a rigidly meritocratic system were what mattered. If the routes to these occupations were well mapped out, and if a range of opportunities existed within each ability group, parents 'will be satisfied when every secondary school offers a number of bridges to jobs which are worth having'. Indeed, the 'Englishman will not ask that the bridges should be all equal in wealth, or should all lead to the same suburb, but he will expect to see them in clear outline and to hear them well-spoken of'.[209] Unfortunately for Eccles, such levels of satisfaction were not attained, and unfair selection at 11 continued to draw rebuke. As for bridges, the terrain was already too convulsed for a lasting set of structures. Eccles was holding on to a Benthamite dream, with its direct mechanistic link between education and employment. By this point, meritocracy was suffering the early effects of dissolution, and in a dissolved landscape bridges no longer stand.

* * *

In 1957, the routine errors involved in selection were published. According to estimates, 12 per cent of children examined at 11 plus were wrongly positioned according to their intelligence, a proportion that corresponded to 78,000 wrongly allocated children in 1955. It was claimed that with contemporary technologies this could be reduced to 10 per cent, but no further. The system was also criticised for the fact that mistakes were not later corrected. Only 2 per cent of children were transferred from secondary modern to grammar schools between the ages of 12 and 15, with less than 0.5 per cent transferred in the opposite direction.[210] Methods of selection at 11 were inaccurate, and, to make matters worse, rigidly obeyed.

Amid this growing controversy, the *British Psychological Society* set up a special working party to consider the matter. They adopted a cautious tone:

> It must be remembered in view of the *complexity* of the environmental, emotional and intellectual considerations involved and the difficulty of assessing them accurately in all individual cases, that some errors will occur in any system of selection applied to human beings and that, unless there is appreciable *administrative elasticity*, there will always be unfortunate borderline cases with consequent frustration for the individuals concerned.[211]

The working party maintained, nevertheless, that intelligence tests were the best tests available. The strategic position occupied by such tests had altered, however. In the early days of a traditional meritocracy, tests were designed as a point of access for the hidden genius. Environmental factors (when acknowledged) were mere obstructions that the genius of sufficient strength would overcome. When engineers such as Lewis Terman[212] decided that waiting for the gifted few to rise of their own accord was insufficient, and argued for the deeper penetration of society by psychometric measurement, it was nevertheless felt that scientific tools could, with sufficient effort and development, cut a steady path towards truth. This perspective would change once environmental factors were no longer viewed as mere obstructions to the pursuit of innate ability. The psychologist, we discover, can no longer ignore the intractable effects of environmental influence. Faced by the limitations these influences impose, the honest professional should encourage greater flexibility: a 'flexible form of organization and grouping' was required, one that 'gives scope for gradual unfolding and the variability of children's abilities and interests'.[213] Again, flexibility within the system was promoted as a solution to its technical problems. Despite doubts over the accuracy of psychometric measurement, as an organising principle, intelligence retained its position in the meritocratic order. Intelligence tests would now accompany systems of human location that would take steps to compensate for any remaining inaccuracies of measurement.

*   *   *

By the 1950s, the terrain open to the social scientist had significantly widened. In the past, we are told, the 'problem of social waste in education could be seen in comparatively simple terms, for gross material factors overshadowed all others'. By 1957 this situation had altered significantly. Though there was 'still scope for attack on gross economic disabilities', social factors 'influencing educational selection' were said to 'reveal themselves in more subtle forms'. As a consequence of this shift in perception, it became legitimate to expect that 'relations between social class, family environment and educational opportunity' could 'only be effectively examined through intensive enquiry' into the 'home environment'.[214]

* * *

A commitment to subtlety now served to restrain the politics of research. Those seeking to interrogate the systemic biases produced by environmental disadvantage were not automatically committed to large-scale proposals for material redistribution. Indeed, such proposals were seen as crude in that they missed the finer operations of environmental influence. A preoccupation with 'gross material factors' was now seen to be symptomatic of the social scientist who lacks subtlety and insight.

* * *

A rise in egalitarian–environmental sensitivities justified the extended reach of investigation. The home environment of the most disadvantaged became increasingly interesting to researchers, whose intrusions were constructed as interruptions of progressive intent. Nevertheless, the main beneficiaries of a concern for the marginalised and dispossessed, the major profiteers of this benevolent endeavour, are often those who make it their business to be concerned. Careers are built on the plight of others.

* * *

The manipulation of individual prospects was transformed from systems of *extraction* (where the promising child was mechanically removed from one level of education and placed in a higher level), or *redistribution* (where all children were redistributed at 11 years regardless of their previous experience), to a regime of *environmental management*, where individual prospects are negotiated at a local level. Research now mapped intellectual ability in its relation to a variable environment. Having once focused on the calibration of instruments of extraction, research passed over to an exploration of the conditions necessary for human flourishing under the constraints of existing society. This involved the identification of unfavourable environmental conditions and an investigation of the most successful methods for their amelioration. There was to be a whole 'programme of research in teaching techniques designed, particularly, to help pupils whose abilities are artificially depressed' by environmental 'handicaps'.[215] Ability remained untapped not simply because large populations of able children lay undiscovered; rather, this was due to a failure in their collective nurture.

* * *

The overall project to distribute ability according to its normal curve continued. With a rising awareness of environmental factors, greater flexibility within the system was to be encouraged. This posed no immediate challenge to fairness and efficiency, which, as interpenetrating ideals, continued to inform the governmental logic of a meritocratic order. The ultimate goal remained that of a fully rationalised spread of ability. Progressive critics remained confined within this logic: promoting fairness through the principle that everyone must be allowed to develop his or her ability to its full potential. The old socialist complaint, that those who succeed in a capitalist order *only do so by climbing on the backs of others*, was little heard by mainstream reformers. Indeed, the notion that the 'able few' come to eminence by sitting on a whole edifice of wealth that has been constructed through the collected labour of the subjugated majority is an idea that could not be confronted directly without admitting that the entire social order was ripe for replacement. In its raw and proper form, this critique is 'useless' to government. It can be adopted and employed by government only through the strategy of a diversion, such as through the well-known argument that those who succeed must therefore pay back their debt to society through charitable work, progressive taxation or 'restrained' incomes.[216]

*   *   *

Though meritocracy embraced fluidity as a corrective strategy, it was only allowed a subordinate role in the meritocratic order. In occupying this position, fluidity brought with it a certain tension. This can be observed in a study of social mobility carried out by the sociologist David Glass in 1954.

In considering why mobility should be encouraged, Glass points to the rise in economic efficiency that is to be expected when 'positions requiring high ability will in fact be held by individuals who possess high ability'. He consequently expresses regret that social mobility is still limited by a private school sector that decides entry according to wealth rather than intelligence. Mobility, he adds, is also limited by the tripartite system of state-funded secondary education. Even though 'a process of osmosis is allowed' following allocation into one of three schools at 11 plus, the necessity for such mobility clearly demonstrates that 'deficiencies of the selection procedure' remain.[217]

Glass moves on to consider the social effects of increased mobility. He observes that 'existence of opportunity to rise in status' according to ability might lessen feelings 'of personal frustration' and bring about 'greater social harmony'. This much is standard discourse. And yet, Glass adds a rather mischievous remark: *'even if there is little actual opportunity to rise in social status, the belief in a myth of opportunity may produce similar results'*.

In a separate observation, Glass suggests that technical perfection in the assessment procedure could breed discontent. Selection procedures that divide the population into deliberate streams would probably reinforce the prestige of certain occupations. The 'feeling of resentment' this would engender may become 'more rather than less acute' because 'apparent justice may be more difficult to bear than injustice'.[218]

Now, it should be clear that Glass speaks from within the logic of a traditional meritocracy. His objectives include the redistribution of ability; the matching of positions requiring high ability to persons possessing such ability; the final removal of the last remaining vestiges of patronage; and the rectification of deficiencies in selection. Nevertheless, his was not a straightforward plea for meritocracy. Whilst expounding upon the necessity of greater social mobility, Glass is perturbed by the consequences of mobility for social stability. He suspects that the distribution of awards will become harder to bear once a system of merit approaches perfection. One's personal limitations are presumably harder to accept than broader systematic failures.

The Road to Serfdom contains a similar argument. In this book, published in 1944, Friedrich Hayek develops his critique of highly administered societies, claiming that England at that point resembled Germany in its tendencies to state control. On the matter of centralised distribution by merit, he warns that, when 'the position of an individual' is no longer determined by 'impersonal forces', 'the attitude of the people towards their position in the social order necessarily changes'. 'Dissatisfaction of everybody with his lot will inevitably grow with the consciousness that it is the result of deliberate human decision' in a 'planned society'.[219] These observations should be taken seriously. Both Glass and Hayek anticipate an alternative system, one that abandons the technocratic aspiration to combine efficiency with fairness, and hence overcomes the problem of resentment.

*   *   *

To *believe* that one lives in a system that allows individuals to realise their talents is said to be good for social stability. This belief produces contentment, or, at least, it avoids discontent. The mischievous suggestion Glass makes is that beliefs are more important than actualities (*the belief in a myth of opportunity may produce similar results*). As we will see, within a few decades, social opportunity was indeed mythologised in this way. Perfected distributions were abandoned by the operational logic of a meritocratic order, and principles of meritocracy were internalised and adopted in the practices of aspiring social subjects.

*   *   *

Today we live amongst the residues of welfare reform, occupying a broken landscape from which we draw meaning. Our memories of a former system – of the institutions and dreams of the welfare state – play a crucial role in the regime that is its replacement. Hence, to speak of the destruction of the welfare state is to exaggerate the case. Welfare has been destroyed only to the extent that it has been co-opted and absorbed. Its relations and dispositions have been further refined, they have been put to more effective use by new frameworks of power.

*   *   *

The various cataclysms anticipated for a meritocracy on the verge of perfection lent themselves to dramatisation. Dilemmas of perfection formed the subject matter of a satirical novel by Michael Young that was published in 1958. This book, *The Rise of the Meritocracy*, which charted the period 1870–2033, both coined the word and identified it with a dystopian social order.[220] Young's intention was to reveal the follies and dangers of a meritocratic life. Whilst the book bore this potential when it was first published, it no longer has the capacity to disturb us today as it once did. Young's satire no longer troubles us because the system he describes has ceased to exist.[221]

*   *   *

The term 'meritocracy' has since been transformed from a pejorative term to a positive ideal, invoked by recent political leaders such as Labour leader Tony Blair in a cynical attempt to win favour. In later life Young was deeply disturbed by this complete and utter reversal in the meaning and moral force of the term he had once invented.[222] All things considered, *The Rise of the Meritocracy* reveals far more about 1958 than it does about 2033. It depicts the end game of a traditional meritocracy.

*   *   *

So, to the story. From the distant perspective of 2033, Young's narrator reflects back to the 1960s and 1970s, and recalls the eventual defeat of those who supported comprehensive reform. This defeat was a victory for those meritocrats who, according to Young, were quick to argue that 'sentimental egalitarianism' would only ever encourage 'mediocrity'.[223]

In Young's satire, stronger partitioning and greater compulsion followed the defeat of comprehensive schools. Able pupils were paid a maintenance allowance to keep them in education whilst less able pupils were encouraged to leave. Grammar schools were improved upon until they outclassed and replaced private schools. Most importantly, intelligence tests were developed and extended as the lionised and most trusted device of the administrative machinery.

The continuity of psychometric science was secured through a direct appeal to the unique ability of this science to correlate high IQ with high performance in grammar school. This circumvented any debate questioning the existence of intelligence as a general entity within the mind.

The methods seemed to work, and that was all that mattered. From a technocratic perspective, comprehensive schooling was only appropriate for a brief historical period, when selection at 11 remained unperfected. Under these conditions, a little fluidity 'actually did some good by making it easier for people to swim from one stream to another'.[224]

From the late 1980s onwards, this sort of fluidity was no longer appropriate, as a higher degree of precision in making allocations was now attainable. Intelligence was measured every five years in order to check predictions and effect small corrections, and yet, with time, even this procedure would be abandoned. Gradually, predictions made during childhood became so accurate that regular retesting throughout life was dropped. The arguments of those who said it should be retained, 'if only to maintain the morale of low-I.Q. subjects who would otherwise be without hope', were ignored. The predictive validity of testing was felt to be unassailable: 'in 2000, the reliable age was 9; in 2015, the reliable age was 4; in 2020 it was 3'.[225] The entire course of education from nursery to university could be divided into a hierarchy of progression routes. Segregation according to intelligence was to be total.

The archaic model of protracted and incremental workplace promotion – from floor cleaner to occasional executive in 20 years – was also gradually abandoned. As industry began to recognise that recruits at 15 or 16 could no longer work their way up through the company (being now of a uniformly inferior intelligence), higher positions were recruited for directly from those attending institutions of higher education. Whilst direct recruitment such as this was an advance on the old model, it nevertheless resulted in hectic competition. Companies descended upon grammar schools and universities in order to scout through the best brains, siphoning them off before their education was complete with the promise of generous salaries.

At this stage in meritocratic development, competition was at best a necessary evil, one that must remain subordinate to the well-planned distributive ideal. Eventually, highly administered societies must obviate the need for competition: 'Effective brain power planning is not only necessary to end one of the kinds of competition between employers that is wasteful, but gives the government strategic power to control the whole economy.'[226] Competition had only been required in former times to the extent that it motivated individuals to help redistribute themselves: 'Before modern society could reach maturity, ambition had to be forced ever upwards.' Once it reached maturity, excessive (unreasonable) ambition became a dangerous condition.[227]

Despite the gradual perfection of the administrative machinery, there nevertheless existed seeds of social discontent within the explicit redistributive justice of the new order. In previous times, individual economic and social fate could be blamed upon circumstance. 'Educational injustice enabled people to preserve their illusions, inequality of opportunity fostered the myth of human equality.'[228] 'If only my life had been different, I would have been able to realise my potential; I would have been better off,' was the old lament. In early meritocracy it was possible to indict circumstance and not oneself. This resulted in a strange sort of inner peace, a type of personal contentment that persisted alongside calls for greater equality. The system was *unjust* because it was *unjustly unequal*.

In the new, more advanced meritocracy, social position was the direct expression of ability *plus* effort, a formula that was objectively defined and completely explicit. Citizens were expected to accommodate themselves to the fact that their social status was a direct expression of their intellectual worth. The system was now *just* because it was *justly unequal*.

We are told that imaginations were nevertheless still haunted by the narrative of Huxley's 'gammas'[229] and Orwell's 'proles'[230] – the two best-known exploited groups in fiction. Fortunately, however, the more intelligent members of the populace began to understand that these horror stories were the mere irrational outbursts of an earlier age. They were unreasonable attacks upon social conditioning, attacks that were written for a different era. These social critiques had no relevance in a well-administered state. Meritocracy, Young's narrator asserts, had become increasingly and unassailably just.

> Enlightened modern methods have nothing in common with these brave new worlds [of Huxley and Orwell]...to square efficiency with justice, and order with humanity, was nothing less than a new stage in the ascent of man, brought within his reach by the early advances in the social sciences.[231]

As the narrator's account draws to a close we find that this new stage in the ascent of man is, nevertheless, under threat. Social unrest is on the increase, and, as we are to discover, revolution is near. It seems that the ascent of man was destined to falter one last time, for apparent justice is at times harder to bear than injustice, and this is a situation that, if left unchecked, will lead the less intelligent classes to revolt. Life for those located further down the normal distribution was, in psychological terms, simply intolerable. They were unable to appreciate the intrinsic sense of the system of which they were an irreducible part. It was beyond their intellectual capacity to do so. The account breaks off, and an editorial footnote tells us that the narrator and author was killed in the upheavals of May 2034. He met his end at Peterloo. So it goes.

The conclusion is this: a society that is *justly unequal* invites rebellion in a way that an *unjustly unequal* society does not. The transparency of administrative systems in an advanced meritocracy provides an obvious target for revolt, especially when compared with the indeterminate and multiple forces of ill fortune that prevail in a less perfected meritocratic society. As

Young appears to suggest, the principles of traditional meritocracy are, in the end, self-defeating.

*   *   *

To readers of the twenty-first century this is an odd tale; they forget that it was intended as a warning. Of course, this warning is now clearly off target, as the society Young warned against was never even remotely achieved. It would be a mistake to dismiss his predictions entirely, however. Even his more outlandish forecasts must be treated with the seriousness they surely deserve. If Young's work reflects the meritocratic philosophy of his times, as we can assume from the vast distance that lies between his imagined future and our present, there must have been an equally momentous change in the rationale that informs our social order. Young's dystopia is instructive precisely for what it failed to predict.[232] In other words, the fact that Young's predictions were not borne out in reality suggests that meritocracies underwent radical adjustment. As yet, they have failed to inspire an insurrectional response of the kind Young described. Indeed, the difficulties anticipated for justly unequal societies never arrived. My claim, then, is this: the cataclysmic effects of perfection that Young so graphically portrayed were eventually avoided through their abandonment. As traditional meritocracies were superseded, the stark problems posed by redistributive justice faded away. The governmental task was reconfigured, becoming in its remit chiefly pedagogic and moral, instructing subjects in the art of living in (and not revolting against) a deeply unsystematic and divided social order.

*   *   *

The Secondary Modern School, published in 1963, also glanced into the future. Within this more prosaic text one finds the following apparently naïve claim: if tripartite education were to disappear, there would be 'an opportunity to dispense with' end-of-school examinations. When secondary schooling is amalgamated and modern schools no longer have to assert their place in the system, the 'significance of paper qualifications' will be reduced.[233] As we now know, paper qualifications were not diminished; they subsequently multiplied.

*   *   *

In 1963, examinations were still associated with the rigidities of tripartite selection. Examinations were, as yet, unable to survive outside this system; they had not developed that capacity. In this sense, modern examinations were still radically opposed to the embrace of fluid orders.

*   *   *

Rigidity in the social structure was redefined as a problem.[234] Insofar as it was connected to systems of examination, these systems would need to be eased up.

*   *   *

Rigidity was problematic for economic reasons. Employment had changed, employees were less likely to have a trade for life, and rapid technological change was making some jobs redundant whilst creating new roles for the employee. Ever a slave to the status quo, the social scientist recommended 'the adaptability of the individual and the flexibility of the labour force'.[235]

*   *   *

This recognition that vocations were in a state of flux conveniently matched post-war conceptions of the individual. Or, stated in reverse, a partial rejection of innate, fixed ability matched changing industrial requirements. In the words of a contemporary government report, it was now accepted that the working population must 'be able to adjust to a rapidly changing environment'.[236] This population was to be reconfigured as a malleable group that could be enhanced through environmental conditioning. The individual economic subject was no longer viewed as a fixed resource. He or she was now seen to be replete with abilities of uncertain provenance and specification. These hidden resources must be allowed to emerge. Individuals must be convinced that, whatever happens, they will be able to draw from as yet hidden talents. The overall point is this: individuals of malleable composition are better able to embrace the vocational and industrial uncertainty of their times.

*   *   *

According to the French sociologist Georges Friedmann, writing in 1955, the individual can no longer be 'considered as an unalterable datum' to which must be allotted its appropriate vocation. It is necessary to take into account the 'evolution in tastes and abilities in the individual', and consideration must also be given to the parallel 'evolution in trades'. 'The myth of an individual with a single occupational value' is now over. 'The evolution of trades and the regrading of workers' in modern industrial societies make rigid job allocation a thing of the past.[237]

*   *   *

English sociologists Jean Floud and Albert Halsey address these problems in *English Secondary Schools and the Supply of Labour*. They repeat the standard refrain, that the 'efficient division of the working population among occupations requires both that there should be the right number of workers in each occupation and that the qualities of workers in each occupation should be as appropriate as possible'. However, the 'relationship between the educational system and occupational structure is not a simple one. Moreover, it changes over time.' The range of vocational opportunities is subject to change as the economy itself undergoes its interminable alterations. From this perspective, a 'fluid labour supply' was urgently needed, both for the nation and for the capitalist order it served. It was regrettable, therefore, that the education system was holding the country back as its major 'source of rigidities'.[238]

These points are repeated in *The Secondary Modern School*:

> The problem today is no longer one of discovering, educating and promoting an *elite*, and ensuring sufficient culture and general literacy for those who, because of the 'facts' of economic life and hereditary endowment, are likely to become hewers of wood and drawers of water.[239]

That low-skilled occupations still continue to exist 'is indisputable', but it is 'no longer true that the line drawn between pupils in Grammar, Technical and Modern schools is meaningful in terms of the demands for skill and training likely to be made by industry, commerce and trade'.[240] Vocational demands had already changed and would continue to change. Educational provision, however, lagged far behind.

* * *

The social commentators who raised these difficulties were clearly wedded to the system that employed them, and, yet, they were far more than its obsequious lackeys. As sociologists, they were closely involved in the transformation and refinement of a regime of government.

* * *

It was now reasonable to reject tripartite education and its occupational assumptions. Comprehensive schooling was, at first, the sole alternative. It would bring these assumptions under one roof, where they could be modified more rapidly in response to the fluctuating needs of industry. Eventually comprehensive schools fell out of favour. In late twentieth-century England a school system that was *systematically chaotic* replaced its comprehensive forebear.

* * *

Despite its comparatively brief existence, the comprehensive project was pivotal in the transformation of meritocracy. It represented the last attempt to rationalise the distribution of talent, and the first move towards a system where the perfect distribution of talent became unimportant. Whilst allowing greater flexibility – so as to achieve a better match between ability and vocational distributions – comprehensives also embraced the problem of complexity. It was in the process of this embrace that education developed the techniques that would allow it to become systematically disordered.

* * *

With the education system prised open, so that fluidity might enter and rise from its formerly subordinate position to occupy a superordinate role, there was no chaotic deluge or descent into liquid disorder. A single examination system would provide the collective logic beneath which fluidity could be directed, so that its flows could be channelled, diverted and accelerated where necessary.

* * *

The earliest comprehensive schools introduced streaming, channelling pupils according to ability along select developmental paths. It was reported that 'from the outset, they saw this not as a permanent classification so much as a means of educational guidance'.[241] Internal movement was still possible. Some schools went further, offering a general course common to all pupils in the first two or three years of secondary school. In these schools, streaming was still in operation, but a common curriculum would allow greater movement in the formative years of secondary schooling. Elsewhere, streaming was replaced by a system of three distinct 'bands', where several un-streamed classes coexisted within each category; movement between bands was encouraged. Alternatively, all pupils were entirely mixed for the first years of secondary school. After this phase, pupils were divided into a range of set courses, from technical, craft and commercial to more academic. Some schools dispersed these choices further, into subject-based divisions.[242]

Since subject choice was 'clearly of great importance to each individual pupil, various systems of "guidance" or "counselling" were introduced, involving teacher and youth employment officer, parent and child'.[243] In effect, ability distributions were now rationalised in a far more flexible environment. The distribution of ability to employment to social position was up for negotiation and renegotiation, through a process in which environmental factors and background were now taken into account.

From the mid-1960s, un-streamed, mixed-ability classes were trialled.[244] It was claimed that streaming set 'arbitrary limits'. An 'untapped source of ability' remained that would not be revealed unless streaming was relaxed.[245] Here the last vestiges of an aristocratic meritocracy were under attack in an effort to ensure no barrier remained between ability and its rightful place.

As a result, the general idea that educational governance should serve hierarchical structures that administer the distribution of talent was all but demolished. A traditional meritocracy had reached the point where efforts to compensate for the influence of environment had finally brought about the prospect of its dissolution.

*   *   *

The comprehensive experiment was not accompanied by a similarly radical overhaul of examinations. For all the attempts to increase flexibility within the school and counteract the effects of environmental disadvantage, final school examinations remained comparatively untouched. They retained the old tripartite hierarchy within their structures. Indeed, comprehensive education was not accompanied by a comprehensive examination system until it was in decline. An older rationale persisted, one that embodied the divisions of a more traditional meritocracy.

*   *   *

In an effort to guide post-war reform, the Ministry of Education published a series of pamphlets. *Pamphlet No. 9* dealt with secondary education and the 'necessary' division of schooling into three types, designed to suit the needs of different types of child.

'No child must be forced into an academic education which bores it to rebellion' if it is more likely to 'get fun out of a carpenter's bench or a bricklayer's trowel, or satisfaction out of the risk and adventure of the mine'. It seemed obvious that different types of school were required for different grades of individual. These divisions would not be socially divisive if 'parity of esteem' could be achieved. Surely, they argued, after two world wars the 'public attitude to the craftsman and the technician' has changed in a way that 'is nothing less than revolutionary'.[246] Parity of esteem (if not parity of pay) is presented here as if it were a real possibility.

Grammar schools would surely benefit once competition for scholarship was replaced by careful allocation. With child type better matched to school type, grammar schools would no longer find themselves having to 'meet the requirements of pupils for whom its own form of education is not really appropriate'. They could focus more fully on their 'proper function', that is, preparation for higher education and the professional classes.[247] Whilst entry examinations were appropriate for all schools, it was felt that exit examinations would only suit grammar schools. These exit examinations had no place in secondary modern schools that catered for a much wider range of abilities. It was seen as 'impracticable to combine a system of external examinations, which presupposes a measure of uniformity, with the fundamental conception of secondary modern school education, which insists on variety'.[248]

Here we should recall that the population had been divided at 11. In principle, the homogeneity of each respective division was thereby increased. Ideally, each group would now be targeted by end-of-school examinations that were precisely calibrated to its distinctive traits. These examinations would represent the final point in a long process of selection, only now subdividing a limited range of ability into successful and unsuccessful candidates. It was reasonable to expect that, as a traditional meritocracy reaches perfection, end-of-school examinations should increasingly function like a yes/no logic gate. In practice, though, this ideal was most easily applied to grammar schools, for these were the only institutions that catered for a relatively small section of the normal distribution. With their relatively homogeneous cohorts, they could withstand a single external examination. In the grammar school, examination would be a qualifying procedure rather than a competitive device for siphoning upper streams of ability from a vast range of candidates. These institutions were to be contrasted with secondary modern schools, which, by definition, schooled a much wider range of abilities. In this context, one examination open to all would have been inappropriate. The modern school would have failed as a confederate in the system of official location had its terminus been marked by a free-for-all. It would have merely educated, rather than also selected, streamed and allocated. Modern schools, being comparatively diverse, would have to be served by different, more variegated systems of assessment.

*   *   *

The problem of variety in the secondary modern school could only be resolved by a shift from external to internal examination – from the unitary assumptions of an external examination board, to the multiple curricular accommodations that could be achieved through situated expertise. Externally administered school-leaving examinations had traditionally focused on the top scholarly echelons, which meant that: 'it was in the main only for these heavily intellectual-cognitive subjects that generally accepted methods of examination had over the years been developed'.[249] For this reason, meritocracy would necessarily depend upon the expertise of teachers to assess the lower grades of ability. Careful assessment 'of all the work done by a pupil in a subject over a term or a year' would be required: 'the more "practical" and "non-academic" the subjects, the more important this is'.[250] Internal expertise would be essential in judging the modern school child. Only at this level of individual detail, by making use of localised, professional knowledge, could meritocracy surmount such prior neglect of the below-average child, and thus subdivide the secondary modern population.

*   *   *

This system was under strain from the outset. External qualifications swiftly became a sought-after commodity. As early as 1946, many modern schools began preparing pupils for the School Certificate (an old grammar school examination established in 1917). This route was swiftly blocked by the Ministry of Education, which forbade external examinations under the age of 16, thus debarring the modern school child, whose education generally finished at 15 years. Only grammar school children should be allowed to take the associated examination. When the School Certificate was replaced in 1951 by a new examination, the O-Level GCE,[251] the chance for modern school entries opened up once again, as the GCE came with a lowered minimum age. Barriers remained, however. The standard of a pass was raised to the level that had formerly counted as a 'credit' on the School Certificate. This would ensure the GCE remained in the grammar schools, qualifying only grammar school pupils for further study.

End-of-school examinations were intended to qualify individuals for specific tasks. They were not regarded as a source of non-specific certificates that could be exchanged for any number of employments. Nevertheless, and in open revolt, the upper streams of modern schools were prepared for the GCE. In 1954, over 5000 modern school pupils were entered; by 1962, this figure reached 36,000.[252] To some extent, these numbers served as a further critique of tripartite education – the GCE should have been well beyond the modern school child had allocations at 11 been correct.[253]

Other external examinations for the modern school also proliferated at this time. In the absence of a single state-sanctioned examination, awarding bodies occupied the terrain left vacant beneath the GCE. In 1960, one particular school introduced 'school-leaving examinations at three separate levels to provide an examination objective for children throughout the ability range: a GCE course for the A stream; a five-year Royal Society of Arts course for the B stream and a four-year Union of Educational Institutes qualification for the C stream'.[254] This modern school managed to sort its ability range into groups, providing each level with its own external examination.

External examinations for the secondary modern school were not, however, the favoured option. Secondary moderns were expected to experiment with a combination of internal examinations and records of achievement. The use of teacher expertise was intended to match practices of internal examination to the greater range of ability in moderns. Despite the encouragement of government agencies, however, internal examinations were not widely implemented.[255] Moreover, external examinations were on the increase, prompting the Minister of Education to ask whether the conventional divisions between internal and external examinations, and modern and grammar schools, should be reconsidered.[256]

In the report that followed, the relatively homogeneous nature of the grammar school was contrasted, once again, with the much wider range of ability catered for within the modern schools. This group could itself be divided, and amongst 'those four-fifths of the nation's children who do not get to grammar schools' three important groups were discerned. The first group was very small; it consisted of those able to take the GCE. The second group was larger, 'for whom an external test is both possible and sensible'. The third group was by far the largest, and 'consists of those for whom an external examination at the age of 16 is an absurdity'.[257] This point was repeated four years later in *Half Our Future*, a specialist report for children of average and below-average ability: 'We are convinced that for a substantial number of pupils [the majority of those below average] public examinations would be entirely inappropriate.'[258] The education of such children 'should be as little abstract as possible'. It should be focused upon their immediate surroundings and 'will be dictated by the character of the place in which the school is'. External examinations would not be able to accommodate this localised focus. In addition, the education of this lower group should place greater emphasis upon speech rather than written work, and 'speech does not lend itself well to external examination' either.[259] Still, if external examinations were introduced to the modern school for the more able groups this would breed problems of its own. The difficulty was one of potential trespass, a familiar problem for a traditional meritocracy.

> ...neither schools nor parents would be able to resist the pressure to give border-line candidates a chance, and that in consequence the border-line itself would be pushed further down year by year. An examination for the top third might soon find its fringe candidates drawn from the half-way mark: an examination designed for the top half might find itself serving all but the bottom quarter.[260]

If these examinations were publicly billed as 'general examinations' rather than 'special examinations with a particular defined purpose such as securing admission to this or that institution or profession', it was feared there would be 'nothing to limit the numbers taking the former'.[261] Examinations designed for particular sectors of the modern school population were likely to grow into a general modern school examination or 'mass examination', which was exactly the result they wished to avoid.[262] Divisions between different types of child within the modern school had to be retained. The whole point of school provision in a rigid meritocracy was to establish such partitions. Human sorting at an earlier stage in school life was designed to make a general end-of-school examination unnecessary.

* * *

In 1965, an external examination appropriate to the modern school was finally introduced. This was designed to claw back initiative once the drive for internal assessment floundered. The CSE[263] was to be administered at a local level by 14 regional examining boards and was to be made available in three modes: Mode III was the most celebrated approach, allowing both syllabus and examination to be internally set and marked. Subjects ranged from more traditional academic courses to areas such as typing, domestic science, needlework, accounts and catering.

* * *

It is conventional in educational circles to view the Mode III CSE as a radical and progressive experiment in the history of English examination. Here was a chance to escape the centralising control of the examining bodies. This was the moment in the history of examination when curricular control was most radically devolved. It was the high watermark of teacher autonomy.[264]

What these commemorations ignore, however, is the profoundly technocratic role the CSE performed. This examination was crucial to the refinement of meritocracy, extending its operations to 'lower grades' of ability and courses of study.

To the extent that the CSE, for all its variations, was still a single examination, it was dogged by the variety question that faced the modern school with its large distribution of ability. In an effort to solve this problem, those passing the examination were graded according to five categories of merit. In this respect, the idea that a modern school should contain multiple qualifying examinations, each acting like a yes/no logic gate for its respective level, was abandoned. The CSE would be awarded from grade 1, which corresponded to a GCE pass, to grade 5, for those of below average ability. By contrast, the grammar school equivalent, the O-level GCE, was initially only offered at pass or fail, which was the appropriate course of action when testing a relatively homogeneous grammar school group.[265]

To provide extra differentiation, the CSE would also be available in the form of single subject examinations. The old School Certificate, by contrast, had only been awarded for select groups of subjects. In 1951, the GCE too made a break with this tradition. Now 'pupils of quite low general ability' were able to take 'isolated papers'.[266] This extended the range of an examination where more 'able' pupils were simply entered for a greater number of subjects. Thus, finer stratification was achieved both in the graded pass marks and in the range of subjects entered for and passed.

* * *

In response to the unplanned proliferation of the GCE beyond the grammar school for which it was intended, a system of examination had finally been developed for lower levels of 'ability'. As comprehensive

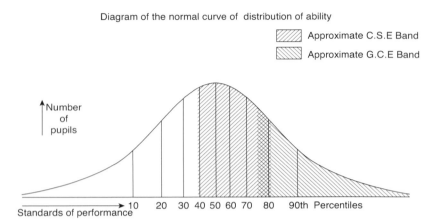

Diagram of the normal curve of distribution of ability

schools spread, gradually replacing modern and grammar schools, the dual GCE/CSE examination system continued. It is in this sense that comprehensive reorganisation represented the last stage in the development of traditional meritocracy, where greater internal fluidity (allowing for late-flourishing ability to achieve its rightful place) operated within a clearly stratified examination structure. The GCE was designed for the top 20 per cent and the CSE for the next 40 per cent of the school population.[267] Those taking CSE exams would be differentiated by the number of subjects for which they were entered, and by the respective grades achieved. The CSE was certainly not intended to be a device for mass testing.

* * *

Increasingly, the prescription that these examinations were each to cater for a specific range of ability was ignored in practice. Once the CSE was introduced, many schools allowed 'almost all pupils to enter for at least one or two subjects'.[268] According to a government survey, some schools were making 'unrealistic demands' of their pupils with 'too many subjects being taken' and pupils 'working to overambitious targets' – in particular those pupils 'of average or low ability'.[269] It was claimed that pupils who should not have been sitting external examinations were allowed by their schools to do so, and that those pupils for whom external examinations were appropriate were, in the expert view, often sitting far too many. It was becoming increasingly difficult to confine the GCE to grammar schools, or to precisely divide a population of above-average comprehensive school pupils into those suitable for the GCE and those who should settle for the CSE. This much the CSE architects had anticipated: the 'gradations would [have to] be much less clear cut', they wrote, where, in addition to a 'group concentrating on the GCE examination', there would have to be 'a group who would in the same year' take GCEs in some subjects and CSEs in others.[270] However, the lower limit of the CSE was likely to generate problems. As the architects feared, there was little to prevent this border-line descending. This descent was understandable enough, for, with the composition of natural ability in doubt, all boundaries had become grey areas. With a rising awareness of the role environmental factors had to play, greater flexibility was demanded. Pupils should be given the chance to attempt an examination even if it seemed futile. They should be given the opportunity to fight against any possible disadvantage in their upbringing and education. It was now unreasonable to divide a population once and for all into GCE and CSE strands based upon selection at 11. Indeed, the CSE architects never intended 'to suggest that intelligence tests made at 11 should determine which children should take a particular examination five years later'.[271]

Ultimately, then, these attempts to refine meritocracy led to its own undoing. By hedging around these thorny issues, the architects of the CSE pandered to the growing disorder of the system. The prescriptive logics of a traditional meritocracy would subsequently break down, opening up end-of-school examinations to all, where the old prescription that there should be a level of homogeneity shared between examinees was the decisive casu-alty of this system change. Traditional meritocracy, and its careful efforts to divide ability, broke apart before an examination system that was becoming increasingly general and widely applied.

* * *

The old two-tier external examination structure was finally replaced in 1986 by the GCSE.[272] This new examination was made available on an individual subject basis and was awarded according to a sequence of grades. Initially, it was intended to be an examination appropriate for the top 60 per cent of the ability range only.[273] Yet, by the early 1990s 94 per cent of each year group were achieving at least one GCSE.[274] The mass examination that was once to be avoided had finally arrived.

* * *

Mass examination has a long history. Its operations can be observed, for example, in early twentieth-century efforts to ensure that scholarship examination was a group test, taken by all. Only recently, however, have its operations been so profoundly generalised that they extend *throughout* the years of schooling, across school types and between nations, allowing global comparisons, and equally global condemnations.

After Fairness

> Our institutions are no longer fit for anything: everyone is unanimous
> about that. But the fault lies not in them but with *us*.[275]
>
> *Friedrich Nietzsche*

The dissolution of meritocracy was accompanied by the arrival of a uniquely
dissolute regime of power. This regime constructs its citizen subjects so that
they live unperturbed by its depraved moral order. They are to be educated
for a life beyond justice, fairness and reason.[276]

*   *   *

Basil Bernstein once famously remarked that 'education cannot compensate
for society'.[277] This mantra is worth repeating when faced by the glib statements of educators who claim to be mending the social rift. Ironically, the
affluent parent understands this statement only too well. This parent knows
that individual success increasingly depends on an augmented education.

*   *   *

Today's aspirational parent is keenly aware of the role of environmental
conditioning, and its potential to enhance or disrupt a child's chances of
success. This parent has diligently absorbed that particular mid-twentieth
century sociological insight. The child now endures parental efforts that
are markedly different from those encountered by his or her nineteenth-
century precursors. Sending one's child to the crammer was a late nineteenth-century fix whereby the child's mind was simply to be filled in a
short space of time with all the information relevant to a particular examination. Avoiding schools that catered for lower classes was seen as a defence
against social and moral depravity; it was a matter of maintaining one's
position within the divisions of social class by preventing any association
with socially 'inferior' children and teachers. Cultured environments were
optimised and defended for the sake of social segregation. In both cases,
this was not about optimising environmental influence for the purposes of
better intellectual development. It remained for the twentieth century to
make this connection.

*   *   *

The twentieth century witnessed an overall switch from investment in
school fees[278] to investment in educationally enhanced home environments. This coincided with numerous longitudinal studies that followed
children from birth to employment, correlating experiences and conditions
in the early years with later life chances.[279] These studies convinced their

readers that the early years of a child's life were crucial to later development; they laboured the point that material and social disadvantage can adversely affect later life chances. During this period, 'a new project came to bear upon the mental development of the young child'. This would seek 'to supplement or replace the pedagogy of citizenship provided by the mother' with better-informed child-rearing techniques.[280] Outside the home there were to be 'education priority areas' where schools could exercise 'positive discrimination' and 'supply a compensating environment' for those with 'social handicaps'.[281] These priority areas were to be for the poor, in other words, who were seen as culturally deprived and in need of remedial action. Of course, the scheme failed to equalise educational opportunity. Its real achievement was to pilot strategies for linking communities and parents to a wider political ordering of social life.

Closer to home, the 1960s saw the rapid growth of the playgroup movement, providing enhanced environments and socialisation for the under-fives.[282] At home, the domestic sphere was overhauled as principles of early-years enhancement were popularised. These were initially visited on middle-class mothers, who were targeted by books, pamphlets and magazine articles. They were encouraged to view every aspect of the home environment in terms of its educational value. Whilst the working-class mother faced ongoing material disadvantage, the bourgeois mother found herself trapped by the scale of her educational task. It was difficult in the face of such discourse to extract herself 'guiltlessly from so monumental a role'.[283]

> The learning environment becomes the entire home, every possible permutation of events, actions and conversations becomes a 'not to be missed' opportunity for a valuable lesson [that] must be directed carefully and sensitively taught...The good mother must always be there. And so, not only the 'formal' lessons or the 'educational game', but imaginative play, mealtimes, housework, conversations, questions, demands, resistance and arguments *all* become the site of learning.[284]

Time collapses for a parent in this position as the separation between time for housework and time for childcare disappears. The parent must focus on the perpetual educational present, where every moment becomes a moment of potential educational significance.[285]

* * *

In recent years, the early years of life have not escaped the interests of capital. Toys have been reclassified according to their educational attributes.

* * *

Spend some time in the toy department. A child of two or more years can own a colourful toaster with two slices of plastic bread that pop up when done. According to the key displayed on the box, this will achieve two objectives: it will help increase social skills and imagination. A child of three or more years can enjoy a plastic cupcake tea party: 'Invite your friends to a scrumptious tea party,' it reads, because this will increase your imagination and instil confidence. Alternatively, a wooden cut and play birthday cake will increase social skills and imagination *and* instil confidence: 'Let's celebrate our birthday every day,' the cake suggests.

*   *   *

Multi-million dollar brands now occupy this lucrative domain. 'Baby Einstein', a franchise owned by Walt Disney, is one such enterprise catering for the overly ambitious parent.[286]

*   *   *

Ambitious parents tend to identify to an excessive degree with the successes of their children. Theirs is a projection of desire that is likely to inflict some measure of psychological pain on its recipient.

*   *   *

We know that vast industries serve the needs of institutionalised violence. In this context, educational toys are remarkable only for the beneficent aura with which they are surrounded.

*   *   *

Educational enhancement is now linked more or less directly to the forces of capital. It is at the level of individual environmental enrichment that advantage is to be secured by those who can afford it. In this context, those who protest on behalf of parents who cannot afford enrichment are inclined to recommend remedies that are located at a similar level.[287] Political debate is thereby increasingly constrained to a time-collapsed realm.

*   *   *

At their limit, such efforts to optimise the environment of the child extend back into the womb. Indeed, some have attempted to create genius *in utero*. In 1962, a South African study suggested that abdominal decompression during pregnancy could enhance intellectual development. Subsequently, there was a brief spike in the number of pregnant women wearing decompression suits, with British scientists joining the fray. Months later, scientists confirmed that they were unable to confirm the intellectual benefits of decompression.[288]

* * *

Rats are more obliging. Mozart reportedly enhances their maze-solving abilities. This is on the condition that they are blasted with it for 12 hours a day both *in utero* and following birth.[289] Mozart's ability 'to transpose universal laws of nature into music' has also been applied to the treatment of German sewage, in the hope that microbe cultures would be similarly enhanced.[290] Again, scientists confirm that they are unable to confirm this claim, though the experiments continue.

* * *

External manipulation of the uterine environment is hardly comparable to eugenics, and yet, alongside other forms of environmental adjustment, it comes closest to eugenic intervention. It, too, is designed to ensure a 'good birth'. Now, one could be pious about this distinction, and argue that manipulation of the womb marks the ultimate limit of nurture and the frontier of nature. Accordingly, when pregnant women take iodine supplements in the hope that they will enhance brain development, they remain within the realm of nurture. This would be the point of distinction. From a political perspective, though, there is no dividing line, and, to the extent that science is wrapped up with the formation and revision of regimes of power, it is inclined to agree. As a geneticist observed shortly after the war, the 'distinction between causes, which are said to be hereditary or part of the individual's nature and those which are environmental or pertaining to nurture, must be based upon a temporal sequence'. In other words, the relation between nature and nurture is really one of *time*. Genetic effects may simply be divided into 'remote' and 'recent'; environmental effects into 'early prenatal', 'late prenatal', 'intranatal' and 'postnatal'.[291] Other post-war scientists agreed,[292] as did the following government report:

> All characteristics have a history of continuous developmental interactions, first of gene products with other gene products, then of more complex molecules with other molecules, then of cells with cells, of tissues with the environment of the mother's uterus, and finally of a whole complex organism with an equally complex environment during the whole of growth after birth.[293]

From this perspective, the antenatal decompression suit represents an intermediate point between two distant locations in time. The basic lesson here, in reducing the contrast between nature and nurture to a difference in time, is this: once our focus shortens onto more recent events (i.e. from a eugenic manipulation of ancestry to an environmental optimisation of the womb or early-years environment), the possibilities for intervention multiply and confounding variables increase. There is no essential difference between the eugenic position and the environmental one from the perspective of power, other than the shortening of time and the rise in complexity. 'Eugenic time', with its focus on the distant ancestral past and the remote, potentially moribund future,[294] is gradually replaced by a foreshortened individualised time, by a decreased angle of vision and a focus upon the educational present. The vast expanses of dynastic time collapse to reveal an intensely myopic concern with individual enhancement.

* * *

The genealogy of biopower may be described in terms of this temporal axis. During the eugenic era, biopower was concerned as much with the biological past and future as it was with the Nature of the present. Once the eugenic programme fell from favour, the temporal axis of biopower began to shorten. The current ecological status of a population, rather than its prior genetic basis or future possibility, became the principal concern.

Broadly speaking, this reconfiguration of power is complicit in the marginalisation of critique: recall Foucault's account of counter-history and its eventual demise.[295] This proto-genealogical critique reworked historical perception to disrupt its present. It constructed rival social histories to undermine the apparent inevitability of things. These rival histories were able to show that another present was possible, and that another future could be hoped for. Always a marginal discourse, counter-history was, nevertheless, largely neutered during the nineteenth century when 'social time' was reconfigured as biological time. Social histories of races were replaced by a new emphasis on the biological histories of bloodlines.

Emerging from this transition and extending well into the twentieth century, the perspective of eugenic time, for all its horrific implications, nevertheless retained a conception of time as something of epochal proportions. This time-based perception has since collapsed. We are increasingly encouraged to think in terms of an individuated timeframe, a realm within which it is possible to forget that each individual exists within a longer social history of events and processes. This means, for example, that the organisation of social institutions has become increasingly irregular. There is no longer any extended socio-historical project to which these institutions can be meaningfully attached. Strategies of power that encourage such shortened historical perspectives leave us more than ever susceptible to the vicissitudes of the present.

* * *

The provision of schooling in England has never been operationally consistent or well ordered. It has evolved through a series of *ad hoc* developments, where each stage has failed to fully regularise the system it hoped to reform.[296] Since the first schools enquiry of 1868,[297] it was always hoped that schooling could be organised along nationally coherent lines. By the end of the twentieth century, however, this assumption ceased to inform educational reform efforts. Divergent modes of educational provision were now expected to 'coexist'[298]; indeed, diversity was to be encouraged. Following the 1988 Education Act, school governance was devolved: budgetary control was handed over to individual schools, some schools were allowed to opt out of local government control, and 'technology colleges' were established with business sponsorship. From 1994, secondary schools were encouraged to develop specialist status and distinct identities. A few years later, the academy programme further multiplied the permutations of schooling. Initially situated in deprived wards and run by corporate sponsors, they were given substantial freedom to innovate: 'transforming education in areas where the status quo is simply not good enough'.[299] In the *Sponsor Prospectus*, future investors are told that they can:

> appoint the majority of the governors and with them lead the strategic direction of the Academy, offering challenge and support to the principal and senior management team... Issues of ethos, specialism and uniform are entirely for you. There are some requirements on the curriculum that you will need to meet [but] the vast majority of the detail will be for you... Each Academy is unique – and so too is its sponsor.[300]

*　*　*

The social divisions generated by local *ad hoc* arrangements have been interpreted by some as heralding a return to the iniquitous days of tripartite education. These claims are mistaken, relying as they do on a statistical analysis of schools, dividing them retrospectively into categories: eight school types have been identified, from those creaming the top 10 per cent to those that are heavily weighted to the bottom 50 per cent, suggesting a finer level of discrimination than tripartite education ever achieved. Significantly, though, the 'names given to secondary schools' do not 'accurately reflect the characteristics of their intakes'.[301] Indeed, one must conclude that these stark divisions in school provision *are no longer organised according to an overall plan*, tripartite, comprehensive or otherwise. Bureaucratic overview has been replaced by systems of organisation 'replete with overlap, multiplicity, mixed ascendancy and/or divergent-but-coexistent patterns of relation'.[302]

*　*　*

The extent to which fluidity has taken hold should not be exaggerated. A fluid meritocracy is still based upon a definite framework of power relations. These were essential when replacing a traditional meritocracy and its embedded techniques. In Britain, early attempts to develop the requisite governmental devices included those made by the Manpower Services Commission. This quasi-autonomous organisation was created in the 1970s to coordinate training and employment services. Though it gave rise to a 'bewildering wealth of schemes and acronyms', its more perspicacious critics identified three major innovations. First, 'the repertoire of concern for justice and efficiency was replaced by emphasis on the need for "employability" '. It was a matter of training and socialising the jobless young, heedless of the environment from which they came. Second, 'particular skills were to be replaced by (examinable) generic skills'.[303] Third, the commission 'took the differentiation already achieved by schooling as its datum line'.[304] Counteracting environmental disadvantage, and working towards greater justice in meritocratic distribution, was no longer the primary objective. The aim was to socialise young workers, prepare them for employment, and provide a common frame of reference for comparison.

* * *

With the rise of biopower, disciplinary techniques were forced to operate outside their former enclosures. Such a technological breach, taking an old technology far beyond its original institutional setting, eventually resulted in the erasure of its more mechanistic elements. Once the strategic hub of disciplinary practice, the modern examination became a principle of movement that extended to the entire population. It was to be the common framework that ties together disparate events.

* * *

When Raymond Cattell imagined a non-mechanistic, religious future for the eugenic cause, he identified the motivated individual as its key agent. As Cattell realised, it would soon be necessary to create a substructure of motivated rather than disciplined individuals. Cattell anticipated that efforts would be made to 'shift regulation entirely to the individual'.[305] The social order he imagined here would require a common cultural framework to take the place once occupied by more prescriptive forms of power. A common understanding and a joint sense of direction would provide self-regulated behaviour with its unified purpose.

Today's eugenic religion is a diffusely meritocratic one. Individuals are to be educated so that they absorb meritocratic desire in their mutual efforts to work against each other in competitive rivalry. Together, but in rivalry, they must attempt to further economic prosperity, generate innovation and drive progress. The common framework that is to act here as both referee and principle of comparison is the framework of assessment.

In a fluid meritocracy it no longer matters whether the distribution of talent matches the provision of educational opportunity, which, in turn, matches the distribution of jobs. Indeed, the strategic aim to achieve overlapping bell curves departs in silence. Crucially, though, individuals must still act as if overlapping distributions and the rationalisation of talent remained the collective aim. They must live with the residues of a traditional meritocracy at the forefront of their minds. These residues provide an aspiring population with its principle of movement:

SEEK AFTER MERIT, AND MERIT WILL BE REWARDED

* * *

Research oriented towards social justice has been marooned by a system that no longer seeks redistributive perfection. *More* social mobility, *less* bias, *more* fairness, *less* discrimination – with a collapse in the time dimension, these are its foreshortened demands. Perhaps the comprehensive school was the final attempt to redistribute ability in a 'socially just' manner. However, in an effort to confront the complexities of the problems it faced, the comprehensive project eventually denied its possibility. The great ideal of 'education for all' *under a single roof* tore itself apart, and, much to its own surprise, the educational Right found itself knocking at an open door.[306]

* * *

The complex dynamics of social life are now given so much respect that those who govern hesitate to mount coordinated interventions that reach deep into the social fabric. Indeed, they now fear the label 'social engineer'. Consequently, attempts to collectively offset environmental disadvantage have receded into piecemeal and disjointed actions.

*   *   *

This is the contemporary exhortation: 'We've tried equality. We've tried social engineering...But what about just letting people get on with it?'[307] Here social mobility has been elevated as if it were some sort of life force that will always be, by its very nature, beyond the control of the social engineer. We interfere with it at our peril.

*   *   *

Our disparate actions are structured by more than mere principles, however. Individuals must learn to comport themselves in a fluid meritocracy. They must be educated so that they understand how precisely it is that they are to focus on the perpetual present. Definite procedures must be woven into the activities of daily life, enabling individual subjects to relate to their meritocratic selves.

*   *   *

During the 1970s, a time of economic hardship, government spending in the public sector was severely rationed. Education, once seen as 'the saviour of the economy', was now 'one of its scapegoats', delivering a poor return on investment.[308] It would have to be slimmed down and reconceived. At a similar time, sociological research was taking an increasingly pessimistic turn, with researchers exploring ever more deeply the environmental effects that are said to thwart educational reform.[309] The problem of social complexity was becoming ever more intricate and increasingly gargantuan, spreading further into the recesses of social life.

*   *   *

Sociological reportage unveiled deep problems of acculturation within schooling, let alone without. *The Divided School* was one such study that unpicked the internal and selective dynamics of a secondary modern school in the late 1970s. The school concerned was ordered along traditional meritocratic lines. Pupils were initially placed in mixed-ability groups, later to be divided according to their English proficiency. In the fourth year, they faced a choice of two examination forms (4A and 4B), one commerce form (4C) and one non-examination form (4L). Forms A and B were able to choose between various groups of fairly traditional subjects, whilst form C, composed 'entirely of girls', kept to a 'secretarial diet of typing and book-keeping'. Form L moved between various 'block activities', including 'large doses' of 'practical activities and games'.[310] Pupils elected which form to join according to a mixture of structurally influenced choices and questionable professional advice. Though the decision-making process served to perpet-uate gender and class biases, it was based on a complex of self-reinforcing relationships that were hard to disentangle:

> Differences in social class origins produce different educational experi-ences. These are reflected in school structure, which is serving societal rather than individual aims, and hence feeds back into social structure. From all of these, singly and collectively, values, attitudes and actions form. Group perspectives develop in reaction to 'pedagogical orienta-tion', which includes aims, methods and organization of teaching, them-selves determined by teacher philosophies and ideologies and sustained or intensified by critical area influences... Most educational decisions in school, including subject choice, are made within this framework.[311]

Social Relations in a Secondary School, published four years earlier, laid down the new agenda for sociological research:

> In contrast to the recent emphasis on the influence of home environ-ment on children in school, this exploratory study deals with some of the in-school processes... It suggests that our preoccupation with comprehen-sive reorganization may blind us to the more fundamental and perennial problems which face our schools and teachers.[312]

In this research project, two school subcultures were identified, dividing the 'academic' higher streams from the 'delinquescent' lower streams. Pupils in the lower streams were thought to suffer from 'status deprivation', leading to a culture that rejected the academic values of the school. In the eyes of their observer, these pupils became 'progressively retarded' as a result of various processes arising from their positioning within the school hierarchy.[313] Early differentiation by ability was compounded by subsequent accultur-ation of the respective groups. There was also a consequent reduction in flexibility of movement between streams following the late discovery of promise. The social environment of the school developed, in other words, systems of social reproduction. Similar subcultures were later observed in grammar schools.

Researchers demanded a more thorough understanding of the 'micro-so-ciological mechanisms'[314] operating within the social system of the school. This would go some of the way towards explaining 'the disappointing performance of working-class boys' since the 1944 Education Act.[315] A separate study reported a class bias in the values held by teachers that would be disabling for those who did not share their middle-class assumptions.[316] Meanwhile, a government-sponsored research project reviewed recent attempts to compensate for environmental disadvantage in poor neighbourhoods. Realising the scale of the task, they drew attention to the 'contradiction between astronomical ends and miniscule means'.[317]

From a sociological perspective, the task of social and educational reform appeared increasingly intractable. On this point, indeed, educational sociologists were busy making a name for their profession. Sociological perception was, however, becoming entangled in its object, a reality in which the newly observed barriers to opportunity were said to run deep. In this respect it colluded in its own obscurity, chasing fine points and details, and rendering bold pronunciations impossible.

* * *

Meanwhile, reactionary and right-wing critique associated itself with a revival of genetic claims concerning the origins of intelligence.[318] This mode of critique adopted a tone that was marked by a return to 'common sense' and simplicity,[319] where the supposed crisis in education was associated with a widespread fear that standards were dropping. There was an accompanying media storm, and, in response, subsequent policy focused resolutely upon a simplistic demand: the apparent need to drive up basic standards. One could argue that this lack of regard, or overlooking, of contextual influences on educational achievement represents a determination on behalf of those in power to avoid thorny socio-economic factors. One might say that this return to common sense and simplicity was nothing but a thin veil cast across a more or less deliberate process of abandonment. These are worthy arguments.

My point, though, is more targeted. This rejection of egalitarian attempts to intervene in social life was so radically influential because it expressed a more fundamental adjustment in strategies of power. Though the rhetoric was simple, promoting standards to the neglect of all else, this moment represented an overall shift in the governing rationality. Concealed by the rhetoric was a more involved transformation through which biopower achieved its greater embrace of complexity. From a biopolitical perspective, interference in social life is always unwise if the processes of social life are not well enough understood. The natural forces inherent within a population are to be respected. Consequently, acting against or even without due respect for such forces would be foolhardy. Initially, biopower lacked the strategic base to follow through with these principles of rule. It relied upon practices of disciplinary power that operated according to very different assumptions, where interference without due regard for pre-existing processes was, at the time, acceptable practice. During the post-war years the dependence of biopower

upon its disciplinary companion became increasingly tenuous until this relationship was eventually broken. Though biopower had always been inclined
towards complexity, it was now possible for the systems of rule it had established to more fully embrace it. In this new climate it made sense to abandon
projects designed to counteract the forces of disadvantage. The 'Nature' of the
social system would now be given greater space to express itself. The accompanying switch to a simplistic rhetoric of standards was, therefore, no accident.
A simplistic policy of standards was far better able to sit astride the shifting
form of a population with all its multiplex internal dynamics.

*   *   *

The pursuit of educational improvement was originally tied up with efforts
to develop a highly accurate diagnostic tool. The government-sponsored
'Assessment of Performance Unit' was set up in 1974 with a remit to identify
cases of 'under-achievement' so that resource allocation could be bettered.
However, it soon became clear that its real role was to monitor standards
and indicate whether, indeed, they were rising or falling.[320] Professional
fears that a national monitoring system was being introduced were allayed
by statements to the effect that the Unit would only ever engage in 'light
sampling' rather than blanket testing. The government provided assurances
that 'as a general rule a school would be selected only once in several decades,
and a child would be unlikely to be involved more than once in his school
life. Indeed, many children would complete their school days without ever
encountering the monitoring process.'[321] Lastly, it was decided that individuals, teachers and schools would not be identifiable from the surveys.[322]

Subsequent attempts by the Unit to measure standards over time by light
sampling were, nevertheless, fraught with technical difficulties. The main
problem was that test content went out of date, preventing absolute measures of change over time. Statistical techniques were developed to calculate
comparative difficulty levels between different tests, but these techniques
were eventually abandoned following doubts over their accuracy.

What these early attempts at monitoring lacked was the facility for national
comparisons. From the perspective of power, it was regrettable that the Unit
given over to such a task was so fastidious. This experiment made it abun-
dantly clear to government that the proliferation of testing depended on its
isolation from scientific restraint. The two basic methodological demands,
that tests are both 'valid' and 'reliable', risked limiting the governmental
scope of testing technologies.[323]

The separation of testing from scientific restraint began in the 1980s with
the publication of end-of-school examination results. This rough comparative model could not be withdrawn in the face of technicist critique, for
such objections were swiftly effaced by the bald certainty of the figures. The
scientist was still free to object that trends in examination results were mere

fluctuations, providing no proof that standards were ever rising or falling. But the role occupied by the scientist had changed, from revered technocrat to hapless technician. The task remaining was to maintain and perpetuate a flawed system.[324]

*   *   *

The introduction of a national curriculum in 1988 established a relatively even surface for comparison. Schooling was now divided into 'key stages' with educational objectives set for each level. Monitoring would occur periodically at each stage, in addition to national leaving examinations at 16 and 18. According to Prime Minister Margaret Thatcher, this was part of a dual strategy.[325] On the one hand, a degree of centralisation would satisfy those who argued that there 'had to be some consistency in the curriculum'. And so, there would be a 'nationally recognized and reliably monitored system of testing at various stages of the child's school career' so that government was in a position to 'take remedial action if necessary'. On the other hand, a degree of decentralisation would 'give power and choice to parents'. Of course, the rhetoric of parental choice is an important liberal illusion – it establishes a clear conscience for those beneficiaries who manage, somehow, to deny the fact that choices are always limited and weighted in favour of the wealthy. Lastly, schools would be woken from their progressive dogmas by the bracing stimulus of 'per-capita funding'.[326] State funding would now follow the child to whatever school he or she elected to attend.

*   *   *

The new monitoring system arrived amid a storm of controversy. Designed by an expert body, the Task Group on Assessment and Testing, its mission was to satisfy two divergent aims. First, it sought to embed forms of assessment that were intended to assist learning. These would become part of the day-to-day processes of the classroom. Second, it would establish a national system for purposes of comparison and monitoring, with periodic assessments at 7, 11 and 14 years. These were to be the Standard Assessment Tasks, or SATs, which would be designed for teachers to implement. The results from these standardised tasks would then be combined with subjective ratings provided by teachers. Finally, moderation would assure that teacher ratings were comparable between classrooms, across schools and nationally.[327]

The system was never implemented as planned, and it is easy to argue in retrospect – indeed, it was argued at the time – that at best the Task Group failed because this expert body had been set an impossible task. The two basic aims that it had been asked to pursue were patently contradictory. This dual purpose, in which learning was to be combined with accountability, contributed to its derailment, leaving the establishment with a below optimal, crude, anti-pedagogic technology of accountability.[328] For its chief architect, the resultant system was compromised to the extent that it was the product of 'many changes made since 1988' that tended to ignore the original blueprint, whereas the original plan had involved a careful balance between monitoring and pedagogic purposes. His lament was that these changes were 'not informed by any overall strategy'.[329] From the perspective of power, however, the system was very successful indeed. This monitoring regime developed without central direction, becoming well tuned to the prevailing disposition of government. Though the scheme initially contained aspects that were recognisably disciplinary, these were swiftly abandoned in favour of more permissive techniques.

* * *

The ambition to embed assessment-directed learning within the classroom marks a significant advance in the gradual process charted so far by which assessment has become part of pedagogic practice. In order to attach practices of assessment to processes of learning, the Task Group intended to make use of 'criterion referencing', whereby scores were intended to relate directly to competences.[330] In its outline form, this scheme was recognisably disciplinary: the developmental process of a 'normal' child was to be divided into parallel components or *elements* that were themselves to be subdivided into a set of *levels*. Together, these levels would describe a developmental hierarchy for each element. Each level was finally to be divided into a set of specific *targets*, which would be designed to match the prescriptions of the new national curriculum. Estimating which targets had been met, in order to ascertain, in turn, the level a child had reached in a certain element, was to become part of the pedagogic process by which a teacher decided what must be done in order to reach the next level of development. This mode of assessment was to occur in context, in the classroom, and was to be carried out by the teacher. The results of such assessments would allow a judgement to be made about a child's position in a sequence of progression, enabling the teacher to provide developmentally specific feedback to the child. Individual bodies were to be distributed, in other words, throughout a carefully defined and minutely divided programme of study, where even the activities of the teacher were to be carefully prescribed.

These disciplinary allusions are, nevertheless, deceptive. The developmental scale employed by the Task Group also contained assumptions concerning what the *average* child is presumed able to achieve at each respective level (with graphical depictions of average progression, including the interval within which the bulk of the normally distributed population was to be found[331]). These calculations betrayed a population-level awareness, and in so doing they augmented and transformed the disciplinary scheme once found in the monitorial school. Recall that disciplinary power treats any large population as if it were a mysterious entity. The population is a formless mass of bodies from which individuals are extracted and then put to use. For biopower, by contrast, the population is a cognisable social organism; it is an independent entity that contains a set of processes to be managed on the basis of what is natural to them. These processes reveal averages and norms that are to be managed as entities in their own right. In this switch from procedures of 'normation' to those of 'normalization', where principles of government are derived from the population under study,[332] we have, then, travelled beyond the explanatory power of Foucault's theory, outlined in *Discipline and Punish*.[333]

*   *   *

The Task Group helped inaugurate a technique of assessment that was to be profoundly non-disciplinary in its form. This technique operates according to a loosely normalised framework of progression. Within this framework, *process* is more important than *position*. Subjects must attend to the activity of progression, with their eventual positioning reduced to an epiphenomenon of that process-based interest. It matters little whether or not the positions that result make administrative sense. When process is more important than position, the *act* of positioning is more important than the *accuracy* of the position attained.

*   *   *

In a disciplinary regime, positioning is the first essential. This emphasis can be observed in the Task Group blueprint, where position is to be minutely defined according to the division of a pupil's attainment into various elements, levels and targets. To borrow from Foucault's remarks on disciplinary power: as activity is subdivided, time 'penetrates the body' along with 'all the meticulous controls of power'. This division of pupils into elements, levels and targets in order to design a set of personalised, short-term objectives seems 'to intensify the use of the slightest moment, as if time, in its very fragmentation, were inexhaustible or as if, at least by an ever more detailed internal arrangement, one could tend towards an ideal point at which one maintained maximum speed and maximum efficiency'. [334] In a disciplinary arrangement, then, whilst process is important, it depends upon a clear definition of position. By contrast, a biopolitical regime is sensitive to the population it seeks to guide. This population is *already positioned*. Principles of government are derived, instead, from observed regularities. These regularities represent natural processes that are, by definition, the product of multiple, unpredictable forces. The average child and the average sequence of progression are no longer amenable to mechanistic rule.

*   *   *

Disciplinary power contained the seeds of its own transformation. Its techniques revealed processes 'that superseded the mechanical body'. The 'simple physics of movement' that informed early disciplinary power was eventually opposed to reveal 'the conditions of functioning' said to be 'proper to an organism'.[335]

In a similar way, the Task Group saw its plans unravel, as they were adapted to the conditions of functioning said to be proper to the learner. The rate of change was much faster, though, for biopolitical assumptions were now well established in educational discourse. The nature of this transformation was barely perceived, however, as these same biopolitical assumptions also restricted the perceptions of educational critique. Educational critics, indeed, were unwittingly involved in perfecting the new regime of power.

According to the relatively closed reflex arc that such critique adopted, it was deemed no longer acceptable to inflict disciplinary techniques on teachers and pupils alike. Critics were quick to denounce the scheme for its 'highly instrumental and mechanistic view of learning' for which 'teachers are simply taken to be operationally responsible'. Such approaches to learning may have worked during the era of the monitorial school, but to those writing in the late twentieth century they appeared 'too mechanistic'. These critics would rather affirm the irreducible complexity of human life, believing, as they now did, that a single route of progression cannot adequately represent the learning process, however intricate and well branched its architecture may be. Assessment must now embrace the fullness of human life and allow bodies their own space to move. Education is today viewed as too 'unpredictable' and for that very reason cannot be governed by approaches that seek to reify daily life.[336]

* * *

The social theorist has come to fear one particular accusation, particularly acutely today. This is the claim that one is guilty of *reification* in one's theoretical work. To reify, we are told, is to commit a basic fallacy in treating abstractions as if they were real.

Whilst discipline once reified without rebuke, in a biopolitical order reification becomes unsupportable. Those who attempt to realise their abstractions are now seen as victims of their own deception. Moreover (and this is why the theorist fears the rebuke so badly), they are judged to be distinctly unsophisticated in making this error. In mistaking their own ideas for reality, they pay too little attention to the complexity of life. In today's world, the social theorist must always defer to reality.

* * *

In the late twentieth century, whilst it was still possible to design highly mechanistic social technologies, critics were quick to mention that they are unlikely to function as planned. Otherwise put: reification is now considered to be impossible (as well as intellectually simple). In failing to realise their abstractions as intended, reifications will have unintended and potentially dangerous consequences. The Nature of the social and educational task is now said to be far too complex for grand ideas.

*   *   *

The architect may lament that 'current national testing in England and Wales falls far short of acceptable requirements of reliability and validity',[337] but these lamentations will go unheeded by power. Such technical requirements are swiftly abandoned once the precise location of a learner within a scale of progression ceases to matter.

The blueprint for national testing underwent a process of radical simplification: Standard Assessment Tasks became summative written tests; teacher assessments were downgraded in favour of SAT results;[338] marking was outsourced; 'targets' came to serve the purpose once envisaged for 'elements',[339] and the careful subdivision of elements into levels became confused.[340] Without the intimate supervision of a teacher – assigning targets, elements and levels – it was impossible for the learner to be informed of his or her precise location on a route of progression. All that remained of the original scheme was the idea of age-independent levels of achievement and regular examinations at the end of each key stage.[341]

The disembodied idea of progress had overtaken the last vestiges of the original scheme. That is, testing was left with a notion of process that was stripped of any precise notion of where one is within a sequence of progression. What remained was a near-sighted view of individual enhancement, of improvement abstracted from any detailed framework of progression or overall plan. This was a matter of pursuing process without precise location, without informative outcome; process existing for its own sake, for the sake of proceeding; process as a natural sequence of changes without purpose or end.

*   *   *

Despite the biopolitical shortcomings of the original scheme, shortcomings that were so quickly and all-too-easily attacked by critics, it did contain some noteworthy recommendations that were more closely attuned to the political context. These recommendations were for the development of so-called 'feedback' and 'feed-forward' techniques.

*   *   *

Feed is a process term, meaning to supply material progressively for an operation. It covers the means, channel, motion or rate of such supply. Feedback and feed-forward techniques suited the prevailing regime of power by prioritising the act of movement (its motion, means and rate). Movement itself became important, rather than the material being dealt with or the eventual output or endpoint such movement served.

*   *   *

Feedback was to be a developmentally tiered process that would modify and condition pupil behaviour. The idea here was to generate information in response to the output of a child's work, returning the output of a system as an input, as a means for improvement and self-correction. The Task Group made the mistake, according to its early critics, of interpreting this process in an overly rigid way. Feedback techniques were mistakenly designed to refer to an already existing sequence of progression. To rectify this mistake, assessment-led learning was reintroduced in the late 1990s under the independent banner of 'formative assessment' or 'assessment for learning'. Under this incarnation, the external validity of a teacher's response to a particular pupil's output was no longer important. There was to be no rigid sequence of levels and tasks within which the pupil must be located. Rather, the response offered by the pedagogue or peer is an impressionistic one, designed to make sense only in the context within which it is made. Feedback was to follow a self-referential loop.

*   *   *

Feed-forward was initially more successful, its intention being to bring about the modification or control of a process using its anticipated results or effects. It would occur during class-to-class transfer, and alongside transfer at 11 from 'feeder schools' to secondary education.[342] Results were passed on to the next teacher or institution, enabling the careful management of school or class intake. These feed-based possibilities were associated with the much wider availability of educational data, following an expansion in its production that has been billed by some as one of the greatest achievements of modern educational research.[343]

*   *   *

The feedstuff of educational process is educational data. In the last decade of the twentieth century, the data stream swelled in Britain as national testing was rolled out. School-level data were made available in performance tables issued by government. The media collated these basic statistics for public consumption, ranking schools according to various indicators of 'success'.

Whilst some complained that league-tables were misleading and technically invalid,[344] a process-based remedy had already been identified.[345] League-tables were to adopt a process-based corrective, called 'value-added'. This would take into account variations in the quality of intake between schools. The relative quality of a school's basic material, its pupils, was to be factored in to estimations of their worth.

A value-added system would build upon the assumed sequence of progression first developed by the Task Group in 1988. According to the tiered scheme it designed, an average pupil aged 8 would be performing at the lower end of Level 3; an average 10-year-old should have achieved Level 3; a 12-year-old Level 4; and a 14-year-old Level 5. In other words, the average child would rise by one such level every two years. Below-average children would be expected to progress more slowly, above-average children more quickly: and so the spread of attainment (the width of the bell curve) would increase with age.[346]

Following statistical analyses of the progressions of actual children, a *likely future* is predicted for each child type according to his or her starting score. Schools and teachers are then judged according to their ability to achieve such likely futures, or, indeed, *exceed expectations*.

Excessive hopes are to be encouraged, whereby average or typical progressions are reduced in status to become mediocre achievements. The value-added represents the difference between a statistically predicted performance and the actual performance. A zero score denotes average progress, whilst scores above zero indicate progress that exceeds expectations.[347] Those schools that enhance individual development beyond what may be predicted by extrapolation from normalised progression routes would have generated 'surplus value'.

* * *

An old eugenic idea returns here in a modified form. According to conventional eugenics, the normal distribution of outcomes was to be enhanced through concerted action across the normal distribution, allowing the distribution to move towards the right. This was a globally administered approach. However, in an institutional order governed by the rationale of added value, when process itself becomes the predominant point of interest, the strategy changes and perspectives shorten. The *rate* of individual progression, rather than the overall distribution of outcomes, is the focus for improvement. Rather than improve the overall intelligence of the human stock by assisting some to breed and by dissuading others, the aim is to improve the *rate of growth* by which intelligence matures. The effects of this obsession with growth on the overall outcome are secondary.

Conventional eugenics generated conceptual devices that suited a traditional meritocracy. A traditional meritocratic order deals in a similar currency of outcomes, mapped in terms of overall distributions in educational attainment that must be fitted to the distribution of jobs. An exaggerated interest in process, meanwhile, suits a fluid meritocracy. Outcomes are still important because the percentage of pupils achieving top grades serves as a supreme benchmark of institutional performance. Yet, the aim, simply, is to increase this statistic. The overall distribution of outcomes is now relatively unimportant so long as it remains above a minimum benchmark of acceptability. Indeed, the meaning of a specific outcome is also less significant. Whether a level 5 in Mathematics at Key Stage 2 is equivalent to a level 5 in Science at Key Stage 3 no longer matters in a value-added system so long as 'all schools have taken the same tests'.[348] Once measures of temporal difference become the main focus, absolute position diminishes in significance. In other words, when the distance between two points is the point of concern, what these points represent in themselves matters less.

Whilst conventional eugenics was outcome-obsessed, it nevertheless bore the potential to become oriented towards process. Eugenic thinkers such as Raymond Cattell were committed to this latter project, believing that the mechanical manipulation of outcomes would be insufficient to secure a eugenic future. Eugenics would only succeed by adopting from Christianity its methods of pastoral supervision and guidance. In the late twentieth century, the educational project faced a similar challenge. It would increasingly depend on process-based techniques, eventually using value-added systems to provide quantitative support to its strategies of pastoral supervision.

* * *

The implementation of value-added systems took time. Cohorts of students would have to first pass through the national curriculum framework and its associated tests, generating sufficient data to calculate student trajectories and progression norms.[349] Well before value-added statistics were made available for general consumption, however, schools willingly adopted value-added systems to optimise their internal processes.[350]

The switch to value-added technologies was not without its critics. Some researchers attempted to counter what they correctly identified as the 'recent overwhelming focus on "process" '. Their claim is this: when research becomes preoccupied with school effectiveness over school contexts, wider structural failings are hidden from view.[351] According to its critics,[352] the pursuit of school effectiveness is part of and complicit in a strategy that is embedding a market ideology in public education, with schools atomised into competing providers.

These criticisms are important, but they are also problematic. The difficulty with such attacks on the marketisation of education, a project traditionally of the Right, is that a process-based regime of power is able to accommodate both conventional left-wing and right-wing interests. This became evident when value-added systems were subsequently contextualised in the early twenty-first century. Even structural factors, traditionally the concern of left-wing politics, could be accounted for by the system.

* * *

In their early form, value-added systems ignored the effects of social inequalities.[353] They only took account of prior attainment, ignoring other external influences on performance. In response to criticism, value-added systems were later contextualised so that so-called structural factors, such as gender, ethnicity and social disadvantage, could be taken into account. Value-added scores were now adjusted so that likely futures matched what might be expected of an average child, of a particular initial ability, *in a particular grouping*. Gross population norms were divided into specific norms that were designed to be appropriate for various subpopulation groups.

Contextual value-added, as it came to be known, required more sophisticated analysis, finer discrimination and more detailed data. The biopolitical embrace of process must, therefore, be accompanied by modes of data collection and analysis that are both more intrusive and more intense in form. Hence, for example, a series of 'unique pupil identifiers' were introduced, allowing successive key stage scores to be matched to individual pupils, all of which could be tracked by a central database. Later, a pupil-by-pupil level annual school census was set in place. This required schools to record and submit particular background characteristics for each pupil. With these enhancements to the data stream, the likely futures for contextualised children could now be calculated.[354] These calculations would encourage individuals and institutions to govern themselves accordingly. Nevertheless, some schools were thought to require additional motivation: these were identified and labelled as 'coasting schools'. The problem, as seen by government, was that 'a substantial minority of children who did well in primary school' subsequently lose 'momentum' in secondary education. Accordingly, local authorities were required to identify coasting schools (which 'often have respectable overall GCSE results' helping to conceal 'poor progress') and provide help and resources, including advisors from more process-oriented schools in the area. It was a matter of cultivating a 'we can do better than this attitude'.[355] Exemplary schools would

> set ambitious targets for their pupils, monitor their progress, personalise the support they receive, and if pupils fall off trajectory they intervene to put them back on course. This focus on progression is backed up by a personalised approach to teaching and learning and focused feedback so that each child knows what they are aiming for and what they have to do to get there.[356]

The expectation is that school managers, teachers and pupils will adopt for themselves the principles of process enhancement and translate these principles into contextually specific efforts to achieve individual gains. Governance is to be context specific, operating at the level of lived experience. Nobody is exempt from this preoccupation with process, however well they may be performing. Indeed, achieving a rate of progression which is the expected rate for one's level and context is redefined as treading water. As the Secretary of Education, Michael Gove, later explained to Parliament, the task is to create an 'aspiration nation'.[357] This point is developed in the accompanying White Paper, which explains that citizens must administer themselves so that they become the 'authors' of their own 'life stories'.[358]

*   *   *

In order to encourage individual practices of process enhancement, value-added systems have been embedded in free software made available to schools. School, group, pupil and question-level data are analysed; comparisons are made with national patterns; performances in specific curriculum areas are monitored; and individual pupil targets are set, informed by progress made by similar pupils nationally. The software is interactive, allowing users to import extra data from optional tests; compile customised reports; and even experiment with hypothetical futures: 'school administrators are able to amend and change data, such as adding and removing pupils or changing grades. This provides the ability for schools to carry out "what if" scenarios.'[359] The potential and predisposition for process-level governance are thereby enhanced.

*   *   *

Process-enhancing schools are modelled for us in the form of easily digestible case studies:

> A Roman Catholic School in Sunderland achieves 10 per cent progress. This is well above the national average of 3 per cent for pupil enhancement. Multiple strategies are employed whilst using a 'rigorous target-setting and data tracking system'. Underachieving cohorts, groups and individuals are identified, following which various strategies and interventions are planned. Academic and pastoral staff 'mentor pupils' whilst progress is monitored, regularly reviewed and relayed to parents. A 'structured monitoring cycle' is then established, including 'observation of lessons, pupil work sampling and scrutiny of teachers' planning'. Lastly, teaching strategies for enhancing process are developed, where there is a facility to share good practice in whole school professional development sessions so that these initiatives can 'become embedded in every curricular area'.[360]

A secondary school in Wandsworth achieves 12 per cent improvement, 'following the successful use of a red/amber/green traffic light analysis'.[361] Here, pupil progress is monitored using predictions derived from previous key stage results. At the end of the first year, pupils are assessed and rated green, amber or red according to their performance in relation to these expectations. Pupils falling just short of their target (amber) or well short (red) are targeted for remedial action.

The schools inspectorate lays great emphasis on progress tracking and target setting as techniques common to successful schools. There is one school in particular where pupils carry 'a regularly updated grid in their planners, downloaded from the system, indicating their current attainment and personal targets'. Regularly updated cohort lists are also 'posted near the school canteen, showing students' current levels'. Such public lists are said to 'generate constructive discussion rather than unease'.[362]

* * *

Process calculations have been supplemented by additional tests that are conducted alongside the national system of SATs, providing a further boost to data power. A large proportion of the school population completes the Cognitive Abilities Test shortly after arriving at secondary school. This testing package is a best-selling product. Those associated with it claim that this test battery is a better predictor of subsequent attainment than national tests. Schools are said to prefer these tests because they have been adminis- tered 'in a consistent fashion for all pupils from all feeder primary schools', rather than under variable circumstances prior to secondary transfer.[363] These independent tests are used to refine the quality of feedstock data and diminish the need to rely upon the statistics provided by feeder schools. In part, this is a quality assurance exercise.

The test comes with its own predictive reports. Such clairvoyant devices are used for purposes of internal management. The reports are also shared when teachers meet parents to take them through a table of probabilities, which predict examination grades three, five and seven years down the line. As a trainee teacher, I once represented pupils to parents in this way, at a parents' evening specially arranged for the task. They came in, one after the other, the statistical predictions were shared and explained, following which they left. We saw tens of parents in this way, almost perishing ourselves from the after-effects of delivering one relentlessly hollow explanation after another. This noxious activity helped encapsulate what education had been reduced to: if a teacher were to don a gas mask, filtering the toxic fumes emitted by this corrupted endeavour, almost all that would remain of education would be the sound of the teacher, breathing.

* * *

Through the educational mask, and with a fixed but empty grin, we see how the child is placed within a likely future, a future that is the product of statis- tical manipulation and population norms. This is a space of zeroed progress, of aspirations to above-average development, to the hope of positive value- added, towards a surplus value that becomes the maximum hope. Much has changed since 1911, when that child stood with her mind obscured before the camera. Children are now rendered transparent: their present aptitudes and future possibilities are seemingly plain to see.

* * *

Researchers confirm that notions of self-worth in children are becoming linked to the test levels these children hope to achieve. These researchers nevertheless give the impression of a static governmental strategy where self-worth is tied to the outcome of a single upcoming test. The problem with these tests, we can infer, is that they reduce complex selves to single scores. In one study, 'Hannah', who fears she will under-perform, thinks she will "be a nothing" '. But, as the authors note, she 'is an accomplished writer, a gifted dancer and artist and good at problem-solving yet none of those skills make her somebody in her own eyes'. These qualities, they argue, are missed by tests that produce 'very simplistic judgements purged of any subtlety and complexity about the sort of learners pupils are judged to be'.[364]

These research findings are corroborated by the discovery elsewhere of an 'extensive invasion of pupils' subjectivity' which is occurring as a result of national tests. Testing regimes have become linked, they claim, to 'the production of amenable pupil identities'.[365] In schools, instructions are increasingly unspoken; pupils are 'well-drilled' and 'police themselves' in lessons dominated by preparation for the upcoming tests.[366] Again, however, critics rely on a constructed binary between reductive or simplistic tests and 'learners who have complex, multiple identities'.[367] Monitoring systems are portrayed as overly mechanistic and disciplinary.[368]

These findings are important, but their critical thrust is misplaced. In a biopolitical era, it is anachronistic at best to defend education against mechanical reduction. Power now seeks to build upon (rather than deny) the complexities of lived experience. Strategies of subjection have opened up to embrace complexity in a way that is missed by critical researchers with their humanistic good intentions. *Progress itself* is sought, a form of progress that has been abstracted from the detailed, subdivided scheme of advancement towards which disciplinary power aspires. Selves must work within a likely future, within a personalised frame of reference. They are complex entities and must be allowed to unfurl within a personalised framework. This is not to say that single test outcomes are no longer of great personal import or that ranking ceases to exist, but it does suggest a supplementary and increasingly dominant logic.

* * *

In the dark-suited realms of organisational governance, this switch to process is already well advanced. The assessment of all children entering English primary schools has become a statutory requirement.[369] This allows a measure of progress between entry at 5 years and the first national tests at 7 years.[370] The Centre for Evaluation and Monitoring at Durham sells the most widely used baseline assessment in England. This standardised assessment system is designed to monitor pupils' educational progress throughout the primary phase. It provides a 'comprehensive profile of each pupil's ability' enabling 'longitudinal monitoring'.[371] Crucially, the assessment is almost completely administered by the provider, minimising the role of teachers. This concurs with the Centre's mission statement, which is to use 'evidence, rather than authority or opinion, as the guide to practice'. This evidence comes from 'controlled trials wherever possible... applying the best standards of science' to 'give accurate answers and keep things *"in perspective"* '.[372] This last point is essential, as the whole purpose of educational process monitoring is to generate perspective. To keep things in perspective means to reduce things in magnitude so that they appear realistic and manageable, in this case, to generate realistic expectations of future performance. The perspective on offer is one that has been statistically adjusted to match the individual.

* * *

Those selling baseline assessments are eager to demonstrate the international scope of their tools. Global comparative studies of educational attainment have been criticised for their failure to measure progress throughout schooling, focusing instead on mere outcome measures. The purveyors of such tools eagerly await their lucrative contracts. From the individual pupil to the nation state, process-based technologies are available for purchase.

* * *

The calculation of likely futures has been extended to the management of risk, where the riskiest school age populations, those that come into contact with the criminal justice system, are assessed by the use of a structured questionnaire. This is deployed to pinpoint the multiple needs and difficulties of 'troubled children'. The results are then used to construct an intervention plan. The nature and frequency of intervention are based upon an individual's calculated probability of reoffending: higher scores indicate increased risk. Initially, only dynamic contributing factors were assessed. Having, by definition, the potential for adjustment, these factors could be addressed directly when planning remedial action. In effect, the test already incorporates sites of intervention within its structure: it both predicts likely futures, and then allows adjustments to be made within the parameters of that prediction.[373] Critics have since argued that the system does not live up to its scientific pretensions; it fails to predict with sufficient accuracy.[374] This misses the point. The objective here is to encourage young offenders to live within a future that has been anticipated for them. Whether or not this future is an accurate prediction is neither here nor there. The objective, simply, is to ensure that they live according to the activities such predictions warrant.

* * *

Process-based technologies are now well embedded within administrative and professional practice. Individuals learn how to keep things in perspective. They adopt perspectives and strategies that will make life realistic and manageable. These dispositions are essential for those who live as we do, in a period of inflated desires.

* * *

Britain once feared the 'excessive desires' of the 'undeserving poor'. In 1807, a Member of Parliament warned that 'giving education to the labouring classes of the poor' would encourage insubordination by teaching the poor to 'despise' the 'employments to which their rank in society had destined them'. Education, it was presumed, would allow the masses to 'read seditious pamphlets, vicious books and publications against Christianity'. Elevating the poor by giving them an education would make them liable to revolt, or so the argument went.[375] In effect, it was feared that mass schooling would give people 'ideas'. In this climate, the educational challenge was to somehow coerce the poor into accepting their lot. Fortunately for these conservative critics, mass education would eventually develop the disciplinary and moral tools to achieve that end.

Today, the problem is its opposite. Individuals are raised on the promise that anyone can reach the stars. In this environment, schools encourage their pupils to believe that personal effort will bring its rewards, that there is no ceiling to the desires of the diligent. The coercive task facing schools today is, therefore, rather different: it is to teach the unlucky majority how to better dream. They must learn to keep things in perspective when failure occurs, and to always try and try again. 'If at first you don't succeed...' so the popular saying goes.

* * *

Multi-million dollar international franchises such as The X Factor encapsulate well the function of hope in contemporary society.[376] In this popular entertainment show, the most ambitious dreams are to be encouraged even though most contestants will fail, for indeed they must fail according to the structure of the contest. The majority entertain hopes that are patently unrealistic. Here, for example, is a typical exchange from 2011, in which the judge delivers his crushing verdict to the aspiring contestant: 'You're not a rock star, you never will be a rock star!' he declares. This creates quite a commotion on the judging panel, in which another judge retorts: 'I think you're out of order for telling someone what they'll never be!'

This indignant riposte went to the crux of the matter. Despite the fact that futures are now routinely predicted in schools, we are nevertheless in denial. Who, today, has the authority to tell us what we are capable of achieving? We must be allowed the freedom to find ourselves, and then, when we have done so, to find and define our own individual path to success. Nobody has the right to limit our hopes; or so it goes.

It is intriguing to see how those contestants who inevitably fail are expected to cope with their descent from the limelight. A form of 'ritual humility' is demanded of them, as they openly thank the judges for their criticisms.[377] Audiences are drawn into the cruelty of this spectacle, where the hopes of the tone-deaf and deluded are very publicly destroyed. The levels of distress they witness must, though, remain within acceptable limits. The show must go on, and so it must remain within the boundaries of that which is considered *acceptably cruel*. This presents a challenge for its producers: to provide entertainment based on the exploitation of hope and yet keep the effects of disappointment in check. Those who fail cannot be allowed to transform their despair into violence against the system that judges them, nor should they be allowed to reach a point where they take it out on themselves.

* * *

It is fortunate that many of the contestants have already been schooled in the manipulation of hope. Facing a symbolic order that works to stoke up unrealistic aspirations, the mundane, everyday perspective-shortening techniques taught at school and elsewhere (through self-help manuals, for example) are vital. These practices of self-absorption ensure that aspiration drives effort within acceptable channels of restraint; they prevent self-loss and subsequent dissatisfaction with the global order.

* * *

The academic is not immune to the manipulation of hope. Each university has its academic 'superstars' to whom the rest of the university is expected to pay homage. These figures are celebrated not so much for the quality of their work, or for the depth of their insights, but for their successes in attracting revenue and prestige. The inaugural address, which is the moment when a professor celebrates his or her procurement of this once-coveted position, is a public event at which the fanfare of academic stardom is most obviously celebrated. This event has developed far beyond its originating medieval code in which the incepting master addressed his peers in their terms. It has become an ostensibly 'open' procedure at which the

public can, alongside a majority academic audience, receive the wisdom of him who 'professes' in laicised terms. More recently, though, this event has been invested by what has become the institutionally embedded injunction to achieve and exude academic stardom. It has become a spectacle. We should note, of course, that, for every academic luminary, there are 100 academic men and women who have had their spirits broken by the reductive demands of the academic machinery, which insists that they enhance productivity for its own sake, measured by values which are not their own. A professing professor who genuinely wished to speak on behalf of that wider intellectual constituency would, out of respect for these diminished peers, adopt a sober tone devoid of all glamour and charm.

*   *   *

When pupils are confronted with a likely future that has been matched to their attributes, they engage in a relationship with this often-diminished prediction that ranges from subservience to pure refusal. In the process of this exchange, they learn to negotiate the terrain that lies between these 'realistic' possibilities and their fonder ambitions. The ability to manage this relationship well is an essential skill. Indeed, the economic subjects of a fluid meritocracy must *repeatedly* construct and reconstruct their hopes in response to the vicissitudes of a chaotic social order. They are expected to negotiate the successes and disappointments of their lives and emerge continuously striving. New stories of hope and aspiration must be told when old stories develop a sour taste. As stories are revised, the discontinuities generated by these revisions must be largely erased. Hopes become fluid and insubstantial, even though individuals pretend each daily hope is what they had always wanted.

* * *

Shortened perspectives facilitate the manipulation of hope. They produce forgetfulness. The school technique known as 'formative assessment' works in this direction perhaps more than any other educational device.

* * *

It is common to place high-stakes, objective, summative and numerical testing approaches in opposition to 'more pedagogic', 'less judgemental', interpersonal and formative techniques.[378] Some educationalists argue that high-stakes tests are basically anti-pedagogic, whilst many would agree that they have at least some anti-pedagogic effects.[379] It is conventional in educational circles to maintain that there is too much quantitative testing in schools, that the examinations system is overbearing, that it warps teaching practice and invades pupil subjectivities, that it defeats the point of education. In this climate, any move towards more pedagogic, qualitative and seemingly humane forms of assessment appears to be fighting against this trend. The 'formative assessment' movement is a celebrated example here. It is seen as an educationally favourable mode of assessment, in stark contrast to the rigmarole of national testing. Turning a pupil into numerical data does violence to the child and denies his or her needs as a learner; formative assessment, so the argument goes, has the potential to rectify this situation, providing teachers and pupils with a more context-specific approach that will gently enhance the educational experience.

From the perspective of power, however, these two paradigms are not opposed, nor are they clearly distinct. Formative assessment furthers the project that began with target-setting and pupil-tracking systems. It builds on their process-based obsessions, extending associated strategies of power further into pupil subjectivity and to a finer level of detail.

* * *

Formative assessment is the natural heir of the mid-nineteenth century moral training school. In that institution, the playground and gallery were combined in a regime of moral supervision. The techniques were interpersonal, relying upon intimate relationships and the high personal esteem with which pupils were to hold their moral exemplar, the schoolmaster. Formative assessment occupies a similarly affective realm, and yet its moral economy has been secularised. Moreover, whilst it still prioritises the context within which the child is to be found, it no longer does so through a simulation of the street. The perceived challenge has changed, from a struggle pitted against the temptations of a fallen social existence, to an endeavour which implicitly fears that individuals will one day reject the secular order in which they find themselves and hence cease to 'realise their potential' according to its reductive demands. The focus is now on the child's unique position as a learner, on promoting the next step within his or her own developmental path. A comparison between the child's inner being and God's will has been replaced by a comparison between the child today and what the child might become tomorrow. This shortened focus is absorbed within the process of learning. The shepherd–flock game, once identified by Foucault,[380] has become a game of ceaseless self-monitoring and self-enhancement under the sign of 'growth'. The moral order of God has been cast aside by the guiding morality of improvement, pursued through assessment, and the natural processes of learning that assessment seeks to assist. This assessment-based morality is an economic morality insofar as it develops an individual's ability to cope with the inflated desires and ambitions for economic advance that are generated in late modernity. It maintains its economic subjects in a state of constant and ultimately pointless activity through its mechanisms of myopia.

*   *   *

This mode of assessment is 'characterised as a cycle involving elicitation of evidence, which when interpreted appropriately may lead to action, which in turn, can yield further evidence and so on'. It yields context-specific interpretations 'that form the basis for successful action in improving performance'.[381] In this self-referential realm, evidence of an incidental, ephemeral and continuous sort is now of use. Formative assessment also requires that evidence be acted upon, though only in a highly specific way: that is, in order to close 'the gap between actual and desired levels of performance'. Thus, employment 'placement decisions' are, by contrast, 'not formative', for the only potential actions here are 'acceptance for, or rejection from, employment or a course of study'.[382] Indeed, this emphasis upon the formative is so thoroughly process-based that, as a mode of assessment, it has finally broken the link to any Benthamite derivative of 'official location'. Promoted here are situated feedback loops designed to enhance the process of learning in all its subtle detail.

*   *   *

We are told by its foremost proponents that, in the field of assessment, the 'day-to-day activities of teachers have historically been of little interest to academic researchers'.[383] Setting themselves against this self-professed history of neglect, the journey they recommend will be a journey into the 'black box' of the classroom, into a void of unknown relationships thus far neglected by a type of assessment research that has been preoccupied with simple input/output variables.

Formative assessment is presented as if it were timeless, presumably to be found in all good teaching throughout the ages. In itself, we are told, it is 'nothing new'. Almost 'all successful teaching' relies heavily on adapting approaches 'in the light of evidence about the success of previous episodes'.[384] In order to be effective, this form of assessment must be conducted in an environment that is carefully managed. The surroundings must be safe and comfortable for the student, thus allowing learning to flourish: 'Good teachers know that this is so.'[385] We can infer from their recommendations that some teaching practices would require significant revision. In effect, if a teaching environment is not employing the natural techniques of formative assessment, it must be in a deviant, suboptimal state – the caring, insightful, responsive type of teacher is the sort that must be encouraged, modelled and enhanced. We are, nevertheless, told by the foremost proponents of formative assessment that research aiming to improve formative teaching practice must not be prescriptive; it should work with what teachers already do and 'build on existing good practice'.[386] We are encouraged to view formative assessment as an already existing *natural* pedagogic process that can be enhanced or, indeed, hindered by educational policy. League-tables and high-stakes assessments are commonly invoked in the literature as harmful in this respect, diverting attention to outcomes and thereby neglecting the day-to-day of learning. Evidence is amassed, nonetheless, to show that formative assessment improves pupils' scores in tests. Moreover, it is reported that '*improved formative assessment helps the (so-called) low attainers more than the rest, and so reduces the spread of attainment whilst also raising it overall*'.[387] In other words, the lower tail of the normal distribution could be significantly shortened, whilst moving the overall distribution to a higher score. This would take place in a gentle, gradual and self-propelling manner: an old eugenic dream.

* * *

With outcomes cast aside, the supervision of process becomes yet again an aim in itself. Formative assessment is also said to enhance self-esteem and remove the damaging effects of ranking and competition amongst peers:

> 'Where the classroom culture focuses on rewards, "gold-stars", grades or place-in-the-class ranking, then pupils look for the ways to obtain the best marks rather than at the needs of their learning.' This generates a 'fear of failure' and leads, reportedly, to efforts by pupils to 'try to build up their self-esteem in other ways'. We are told that, on the contrary, what 'is needed is a culture of success, *backed by the belief that all can achieve*'.[388]

As far as possible, when delivering feedback, comparisons with other pupils should be avoided. The negative effects of ranking on the lowest achievers, leading them 'to see themselves as unable to learn' and thus remove themselves from the system, eventually to become 'alienated from society', the 'sources and victims of serious social problems'...are effects that are said to diminish with the arrival of formative solutions.[389] Even though this causal string from test failure to social deviance is doubtful, to say the least, there is a shift in governmental strategy at work here: confrontations with failure should be avoided, and the idea of failure itself must be suppressed beneath an ethic of Panglossian self-exertion.

We are told that 'helpless children' who 'seem to accept that they will fail because they are not clever enough; believe that if something seems to be too hard there is nothing they can do about it'. They 'tend therefore to avoid challenge'. These unwilling contenders must be transformed into 'mastery children' who 'are motivated by the desire to learn; will tackle difficult tasks in flexible and reflective ways; are confident of success, believing that they can do it if they try'. Mastery children 'believe that you can improve your intelligence' with sufficient determination.[390]

* * *

Once the social engineer retreats, only those who believe improvement is a perpetual possibility can be depended upon to make the effort required to constantly reposition themselves in the social hierarchy.

* * *

Transforming the hapless ways of helpless children is not easy. Such children may have to pass through an intermediate phase on the way from 'learned helplessness' to mastery. In this transitional phase, 'they find strategies that place the blame on others or factors beyond their control'.[391] Here, in such children, one can perhaps observe the operations of a nascent political critique. And yet, the moment this conflagration begins to take form, the critical impulse that prompted it must be snuffed out. This is achieved by breaking down learning into the minute and achievable steps of formative improvement. By encouraging pupils to take a greater responsibility for their learning, it is hoped they will no longer extend a critical gaze elsewhere. The vulnerable child must become resilient rather than rebellious.

* * *

According to the pathological constructs of a recent government report, these strategies are particularly important in deprived communities. Such communities are said to be lacking in aspiration, or so the mantra goes. The goals young people set for their future, and the ways in which they pursue them, are said to require adjustment. This kind of intervention is particularly wicked because the wider causal factors that led to subjugation in the first place have been so effectively personalised. The systemic violence that produces poverty is hidden behind an ideology of personal responsibility.

In these contexts, aspirations of a highly specific sort are to be encouraged. Here the period between 11 and 14 years is seen as 'a key age range, when young people move from idealistic to more realistic ambitions'. During this period, it is important that deprived children 'develop ambitious, *achievable* aspirations'. Many of the proposed interventions are to be enacted through agencies existing outside schooling, demonstrating the broader purchase of a governmental strategy that seeks to enhance process-based solutions. One suggestion on offer is to provide appropriate role models, sourced locally. We are told that aspiration must be carefully channelled through a coordinated programme of 'locally-tailored behavioural change' that is limited to an estimation of what someone should reasonably expect to achieve in their current circumstances.[392]

*   *   *

Formative assessment involves far more than feedback from the teacher. It requires that teachers instruct pupils in the techniques of formative assessment itself. Here, again, pastoral power is recast for our late modern context.

Recall that the moral training school sought to enlist the power of peers in pastoral supervision: 'The power of the Sympathy of Numbers' is a 'principle of the highest importance', Stow argued. 'To lay hold of this principle... is the great desideratum.'[393] According to the scheme mapped out by those who promote its contemporary (formative) analogue, the sympathy of numbers is to be employed by setting up formative peer-to-peer assessment scenarios. These are to be performed in a collaborative spirit. Mutually beneficial feedback conversations will allow pupils to assist each other in achieving personal advancement: 'Individual pupils learn how to communicate with their peers in non-judgemental ways', soon discovering that 'if they want constructive feedback they have to be sensitive about the kind of feedback they give others'.[394] (A similar policy is enforced between X Factor finalists, permitting 'only public statements of mutual appreciation and camaraderie'.[395]) The assessment process is socialised and rendered humane as individuals learn to work in an environment of individual striving without the pernicious effects of rivalry. They are to be trained in the techniques of cooperative activity whilst atomised within practices of self-enhancement.

Reviewing the work of peers also allows pupils to reflect back upon 'the relative merits of their own performance'.[396] Indeed, the development of these peer-reviewing skills 'may even be a prior requirement for self-assessment'. Relating their work to a range of potential outputs enables pupils to 'develop the objectivity required for effective self-assessment'.[397] Assessing others is viewed as a technique for improving self-interrogation.

* * *

Self-assessment is considered to be the foundational activity in a regime of formative assessment, allowing pupils to develop a constructive and active approach to their own enhancement. Along with formative teaching, we are told that self-assessment is nothing new; in fact, it is an entirely natural process particularly prevalent in the better learner: 'many high attainers already intuitively self-assess'.[398] However, these processes of self-development are not to be left free from constraint. Crucially, for self-assessment to be effective, pupils must be told what they are expected to achieve; they must be made aware of their learning goals. This is a display of professional openness on behalf of the teacher that appears intrinsically democratic. It is described as the 'first and most difficult task' in the teaching of self-assessment to students.[399]

There can be a certain degree of negotiation and reformulation of goals, which helps to ease their internalisation, but ultimately these learning goals

are translated from external sources. The situation is also assisted by the professional language used to describe it: one pioneer teacher refers to the 'pupils taking *ownership* of their own learning', how she lets them 'know what the intention of the lesson is and what they need to do to *achieve it*' so that they can take '*responsibility* for their own learning'.[400] These three terms, upon which such emphasis is laid, may sound empowering. However, they disguise a process by which goals are transmitted to the student for subsequent internalisation. Though such an approach may well be pedagogically effective and may, indeed, be empowering to a degree, there is also a subtext here. The deeper agenda of self-assessment is to develop the ability to enhance personal performance *within a logic that is externally set*. Pupils learn to perform work on themselves according to an external design, whether this be the logic of the school or of the wider social order into which they are inducted.

* * *

In the Commissioners' report of 1895, it was noted that as a result of parental efforts to find lucrative scholarships for their children, boys were 'hawked about from school to school, and early come to think of themselves as articles of commerce'.[401] This was a result of their conveyance from one institution to the next, taking tests that might result in scholarship funding, should they be judged worth the investment. Today, in an era of incessant product rebranding and development, the situation has altered. Using techniques of formative self-assessment, pupils learn to commodify themselves through repackaging and upskilling. They are taught how to improve their chances of employment and promotion through self-analysis and self-help. Trained to assess their current position in the market, they make adjustments to realise what are deemed to be their realisable goals.

* * *

Despite claims to the contrary,[402] competition does not disappear within the explicitly constructive and encouraging ethic of formative assessment. Indeed, competition thrives on the carefully constructed optimism of its contestants. To this end, those assessments that are judged most 'benign' are those that are the most effective in creating the hopeful and cheery demeanours that repeat contestants will require.

Pupils are trained in the techniques of cheerful and cooperative rivalry. They learn to compete in apparent harmony with one other, each involved in personal formative cycles, occupied in unison within individual feedback–action loops. They learn to become industrious self-improvers, accepting and implementing external goals. Competition is humanised and disguised and thereby intensified by this formative technology.

* * *

Competition is no longer subordinate to a technocratic order. The competitive drive has been elevated from its formerly subordinate position. It has been raised from necessary evil to central doctrine. Competition has now achieved its disembodied form; it has finally been separated from past efforts to rationalise ability. Without these constraints, competitors are encouraged to drift off in a state of self-absorbed self-actualisation.

*   *   *

In a fluid meritocracy it is important to maintain a basic level of confidence in technologies of assessment. As the Education Secretary, Michael Gove, made plain: 'Qualifications are the currency of education – and just like the money markets – confidence is everything.'[403] Confidence is, indeed, essential for a social order dependent on the collective actions of hopeful individuals.

Though confidence was also a prerequisite for a traditional meritocracy, it was manufactured differently. Confidence was a function of statistics; the objective of test designers was to reduce statistical confidence intervals and thus enhance the accuracy of their allocations. The last major anachronism of the 1988 Task Group was its appeal to this older method of confidence procurement. In the section entitled 'Ensuring confidence in national assessment', the Task Group committed itself to developing a system 'in which a wide variety of users can have confidence. This confidence arises from the reliability of the observations made and the validity of the interpretations placed on them. Both reliability and validity contribute to a statistical estimate of confidence.'[404] Confidence would be maximised, they say, through careful test design, leading to high-scoring statistical estimates of test accuracy. Gaining public confidence through other means is not considered.

With the dissolution of meritocracy, today's test designers are forced to operate differently. Their objective is no longer simply to prove but also to *demonstrate* to the public that examinations should command their respect. The language of statistics and scientific kudos is still important, but it is, nevertheless, subordinate to impression. Following the introduction of league-tables and the elevation of parental choice, added clout has been afforded to media reports claiming a decline in standards or other such educational flaws. The annual summer panic perpetuated by the media surrounding the validity of examination results is symptomatic of their affective significance.

In response to this cycle of hysteria, a quasi-independent government body was established to regulate examinations.[405] The assigned task is to reassure the public and maintain confidence. The examinations' regulator occupies its role as the visible security presence on the landscape of examination provision.

Public confidence occupies a position of great strategic importance in an era of manufactured freedoms. In a fluid meritocracy, citizens must believe that examinations can open doors; they must believe that examinations can effectively discriminate between competitors, and recognise real talent when they encounter it. Here the danger posed by poor confidence is that it could lead to more than mere dissatisfaction. A fluid meritocracy is vulnerable to the disruptions of personal disaffection. These have the potential to detach individuals from its mechanisms of myopia.

Its systems are, nevertheless, fairly resilient. Our confidence in the overall moral order of meritocracy is sealed within a logic of assessment that we have all individually absorbed; it is trapped within a form of self-perception that can see intrinsic sense in gateways, graded hierarchies and technologies of numerical separation.

*   *   *

Typically, end-of-school examination passes rise in proportion, year-on-year. Hence, it is most often feared that the tests are becoming easier, that they are losing their ability to separate 'the wheat from the chaff', as they say. In 2012 the unexpected occurred and they fell.[406] This reduction in those achieving top marks was worth less than a percentage point, and yet the effects were personally felt and raw: individual futures were said to be at stake and school futures were said to be far from secure. One headteacher described the day after results that year as 'the darkest day in my time as a school leader'. 'We fell off a cliff,' he said. Following days of public discontent, Michael Gove sought to quell the outcry by declaring: 'my heart goes out to those students who sat the exam this year'. A benevolent gesture, perhaps, but the anger registered online was far from abated. One particularly vexed commentator simply dismissed Gove as 'a swollen bollock of a man'. Instantly, his offer of a heart appeared distinctly mean. A bollock would have been more appropriate.

*   *   *

The obsession with standards, shared by politicians, academics and public alike, is a difficult one to confront. Those who challenge the dubious nature of this obsession find themselves attacked as if they were guilty of underestimating pupil and institutional potential. This discourse is deeply uncompromising. It is held in place by a strong ideological commitment to the ethic of improvement.[407] The implicit assumption here is that education has come to sit astride a unilinear curve of educational enhancement. The presumption that this singular route to improvement is so straightforwardly true, correct and proper as to be rationally unassailable is combined with the belief that examinations are still worthy of their task. For this reason, when our faith in examination falters, the whole edifice shakes.

*   *   *

The educational heart flutters most upon the day that examination results are revealed. It seems deeply significant that individuals are most worked up when a course of education reaches its end. In itself education invites little passion, being divorced from any teleology or system of value, emancipatory or otherwise. The heart education helps nurture has, in other words, been profoundly misdirected, becoming little but a hollow muscular pump in pursuit of its pulse.

*   *   *

The switch from traditional to fluid meritocracy is marked by a series of transitions. Competition was once seen as a necessary evil; now it is to be encouraged. Aspiration was once an irrational impulse to be avoided, but this, too, has changed. Technologies once sought to rationalise desire, where the 'wish or the whim of the parent and of the child' was to be overruled; these undesirable whims included 'selfish' desires for a 'quick financial return', potentially misplaced though 'fond ambitions', 'gossip' and 'fantasies'. It was felt that those who lacked 'psychological insight' could not possibly be relied upon to make a 'satisfactory choice'.[408] Now, aspiration is to be encouraged. We are allowed our fond ambitions and fantasies; in fact, these impossible hopes are encouraged by the symbolic order. Anyone can be launched into fame and millionaire status, or so we are led to believe.

*   *   *

Aspiration is, nevertheless, subject to a series of constraints. These practices of self-control are taught in schools, where children learn to compete in cooperative rivalry; where they learn to provide instructive and encouraging feedback to one another whilst also focusing on their own enhancement. They are to keep things in perspective by living within the jurisdiction of a predicted future. Traditional meritocracies faced a basic dilemma: how would they cope once unjust inequalities were replaced by rationalised inequalities, once citizens understood their social position to be a precise measure of their social worth? This problem disappeared once justly distributed inequalities were no longer sought after. Societies that are 'unjustly unequal' are easier to bear than those that are 'justly unequal'.

*   *   *

In 2010 three Italian academics predicted that random job promotion is the best and most effective form of progression in large bureaucratic organisations.[409] This study is worth dwelling upon. Whether or not the mathematical methods and assumptions they employ are to be believed is beside the point. The fact that this study was conducted in the first place is important. It betrays the prevailing assumptions of a biopolitical order, according to

which natural social systems are often far better 'left alone'. Random allocation does not contradict the administrative logic of a fluid meritocracy, for
this is a social system that *embraces disorder*.

Still, these statisticians have managed to generate findings that sound
absurd. If the system of random promotion they envisage were to be implemented, it would strike its citizens as profoundly immoral. Random allocations contradict the present economic morality, according to which
subjects must try with patience to succeed, believing that their efforts will
be rewarded.

* * *

A fluid meritocracy serves what is now seen as the natural ecology of human
existence, in which each individual strives towards the realisation of his
or her individual potential. Whilst this natural ecology appears relatively
benign, it is sustained by the systemic manufacture of affective dispositions, which form a closely guarded space in which a struggle for existence
is deliberately fabricated. Statistical forecasts are combined in this otherwise foreshortened realm with interpersonal modes of governance and self-
absorbed subjects.

* * *

Those who live within this realm of naturalised selection are oddly pre-
Darwinian in their perception of it. They rarely perceive the brutal struggle
upon which it depends. Of course, in a fluid meritocracy the struggle for
existence is of an artificial kind: selection has been naturalised in the sense
that it occurs in a carefully socialised space of mutual rivalry. Children learn
to become benevolent competitors, absorbed within formative cycles of self-
enhancement. As socialised adults, they are unable to perceive the selective
violence that occurs around them.

* * *

Measured against the comparatively permissive ideologies of biopolitical
governance, the social engineer has been denigrated and reduced to one
of the more dangerous beasts modernity had to offer. Social engineering
is to be rejected as a violent, potentially totalitarian mode of intervention.
Societies cannot fight injustice as they once did, or so we are led to understand. Whilst it may still be possible to remove barriers and provide limited
and sporadic forms of assistance, it would be an imposition to redistribute
people. Individuals must be given the tools, perspectives and incentives to
redistribute themselves. Societies are complex entities; they are composed
of interminable dynamics and contain detailed networks of social interaction that we dominate at our peril, so they say. Advanced societies are those

societies that recognise this fact, we are told. They are innately meritocratic, as movement by merit is one of the many irreducible social processes contained within them. This meritocratic process cannot be subjected to technocratic command. It must be allowed a certain degree of breathing space. Meritocratic processes can only be encouraged and nurtured through the careful socialisation of future competitors. Advanced societies have learned these lessons at a heavy cost. It is to our collective benefit, or so we are encouraged to believe, that we have reached this stage in human development, where government has finally learned to rule us through our freedoms.

Arguments such as these make implicit sense. We imagine social life in its natural state as desirable for the very reason that it has not been interfered with (or so we believe). Interference, especially state interference, is increasingly ruled out by consensus as inherently bad. State institutions are viewed as inflexible and intrinsically oppressive. Such is our contemporary biopolitical bias.

By analogy, this bias informs our contemporary experience of animal captivity, where 'well-meaning but misinformed people think animals in the wild are "happy" because they are "free" '. In captivity, 'the animal becomes a shadow of itself, its spirit broken'…Of course, captivity does entail its own cruelties, and yet we consistently forget that animals in the wild 'lead lives of compulsion and necessity within an unforgiving social hierarchy in an environment where the supply of fear is high and the supply of food is low and where territory must constantly be defended and parasites forever endured'.[410]

* * *

We do not recognise the powers imposed upon us during this reign of freedom. We will not admit the artifices upon which our freedom depends, where these artifices are most pernicious precisely where they appear most benevolent.

* * *

Power often masks itself in frivolous activities, demanding an explanation of those who refuse to play along. Beware of the carnival, I say. Not only does it distract us from the violence and exploitation that underpins all human relations,[411] not only is the carnival a thick veneer concealing what lies beneath – relations of power also lurk at the surface of such events. These can only be identified at the cost of ridicule or expulsion, or both. The carnival goers will not allow you to take them seriously. You must not confront them with your seriousness.

* * *

Worse than the carnival, perhaps, is a form of *malevolent simplicity* that pervades institutional life. Principles and procedures designed ostensibly to protect us are dogmatically followed. This happy simplicity allows one's co-workers and superiors to rest content *and ignore* the complex violence of the workplace. Educators and other benevolent professionals are particularly vulnerable, as this violence most often feeds on and manipulates the educational conscience they have been forced to internalise.

*   *   *

This 'history of the present' has reached its destination and should have nothing more to say.[412] Genealogy makes a deliberate choice; it refuses to speak of the future, seeking instead to destabilise the present. If it were to remark upon the future, it would have to develop normative commitments that would retroactively jeopardise the project in which it is engaged. According to this project, genealogy seeks to break down our various infatuations with the present, and our longings for the golden ages of the past. It demonstrates the profound historical contingency of all we hold dear and seeks to destabilise all that we think of as stable or proper. Beyond this it will not go.

As Paul Veyne approvingly reports, Foucault offers 'critique, that is all: nothing more positive'. Foucault helps to 'bring doubt to bear upon our present' but 'as a thinker, he will go no further'. He will not argue for any cause; indeed, his genealogy of 'human finitude creates havoc, irremediably separating the scholar from the partisan'.[413] To demonstrate our contingency is the genealogical aim, and this demands of it an ethos that is one of 'militancy grounded in scholarly moderation'.[414] Genealogy refuses to suggest or even hint at alternative forms of social life. After showing that change might occur at levels so fundamental that we find them hard to imagine, it leaves the process of change to others.

* * *

It is regrettable that such stipulations have been translated by their proponents into an intellectual rationale that serves to justify political inactivity. Only the activities of intellectual work are allowed to proliferate here. We must concede, of course, that conventional genealogy exhibits an admirable work ethic, according to which its pursuit of knowledge is to be 'a *regressus in infinitum*', where 'that which comes to a standstill (at a supposed *causa prima*, at something unconditioned, etc.) is laziness, weariness...'[415]

Intellectual workers of this tradition nevertheless exhaust themselves in their endless cycles of research. They are too kaput to apply their destabilising impulse to the activity of intellectual work itself.

* * *

Genealogy incites. Aware of its (necessary) incompleteness, genealogy engages in combat without intellectual restraint. It distances itself from the expert who believes that truth must precede intervention. Understanding itself to be already located within conflict, genealogy becomes reconciled to this compromised position. It is an insurrectional device, designed for rebellion.

* * *

Social orders are contingent entities. They depend on shifting configurations of power that are subject to change. The dominant principles of present-day meritocracy may be highly influential and constraining, but they can be disrupted. Regimes of power are always, by definition, failing enterprises. The challenge is to understand how these failures are so frequently reabsorbed by the governing order. We are still learning how to resist.

* * *

When medieval moral training fell into abeyance, it was replaced by systems of modern examination that adopted the pretence of scientific neutrality. This pretence must be refuted at its most basic level. Modern examination was not a straightforward measuring device; it was not without its own forms of moral training.

* * *

The measurement of individuals and the management of bodies generated a view of the population as a whole. The principles of government were now derived from the populations governed. This circular and reductive operation led to profoundly ambivalent strategies of power that were able to justify great violence in the name of life.

*   *   *

The 'golden age' of meritocracy, a time when efforts were made to match the normal distribution of abilities to the normal distribution of jobs, was closely associated with the rise of eugenic thought. This system of power has since been replaced by the logics of a fluid meritocracy. We have come to live in environmental times, in the sense that we have learned to position ourselves within our immediate environment, accepting the reality of the external world, and learning to deal with it as best we can. Individual enhancement is favoured at the expense of overall meritocratic reallocation.

*   *   *

It is easy, when convinced, to feel the futility and overall lack of purpose inherent within a system of fluid merit. Its highly individualised, process-oriented modes of social action appear aimless and absurd. This impression of futility derives, however, from an implicit comparison between fluid times and their more solid traditional precursors, from comparison with a period when the formula 'merit = ability + effort' was an active device in the technocratic order. Nevertheless, having understood the complex gene-alogy of this more concerted and comprehensively administered system, we realise that this is a problematic point of comparison. The historic connec-tion between more concerted efforts to rationalise ability and eugenics raises considerable doubt. The link between such a conception of meritoc-racy and deterministic and fixed conceptions of human worth, with all the excesses this inspired, enables us to see that the 'golden age' of meritocracy was far from desirable. We become confused by this social and educational principle of meritocracy, unable to estimate its worth. Fluid meritocracy is absurd and insidious, but traditional meritocracies were deterministic and potentially demagogic.

*   *   *

Embrace your confusion. Meritocracy can no longer be invoked as your abstract ideal. It can no longer be relied upon as a standard against which we must make things 'better'.

*   *   *

These are broad dispensations of power. They lie beyond the grasp of reform. The overall system is under question here.

*   *   *

Radical alternatives have been imagined, the most famous of which we attribute to Marx. An advanced communist society would, he tells us, 'inscribe on its banner' the following statement: [416]

FROM EACH ACCORDING TO HIS ABILITIES, TO EACH ACCORDING TO HIS NEEDS

This meritocratic formula seeks to generate a *total* rupture between questions of ability and reward. That would go against the core principles of both traditional and fluid meritocracies. Since Marx wrote, the conditions required for the creation of such a rupture between abilities and rewards have demonstrably changed. In the event of a communist revolution, it is conceivable that a traditional meritocracy could be retuned as two parallel systems: one concerned with the administration of ability, the other with the administration of need. The challenges posed by a fluid meritocracy are very different, however. Abilities and hoped-for rewards intermingle now at a deeply personal level. Hopes are carefully conditioned, so that they are both excessive and realistic, whilst abilities are constantly refashioned in a cynical effort designed to reap successive rewards. Practices of self-fashioning seek to exploit economic opportunities directly as they arrive. In the event of a communist revolution, then, an entire economic morality and its connected practices of living would have to be recast.

* * *

When our faith in God departs, we should seriously consider whether the entire edifice of Christianity should be jettisoned as well. This was the question Nietzsche provoked, for without its deity the religion in question should no longer make sense. For Nietzsche, it was deeply disappointing that Christian ideals continue to organise secular life.[417] These ideals have either been allowed to remain, in an attenuated form, or have been replaced by other ideals that, nevertheless, fail to bring into question the transcendental framework on which Christianity relied. Nietzsche claimed that we lack the commitment that is required for the kind of 'revaluation of all values' that must surely ensue when a moral order is hollowed out by the death of its God.[418] Our difficulty, in other words, is that we live in 'a society that no longer has the strength to *excrete*' those commitments and values it begins to doubt.[419]

In a similar way, the hollowed out, echoingly empty edifice of meritocracy should be abandoned, since the guiding principles of justice and efficiency have already departed. The difficulty is that, having travelled beyond justice and efficiency, we have arrived in a state of abject self-absorption wherein we have lost the ability to jettison the moral order these ideals helped create. We remain psychologically attached to the present and its derelict moral code. This embrace is one from which we lack the will and imagination to release ourselves. We have been educated to bear the selves we now occupy. We have learned to live according their fabricated desires.

To rebel against our educational present we must explore its perversions, its cynicisms. We should disabuse ourselves of our well-meaning but shallow commitments. To resist, we must become uncomfortable. This resistance will be an *excoriating experience*, where those who rebel feel ill at ease in their skin.

Notes

List of Figures

1. 'Whitely Woods Open Air School, Sheffield. Measuring a pupil, 1911' (Turner, David. The Open Air School Movement in Sheffield. *History of Education*, 1972, 1(1). Reprinted by permission of the publisher, Taylor & Francis Ltd.).
2. 'Boys dressed in Hindu costume for Empire Day celebrations, children from Abbeydale Council School, 1906' (Reprinted by permission of picturesheffield. com. Ref No: s02835).
3. 'Walter Harrison with his father's horse and cart on the corner of Grimesthorpe Road/Earl Marshall Road with Grimesthorpe School in the background' (Reprinted by permission of picturesheffield.com. Ref No: s15876).
4. 'Free Writing School, School Croft, Sheffield' (Reprinted by permission of picturesheffield.com. Ref. No: s06568).
5. 'Interior of the Central School of the British & Foreign School Society, Borough Road' (BFSS. *Manual of the System of Primary Instruction*. London: BFSS, 1839. Reprinted by permission of British & Foreign School Society Archive, Brunel University).
6. 'Positions of the Scholars' (ibid. Reprinted by permission of British & Foreign School Society Archive, Brunel University).
7. 'Tinsley Church of England School, Bawtry Road, Tinsley, Sheffield' (Reprinted by permission of picturesheffield.com. Ref. No: v01664).
8. 'Teacher Mr Wood and pupils; Boys School Classroom, St John's School' (Reprinted by permission of picturesheffield.com. Ref. No: u05913).
9. 'Western Road School, Western Road, Crookes, Sheffield' (Reprinted by permission of picturesheffield.com. Ref. No: s06608).
10. 'Plate V. The fire-balloon' (Feasey, Jesse Eaton. *Outdoor School Work*. Bath: Sir Isaac Pitman & Sons, 1919).
11. 'Plate II. Siphoning water over a wall' (ibid.).
12. 'Standard Scheme of Descent' (Galton, Francis. The Possible Improvement of the Human Breed under the Existing Conditions of Law and Sentiment. In: *Essays in Eugenics*. London: The Eugenics Education Society, 1909 [1901]).
13. (Reprinted by permission of Sheffield Archives: Acc. 2001/27)
14. (Reprinted by permission of Sheffield Archives: Acc. 2001/27)
15. (Reprinted by permission of Sheffield Archives: Acc. 2001/27)
16. Picture taken by the author.
17. (Reprinted by permission of Sheffield Archives: Acc. 2001/27)
18. 'Industrial Classification' (Goddard, Henry. *Feeble-Mindedness its Causes and Consequences*. New York: Macmillan, 1914).
19. (Reprinted by permission of Sheffield Archives: Acc. 2001/27)
20. (Reprinted by permission of Sheffield Archives: Acc. 2001/27)
21. 'That's the way to London' (Feasey, Jessie Eaton. *In the Garden*. Bath: Sir Isaac Pitman & Sons, 1910).
22. 'Diagram of the normal curve of distribution of ability' (Ministry of Education. *Scope and Standards of the Certificate of Secondary Education*, 1963, p. 4).

23. 'Feeling the direction of the wind with a wet finger' (Feasey, Jessie Eaton. *Garden and Playground Nature Study*. Bath: Sir Isaac Pitman & Sons, 1911).
24. (Reprinted by permission of Sheffield Archives: Acc. 2001/27)
25. 'Mad hatters Tea Party, High Wincobank Council School. Miss M. Hemmingfield as Alice' (Reprinted by permission of picturesheffield.com. Ref. No: s02920).
26. 'Singing songs out of doors' (Feasey. *Outdoor School Work*).

Preface

1. Nietzsche, Friedrich. *The Birth of Tragedy*. London: Penguin, 2003 [1872], p. 97.
2. These arguments draw from: Allen, Ansgar. The solitary academic: a dying breed. *openDemocracy – OurKingdom*, 2013 (14 February).
3. Plato. *The Last Days of Socrates*. London: Penguin, 1993.
4. Xenophon hints at more lowly reasons, suggesting Socrates was more influenced by a fear of senile old age. Xenophon. *Conversations of Socrates*. London: Penguin, 1990.
5. Bailey, Michael and Freedman, Des. *The Assault on Universities: A Manifesto for Resistance*. London: Pluto Press, 2011.
6. Nietzsche, Friedrich. *On the Genealogy of Morals*. Oxford: Oxford University Press, 1996 [1887], p. 10.
7. Nietzsche, Friedrich. The Wanderer and His Shadow. In: *Human, All Too Human*. Cambridge: Cambridge University Press, 1996 [1880], p. 327.

I Bodies

1. Green, J. A. The University of Sheffield. In: Porter, ed. *Handbook & Guide to Sheffield: Prepared for the Members of the "British Association for the Advancement of Science," on the occasion of their visit to Sheffield*. Sheffield: J. W. Northend, 1910, p. 152. J. A. Green, M.A., was Professor of Education at the university.
2. Turner. *Open Air School*, p. 75.
3. Pongratz, Ludwig. Voluntary Self-Control: Education reform as a governmental strategy. In: Masschelein, Bröckling and Pongratz, ed. *The Learning Society from the Perspective of Governmentality*. Oxford: Blackwell, 2007, p. 63.
4. InvisibleCommittee. *The Coming Insurrection*. Los Angeles: Semiotexte, 2009, p. 18.
5. Lyotard, Jean-François. *The Postmodern Condition: A Report on Knowledge*. Manchester: Manchester University Press, 2005 [1979], p. 15.
6. Barthes, Roland. *Camera Lucida: Reflections on Photography*. London: Vintage, 2000 [1980], p. 3.
7. To pick an example, Henrik Ibsen was giving it a tongue-lashing in 1869. See Ibsen, Henrik. The League of Youth. In: *A Doll's House and Other Plays*. London: Penguin, 2003 [1869].
8. Sloterdijk, Peter. *Critique of Cynical Reason*. Minneapolis: University of Minnesota Press, 2001.
9. Staten, Henry. *Nietzsche's Voice*. Ithaca, NY: Cornell University Press, 1990.
10. There are always exceptions. Kurt Vonnegut, once honorary president of the American Humanist Association, would be one.
11. Staten. *Nietzsche's Voice*, pp. 78–9.
12. Gray, John. *Enlightenment's Wake*. London: Routledge, 2008, p. 26.

13. Staten. *Nietzsche's Voice*, pp. 78–9.
14. This has not gone unnoticed. As Bowles and Gintis once observed, 'the educational system legitimates economic inequality by providing an open, [apparently] objective, and ostensibly meritocratic mechanism for assigning individuals to unequal economic positions'. (See Bowles, Samuel and Gintis, Herbert. *Schooling in Capitalist America*. Chicago: Haymarket Books, 2011 [1976], p. 103.)
15. Haskins, Charles. *The Rise of Universities*. New York: Henry Holt and Company, 1923, pp. 3–4.
16. Ibid.
17. Ariès, Philippe. *Centuries of Childhood*. London: Penguin, 1973 [1960].
18. Haskins. *Rise of Universities*. p. 46.
19. For accounts of the medieval university career and accompanying systems of examination, see Rashdall, Hastings. *The Universities of Europe in the Middle Ages: Volume I*. Oxford: Clarendon Press, 1895, pp. 433–62; Rashdall, Hastings. *The Universities of Europe in the Middle Ages: Volume II*. Oxford: Clarendon Press, 1895, pp. 440–446; Haskins, *Rise of Universities*. pp. 37–68; Leff, Gordon. *Paris and Oxford Universities in the Thirteenth and Fourteenth Centuries*. London: John Wiley and Sons, 1968, pp. 146–60; Cobban, Alan. *The Medieval English Universities: Oxford and Cambridge to c. 1500*. Aldershot: Scholar Press, 1988, pp. 161–71.
20. See Rashdall. *Universities of Europe I*, p. 462.
21. Carr, Wilfred. Professing Education in a Postmodern Age. *Journal of Philosophy of Education* 1997; 31(2); Clark, William. *Academic Charisma and the Origins of the Research University*. Chicago: University of Chicago Press, 2006.
22. MacIntyre, Alasdair. *Three Rival Versions of Moral Enquiry*. London: Duckworth, 1990, p. 64.
23. Ibid., p. 62.
24. Ibid.
25. Ibid., p. 181.
26. Goddard, Roy and Payne, Mark. Criticality and the practice-based MA. *Journal of Education for Teaching* 2013, 39(1), p. 127.
27. If you would prefer to read a more straightforward history of examination, I refer you to: Roach, John. *Public Examinations in England 1850–1900*. Cambridge: Cambridge University Press, 1971; Montgomery, Robert. *Examinations: An Account of their Evolution as Administrative Devices in England*. London: Longmans, 1965; Montgomery, Robert. *A New Examination of Examinations*. London: Routledge and Kegan Paul, 1978.
28. MacIntyre. *Versions of Moral Enquiry*.
29. Bentham, Jeremy. *Constituional Code – Volume I*. Oxford: Clarendon Press, 1830 [1983], p. 310.
30. Ibid., p. 330.
31. Ibid., p. 331.
32. Ibid., p. 329.
33. Ibid., p. 331.
34. Ibid., p. 332.
35. Ibid., p. 333.
36. Costello, William. *The Scholastic Curriculum at Early Seventeenth-Century Cambridge*. Cambridge, Massachusetts: Harvard University Press, 1958.
37. Montgomery. *Examinations*, p. 6.
38. Gascoigne, John. Mathematics and Meritocracy: The Emergence of the Cambridge Mathematical Tripos. *Social Studies of Science* 1984; 14.

39. Hoskin, Keith. The Examination, Disciplinary Power and Rational Schooling. *History of Education* 1979, 8(2), p. 144. The significance attributed to 1792 has been questioned. It has been argued that a certain degree of 'impression marking' lasted until exams were finally stabilised in the 1840s. See Stray, Christopher. The Shift from Oral to Written Examination: Cambridge and Oxford 1700–1900. *Assessment in Education* 2001, 8(1), p. 41. For my purposes the precise dating of events matters little.
40. Stray. *Oral to Written Examination*, p. 39.
41. Macaulay, Thomas. Government of India Bill – Ajourned Debate (Second Night) Friday June 24. *Hansard's Parliamentary Debates Third Series CXXVIII*. London: Cornelius Buck, 1853, p. 756.
42. Lindqvist, Sven. 'Exterminate All the Brutes'. *Saharan Journey*. London: Granta, 2012.
43. India Act. An Act to provide for the Government of India – 20th August 1853. In *A Collection of the Public General Statutes passed in the Sixteenth and Seventeenth Year of the Reign of Her Majesty Queen Victoria*. Eyre and Spottiswoode, 1853, p. 487.
44. Preparations were made for an examination on 16 July 1855. Parliamentary Papers. *Reports, August 1855, to Coms. for Affairs of India by Examiners of Candidates for Civil Service of India; Correspondence relating to Appointment and Proceedings of Examiners*. (513) XL.135. House of Commons Papers, 1855.
45. Parliamentary Papers. *Report on the Organisation of the Permanent Civil Service, together with a letter from the Rev. B. Jowett*. XXVII.1. House of Commons Papers, 1854.
46. Parliamentary Papers. *Report, November 1854, from Committee on Examinations of Candidates for Civil Service of East India Company*. (34) XL.105. House of Commons Papers, 1854. p. 11.
47. Roach. *Public Examinations*.
48. Victoria, Alexandrina. In: Benson and Esher, ed. *The Letters of Queen Victoria: A Selection of Her Majesty's Correspondence Between the Years 1831 and 1861*. New York: Longmans, Green and Co, 1907, pp. 12–13 (emphasis mine).
49. Ibid., pp. 13–14.
50. Parliamentary Papers. 1854. (34) XL.105. p. 15.
51. Parliamentary Papers. 1854. XXVII.1. p. 24.
52. Parliamentary Papers. 1854. (34) XL.105. p. 15.
53. Foucault, Michel. *Discipline and Punish: The Birth of The Prison*. London: Penguin, 1975 [1991], p. 30.
54. Nietzsche, Friedrich. *Thus Spoke Zarathustra*. London: Penguin, 1969 [1883], p. 42.
55. Peim, Nick. Education, Schooling, Derrida's Marx and Democracy: Some Fundamental Questions. *Studies in Philosophy and Education* 2013, 32(2).
56. The argument that follows draws from: Allen, Ansgar. The Examined Life: On the Formation of Souls and Schooling. *American Educational Research Journal* 2013, 50(2).
57. Foucault. *Discipline and Punish*, p. 30.
58. Foucault, Michel. The Subject and Power. In: Dreyfus and Rabinow, ed. *Beyond Structuralism and Hermeneutics*. 2nd ed. Chicago: University of Chicago Press, 1983, p. 208.
59. Foucault. *Discipline and Punish*, p. 29.
60. Tröhler, Daniel, Popkewitz, Thomas and Labaree, David. *Schooling and the Making of Citizens in the Long Nineteenth Century*. New York: Routledge, 2011, p. 20.

61. Nietzsche. *On the Genealogy of Morals*.
62. Foucault, Michel. Nietzsche, Genealogy, History. In: Faubion, ed,. *Essential Works of Foucault 1954–1984. Volume 2*. London: Penguin, 2000 [1971].
63. Ibid., p. 374.
64. Ibid., p. 376.
65. Ibid., p. 377.
66. Nietzsche. *On the Genealogy of Morals*, pp. 57–8.
67. In adopting this institutional focus I am aware of the risks. As Foucault would argue, 'one must analyze institutions from the standpoint of power relations, rather than vice versa'. To adopt the latter position may give 'an exaggerated privilege' to 'functions that are essentially reproductive' as well as to coercive and legalistic frameworks of power. The danger is a neglect of those operations of power that are far more dispersed and productive, of relations that find anchorage outside the institutions concerned. (See: Foucault. *The Subject and Power II*, p. 222.)
68. Ibid.
69. Caruso, Marcelo. Order through the Gaze: A Comparative Perspective of the Construction of Visibility in Monitorial Schooling. *Encounters in Education*, 2008, 9; Miller, Pavla. *Transformations of Patriarchy in the West, 1500–1900*. Bloomington, Indiana: Indiana University Press, 1998; Upton, Dell. Lancasterian Schools, Republican Citizenship, and the Spatial Imagination in Early Nineteenth-Century America. *Journal of the Society of Architectural Historians*, 1996, 55(3).
70. Curtis, Bruce. *Building The Educational State: Canada West, 1836–1871*. London, Ontario: The Althouse Press, 1988; Perry, George. 'The Grand Regulator': State Schooling and the Normal-School Idea in Nova Scotia, 1838–1855. *Acadiensis*, 2003, 32(2).
71. Rayman, Ronald. Joseph Lancaster's Monitorial System of Instruction and American Indian Education, 1815–1838. *History of Education Quarterly*, 1981, 21(4).
72. Jones, Dave. The genealogy of the urban schoolteacher. In: Ball, ed. *Foucault and Education: Disciplines and Knowledge*. London: Routledge, 1990.
73. Kay-Shuttleworth, Sir James. *Four Periods of Public Education as reviewed in 1832–1839–1846–1862*. Brighton: Harvester, 1862 [1973], p. 296.
74. Parliamentary Papers. *Education Commission. Reports of the assistant commissioners appointed to inquire into the state of popular education in England. Vol. 1*. XXI Pt.I.1. House of Commons Papers, 1861, p. 94.
75. Ibid., p. 91.
76. Ibid., p. 92.
77. Ibid., p. 93.
78. Ibid., p. 94.
79. Foucault. *Discipline and Punish*.
80. See, for example: Miller, P. J. Factories, monitorial schools and Jeremy Bentham: The origins of 'the management syndrome' in popular education. *Journal of Educational Administration and History*, 1973, 5(2), p. 10; Margolis, Eric and Fram, Sheila. Caught Napping: Images of Surveillance, Discipline and Punishment on the Body of the Schoolchild. *History of Education*, 2007, 36(2), p. 198; Gore, Jennifer. Disciplining Bodies: On the Continuity of Power Relations in Pedagogy. In: Popkewitz and Brennan, ed. *Foucault's Challenge: Discourse, Knowledge and Power in Education*. New York: Teachers College Press, 1998, p. 232.
81. Bentham, Jeremy. Panopticon; or, the inspection-house. In: Bowring, ed,. *The Works of Jeremy Bentham*. Edinburgh: William Tait, 1791 [1843].

82. Foucault. *Discipline and Punish*, p. 205.
83. 'The procedures of power resorted to in modern societies are far more numerous and diverse and rich. It would be false to say that the principle of visibility has dominated the whole technology of power since the 19th century' (Foucault, Michel. The Eye of Power. In: Lotringer, ed. *Foucault Live: Collected Interviews, 1961–1984*. New York: Semiotext(e), 1996 [1977], p. 227).
84. Foucault. *Discipline and Punish*, pp. 218–19.
85. Ibid., p. 167.
86. Elsewhere, work has tended towards this position. See Hoskin, Keith. Foucault under examination: The crypto-educationalist unmasked. In: Ball, ed. *Foucault and Education: Disciplines and Knowledge*. London: Routledge, 1990.
87. Rayman. *Lancaster and American Indian Education*, p. 399.
88. Bell, Andrew. *The Madras School, or Elements of Tuition: Comprising the Analysis of an Experiment in Education, Made at the Male Asylum, Madras*. London: Murray, 1808, p. vii.
89. BFSS. *Report of the British and Foreign School Society*. London: Taylor, 1814, p. 44.
90. BFSS. *Report of the British and Foreign School Society. The general meeting. November 1815*. London: Taylor, 1815, pp. 3–4.
91. Ibid., p. 43.
92. Bell. *The Madras School*, p. viii.
93. The National Society (after Bell) and British and Foreign School Society or BFSS (after Lancaster).
94. Bell, Andrew. *The Report of the Military Male Orphan Asylum at Madras, a New Edition*. London: Murray, 1812, p. xx.
95. Ibid., p. 20.
96. Ibid., p. 19.
97. BFSS. *Manual 1839*, p. 9.
98. Bell. *The Report of the Asylum*, pp. 20–4.
99. Lancaster, Joseph. *The British System of Education*. London: Royal Free School, 1810, p. 23.
100. Bell. *The Madras School*, p. 5.
101. Bell. *The Report of the Asylum*, p. 39.
102. Bell. *The Madras School*, p. 3.
103. Lancaster, Joseph. *Improvements in Education, as it Respects the Industrious Classes of the Community*. London: Darton & Harvey, 1803, pp. 17–18.
104. Fromm, Erich. *The Fear of Freedom*. London: Routledge, 1942 [2001], p. 50.
105. Foucault. *Discipline and Punish*, p. 154.
106. Bell. *The Report of the Asylum*, pp. 38–9.
107. Bell. *The Madras School*, p. 3.
108. Ibid., pp. 6, 11.
109. Bell. *The Report of the Asylum*, p. 40.
110. Bell. *The Madras School*, p. 16.
111. Gladman, F. J. *School Work: Control and Teaching, Organization and Principles of Education*. London: Jarrold & Sons, 1898, p. 368.
112. Ibid., p. 373.
113. Lancaster. *The British System*, p. 25.
114. Gladman. *School Work*, p. 374.
115. Ibid., p. 375.
116. BFSS. *Manual 1839*, p. 10.
117. Ibid., pp. 55–6.

118. Bell. *The Madras School*, p. 32.
119. BFSS. *Sixteenth report of the British and Foreign School Society*. London: Vogel, 1821, p. 49.
120. BFSS. *Fourteenth report of the British and Foreign School Society*. London: Bensley and Son, 1819, p. 41.
121. Bell. *The Madras School*, p. 15.
122. Bell. *The Report of the Asylum*, p. 42.
123. Ibid., p. 84.
124. Bell. *The Madras School*, p. 19.
125. Ibid., p. 20.
126. Though here, too, ingenious techniques were used. In one school at Edinburgh, the accusation of poor teaching by the respective class monitors could be raised at an appeal, and, if proven, those who registered the complaint took the place 'of those who have not observed the blunder, and the Monitor himself loses a place' (BFSS. *Report 1814*, p. 59).
127. Bell. *The Madras School*, p. 23.
128. Ibid., p. 20.
129. Ibid., pp. 46–7.
130. Lancaster. *The British System*, pp. 27–8.
131. Bell. *The Madras School*, p. 28.
132. Ibid., p. 31.
133. Salmon, David. *Joseph Lancaster*. London: Longmans, Green, and Co., 1904, p. 10.
134. Lancaster. *The British System*, pp. 35–6.
135. Ibid., pp. 34–5.
136. Ibid., p. 26.
137. Ibid., pp. 35–7.
138. Lancaster. *Improvements in Education*, p. 50.
139. Bell. *The Madras School*, p. 24.
140. Ibid., p. 16.
141. Hunter, Ian. Subjectivity and Government. *Economy and Society*, 1993, 22(1), p. 130.
142. Ibid.
143. Ibid., p. 131.
144. Foucault. *Discipline and Punish*, p. 191.
145. Ibid., p. 189.
146. Ibid., pp. 226–7 (emphasis mine).
147. Ibid., p. 148.
148. Cruickshank, Marjorie. David Stow, Scottish pioneer of teacher training in Britain. *British Journal of Educational Studies*, 1966, 14(2), p. 206.
149. Stow, David. *The Training System, Moral Training School, and Normal Seminary. Tenth Edition*. London: Longman, Brown, Green and Longmans, 1854, p. 61.
150. Ibid., p. 60.
151. Ibid., pp. 62–3.
152. Ibid., p. 63.
153. Cruickshank. *David Stow*, p. 206.
154. Kay-Shuttleworth. *Four Periods of Public Education*, pp. 583–5.
155. Bell. *The Report of the Asylum*, p. 42.
156. Upton. *Lancasterian Schools*.
157. Stow. *The Training System*, p. 153.

158. Lancaster. *Improvements in Education*, p. 7.
159. Stow. *The Training System*, pp. 6, 8.
160. Shaw, George Bernard. *An Unsocial Socialist*. London: John Murray, 2012 [1884].
161. Tröhler, Popkewitz and Labaree. *Schooling and the Making of Citizens*, p. 15.
162. Foucault, Michel. 'Omnes et Singulatim': Toward a Critique of Political Reason. In: Faubion, ed. *Essential Works of Foucault 1954–1984. Volume 3*. London: Penguin, 2002 [1979]; Foucault. *The Subject and Power II*.
163. Kay-Shuttleworth. *Four Periods of Public Education*, pp. 295–6.
164. Jones. *The Urban Schoolteacher*, p. 61.
165. These 'normal schools' were set up by pioneers such as Kay-Shuttleworth at Battersea and Stow at Glasgow. Kay-Shuttleworth. *Four Periods of Public Education*, p. 312.
166. Hunter, Ian. *Culture and Government: The Emergence of Literary Education*. London: Macmillan, 1988, p. 59.
167. Stow. *The Training System*, p. 203.
168. Ibid., p. 156.
169. Ibid., p. 153.
170. Ibid., p. 206.
171. Symons, Jelinger. *School Economy, A Practical Book on The Best Modes of Establishing and Teaching Schools, and of Making them Thoroughly Useful to the Working Classes by Means of Moral and Industrial Training*. London: Parker and Son, 1852, p. 121.
172. Ibid., p. 120.
173. Ibid., p. 116.
174. 'The teacher must be what he wishes to make the children', ibid., p. 126.
175. Stow. *The Training System*, p. 156.
176. Foucault, Michel. *The Will to Knowledge*. London: Penguin, 1998 [1976], p. 60.
177. BFSS. *Report 1819*, pp. 49–50.
178. BFSS. *A Handbook to the Borough Road Schools*. London: BFSS, 1856, p. 146.
179. Ibid., p. 128.
180. Kay-Shuttleworth. *Four Periods of Public Education*, p. 38.
181. Stow. *The Training System*, p. 339.
182. Ibid., p. 322.
183. Ibid., pp. iv–v.
184. Jones. *The Urban Schoolteacher*, p. 73; Turner. *Open Air School*.
185. Hunter. *Culture and Government*, p. 34.
186. Ecclestone, Kathryn and Hayes, Dennis. *The Dangerous Rise of Therapeutic Education*. London: Routledge, 2008.
187. Gide, André. *The Immoralist*. London: Penguin, 1981 [1902].
188. Nietzsche, Friedrich. *Human, All Too Human*. London: Penguin, 2004 [1878], p. 14.

II   Populations

1. Sullivan, Thomas. Merit Ranking and Career Patterns: The Parisian Faculty of Theology in the Late Middle Ages. In: Courteney and Miethke, ed. *Universities and Schooling in Medieval Society*. Leiden: Brill, 2000, p. 128.
2. Foucault. *Discipline and Punish*, p. 222.
3. Foucault, Michel. *The Birth of Biopolitics: Lectures at the Collège de France 1978–1979*. Basingstoke: Palgrave Macmillan, 2008 [1979], p. 67.

4. Foucault, Michel. *Security, Territory, Population: Lectures at the Collège de France 1977–1978.* Basingstoke: Palgrave Macmillan, 2004 [1978], p. 48.
5. Foucault. *The Will to Knowledge*; Foucault, Michel. *Society Must Be Defended: Lectures at the Collège de France 1975–76.* London: Penguin, 2003 [1976]; Foucault. *Security, Territory, Population.*
6. Foucault. *Discipline and Punish*, p. 137 (emphasis mine).
7. Nietzsche. *On the Genealogy of Morals*, p. 39.
8. Nietzsche. *Human, All Too Human*, p. 22.
9. A variation on Nietzsche's 'snares and nets for careless birds', perhaps (ibid. p. 4.).
10. Nietzsche, Friedrich. Twilight of the Idols or How to Philosophize with a Hammer. In: *Twilight of the Idols and The Anti-Christ.* London: Penguin, 2003 [1889], p. 34.
11. In particular I refer here, and for the remainder of this chapter, to the grouping that was announced by and through *The Foucault Effect*, published in 1990 – the influence of which was celebrated at *The Foucault Effect 1991–2011* conference at Birkbeck College in London – and has been expressed most consistently, but not exclusively, through articles published in the journal *Economy and Society*, based at the London School of Economics. (See: Burchell, Graham, Gordon, Colin and Miller, Peter. *The Foucault Effect: Studies in Governmentality.* London: Harvester Wheatsheaf, 1991.) The tendencies I associate with this scholarship are not limited to this largely British grouping. It can be observed in the work of many 'Western' scholars across parts of continental Europe, Australia and North America who are influenced by Foucault, and is particularly prominent within traditions of neo-Foucauldian scholarship that work from the problematic of 'governmentality'. My reflections relate to a line of development in Foucault's thought that is located within the intellectual contexts of those polities that define themselves as liberal democracies, which is to say, those societies in which radical Left social analyses have been in decline. Elsewhere, in, say, a post-colonial context such as Latin America, Foucault may have been taken up very differently.
12. Foucault, Michel. Interview with Michel Foucault. In: Faubion, ed. *Essential Works of Foucault 1954–1984. Volume 3.* London: Penguin, 2002 [1978], p. 240.
13. Foucault, Michel. *The Archaeology of Knowledge.* London: Routledge, 2002 [1969], p. 19.
14. Foucault, Michel. What Is an Author? In: Faubion, ed. *Essential Works of Foucault 1954–1984. Volume 2.* London: Penguin, 2000 [1969], p. 221.
15. Ibid., p. 215.
16. [For example, the link between disciplinary power and pastoral power is difficult to establish for this very reason.
17. Nietzsche. *Thus Spoke Zarathustra*, p. 103.
18. Thiele, Leslie. The Agony of Politics: The Nietzschean Roots of Foucault's Thought. *American Political Science Review*, 1990, 84(3), p. 923.
19. Foucault, Michel. Structuralism and Post-structuralism. In: Faubion, ed. *Essential Works of Foucault 1954–1984. Volume 2.* London: Penguin, 2000 [1983], p. 451.
20. Foucault. *Society Must Be Defended*, p. 13.
21. Foucault, Michel. The Subject and Power. In: Faubion, ed. *Essential Works of Foucault 1954–1984. Volume 3.* London: Penguin, 2002 [1982], p. 336.
22. Ibid., pp. 336–7.
23. Foucault. *Security, Territory, Population*, p. 2.
24. Foucault. *The Will to Knowledge*, p. 93.
25. Ibid., p. 82.

26. Huffer, Lynne. Mad for Foucault: A Conversation. *Theory, Culture & Society* 2010, 27(7–8), p. 332.
27. In other words, this becomes an exemplary case of a kind of self-rule that Foucault set out to critique.
28. Foucault, Michel. The Ethics of the Concern for Self as a Practice of Freedom. In: Rabinow, ed. *Essential Works of Foucault 1954–1984. Volume 1.* London: Penguin, 2000 [1984], p. 292.
29. Thiele. *The Agony of Politics*, p. 908.
30. Foucault. *The Subject and Power I*, p. 342.
31. Foucault. *The Will to Knowledge*, p. 96.
32. Ibid.
33. Foucault. *Society Must Be Defended*, p. 30.
34. Foucault. *Power Affects the Body*, p. 210.
35. Ibid., p. 211.
36. Ibid.
37. Foucault. *Society Must Be Defended*, p. 54.
38. Ibid., p. 16.
39. Foucault had in mind 'less of a face-to-face confrontation that paralyses both sides than a permanent provocation' (Foucault. *The Subject and Power I*, p. 342.).
40. Foucault. *Society Must Be Defended*, p. 54.
41. Ibid., p. 55.
42. Ibid., p. 31.
43. Foucault, Michel. *Psychiatric Power: Lectures at the Collège de France 1973–1974.* Basingstoke: Palgrave Macmillan, 2008 [1974], p. 14.
44. Nietzsche. *Human, All Too Human*, p. 13; Nietzsche, Friedrich. *Beyond Good and Evil: Prelude to a Philosophy of the Future.* Oxford: Oxford University Press, 1998 [1886], p. 5.
45. Nietzsche. *Beyond Good and Evil*, p. 6.
46. Foucault. *Society Must Be Defended*, p. 173.
47. Nietzsche. *On the Genealogy of Morals*, p. 44.
48. Marx, Karl. *Capital: Volume I.* London: Penguin, 1990 [1867], p. 926.
49. Benjamin, Walter. *Illuminations.* London: Pimlico, 1999, p. 248.
50. At times Foucault lays great emphasis on the violence of power, such as in the lectures of 1976. (See: Foucault. *Society Must Be Defended*.) Elsewhere, and particularly in his later work, Foucault is more explicit in stating that violence 'does not constitute the principle or the basic nature of power'. (See: Foucault. *The Subject and Power II*, p. 220.)
51. Foucault. *Society Must Be Defended*, p. 54.
52. Here there are immediate difficulties because Foucault was not consistent in his use of these terms. Strategies are presented as tactics, and tactics as strategies.
53. Foucault. *The Will to Knowledge*, p. 95 (emphasis mine).
54. Nietzsche. *Human, All Too Human*, p. 215.
55. Foucault. *Power Affects the Body*, p. 211.
56. Foucault. *The Will to Knowledge*, p. 100.
57. Žižek, Slavoj. *The Ticklish Subject: The Absent Centre of Political Ontology.* London: Verso, 2008 [1999], p. 303.
58. Certeau, Michel de. *The Practice of Everyday Life.* Berkeley: University of California Press, 1988 [1984].
59. Wells, H. G. *The Time Machine.* London: Penguin, 2005 [1895], pp. 4–5.
60. Foucault. *Power Affects the Body*, p. 211.

61. Foucault. *What is Enlightenment?* pp. 315–16.
62. Foucault, Michel. An Interview with Michel Foucault. *History of the Present* 1985 [1975]; 1, p. 14.
63. Guevara, Che. *Guerilla Warfare*. London: Souvenir Press, 1961 [2003].
64. This becomes particularly clear in Guevara's Epilogue to *The African Dream*, in which he examines his failed attempt at revolutionary war in the Congo in 1965 (Guevara, Che. *The African Dream: The Diaries of the Revolutionary War in the Congo*. London: The Harvill Press, 2001, pp. 221–4). According to Guevara's analysis, the Cuban model of agrarian reform was not appropriate in a context where feudalism was absent. The social environment of the Congo required a revised approach. However, as the revolutionaries failed to examine the 'type of exploitation to which the peasants were subjected', they were unable to connect with their plight (ibid., p. 223.)
65. Debray, Régis. *Revolution in the Revolution? Armed Struggle and Political Struggle in Latin America*. Harmondsworth: Penguin, 1968 [1967], pp. 59–60.
66. Foucault. *Interview with Michel Foucault*, p. 242.
67. Foucault. *Power Affects the Body*, p. 213.
68. Rayner, Timothy. Between fiction and reflection: Foucault and the experience-book. *Continental Philosophy Review* 2003; 36(1), p. 39.
69. 'It can't exactly be a novel' (Foucault. *Interview with Michel Foucault*, p. 243).
70. Ibid., p. 242.
71. Ibid., p. 288.
72. Foucault, Michel. On Popular Justice: A Discussion with Maoists. In: Gordon, ed. *Power/Knowledge: Selected Interviews & Other Writings 1972–1977*. New York: Pantheon, 1980 [1972].
73. Žižek, Slavoj. *In Defense of Lost Causes*. London: Verso, 2007, p. 195.
74. Foucault, Michel. Truth and Power. In: Faubion, ed. *Essential Works of Foucault 1954–1984. Volume 3*. London: Penguin, 2002 [1977], p. 123.
75. Foucault. *Society Must Be Defended*, p. 261.
76. Foucault, Michel. Useless to Revolt? In: Faubion, ed. *Essential Works of Foucault 1954–1984. Volume 3*. London: Penguin, 2002 [1979], p. 450.
77. Foucault. *Nietzsche, Genealogy, History*, p. 369.
78. Foucault, Michel. Revolutionary Action: 'Until Now'. In: Bouchard, ed. *Language, Counter-memory, Practice: Selected Essays and Interviews by Michel Foucault*. New York: Cornell University Press, 1980 [1971], p. 233.
79. Foucault. *Discipline and Punish*, p. 27.
80. Foucault. *Questions of Method*, p. 236.
81. Lemke, Thomas. Critique and Experience in Foucault. *Theory, Culture & Society*, 2011; 28(4), pp. 29–30.
82. Foucault. *Interview with Michel Foucault*, pp. 281–2.
83. Macey, David. *The Lives of Michel Foucault*. London: Hutchinson, 1993.
84. Foucault. *Useless to Revolt?* p. 450.
85. Foucault. *Interview with Michel Foucault*, p. 280.
86. Osborne, Thomas. Critical Spirituality: On Ethics and Politics in the Later Foucault. In: Ashenden and Owen, ed. *Foucault contra Habermas: Recasting the Dialogue between Genealogy and Critical Theory*. London: Sage, 1999, p. 51.
87. Foucault. *Interview with Michel Foucault*, pp. 280–1.
88. Foucault, Michel. *The Government of Self and Others: Lectures at the Collège de France 1982–1983*. Basingstoke: Palgrave Macmillan, 2010 [1983], p. 18.
89. Foucault. *What is Enlightenment?* p. 315.

90. Foucault. *Society Must Be Defended*, p. 55.
91. Ibid., p. 58.
92. Macey, David. Some Reflections on Foucault's Society Must Be Defended and the Idea of 'Race'. In: Morton and Bygrave, ed. *Foucault in an Age of Terror: Essays on Biopolitics and the Defence of Society*. Basingstoke: Palgrave Macmillan, 2008, p. 129.
93. Foucault. *Society Must Be Defended*, p. 55.
94. Ibid., p. 56.
95. Ibid., p. 52.
96. Ibid.
97. Ibid., p. 164.
98. Ibid., p. 173.
99. Ibid., pp. 160–2.
100. Ibid., p. 171.
101. Ibid., p. 65.
102. Ibid., p. 207.
103. Ibid., p. 58.
104. Ibid., p. 170.
105. Ibid., pp. 207–8.
106. Foucault, Michel. What is Critique? In: Schmidt, ed. *What is Enlightenment? Eighteenth-Century Answers and Twentieth-Century Questions*. Berkeley: University of California Press, 1996 [1978], p. 386.
107. Orwell, George. *Nineteen Eighty-Four*. Harmondsworth: Penguin, 1955 [1949], p. 31.
108. Foucault. *Society Must Be Defended*, pp. 56–7.
109. Ibid., pp. 58–9, 60, 78–9, 88 and 111.
110. Ibid., p. 80.
111. Ibid., pp. 83, 261–3; Foucault, Michel. The Confession of the Flesh. In: Gordon, ed. *Power/Knowledge: Selected Interviews & Other Writings 1972–1977*. New York: Pantheon, 1990 [1977], pp. 223–5.
112. Foucault. *Society Must Be Defended*, p. 216.
113. Ibid., p. 81.
114. Faubion, James. Introduction. In: Faubion, ed. *Essential Works of Foucault 1954–1984. Volume 3*. London: Penguin, 2002, p. xxii.
115. Foucault. *What is Critique?* p. 384.
116. Foucault. *The Birth of Biopolitics*.
117. Foucault. *What is Critique?* p. 384.
118. Osborne. *Critical Spirituality*, p. 53.
119. Rose, Nikolas. *Powers of Freedom: Reframing Political Thought*. Cambridge: Cambridge University Press, 1999, p. 284.
120. Ibid., pp. 59–60.
121. Osborne. *Critical Spirituality*, p. 54.
122. Habermas, Jürgen. Some Questions Concerning the Theory of Power: Foucault Again. In: Kelly, ed. *Critique and Power: Recasting the Foucault/Habermas Debate*. Cambridge, Massachusetts: The MIT Press, 1994 [1987], p. 95.
123. Foucault. *Society Must Be Defended*, pp. 16–17.
124. Foucault. *Revolutionary Action*, p. 230.
125. Ibid.
126. Foucault. *What is Enlightenment?* p. 313.

127. Foucault, Michel. Preface. In: Deleuze and Guattari, ed. *Anti-Oedipus: Capitalism and Schizophrenia*. London: Continuum, 2007 [1972], p. xiv.
128. Miller, Peter and Rose, Nikolas. *Governing the Present: Administering Economic, Social and Personal Life*. Cambridge: Polity, 2008, p. 6.
129. Foucault. *Questions of Method*, p. 227.
130. Collier, Stephen. Topologies of Power: Foucault's Analysis of Political Government beyond 'Governmentality'. *Theory, Culture & Society* 2009, 26(6), pp. 79–80.
131. Ibid., p. 80.
132. Nietzsche. *Beyond Good and Evil*, p. 95.
133. Foucault. *Society Must Be Defended*, p. 6.
134. Foucault. *Power Affects the Body*, p. 211.
135. Foucault. *The Subject and Power II*, p. 223.
136. Foucault. *Power Affects the Body*, p. 211.
137. Ibid.
138. Foucault. *Security, Territory, Population*, p. 3.
139. Foucault. *Society Must Be Defended*, p. 56.
140. The concept of biopower represents a significant, though short-lived, departure in Foucault's work, one that flows directly from his treatment of discipline. Biopower is introduced only very briefly in a lecture on 17 March 1976, in a few pages towards the end of *The Will to Knowledge*, and in the first three lectures of 1978 (Foucault. *The Will to Knowledge*; Foucault. *Society Must Be Defended*; Foucault. *Security, Territory, Population*). A more detailed treatment of biopower was deferred, but this 'deferral was also an erasure' as Foucault moved on to his analysis of 'governmentality'. (See: Macey, David. Rethinking Biopolitics, Race and Power in the Wake of Foucault. *Theory, Culture & Society*, 2009, 26(6), p. 189.) Due to this sudden switch, Foucault's theory of biopower has often been neglected, and, when it is addressed, biopower is often applied as an imprecise descriptive term in a way that courts theoretical controversy. (See: Rabinow, Paul and Rose, Nikolas. Biopower Today. *Biosocieties*, 2006, 1(2).) The interpretation of biopower is fraught with difficulty, and it does not help that Foucault himself treated the concept 'as an approximation' (Macey. *Rethinking Biopolitics*, p. 188). Confronted by problems such as these, any account of biopower will be a selective montage. The relationship of biopower to disciplinary power also remains unclear. This sort of difficulty is to be expected when working with Foucault. It was his way to pick up threads from previous work and pursue them carefully, whilst dropping other, formerly coexisting lines of enquiry. The switch from *Discipline and Punish* to the analysis of biopower is no exception. We can see in the former work certain potentialities for population-level knowledge, and respect for the proper functioning of the organism, that were later to be the hallmarks of biopower. Therefore, in examining the relationship between these two strategies of power, we are forced to partially disassemble the text of Foucault's earlier book, *Discipline and Punish*, and establish a fresh analytic boundary within it. When this book was written, it inadvertently addressed certain topics that are more appropriate to the later concept of biopower. Here the modern examination can be seen as the connecting term, forming the strategic hub of disciplinary power whilst also representing the source of population-level knowledge. For the moment, though, in order to establish the novelty of biopower as a domain of calculation and force, it is necessary to pursue the differences between disciplinary power and biopower.

141. Foucault. *The Will to Knowledge*, pp. 141–2. (Foucault was vague when it came to dates, situating the early development of biopower within either the eighteenth, the late eighteenth or the nineteenth century: see, respectively, ibid., p. 141; Foucault. *Society Must Be Defended*, p. 250; ibid., p. 241.) But this transformation to biopower did not occur 'all at once', and Foucault was 'simply pointing out some of biopolitics' starting points, some of its practices, and the first of its domains of intervention' (ibid., pp. 241–5).
142. Foucault. *The Will to Knowledge*, p. 135.
143. Foucault. *Discipline and Punish*, pp. 3–6.
144. Foucault. *Society Must Be Defended*, p. 241.
145. There is some terminological ambiguity here. At one point biopower is used by Foucault as the umbrella term for two staggered developments: (a) disciplinary power (the 'anatomo-politics of the body'), followed by (b) a regulatory 'biopolitics of the population' (Foucault 1976b, p. 139; 1976a, p. 260). Elsewhere (Foucault 1976a, p. 242), the two areas (discipline and biopower) appear to be more distinct and function without the use of a connecting term. In this context 'biopower' and 'biopolitics' are used almost synonymously (Foucault 1976a, p. 243; 1978b, p. 22). I treat discipline and biopower according to the second usage, that is, as two separate but interrelating realms.
146. Foucault. *Society Must Be Defended*, p. 249.
147. Ibid., p. 242.
148. Thiele. *The Agony of Politics*, p. 908.
149. Foucault. *Society Must Be Defended*, p. 250.
150. Ibid., p. 242.
151. Ibid., pp. 242–3.
152. Ibid., p. 243.
153. Foucault. *Discipline and Punish*, p. 156.
154. Ibid., p. 177.
155. Foucault. *Security, Territory, Population*, p. 12.
156. Ibid., p. 46.
157. Ibid., p. 45.
158. Foucault. *Society Must Be Defended*, p. 246.
159. Foucault. *Security, Territory, Population*, p. 19.
160. Foucault. *Society Must Be Defended*, p. 246.
161. Ibid.
162. Foucault. *Security, Territory, Population*, p. 6.
163. Ibid., p. 57. (For this earlier, now 'incorrect' usage of normalization, see Foucault. *Discipline and Punish*, pp. 177–84.)
164. Foucault. *Security, Territory, Population*, p. 56.
165. Ibid., p. 63.
166. Ibid., p. 62.
167. See: *The Oxford English Dictionary*. Clarendon Press: Oxford, 1989.
168. Foucault. *Society Must Be Defended*, p. 253.
169. Kaplan, Laura and Kaplan, Charles. Democracy, Meritocracy, and the Cognitive Elite: The Real Thesis of The Bell Curve. *Educational Theory*, 1997, 47(3).
170. Foucault. *Security, Territory, Population*, p. 66.
171. Ibid., p. 70.
172. Ibid., p. 79.
173. Ibid., p. 75.
174. Ibid., p. 70.

175. Foucault. *Society Must Be Defended*, p. 246.
176. Hacking, Ian. *The Taming of Chance*. Cambridge: Cambridge University Press, 1990.
177. Foucault. *Security, Territory, Population*, p. 71.
178. Ibid, pp. 71–2.
179. Foucault. *Discipline and Punish*, p. 191; Foucault. *Security, Territory, Population*, p. 79.
180. Foucault. *Security, Territory, Population*, p. 105.
181. Burman, Erica. *Deconstructing Developmental Psychology*. 2nd ed. Hove: Routledge, 2008, p. 26.
182. Foucault. *Society Must Be Defended*, p. 242.
183. Foucault. *Security, Territory, Population*, p. 107.
184. This refers to the 1942 UK *Beveridge Report*, which identified five evils in society (squalor, ignorance, want, idleness and disease) and proposed widespread reform to the system of social welfare. It formed the basis for post-war social policy, including the expansion of National Insurance and the creation of the National Health Service.
185. Foucault, Michel. The Political Technology of Individuals. In: Martin, Gutman and Hutton, ed. *Technologies of the Self: A Seminar with Michel Foucault*. University of Massachusetts Press, 1988 [1982], p. 147.
186. Ibid.
187. 'To speak in such terms is to make enormous claims. To prove the point would really take a whole series of lectures', a series that was never delivered (Foucault. *Society Must Be Defended*, p. 261).
188. Ibid., p. 254.
189. Foucault. *The Political Technology of Individuals*, p. 160.
190. Foucault. *The Will to Knowledge*, pp. 136–7.
191. Foucault. *Society Must Be Defended*, p. 254.
192. Ibid., p. 255.
193. Ibid., p. 256.
194. Galton, Francis. *Memories of My Life*. 3rd ed. London: Methuen & Co, 1909, p. 323.
195. Barkan, Elazar. *The Retreat of Scientific Racism: Changing Concepts of Race in Britain and the United States between the World Wars*. Cambridge: Cambridge University Press, 1992.
196. Darwin, Charles. *The Origin of Species: By Means of Natural Selection or the Preservation of Favoured Races in the Struggle for Life*. London: John Murray, 1906 [1859].
197. Hawkins, Mike. *Social Darwinism in European and American Thought 1860–1945*. Cambridge: Cambridge University Press, 1997, p. 4.
198. Darwin, Charles. C.D. to A.R. Wallace. Moor Park, May 1st, 1857. In: Darwin, ed. *Charles Darwin: His Life Told in an Autobiographical Chapter, And in a Selected Series of his Published Letters*. London: John Murray, 1902 [1857], p. 183.
199. Hawkins. *Social Darwinism*, p. 37.
200. Darwin, Charles. *The Descent of Man and Selection in Relation to Sex*. 2nd ed. London: John Murray, 1909 [1871], pp. 205–6.
201. Ibid., p. 206.
202. Galton. *Memories of My Life*, p. 322.
203. Spencer, Herbert. *The Man versus the State*. London: Williams & Norgate, 1907 [1884], p. 19.

204. Galton, Francis. *Inquiries into Human Faculty and its Development*. London: J.M. Dent & Sons Ltd, 1928 [1883], p. 17.
205. Galton. *Memories of My Life*, pp. 287–8.
206. Galton, Francis. Hereditary Talent and Character. *Macmillan's Magazine* 1865, 12, p. 157.
207. Galton, Francis. *Hereditary Genius: An Inquiry into its Laws and Consequences*. London: Macmillan and Co., 1869.
208. Galton. *Hereditary Talent and Character*, p. 327.
209. Galton. *Hereditary Genius*, p. 6.
210. Ibid.
211. Ibid., p. 7.
212. Galton. *Inquiries into Human Faculty*, p. 28.
213. Plato. *Last Days of Socrates*.
214. Galton. *Memories of My Life*, p. 245.
215. Galton, Francis. On the Anthropometric Laboratory at the late International Health Exhibition. *Journal of the Anthropological Institute* 1885, 14, p. 205.
216. Fancher, Raymond. *The Intelligence Men: Makers of the IQ Controversy*. New York: Norton, 1985, p. 37.
217. Galton. *Hereditary Genius*. pp. 19, 25.
218. Ibid., p. 26.
219. Ibid., p. 29.
220. Ibid., p. 30.
221. Ibid., pp. 31–2.
222. The subjects in question were those recently tested 'for admission into the Royal Military College at Sandhurst, December 1868' – which is an early example of modern examination employed as a meritocratic device (ibid., p. 32).
223. Ibid., p. 34.
224. Hacking. *The Taming of Chance*, p. 108.
225. Porter, Theodore. *The Rise of Statistical Thinking 1820–1900*. Princeton: Princeton University Press, 1986, p. 100.
226. Mackenzie, Donald. *Statistics in Britain 1865–1930*. Edinburgh: Edinburgh University Press, 1981, p. 57.
227. Galton. *Memories of My Life*, p. 305.
228. Galton. *The Possible Improvement of the Human Breed*.
229. Ibid., p. 4.
230. Ibid., p. 3.
231. Ibid., pp. 9–11.
232. Ibid., p. 20.
233. Ibid., p. 11.
234. Though lower 'T' class parents produce more 'T' and 'U' class offspring than higher 'U' class parents do, this is due to the higher number of 'T' class parents in the population and is at the expense of producing many descendants of comparatively lower classification (ibid.).
235. Ibid., p. 18.
236. Galton. *Memories of My Life*, p. 318.
237. Ibid., p. 312.
238. Foucault. *Security, Territory, Population*, p. 60.
239. Galton. *Memories of My Life*, p. 312.
240. Galton. *Hereditary Talent and Character*, p. 157.
241. Galton. *Memories of My Life*, p. 313.

242. Galton, Francis. Preface. *The Possible Improvement of the Human Breed under the Existing Conditions of Law and Sentiment.* London: The Eugenics Education Society, 1909.
243. Galton. *Memories of My Life,* p. 311.
244. Galton. *The Possible Improvement of the Human Breed,* p. 25.
245. Fisher, Ronald. Some Hopes of a Eugenicist. *Eugenics Review,* 1914, 5, p. 310.
246. Pearson, Karl. Foreword. *Annals of Eugenics,* 1925, 1, p. 3.
247. Turner, Frank. The Victorian Conflict between Science and Religion: A Professional Dimension. *Isis,* 1978, 69(3).
248. Galton. *Hereditary Talent and Character,* p. 322.
249. Porter. *The Rise of Statistical Thinking,* p. 51.
250. Pearson, cited in Mackenzie. *Statistics in Britain,* p. 75.
251. Pearson, Karl. *The Ethic of Freethought and other Addresses and Essays.* 2nd (revised) ed. London: Adam and Charles Black, 1901, p. x.
252. Foucault. *The Birth of Biopolitics,* p. 16.
253. Pearson. *The Ethic of Freethought,* p. 105.
254. Ibid., p. 110.
255. Ibid., p. 107.
256. Ibid., p. 116.
257. Ibid., p. 429.
258. Terman, Lewis. *The Measurement of Intelligence: An Explanation of and a Complete Guide for the Use of the Stanford Revision and Extension of the Binet-Simon Intelligence Scale.* London: Harrap, 1919, p. 84.
259. The potential contribution of schools configured as laboratories was not lost on Galton, who suggested that statistics should be obtained 'from schools of all description' from 'public schools...down to those of pauper children' (Galton, Francis. Proposal to apply for anthropological statistics from schools. *Anthropometry,* 1874, 3).
260. Rose, Nikolas. *Governing the Soul: The Shaping of the Private Self.* 2nd ed. London: Routledge & Kegan Paul, 1999, pp. 140–2.
261. The '*g*' to '*s*' ratio for Classics was estimated at 99:1, whereas for Mathematics it was 74:26, reflecting the relatively high status of Classics in 1904 (Spearman, Charles. General Intelligence, Objectively Determined and Measured. *The American Journal of Psychology,* 1904, 15(2), p. 276).
262. Ibid., p. 277.
263. Hart, Bernard and Spearman, Charles. General Ability, Its Existence and Nature. *The British Journal of Psychology,* 1912, 5(1).
264. Mill, cited in: Ryan, Alan. J. S. Mill on education. *Oxford Review of Education* 2011, 37(5), p. 355 (emphasis mine).
265. Goddard. *Feeble-Mindedness,* p. 571.
266. Terman. *The Measurement of Intelligence,* p. 5.
267. Ibid., p. 7.
268. Ibid., p. 11.
269. Pearson. *The Ethic of Freethought,* p. 107.
270. Terman. *The Measurement of Intelligence,* p. 12.
271. Ibid., pp. 12–13.
272. Ibid., p. 16.
273. Goddard. *Feeble-Mindedness,* pp. 91–4.
274. Ibid., p. 573.
275. Ibid., pp. 2–3.

276. We are told that the 'type of measurement which the Binet Scale yields is *amenable to statistical treatment only in a very restricted way.* Thus the mean or standard deviation, the probable error of mean or deviation, the co-efficient of correlation with its probable error either cannot be obtained at all for Binet judgements, or are of slight value because of the non-quantitative character of the judgements. By contrast, Point Scale measurements can be statistically treated in all the varied and biologically significant ways' (Yerkes, Robert. The Binet version versus the point scale method of measuring intelligence. *Journal of Applied Psychology,* 1917, 1, p. 115).

277. Ibid., p. 115.

278. After World War I psychologists were removed from such military planning. In the military context a more significant contribution was the development of a specialised personnel system (based on a record of skills rather than IQ scores) which had the capacity to link occupational requirements to skills and to distribute the skilled specialists in a systematic way to where they were required (Rose. *Governing the Soul*, pp. 18–19).

279. Recall that IQ = (mental age/chronological age) × 100. A normal child's mental and chronological age are said to be equivalent, giving a ratio of 1, and an IQ of 100.

280. Rose. *Governing the Soul*, p. 194.

281. Vacher de Lapouge 1896, cited in Pichot, André. *The Pure Society: from Darwin to Hitler.* London: Verso, 2009, pp. 127–8.

282. Foucault. *Security, Territory, Population*, p. 107.

283. Ibid.

284. Parliamentary Papers. *Report and Minutes of Evidence of the Departmental Committee on Defective and Epileptic Children.* XXVI.1. House of Commons Papers, 1898, pp. 3–4 (emphasis mine).

285. Sutherland, Gillian. *Ability, Merit and Measurement: Mental Testing and English Education 1880–1940.* Oxford: Clarendon Press, 1984, pp. 12–13.

286. Parliamentary Papers. *Report of the Royal Commissioners on the Care and Control of the Feeble-minded.* XXXIX.159. House of Commons Papers, 1908, p. 3.

287. Simmons, Harvey. Explaining Social Policy: The English Mental Deficiency Act of 1913. *Journal of Social History*, 1978, 11(3).

288. Jones, Kathleen. *A History of the Mental Health Services.* London: Routledge & Kegan Paul, 1972.

289. Parliamentary Papers. 1908. XXXIX.159, p. 6.

290. Ibid., p. 7 (emphasis mine).

291. Ibid., p. 199.

292. Sutherland. *Ability, Merit and Measurement*, p. 57.

293. Black, Edwin. *War against the Weak: Eugenics and America's Campaign to Create a Master Race.* New York: Thunder Mouth Press, 2004, p. 67.

294. Ibid.

295. Foucault. *Discipline and Punish*, p. 300.

296. Black. *War against the Weak.*

297. King, Desmond and Hansen, Randall. Experts at Work: State Autonomy, Social Learning and Eugenic Sterilization in 1930s Britain. *British Journal of Political Science*, 1999, 29(1).

298. *Report of the Committee on Sterilisation.* XV.611. House of Commons Papers, 1934, p. 56.

299. Cattell, Raymond. *The Fight for our National Intelligence.* London: King & Son, 1937, p. 163.

300. Ibid., pp. 1–3.
301. Ibid., p. 161.
302. Foucault. *Society Must Be Defended*, p. 82.
303. Hitler, Adolf. *Mein Kampf.* London: Pimlico, 2000 [1924], pp. 258–9.
304. Ibid., p. 348.
305. Ibid.
306. Ibid., p. 261.
307. Orwell, George. Review: Adolf Hitler, Mein Kampf, 21 March 1940. In: *Orwell and Politics*. London: Penguin, 2001 [1940], p. 85.
308. Foucault. *The Will to Knowledge*, pp. 148–9.
309. Foucault. *Society Must Be Defended*, p. 82.
310. Pichot. *The Pure Society.*
311. Ibid., p. 180.
312. Ibid., p. 206.
313. Black, Edwin. *IBM and the Holocaust: The Strategic Alliance between Nazi Germany and America's Most Powerful Corporation*. London: Little, Brown and Company, 2001.
314. Ibid., p. 21.
315. Heidinger 1934, cited in Black. *War against the Weak*. p. 309.
316. Foucault. *The Subject and Power I*, p. 328.
317. Foucault. *Society Must Be Defended*, p. 259.

III Meritocracies

1. Eagleton, Terry. *After Theory*. London: Penguin, 2004, p. 66.
2. Foucault, Michel. On the Ways of Writing History. In: Faubion, ed. *Essential Works of Foucault 1954–1984. Volume 2*. London: Penguin, 2000 [1967], p. 281.
3. Foucault, Michel. Return to History. In: Faubion, ed. *Essential Works of Foucault 1954–1984. Volume 2*. London: Penguin, 2000 [1972], p. 423.
4. Foucault. *On the Ways of Writing History*, p. 283.
5. This also inverts the conception of the event. 'In traditional history it was thought that events were all that was known, what was visible, what was directly or indirectly identifiable, and the work of the historian was to search for their cause or meaning. The cause or meaning was essentially hidden. The event, on the other hand, was essentially visible, even if one sometimes lacked the documents to establish it with certainty' (Foucault. *Return to History*, p. 427). For Foucault, and the historical approach with which he identifies, the event becomes something that is hidden behind the interpretative historical frameworks that we all too easily rely upon in generating our historical narratives.
6. Ibid., pp. 429–31.
7. Rose, Nikolas. *The Politics of Life Itself: Biomedicine, Power and Subjectivity in the Twenty-First Century*. Princeton: Princeton University Press, 2007, p. 55.
8. Rose, Nikolas. *The Psychological Complex: Psychology, Politics and Society in England, 1869–1939*. London: Routledge, 1985, p. 85.
9. Ibid., p. 145.
10. Ibid., p. 135.
11. Searle, Geoffrey. Eugenics and Politics in Britain in the 1930s. *Annals of Science*, 1979, 36.
12. Mackenzie. *Statistics in Britain*, p. 45.
13. Galton. *Memories of My Life*, p. 311.
14. Galton. *The Possible Improvement of the Human Breed*, p. 25.

15. Darwin, Leonard. *The Need for Eugenic Reform*. London: Murray, 1926, p. 519.
16. Galton, Francis. The Part of Religion in Human Evolution. *The National Review*, 1894, 23. p. 755.
17. Ibid., p. 759.
18. Ibid., p. 763.
19. Kidd, Benjamin. *Social Evolution: with Appendix Containing a Reply to Criticisms*. London: Macmillan, 1898.
20. Ibid., p. 133.
21. Galton, Francis. Eugenics and the Jew: Interview for the Jewish Chronicle with Sir Francis Galton. *The Jewish Chronicle*, 1910, 30 July, p. 16.
22. Cattell. *The Fight for our National Intelligence*, p. 94.
23. Ibid., p. 131.
24. Ibid., p. 130.
25. Cattell, Raymond. *Psychology and the Religious Quest: An Account of the Psychology of Religion and a defence of Individualism*. London: Nelson, 1938, p. 99.
26. Cattell. *The Fight for our National Intelligence*, p. 69. (Note that these sentiments are still biopolitical. Cattell is *not* seeking to replace nature by something completely artificial. Rather, he wishes to enhance and further develop natural processes. His entire logic sits firmly within the biopolitical injunction to study nature and work within and upon its pre-existing traits and logics.)
27. Cattell, Raymond. *Psychology and Social Progress: Mankind and Destiny from the Standpoint of a Scientist*. London: Daniel, 1933, p. 158.
28. Ibid., p. 156.
29. Foucault. *Omnes et Singulatim*, p. 311.
30. Ibid., p. 310.
31. Cattell. *Psychology and the Religious Quest*, p. 186.
32. Cattell. *The Fight for our National Intelligence*, p. 130.
33. Cattell. *Psychology and Social Progress*, p. 219.
34. Ibid., pp. 200–1.
35. Ibid., p. 200.
36. Ibid., p. 183.
37. Pearson. *The Ethic of Freethought*.
38. Cattell. *Psychology and the Religious Quest*, p. 75.
39. Ibid., p. 104.
40. Cattell. *Psychology and the Religious Quest*, p. 77.
41. Ibid., p. 120.
42. Romans 8:28.
43. Cattell. *Psychology and the Religious Quest*, p. 104.
44. Galton. *The Possible Improvement of the Human Breed*.
45. Searle, Geoffrey. *The Quest for National Efficiency: A Study in British Politics and Political Thought, 1899–1914*. Oxford: Blackwell, 1971.
46. Allen, Garland. The social and economic origins of genetic determinism: a case history of the American Eugenics Movement, 1900–1940 and its lessons for today. *Genetica*, 1997, 99.
47. Searle. *Eugenics and Politics in Britain in the 1930s*.
48. Weiss, Sheila. The Race Hygiene Movement in Germany. *Osiris*, 1987, 3, p. 210.
49. NSDAP poster, 1938.
50. Bentham. *Constitutional Code*. (This system was introduced earlier in *Bodies: Modern Examination*.)
51. Phillips, Melanie. *All Must Have Prizes*. London: Warner, 1996.

52. Foucault. *Discipline and Punish*, p. 164.
53. Goddard. *Feeble-Mindedness*, p. 578.
54. Ibid., p. 571.
55. Ibid., p. 581.
56. Ibid., p. 583.
57. Ibid., p. 588.
58. Burt, Cyril. The Principles of Vocational Guidance. *British Journal of Psychology*, 1924, 14(4), p. 337.
59. Ibid., p. 346.
60. Ibid., p. 349.
61. Ibid., p. 339.
62. Ibid., p. 340.
63. Foucault. *Discipline and Punish*, p. 164.
64. Burt. *The Principles of Vocational Guidance*, p. 346.
65. Goddard, Henry. *Human Efficiency and Levels of Intelligence*. Princeton: Princeton University Press, 1920, p. 60.
66. Presumably by 'socialism' Henry Goddard has some notion of general equality in mind, though really existing socialism also had its hierarchies and systems of merit.
67. Goddard. *Human Efficiency*, p. 102.
68. Ibid., pp. 126–7.
69. Foucault. *Discipline and Punish*, p. 222.
70. Ibid., pp. 222–3.
71. Sutherland. *Ability, Merit and Measurement*, p. 102.
72. Hartog, Philip. *Examinations and their Relation to Culture and Efficiency: with a Speech by the late Earl of Cromer*. London: Constable, 1918, p. 42.
73. Ibid., p. 41.
74. Ibid., p. 37–8.
75. Parliamentary Papers. 1854, (34) XL.105, p. 12.
76. Sutherland. *Ability, Merit and Measurement*, p. 112.
77. Parliamentary Papers. *Papers relating to Selection and Training of Candidates for Indian Civil Service*. (C. 1446) LV.277. House of Commons Papers, 1876, p. 15.
78. Ibid., p. 20.
79. The remaining 22 per cent was filled with the 'sons of merchants, bankers, farmers, and tradesmen' (ibid., p. 35).
80. Parliamentary Papers, 1854, XXVII.1, pp. 8–9.
81. Eagleton. *After Theory*, p. 77.
82. Sutherland. *Ability, Merit and Measurement*, p. 101.
83. Parliamentary Papers, 1854, XXVII.1, p. 8.
84. Ibid., p. 10.
85. Roach. *Public Examinations*.
86. Parliamentary Papers. *Seventeenth report of Her Majesty's Civil Service Commissioners, together with appendices*. (C. 672) XIX.1. House of Commons Papers, 1872, p. vi.
87. Parliamentary Papers. *Second report of the Royal Commission appointed to inquire into the working of the different offices of state at home and abroad*. (C. 5545) XXVII.1. House of Commons Papers, 1888, p. 531.
88. Ibid., p. 528.
89. Parliamentary Papers. *First report of the Royal Commission appointed to inquire into the civil establishments of the different offices of state at home and abroad*. (C.5226) XIX.1. House of Commons Papers, 1887, p. 153. (A 'board school education' is

not to be confused with the higher-class boarding schools. During this period, School Boards were public bodies that established and administered elementary schools, i.e. schools for the working class.)

90. Roach. *Public Examinations*, p. 225.
91. Parliamentary Papers, 1876, (C. 1446) LV.277, p. 16.
92. Ibid., p. 20.
93. Roach. *Public Examinations*, p. 218.
94. Parliamentary Papers. *Royal commission on secondary education. Vol. 1. Report of the commissioners*. (C. 7862) XLIII.1. House of Commons Papers, 1895, p. 220.
95. Parliamentary Papers. *Schools Inquiry Commission. Vol. I. Report of the commissioners*. (C.3966) XXVIII Pt.I.1. House of Commons Papers, 1868, p. 16.
96. Ibid., p. 86.
97. Ibid., p. 83.
98. Ibid., p. 84.
99. Ibid., p. 79.
100. Ibid., p. 81.
101. Ibid., p. 90.
102. Ibid., p. 83.
103. Parliamentary Papers. *Schools Inquiry Commission. Vol. IV. Minutes of Evidence*. (C.3966) XXVIII Pt.III.1. House of Commons Papers, 1868, p. 263.
104. Parliamentary Papers. *Schools Inquiry Commission. Vol. XII. Special Reports of Assistant Commissioners*. (C.3996) XXVIII Pt.X.1. House of Commons Papers, 1868, p. 180.
105. Parliamentary Papers, 1868, (C.3966) XXVIII Pt.III.1, p. 263.
106. Parliamentary Papers, 1868, (C.3996) XXVIII Pt.X.1, p. 239.
107. Parliamentary Papers, 1868. (C.3966) XXVIII Pt.I.1, pp. 92–3.
108. Ibid., pp. 574–5.
109. Philpott, Hugh. *London at School: The Story of the School Board 1870–1904*. London: Fisher Unwin, 1904, p. 153.
110. Parliamentary Papers. 1868. (C.3966) XXVIII Pt.I.1, p. 95.
111. Ibid., p. 96.
112. Ibid., p. 27.
113. Ibid., p. 96.
114. Simon, Brian. *The State and Educational Change*. London: Lawrence & Wishart, 1994, p. 38.
115. Parliamentary Papers, 1895, (C. 7862) XLIII.1, p. 282.
116. Parliamentary Papers, 1868, (C.3966) XXVIII Pt.I.1, p. 583.
117. Ibid., p. 578.
118. Ibid., p. 81.
119. Parliamentary Papers, 1895, (C. 7862) XLIII.1, pp. 67–8.
120. Ibid., p. 290.
121. Philpott. *London at School*.
122. Parliamentary Papers, 1895, (C. 7862) XLIII.1, p. 64.
123. Ibid., p. 300.
124. Board of Education. *Memoranda on Promotion in Elementary Schools in London*, 1919, p. 5.
125. Parliamentary Papers, 1868, (C.3966) XXVIII Pt.I.1, pp. 79–80.
126. Forster, William. Elementary Education Bill – First Reading. *Hansard's Parliamentary Debates Third Series CXCIX*. London: Cornelius Buck, 1870, pp. 465–6.

127. Parliamentary Papers. *Second report of the Royal Commission appointed to inquire into the working of the Elementary Education Acts.* (C.5056) XXIX.1. House of Commons Papers, 1887, p. 270.

128. Parliamentary Papers, 1895, (C. 7862) XLIII.1, p. 138.

129. Galton. *Hereditary Genius*; Galton. *Hereditary Talent and Character*; Galton, Francis. Hereditary Genius: the Judges of England between 1660 and 1865. *Macmillan's Magazine,*1869.

130. Nietzsche. *Twilight of the Idols*, p. 105.

131. Terman. *The Measurement of Intelligence*, p. 5.

132. Ibid., pp. 12–13.

133. As the *Departmental Committee on Scholarships and Free Places* reported, this step 'was important not so much for any immediate increase in the number of "free places" it produced, but for the principle it expressed'. The proportion of ex-elementary students was initially set at no less than 25 per cent of the previous year's intake. The immediate effect was to increase the percentage of free pupils from elementary schools from 24 to more than 27 per cent. (Board of Education. *Report of the Departmental Committee on Scholarships and Free Places*, 1920, p. 4.)

134. This was finally enforced in law with the Education Act of 1944: 'The statutory system of public education shall be organised in three progressive stages to be known as primary education, secondary education, and further education' (Education Act 1944. An Act to reform the law relating to education in England and Wales – 3rd August 1944. In *The Public General Acts and the Church Assembly Measures of 1944*. HMSO, 1944, p. 227).

135. Lindsay, Kenneth. *Social Progress and Educational Waste: Being a Study of the 'Free Place' and Scholarship System*. London: Routledge, 1926, p. 9.

136. Ibid.

137. Ibid., p. 7.

138. Ibid., p. 10.

139. Ibid., pp. 14–15.

140. Ibid., p. 33.

141. Ibid., p. 20.

142. Board of Education. *Report of the Departmental Committee on Scholarships and Free Places*, pp. 19–20.

143. Ibid., pp. 24–5.

144. Ibid., p. 21.

145. Ibid., pp. 24–7.

146. Sutherland. *Ability, Merit and Measurement.*

147. Vernon, Philip. *Secondary School Selection: A British Psychological Society Inquiry.* London: Methuen, 1957, p. 25.

148. Board of Education. *Report of the Consultative Committee on Psychological Tests of Educable Capacity and their possible use in the public education system*, 1924.

149. Board of Education. *Report of the Consultative Committee on The Education of the Adolescent*, 1926, p. 78.

150. Ibid.

151. Parliamentary Papers, 1895, (C. 7862) XLIII.1, p. 167.

152. Terman. *The Measurement of Intelligence*, p. 12.

153. Foucault. *Discipline and Punish*, p. 189.

154. Board of Education. *Curriculum and Examinations in Secondary Schools*, 1943, p. 4.

155. Board of Education. *Report of the Departmental Committee on Scholarships and Free Places.*
156. Hartog. *Examinations and their Relation to Culture and Efficiency*, pp. 6–7.
157. Board of Education. *Report of the Consultative Committee on The Education of the Adolescent*, pp. 81–2.
158. For a rare exception, see: Foucault. *Discipline and Punish*, p. 162.
159. Board of Education. *Report of the Consultative Committee on Psychological Tests*, p. 99.
160. Ibid., p. 130.
161. Ibid., p. 100.
162. Otis, Arthur. The Selection of Mill Workers by Mental Tests. *Journal of Applied Psychology*, 1920, 4, pp. 340–1.
163. Board of Education. *Report of the Consultative Committee on Psychological Tests*, pp. 141–2.
164. Ibid., p. 118.
165. Ibid., p. 123.
166. Ibid., p. 118.
167. Ibid., p. 141.
168. Board of Education. *Curriculum and Examinations in Secondary Schools.*
169. Norwood, Cyril. *The English Tradition of Education.* London: Murray, 1929, p. 188.
170. Ibid., pp. 4–6.
171. Ibid., p. 188.
172. Ibid., p. 197.
173. Board of Education. *Curriculum and Examinations in Secondary Schools*, p. 17.
174. Ibid.
175. Sutherland. *Ability, Merit and Measurement.*
176. Haldane, J. B. S. *The Inequality of Man and Other Essays.* Harmondsworth: Penguin, 1937 [1932], p. 35.
177. Board of Education. *Report of the Consultative Committee on The Education of the Adolescent*, p. 77.
178. Board of Education. *Curriculum and Examinations in Secondary Schools*, pp. 19–20.
179. It should be noted that this rather neat summary is retrospective and descriptive, reflecting 'what most commonly happens now'. By the time this report was published, it was also assumed that intelligence 'is largely an acquired characteristic'. Thus, the distribution of pupil types and references to ability are to be taken as 'descriptive rather than diagnostic; they indicate the facts about the pupils' relative performance in school, but not whether that performance could be modified given different educational opportunities' (Ministry of Education. *Half Our Future: Report of the Central Advisory Council for Education (England)*, 1963, pp. 3–4).
180. Board of Education. *Curriculum and Examinations in Secondary Schools*, p. 2.
181. Paraphrased from: ibid., pp. 2–3.
182. This hierarchy is confirmed by Vernon, who reports that after the 1944 Education Act it was common to 'draw up a single order-of-merit, and to send the top slice to the grammar schools, and the next slice to technical and/or commercial schools' where the latter existed. The remainder would be sent to the secondary modern (Vernon. *Secondary School Selection*, p. 34).
183. Board of Education. *Report of the Consultative Committee on Secondary Education.* 1938, p. 293.

184. Ibid., p. 168.
185. Ibid., p. 293.
186. Board of Education. *Curriculum and Examinations in Secondary Schools. New Secondary Education: Pamphlet No. 9*, 1947.
187. Ministry of Education. *Half Our Future*, p. 83.
188. McCulloch, Gary. *Failing the Ordinary Child? The Theory and Practice of Working-class Secondary Education*. Buckingham: Open University Press, 1998, p. 62.
189. 'We should deplore, for example, any practice of publishing lists of external examination results, thereby indirectly promoting local competitive rivalries' (Ministry of Education. *Half Our Future*, p. 83).
190. Sutherland. *Ability, Merit and Measurement*.
191. Pluchino, Alessandro, Rapisada, Andrea and Garofalo, Cesare. The Peter Principle Revisited: A Computational Study. *Physica A: Statistical Mechanics and its Applications*, 2010, 389(3). (On 30 September 2010 this study was awarded the Ig Nobel Prize, an award that celebrates so-called improbable truths.)
192. Hobbes, Thomas. *Leviathan, or The Matter, Forme, & Power of a Common-Wealth Ecclesiasticall and Civill*. London: Penguin, 1985 [1651], p. 185.
193. Sharpe, S. Psychologists and Intelligence Testing in English Education, 1900–1940. In: Broadfoot, ed. *Selection, Certification & Control: Social Issues in Educational Assessment*. Lewes: The Falmer Press, 1984.
194. Jensen, Arthur. How much can we boost I.Q. and scholastic achievement? *Harvard Educational Review*, 1969, 39(1); Herrnstein, Richard. *I.Q. in the Meritocracy*. London: Allen Lane, 1973; Eysenck, Hans. *The Inequality of Man*. London: Temple Smith, 1973; Herrnstein, Richard and Murray, Charles. *The Bell Curve: Intelligence and Class Structure in American Life*. New York: The Free Press, 1994.
195. United Nations Educational, Scientific and Cultural Organization. *The Race Concept: Results of an Inquiry*, 1952, p. 102.
196. Ibid., p. 100–1.
197. Pichot. *The Pure Society*, pp. 132–8.
198. Barkan. *The Retreat of Scientific Racism*, p. 342.
199. United Nations Educational, Scientific and Cultural Organization. *The Race Concept*, p. 5.
200. See, for example: Bauman, Zygmunt. *Modernity and the Holocaust*. Cambridge: Polity, 2008 [1989].
201. United Nations Educational, Scientific and Cultural Organization. *The Race Concept*, p. 10.
202. Ministry of Education. *15 to 18: Report of the Central Advisory Council for Education (England)*, 1959, pp. 22, 417.
203. Centre for Contemporary Cultural Studies. *Unpopular Education: Schooling and Social Democracy in England since 1944*, 1981, pp. 72–3.
204. Rubinstein, David and Simon, Brian. *The Evolution of the Comprehensive School 1926–1972*. London: Routledge & Kegan Paul, 1973.
205. Ball, Stephen. *The Education Debate*. Bristol: Policy Press, 2008.
206. There were more radical critiques that were not so easily co-opted by government. In 1953, Brian Simon argued that the concept of 'intelligence' represented an entirely arbitrary standard of comparison. In 1958, he argued that the 'whole conception of "intelligence" was class conditioned; inevitably, therefore, "intelligence" test results indicated that the middle class tends to be "intelligent" while the working class tends to be stupid'. Simon went on to

argue that the normal distribution was itself dubious: it was used as a bench-mark standard in order to validate new tests, and thus the 'dogma of normal distribution' became self-reinforcing. (Simon, Brian. Intelligence testing and the comprehensive school. In: Simon, ed. *Intelligence, Psychology, Education: A Marxist Critique*. London: Lawrence & Wishart, 1978, pp. 155–7.)

207. Halsey, Albert and Gardner, L. Selection for Secondary Education and Achievement in Four Grammar Schools. *The British Journal of Sociology*, 1953, 4(1).

208. Ministry of Education. *Early Leaving*, 1954.

209. McCulloch. *Failing the Ordinary Child?* p. 94.

210. Yates, Alfred and Pidgeon, D. *Admission to Grammar Schools: Third Interim Report on the Allocation of Primary School Leavers to Courses of Secondary Education NFER*. London: Newnes, 1957.

211. Vernon. *Secondary School Selection*, pp. 7–8 (emphasis mine).

212. Terman. *The Measurement of Intelligence*.

213. Vernon. *Secondary School Selection*, p. 169.

214. Floud, Jean, Halsey, Albert and Martin, F. *Social Class and Educational Opportunity*. London: Heinemann, 1957, pp. 144–6.

215. Ministry of Education. *Half Our Future*, p. xvi.

216. In the realm of political theory, this has been expressed in Rawls' 'difference principle'. See Rawls, John. *A Theory of Justice*. Cambridge, Massachusetts: Harvard, 1971.

217. Glass, David. *Social Mobility in Britain*. London: Routledge & Kegan Paul, 1954, p. 24.

218. Ibid., pp. 25–6 (emphasis mine).

219. Hayek, Friedrich. *The Road to Serfdom*. London: Routledge, 1944, pp. 79–80.

220. Young, Michael. *The Rise of the Meritocracy 1870–2033: An Essay on Education and Society*. London: Thames & Hudson, 1958.

221. Here I draw from: Allen, Ansgar. Michael Young's *The Rise of the Meritocracy*: A Philosophical Critique. *British Journal of Educational Studies*, 2011, 59(4).

222. Young, Michael. Looking back on Meritocracy. In: Dench, ed. *The Rise and Rise of Meritocracy*. Oxford: Blackwell, 2006 [1994]; Young, Michael. Down with Meritocracy. *The Guardian*, June 29 2001.

223. Young. *The Rise of the Meritocracy*, pp. 32–3. (This argument against 'sentimental egalitarianism' would occupy the invective of much reactionary critique. The so-called 'Black Papers' were notorious for taking this approach (Cox, Brian and Dyson, Anthony. *Fight for Education: A Black Paper*. London: Critical Quarterly Society, 1969; Cox, Brian and Dyson, Anthony. *Black Paper Two: The Crisis in Education*. London: Critical Quarterly Society, 1970). Young's second predic-tion, that comprehensive schooling would rise and fall in this period, was also borne out. Although this seems an exceptional act of clairvoyance, the compre-hensive movement was still young and fragile in 1958 and its success was by no means guaranteed.

224. Young. *The Rise of the Meritocracy*, p. 59.

225. Ibid., p. 143.

226. Ibid., p. 67.

227. Ibid., p. 102.

228. Ibid., p. 85.

229. Huxley, Aldous. *Brave New World*. London: Vintage, 2007 [1932].

230. Orwell. *Nineteen Eighty-Four*.

231. Young. *The Rise of the Meritocracy*, p. 92.
232. There were, of course, trends, current at the time of writing, which Young deliberately avoided. He lays great emphasis upon determinism and Nature, two themes that could easily be exaggerated to dystopian effect: we must cultivate our 'humility towards Nature', the narrator tells us, for science 'penetrates her secrets not for the sake of human dominance' but 'in order to discover the laws which man must *obey*' (ibid., pp. 32, 53). Such descent into the sort of eugenic phraseology that Pearson, Galton and Cattell would have recognised served a narrative purpose. However, had Young given the problem of environmental conditioning and complexity a greater role, he might have been less constrained in his predictions by the logic of traditional meritocracy. Whether it was possible to predict the upcoming transformation of meritocracy at that point in time is, nevertheless, a moot point.
233. Taylor, William. *The Secondary Modern School*. London: Faber & Faber, 1963, p. 29.
234. (The 'growing importance of "being qualified" has implications which, without educational reform, may lead to an undesirable degree of rigidity in the social structure' (ibid., p. 30).)
235. Ibid., p. 23.
236. Ministry of Education. *15 to 18*, p. 449.
237. Friedmann, Georges. *Industrial Society: the Emergence of the Human Problems of Automation*. Illinois: The Free Press, 1955, pp. 230–1.
238. Floud, Jean and Halsey, Albert. English Secondary Schools and the Supply of Labour. In: Halsey, Floud and Arnold Anderson, ed. *Education, Economy and Society: A Reader in the Sociology of Education*. New York: The Free Press of Gencoe, 1961, pp. 80–5.
239. Taylor. *The Secondary Modern School*, p. 27.
240. Ibid.
241. Rubinstein and Simon. *The Evolution of the Comprehensive School*, p. 75.
242. See statistics in: Benn, Caroline and Chitty, Clyde. *Thirty Years On: Is Comprehensive Education Alive and Well or Struggling to Survive?* London: Penguin, 1997, pp. 269–72.
243. Rubinstein and Simon. *The Evolution of the Comprehensive School*, p. 79.
244. For an account of one such institutional transfer, see: Ball, Stephen. *Beachside Comprehensive: A Case-Study of Secondary Schooling*. Cambridge: Cambridge University Press, 1981.
245. Rubinstein and Simon. *The Evolution of the Comprehensive School*, p. 98.
246. *New Secondary Education: Pamphlet No. 9*, p. 4.
247. Ibid., p. 26.
248. Ibid., p. 46.
249. Hargreaves, David. *The Challenge for the Comprehensive School*. London: Routledge & Kegan Paul, 1982, p. 55.
250. Ministry of Education. *15 to 18*, p. 83.
251. This was the Ordinary Level General Certificate of Education, not to be confused with the Advanced or A-Level GCE.
252. Rubinstein and Simon. *The Evolution of the Comprehensive School*.
253. It was hard to argue that a small number of GCE successes at the modern school demonstrated a facility of self-correction in the tripartite system of schooling. First, pass rates when compared with grammar schools were low. Therefore the GCE was 'still some way from offsetting the known "error" in secondary school

selection, which is generally agreed to be in the order of 10 per cent of the total age group' (Taylor. *The Secondary Modern School*, p. 120). Second, there was a class bias favouring the middle classes in those modern school pupils who sat the GCE (Ministry of Education. *15 to 18*, p. 74; Taylor. *The Secondary Modern School*, pp. 122–3).

254. Brooks, Val. The Role of External Examinations in the Making of Secondary Modern Schools in England 1945–65. *History of Education*, 2008; 37(3), p. 461.

255. 'By 1960, only about 30 of the 146 education authorities could claim to have any schools conducting internal examinations which led to some form of certificate' (Montgomery. *Examinations*, p. 194).

256. (See the Minister's 1957 letter in an appendix to the Crowther Report (Ministry of Education. *15 to 18*, pp. 484–5).)

257. Ibid., pp. 87–8.

258. Ministry of Education. *Half Our Future*, p. 81.

259. Ministry of Education. *15 to 18*, p. 82.

260. Ibid., p. 83.

261. Ibid.

262. Ministry of Education. *Secondary School Examinations other than the G.C.E.* 1960, p. 24.

263. (Certificate of Secondary Education.)

264. See Montgomery. *Examinations*, p. 30; Lawton, Denis. *The Politics of the School Curriculum*. London: Routledge & Kegan Paul, 1980, pp. 84–100; Brooks, Val. The Resurgence of External Examining in Britain: A Historical Review. *British Journal of Educational Studies*, 1993, 41(1). (Elsewhere, the CSE is portrayed as hopelessly undermined by the high status of the GCE. According to this revised view, the radical moment lies much earlier, in the unheeded recommendations for internal assessment in *all* schools that were made in the wartime Norwood Report. Brooks. *The Role of External Examinations in the Making of Secondary Modern Schools in England 1945–65*; Board of Education. *Curriculum and Examinations in Secondary Schools*.)

265. Both the Ordinary Level GCE (to be taken at 16 years) and the Advanced Level GCE (to be taken at 18 years) were 'meant to be essentially qualifying rather than competitive'. However, as a result of rising demand for university places, from the very beginning there were pressures to introduce subdivisions in the pass certificate (Montgomery. *Examinations*, p. 142).

266. Ibid., p. 204.

267. See diagram reproduced from: Ministry of Education. *Scope and Standards of the Certificate of Secondary Education*, p. 4.

268. Hargreaves. *The Challenge for the Comprehensive School*, p. 49.

269. Department of Education and Science. *Aspects of secondary education in England: A survey by HM Inspectors of Schools*, 1979.

270. Ministry of Education. *The Certificate of Secondary Education: A Proposal for a New School Leaving Certificate other than the G.C.E.* 1961, p. 10.

271. Ibid., p. 7.

272. The General Certificate of Secondary Education replaced the CSE and the GCE O-level. The GCE A-level remained as an academic examination to be taken at 18 years.

273. Lawton. *The Politics of the School Curriculum*, p. 102.

274. Benn and Chitty. *Thirty Years On*, p. 518.

275. Nietzsche. *Twilight of the Idols*, p. 104.

276. This chapter in particular draws from previously published work. See: Allen, Ansgar. Cultivating the myopic learner: the shared project of high and low-stakes assessment. *British Journal of Sociology of Education*, 2012, 33(5); Allen, Ansgar. Life without the 'x' factor – meritocracy past and present. *Power and Education*, 2012, 4(1); Allen. *Michael Young's The Rise of the Meritocracy*; Allen, Ansgar. Forget Meritocracy. *Research Intelligence*, 2013, (120 Spring); Allen, Ansgar. The heart of British schools and Gove's 'dark place'. *openDemocracy – OurKingdom*, 2012 (3 September); Allen, Ansgar. 'You never will be a rock star'. *openDemocracy – OurKingdom*, 2011 (11 November).

277. Bernstein, Basil. Education cannot compensate for society. *New Society*, 1970, 387.

278. (The proportion of free places increased between the wars; schooling became free for all in England and Wales after the 1944 Education Act.)

279. See Rose. *Governing the Soul*, pp. 187–90.

280. Ibid., p. 191.

281. Department of Education and Science. *Children and their Primary Schools*, 1967, p. 57.

282. See Rose. *Governing the Soul*, p. 199.

283. Walkerdine, Valerie and Lucey, Helen. *Democracy in the Kitchen: Regulating Mothers and Socialising Daughters*. London: Virago, 1989, p. 82.

284. Ibid., pp. 82–3.

285. Working-class parents have not been exempt from efforts to influence their perception of the home environment and its educational significance. Bernstein and Young defined this terrain comparatively early on in their study on social class and the uses of toys. Working-class mothers, it was claimed, were less likely to see toys in terms of their educational potential. It was suggested that 'class determined differences in the conception of the uses of toys have a bearing upon both the development of measured intelligence and the ability of a child to profit from the infant school experience' (Bernstein, Basil and Young, Douglas. Social Class Differences in Conceptions of the Uses of Toys. *Sociology*, 1967, 1, p. 139). Government schemes have since attempted to provide assistance through the distribution of educational toys to those least able to afford them, with Sure Start centres establishing toy libraries in poor areas.)

286. Partly as a result of royalties paid for the use of Einstein's name by Disney, the Einstein estate ranked fourth on the forbes.com list of top-earning dead celebrities in 2008.

287. Ball, Stephen. New class inequalities in education: Why education policy may be looking in the wrong place! Education policy, civil society and social class. *International Journal of Sociology and Social Policy*, 2010, 30(3/4).

288. Hofmeyr, G. Should abdominal decompression be consigned to the history books? *British Journal of Obstetrics and Gynaecology*, 1990, 97(6).

289. Rauscher, F, Robinson, K and Jens, J. Improved maze learning through early exposure in rats. *Neurological Researcher*, 1998, 20(5).

290. Connolly, Kate. Sewage plant plays Mozart to stimulate microbes. *The Guardian*, 2 June 2010.

291. Penrose, Lionel. *The Biology of Mental Defect*. London: Sidgwick and Jackson, 1949, pp. 61–2.

292. Heim, Alice. *The Appraisal of Intelligence*. London: Methuen, 1954.

293. Department of Education and Science. *Children and their Primary Schools*, p. 13.

294. Cattell claimed that without eugenic intervention in 300 years half of the population would be mentally defective (Cattell. *The Fight for our National Intelligence*, p. 163).
295. Foucault. *Society Must Be Defended.*
296. The provision of comprehensive schools was particularly diverse. By the late 1960s, 'far from introducing a monolithic system of education throughout the country, as was once alleged to be the inevitable result of comprehensive education, a main characteristic of the present phase is the *variety* of systems now being established' (Rubinstein and Simon. *The Evolution of the Comprehensive School*, p. 116). According to David Hargreaves, writing a decade later, there was still a 'remarkable diversity among comprehensive schools, whose style and character is much less monolithic and predictable than that of the old grammar schools' (Hargreaves. *The Challenge for the Comprehensive School*, p. 66).
297. Parliamentary Papers, 1868, (C.3966) XXVIII Pt.I.1.
298. Issued in 1970, circular 10/70 insisted on co-existence, revoking circular 10/65 which encouraged comprehensive organisation. Nevertheless, during her term as education secretary, Margaret Thatcher was unable to instigate an immediate 'swing away from comprehensive education' (Thatcher, Margaret. *The Path to Power*. New York: HarperCollins, 1995, p. 174.), and was forced to approve more reorganisations for comprehensive schooling than any secretary of state before or since (Taylor, William. *The Five Giants: A Biography of the Welfare State*. London: HarperCollins, 2001).
299. Department for Education and Skills. *Academies: Sponsor Prospectus*, 2006, p. 2.
300. Ibid., pp. 16–17, 4.
301. Newsam, Peter. Diversity and Admissions to English Secondary Schools. *Forum*, 2003, 45(1), p. 17; Brighouse, Tim. Comprehensive Schools Then, Now and in the Future: is it time to draw a line in the sand and create a new ideal? *Forum*, 2003, 45(1).
302. Ball, Stephen. Academies in Context: Politics, business and philanthropy and heterarchical governance. *Management in Education*, 2009, 23(3), p. 100.
303. Centre for Contemporary Cultural Studies. *Unpopular Education*, p. 230.
304. Ibid., p. 237.
305. Cattell. *Psychology and Social Progress*, p. 158.
306. Centre for Contemporary Cultural Studies. *Unpopular Education*, p. 177.
307. Pollard, Stephen. It's all about moving on up. *New Statesman*, 10 April 1998.
308. Centre for Contemporary Cultural Studies. *Unpopular Education*, p. 173.
309. Major contributions included: Bernstein, Basil. *Class, Codes and Control Volume 1: Theoretical Studies towards a Sociology of Language*. London: Routledge & Kegan Paul, 1974; Bernstein, Basil. *Class, Codes and Control Volume 3: Towards a Theory of Educational Transmissions*. London: Routledge & Kegan Paul, 1975; Bourdieu, Pierre and Passeron, Jean-Claude. *Reproduction in Education, Society and Culture*. London: Sage, 1977; Bowles and Gintis. *Schooling in Capitalist America*.
310. Woods, Peter. *The Divided School*. London: Routledge & Kegan Paul, 1979, p. 6.
311. Ibid., p. 29.
312. Hargreaves, David. *Social Relations in a Secondary School*. London: Routledge & Kegan Paul, 1967.
313. Ibid., pp. 183–4.
314. Lacey, Colin. *Hightown Grammar: the School as a Social System*. Manchester: Manchester University Press, 1970.
315. Ibid., p. xi.

316. King, Ronald. *Values and Involvement in a Grammar School*. London: Routledge & Kegan Paul, 1969.
317. Department of Education and Science. *Educational Priority Volume 1: E.P.A. Problems and Policies*, 1972, p. 5.
318. Jensen. *How much can we boost I.Q. and scholastic achievement?*; Herrnstein. *I.Q. in the Meritocracy*; Eysenck. *The Inequality of Man*.
319. See, for example: Cox and Dyson. *Fight for Education: A Black Paper*; Cox and Dyson. *Black Paper Two: The Crisis in Education*.
320. Lawton. *The Politics of the School Curriculum*, pp. 50–66.
321. Department of Education and Science. *A Language for Life*, 1975.
322. Despite concerns over the surveillance potential of the Unit, at a local level surveillance was already under development. In 1981, the majority of local government authorities used assessments for monitoring purposes. In 1985, in the London Borough of Croydon a testing programme was introduced that assessed Mathematics and reading at 7, 9 and 11 years. Results were collated, giving each school a profile in relation to the Croydon average; the inspectorate visited any school with abnormal scores. See: Gipps, Caroline. The Debate over Standards and the Uses of Testing. *British Journal of Educational Studies*, 1988, 36(1).
323. These terms are so important in the field of assessment that attempts have been made by those concerned with the detrimental impact of testing to expand their definition. It has been suggested that moral measures could be incorporated into a subjective or rationally calculable definition of test validity. Following the work of Samuel Messick, these approaches attempt to expand the meaning of validity beyond its narrow technical definition (is a test measuring what it intends to measure?) to incorporate the consequences of a test (are the effects of testing good or bad?); that is, social consequences must be calculated *alongside* more traditional technical concerns (Wiliam, Dylan. National Curriculum Assessments and Programmes of Study: validity and impact. *British Educational Research Journal*, 1996, 221; Stobart, Gordon. The Validity of National Curriculum Assessment. *British Journal of Educational Studies*, 2001, 49(1); Messick, Samuel. Test validity and the ethics of assessment. *American Psychologist*, 1980, 35.)
324. This reduction of the expert to a technician of refinement coincided with a shift in the research environment during the 1990s. There were calls for educational research to address practical issues that would have direct and immediate influence on educational policy (Oancea, Alis. Criticisms of educational research: key topics and levels of analysis. *British Educational Research Journal*, 2005, 31(2).
325. This educational reform depended on the enfeeblement of Local Education Authorities, which served as an intermediary between government and schools.
326. Thatcher, Margaret. *The Downing Street Years*. London: HarperCollins, 1993, pp. 590–1.
327. Department of Education and Science. *National Curriculum: Task Group on Assessment and Testing – A Report*, 1988.
328. See, for example, Kimberley, Keith, Hextall, Ian, Torrance, Harry and Moon, Bob. Review Symposium: National Assessment and Testing: the TGAT Report. *British Journal of Sociology of Education*, 1989, 10(2); Troman, Geoff. Testing Tensions: the politics of educational assessment. *British Educational Research Journal*, 1989, 15(3); Gipps, Caroline. National Curriculum Assessment: a research agenda.

British Educational Research Journal, 1992, 18(3); Torrance, Harry. Research in Assessment: a response to Caroline Gipps. *British Educational Research Journal*, 1992, 18(4).

329. Black, Paul. Whatever Happened to TGAT. In: Cullingford, ed. *Assessment versus Evaluation*. London: Cassell, 1997, p. 45.

330. In criterion referencing, grading is based on 'the quality of the performance of a pupil irrespective of the performance of' others, requiring 'clear descriptions of the performances being sought'. This is to be contrasted with 'norm referencing', where 'pupils are placed in rank order and pre-determined proportions are placed in the various grades'. Here grades depend upon a comparison between one pupil's performance and the performances 'of all the other pupils in the group'. They do not depend on 'the absolute quality of the performance'. (Department of Education and Science. *Task Group on Assessment and Testing – A Report*, p. 4.)

331. Ibid., p. 33; Allen. *Cultivating the Myopic Learner*, p. 645.

332. As critics observed, the absolute distinction between criterion and norm-referenced assessment could not be sustained. See: Croll, Paul. Norm and Criterion Referenced Assessment: Some reflections in the context of assessment and testing in the National Curriculum. *Redland Papers*, 1990, 1; Wiliam, Dylan. Value-added Attacks: technical issues in reporting national curriculum assessments. *British Educational Research Journal*, 1992, 18(4).

333. Foucault. *Discipline and Punish*.

334. Ibid., p. 152.

335. Ibid., pp. 155–6.

336. Kimberley, Hextall, Torrance and Moon. *Review Symposium*, pp. 245–7.

337. Black, Paul. Learning, League Tables and National Assessment: opportunity lost or hope deferred? *Oxford Review of Education*, 1998, 24(1), p. 57.

338. This was despite research findings indicating an 'increased consistency amongst teachers in the way that they interpret and apply the Key Stage assessment levels' (Reeves, David, Boyle, William and Christie, Thomas. The Relationship between Teacher Assessment and Pupil Attainments in Standard Test Tasks at Key Stage 2, 1996–98. *British Educational Research Journal*, 2001, 27(2)).

339. See Black. *Assessment versus Evaluation*, p. 35.

340. Though Paul Newton takes a more generous view, the overall process he observes is the same: 'In recent years…learning objectives have moved from the "specific competence" end of the continuum toward the "general competence" end. Indeed, precisely this kind of recognition was made within the national curriculum context during the mid-1990s, with the shift from performance criteria to performance descriptions' (Newton, Paul. The defensibility of national curriculum assessment in England. *Research Papers in Education*, 2003, 18(2), p. 106).

341. Black, Paul and Wiliam, Dylan. 'In Praise of Educational Research': formative assessment. *British Educational Research Journal*, 2003, 29(5), p. 625.

342. Department of Education and Science. *Task Group on Assessment and Testing – A Report*.

343. 'What is the biggest impact that educational research has had on education and society over the past 20 years? Opinions will clearly differ, but we want to make a case for awarding the prize to…the development of sophisticated techniques for analysing individual data within a hierarchical context, and the growing availability of good datasets to which these techniques can be applied.' (Schagen, Ian and Hutchison, Dougal. Adding Value in Educational Research – the marriage

of data and analytical power. *British Educational Research Journal*, 2003, 29(5), p. 749.)

344. Morrison, H, and Cowan, P. The State Schools Book: a critique of a league table. *British Educational Research Journal*, 1996, 22(2).

345. Wiliam. *Value-added Attacks*.

346. Department of Education and Science. *Task Group on Assessment and Testing – A Report*,p. 33.

347. The system was later zeroed arbitrarily at a score of either 100 or 1000 to avoid negative scores.

348. Ray, Andrew. *School Value Added Measures in England: A Paper for the OECD Project on the Development of Value-Added Models in Education Systems*. London: Department for Education and Skills, 2006, p. 18.

349. Following a feasibility study, value-added statistics were added to performance tables for secondary schools in 2002 and for primary schools in 2003. (Fitz-Gibbon, Carol. *The Value Added Project Final Report: Feasibility Studies for a National System of Value-added Indicators*. London: School Curriculum and Assessment Authority, 1997.)

350. Local Education Authorities initially facilitated the introduction of value-added systems. They were later joined by research groups at the Institute of Education in London, the National Foundation for Educational Research, and researchers based at the University of Newcastle-upon-Tyne (later Durham University), who provided value-added analysis as a service to schools. (Schagen and Hutchison. *Adding Value in Educational Research – the marriage of data and analytical power*.)

351. Gibson, Alex and Asthana, Sheena. Schools, Pupils and Examination Results: contextualising school 'performance'. *British Educational Research Journal*, 1998, 24(3), p. 271.

352. Gibson, Alex and Asthana, Sheena. School Performance, School Effectiveness and the 1997 White Paper. *Oxford Review of Education*, 1998, 24(2).

353. Here, social disadvantage was found to have a negative impact not only on outcomes, *but also* on the potential for both school improvement and individual progress. (Levačić, Rosalind and Woods, Philip. Raising School Performance in the League Tables (Part 1): Disentangling the Effects of Social Disadvantage. *British Educational Research Journal*, 2002, 28(2); Feinstein, Leon. Inequality in the Early Cognitive Development of British Children in the 1970 Cohort. *Economica*, 2003, 70(277).)

354. Contextual value-added statistics were added to school performance tables in phases from 2006 onwards. These would take into account the following factors in addition to prior attainment: gender, ethnicity, age, special educational needs, first language, mobility, whether a pupil is or has been in care, free school meals and a rating from the Income Deprivation Affecting Children Index provided by the Office of the Deputy Prime Minister.

355. Department for Children, Schools and Families. *Gaining Ground: Improving Progress in Coasting Secondary Schools*. 2008, pp. 1–3.

356. Ibid., p. 2.

357. Gove, Michael. House of Commons, 24 November 2010.

358. Department for Education. *The Importance of Teaching: The Schools White Paper*. 2010.

359. RM Assessment. *RAISEonline – the online reporting tool*. http://www.rmassessment.co.uk/case-studies/raiseonline. 2013.

360. Department for Children, Schools and Families. *Gaining Ground*, p. 11.

361. Ibid., p. 13.
362. Ofsted. *Twelve Outstanding Secondary Schools: Excelling against the Odds*. London: Ofsted, 2009, p. 25.
363. Strand, Steve. Comparing the predictive validity of reasoning tests and national end of Key Stage 2 tests: which tests are the best? *British Educational Research Journal*, 2006, 32(2), p. 233.
364. Reay, Diane and Wiliam, Dylan. 'I'll be a nothing': structure, agency and the construction of identity through assessment. *British Educational Research Journal*, 1999, 25(3), pp. 345–9.
365. Hall, Kathy, Collins, Janet, Benjamin, Shereen, Nind, Melanie and Sheehy, Kieron. SATurated models of pupildom: assessment and inclusion/exclusion. *British Educational Research Journal*, 2004, 30(6), p. 814.
366. Ibid., p. 806.
367. Ibid., p. 802.
368. National tests are criticised for creating an inversion of visibility, and subjecting pupils to 'panoptic surveillance' (Reay and Wiliam. *'I'll be a nothing'*, p. 348).
369. Detailed profiles are compiled for all pre-school children. This profile accompanies pupils upon transfer to primary school. The mandatory profiles are based on observation rather than objective testing. Despite this switch in policy towards rich, qualitative profiling, 'objective' baseline tests are still used by many schools. Both modes of assessment allow learning strategies to be devised for individual children, though objective tests provide standardised procedures allowing the calculation of individual targets. Such data are used in the development of school-level strategies that maximise the raw material. For an evaluation of the scheme in its early form, see: Lindsay, Geoff and Lewis, Ann. An Evaluation of the Use of Accredited Baseline Assessment Schemes in England. *British Educational Research Journal*, 2003, 29(2); Torrance, Harry. When is an 'Evaluation' not an Evaluation? When it's Sponsored by the QCA? A Response to Lindsay and Lewis. *British Educational Research Journal*, 2003, 29(2). The 'Foundation Stage Profile' subsequently replaced this scheme in 2003, later becoming the 'Early Years Foundation Stage Profile'. See: QCA. *Early Years Foundation Stage Profile Handbook*. London: QCA, 2008.
370. (In those cases where standardised tests are implemented by schools.)
371. Centre for Evaluation & Monitoring. *PIPS – Benefits*. http://www.cem.org/pips/benefits. 2013.
372. *Centre for Evaluation & Monitoring. Mission Statement. http://www.cem.org/mission-statement.* 2013. (emphasis mine)
373. YJB. *Asset – Youth Justice Board*, 2006, p. 1.
374. Bateman, Tim. Punishing Poverty: The 'Scaled Approach' and Youth Justice Practice. *The Howard Journal of Criminal Justice*, 2011, 50(2).
375. Davies Giddy, cited in: Donald, James. *Sentimental Education: Schooling, Popular Culture and the Regulation of Liberty*. London: Verso, 1992, p. 20.
376. Here I draw from: Allen. *'You never will be a rock star'*.
377. Hackley, Chris, Brown, Stephen and Hackley, Rungpaka. The X-Factor enigma: Simon Cowell and the marketization of existential liminality. *Marketing Theory*, 2012, 12(4), p. 454.
378. The distinction between summative and formative assessment is generally traced back to: Scriven, Michael. The methodology of evaluation. In: Tyler, Gagne and Scriven, ed. *Perspectives of Curriculum Evaluation*. Chicago: Rand McNally, 1967.

379. See, for example: Thomas, R. *High Stakes Testing: Coping with Collateral Damage.* Mahwah: Lawrence Erlbaum Associates, 2005.
380. Foucault. *Omnes et Singulatim.*
381. Wiliam, Dylan and Black, Paul. Meanings and Consequences: a basis for distinguishing formative and summative functions of assessment. *British Educational Research Journal*, 1996, 22(5), p. 537.
382. Ibid., p. 543.
383. Ibid., p. 537.
384. Ibid., p. 538.
385. Weeden, Paul, Winter, Jan and Broadfoot, Patricia. *Assessment: What's in it for Schools?* Abingdon: RoutledgeFalmer, 2002, p. 16.
386. Black, Paul and Wiliam, Dylan. *Inside the Black Box: Raising Standards through Classroom Assessment.* London: Kings College London School of Education, 1998.
387. Ibid., p. 4.
388. Ibid., pp. 8–9 (emphasis mine).
389. Ibid., p. 4.
390. Weeden, Winter and Broadfoot. *Assessment: What's in it for Schools?* pp. 53–5.
391. Ibid.
392. Department for Children, Schools and Families. *Aspiration and attainment amongst young people in deprived communities: Analysis and discussion paper, December 2008*, 2008, p. 2 (emphasis mine).
393. Stow. *The Training System*, p. 153.
394. Weeden, Winter and Broadfoot. *Assessment: What's in it for Schools?* p. 89.
395. Hackley, Brown and Hackley. *The X-Factor enigma*, p. 454.
396. Weeden, Winter and Broadfoot. *Assessment: What's in it for Schools?* p. 90.
397. Black, Paul, Harrison, Christine, Lee, Clare, Marshall, Bethan and Wiliam, Dylan. *Assessment for Learning: Putting it into Practice.* Maidenhead: Open University Press, 2003, pp. 50–2.
398. Weeden, Winter and Broadfoot. *Assessment: What's in it for Schools?* p. 76.
399. Black, Harrison, Lee, Marshall and Wiliam. *Assessment for Learning*, p. 49.
400. Ibid.
401. Parliamentary Papers, 1895, (C. 7862) XLIII.1, p. 173.
402. Phillips. *All Must Have Prizes.*
403. Gove, Michael. Speech: Michael Gove to Westminster Academy, 6 September 2010.
404. Department of Education and Science. *Task Group on Assessment and Testing – A Report*, p. 21.
405. In 2008, the Office of Qualifications and Examinations Regulation (Ofqual) was formed to reassure the public and maintain confidence in the examination system. It is significant that Ofqual was not amongst the 192 quangos announced for abolition by the Conservative–Liberal coalition government in October 2010 (see 'Bonfire of the Quangos.' *The Independent*, 15 October 2010). Indeed, Michael Gove, the Secretary of State for Education, reassured: 'We will legislate to strengthen Ofqual.' (Gove. Speech: Michael Gove to Westminster Academy, 6 September 2010.)
406. Here I draw from: Allen. *The heart of British schools and Gove's 'dark place'.*
407. Flint, Kevin and Peim, Nick. *Rethinking the Education Improvement Agenda: A Critical Philosophical Approach.* London: Continuum, 2012.
408. Burt. *The Principles of Vocational Guidance*, p. 339.
409. Pluchino, Rapisada and Garofalo. *The Peter Principle Revisited.*

410. Martel, Yann. *Life of Pi*. Illustrated ed. Edinburgh: Cannongate, 2007, pp. 15–16.
411. Webb, Darren. Bakhtin at the Seaside: Utopia, Modernity and the Carnivalesque. *Theory, Culture & Society*, 2005, 22(3).
412. Foucault. *Discipline and Punish*, p. 31.
413. Veyne, Paul. *Foucault: His Thought, His Character*. Cambridge: Polity, 2010, pp. 118–19.
414. Dean, Mitchell. *Governmentality: Power and Rule in Modern Society*. London: Sage, 1999, p. 44.
415. Nietzsche, Friedrich. *The Will to Power*. New York: Vintage, 1968, p. 309.
416. Marx, Karl. Critique of the Gotha Programme. In: Carver, ed. *Marx: Later Political Writings*. Cambridge: Cambridge University Press, 1996 [1875], p. 215.
417. Nietzsche. *Twilight of the Idols*, pp. 80–1.
418. Ibid., p. 31.
419. Nietzsche. *The Will to Power*, p. 32.

Index

Printed and bound by CPI Group (UK) Ltd, Croydon, CR0 4YY